The Changing Capital Markets of East Asia

In recent years much attention has been given to the unparalleled economic development of East Asia. In *The Changing Capital Markets of East Asia* the authors look at the growing sophistication of capital markets in this area and discuss the possible economic and political consequences.

This book has received substantial financial support from the Asia Research Centre, Murdoch University. The Centre's central project is to analyse the emergence of middle classes in the region, and what this may mean to the societies of these rapidly developing countries. Its research focus is academic, but with a strong emphasis on providing work of practical value to decision makers in business and government. In supporting *Capital Markets*, the Centre has helped bring together the perspectives of both academics and practitioners on various aspects of the region's capital markets.

The book analyses recent changes in the emerging capital markets of the region and the implications these may have for international and regional capital markets in general. Early chapters present the dominant global trends impacting on the development of East Asian capital markets. The middle section goes on to look at the practical aspects of capital market activity, from equity market emergence to the accounting and taxation frameworks applicable to businesses dealing in these markets. The closing chapters provide national case studies of South Korea's and Taiwan's capital market conditions as affected by regional and domestic political economic forces. The theme of the book is more strategic than technical and the work does not confine itself to a basic market analysis.

The Changing Capital Markets of East Asia presents a valuable guide for all those interested in what causes and determines change in the private and public finance spheres.

Ky Cao is a Director of Finance International Pty Limited, a financial consultancy firm based in Perth and Los Angeles. He was formerly a Senior Fellow at the Asia Research Centre and Senior Economist at Syntec Economic Services in Melbourne.

Routledge Studies in the Growth Economies of Asia

The Changing Capital Markets of East Asia

Edited by Ky Cao

London and New York

First published 1995
by Routledge
11 New Fetter Lane, London EC4P 4EE

Simultaneously published in the USA and Canada
by Routledge
29 West 35th Street, New York, NY 10001

© 1995 Ky Cao; individual chapters to the contributors

Typeset in Garamond by LaserScript, Mitcham, Surrey
Printed and bound in Great Britain by
Mackays of Chatham PLC, Chatham, Kent

British Library Cataloguing in Publication Data
A catalogue record for this book is available from the British Library

Library of Congress Cataloguing in Publication Data
A catalogue record for this book has been requested

ISSN 1359–7876
ISBN 0–415–12285–6

Contents

Figures

Tables

List of contributors

Jane Brooks works with G.K. Goh (H.K.) Ltd, an international brokerage specialising in research on the East Asian stock markets. Jane has been following China affairs for thirteen years, including her postgraduate work in London and Beijing. Previously, she worked for Baring Asset Management and Hoare Govett Asia.

Ky Cao is a Director of Finance International Pty. Limited, a financial consultancy firm based in Perth and Los Angeles. He was formerly a Senior Fellow at the Asia Research Centre and Senior Economist at Syntec Economic Services in Melbourne. Ky holds a Master of Economics degree from the University of Western Australia.

Jou Juo Chu is Visiting Associate Professor at the Chinese Cultural University, Taipei, and formerly a Research Fellow at the Asia Research Centre. JJ gained her PhD from Oxford University and many of her works have been on the development of Taiwan's new national identity that has accompanied the country's economic success.

Phil Hancock and **Greg Tower** are Senior Lecturers in the Commerce Programme, Murdoch University. Their areas of research include international accounting standards and stock exchange legislation.

Gitte Heij holds a Master of Tax Law degree from the University of Groningen and had worked at the ING (formerly NMB) Bank, International Division, in the Netherlands and the International Bureau of Fiscal Documentation, before coming to the Asia Research Centre in 1992 as a Research Fellow. Her expertise is in corporate tax structures of East Asia.

You-Il Lee is a PhD student at the Asia Research Centre. Part of his thesis is on Korean foreign investment in the Asia–Pacific region and comparative Korean–Japanese industrial organisation.

Catherine Roc is Market Strategist at J.P. Morgan Securities Limited, Sydney. She moved to Australia in 1992 after spending some time at J.P. Morgan GmbH in Frankfurt, Germany. Catherine holds a Master of

Economics degree from the University of Sydney, an Advanced Certificate in International Economics from the Kiel Institute of World Economics and a Diplome of IEP from the Institut d'Etudes Politiques de Paris.

Moon-Joong Tcha is a Research Fellow at the Economic Research Centre, University of Western Australia. Moon-Joong holds a PhD in economics from the University of Chicago and his fields of interest cover international trade and capital flows in the Asia–Pacific.

Joe Zhang is an Investment Banker at Swiss Bank Corporation (Asia) Limited, Hong Kong. Joe was Lecturer in Banking and Finance at the University of Canberra and has previously held senior positions in the People's Bank of China, the PRC's central bank. Joe has a Master of Economics degree from the Australian National University.

Joan Zheng is Senior Economist at Baring Securities (Hong Kong) Limited and former Lecturer in Finance at the University of Canberra. She has previously worked at Swan Consultants and the Industry Commission (Canberra) and in the People's Bank of China.

General editorial assistance by **Cisca Spencer** is gratefully acknowledged. Cisca is currently Senior Research Fellow at the Asia Research Centre, Murdoch University. She previously worked at the Department of Foreign Affairs and Trade in Canberra.

Chapter 1

Introduction

Ky Cao

THE EQUILATERAL TRIANGLES

Whether described as a Triad in Ohmae's terms,[1] or the Three Thirties as in financial markets parlance, world economic activity has consolidated over the last decade into a three-legged phenomenon involving North America, West Europe and East Asia. Each region now commands more or less a third of total world GNP, hence the term 'Three Thirties'. Of the three regions, East Asia has attracted the most interest since it is the recent recruit, setting aside Japan, to the world's prosperity club.

Before going into further discussion, it would be useful to define East Asia, or 'the region', for the purposes of this book. Technically, we are focusing loosely on the eight better known countries of East Asia excluding Japan, namely China (the PRC), Taiwan, Hong Kong, South Korea, Indonesia, Thailand, Malaysia and Singapore. These are not covered evenly, and not every one of them is included in each of the chapters that follow. The inconsistent availability of quality data between them has meant that some countries are bound to be less analysable than others in certain areas. Roc, Heij, and Hancock and Tower provide as broad a comparative cross-country study of, respectively, stock market development, taxation and accounting issues, as practicable. Others, by design, give a vertical look at specific issues in particular countries. Brooks discusses in depth the PRC's equities market, backed up by Zhang and Zheng's presentation of the PRC's regulatory framework in the banking sector. Chu, on the other hand, describes the political economic change that has accompanied Taiwan's financial deregulation over the past twenty years, while Lee and Tcha study South Korea's recent foreign direct investment experience in Southeast Asia.

Australia comes frequently into the picture from a particular angle, that of belonging strategically and economically to the region as well as being the country where much of the research for this book has been done. References, at times extensive, to countries not included in the above 'region' are made for comparative purposes, in particular to Japan in

Chapter 2. Japan's special position is that of a superpower whose perceived alternative 'Asian' economic model had been touted in the 1980s as a contrast to the West, or the major English speaking economies of North America and Britain. This 'alternative' role model, and Japan's obvious postwar success, gives the country a leading influence in shaping East Asian economic thought and development policy.

The structural change that Japan has undergone in recent years, however, has had a significant impact on the direction that many East Asian countries are taking with regard to capital markets development and economic integration. Although the structure of industrial organisation has always differed between Japan on the one hand, and China or East Asian NIEs (newly industrialised economies) on the other, surprise has been expressed in some quarters that Japan is not being seen as the role model for East Asia's financial system development – as if it ever was. The China basin (Northeast Asia excluding Japan) and Southeast Asia have been undertaking fundamental and well documented political, social and economic change. How the emerging capital markets of the region fit into the patterns of international and regional economic integration, and the manner in which these markets reflect economic and socio-political change in the domestic economies, constitutes the subject of this book's study.

In May 1993 a reputable team of analysts from the University of California, San Diego, forecast that the Pacific Rim countries (excluding Japan) that make up the Pacific Economic Cooperation Council (PECC) would grow by 4.2 per cent in 1993 and the same in 1994, up from 3.3 per cent in 1992.[2] This would happen despite the perceived weak US and Japanese economies, which were expected to grow by 3.2 per cent and 2.3 per cent respectively in 1993, and 2.3 per cent and 3.2 per cent in 1994. China, on the other hand, was predicted to come in at 10.1 per cent in 1993 and 9.5 per cent in 1994. 'This giant's growth', team leader Krause said of China, 'is having a huge impact on the region.' As it turned out, the team's optimistic punting was actually an underestimation of the Asian 'giant', whose GDP growth reached 13.5 per cent for 1993 and caused a governmental clampdown on credit availability in early 1994.

Notwithstanding individual country forecasts, similar views concerning the region have been expressed before and since. The OECD's *1993 Economic Outlook* saw East Asia outperforming the rest of the world in the next year or two, predictions that were confirmed in its 1994 *Outlook*. The World Bank projected East Asia's growth to continue to lead the world over the following decade, as shown in Table 1.1. East Asia gradually detached itself from the global (Western dominated) economy from the early 1980s, when the region developed its own momentum, generated partly by the Japanese upturn (the longest since Meiji and probably Tokugawa times) but mostly by its own transnational trade and investment activity. *Time Australia*, in a 1992 special survey of Asia, reported that Pacific Rim countries were their own best customers: about 65 per cent of Asia–Pacific trade was intraregional, compared to 62 per cent for the European Community, and 'achieved without the discriminatory methods of the EC . . .' It went on to say that, while the IMF had lowered its forecast of world economic growth in 1993, the Asian Development Bank predicted average growth among its twenty-five developing member nations at triple the world rate.[3]

The World Bank's Chief Economist for the East Asia and Pacific region, V. Thomas, noted in late 1993 that imports by the Chinese Economic Area (CEA – consisting of China, Hong Kong and Taiwan) were almost two-thirds as large as Japan's, and could exceed the latter by 2002. He added that in view of the structural ratios such as the share of population in

Table 1.1 Real GDP growth

	Trend 1974–90	*Recent estimates 1991–93*	*Forecast 1994–2003*
G-7	3.3	1.2	2.7
Europe and Central Asia	3.1	–9.8	2.7
East Asia	7.3	8.3	7.6

Source: World Bank, Global Economic Prospects and the Developing Countries, April 1994

Table 1.2 Stock market capitalisation, in US$ billion

	January 1993	*June 1994*
New York	3,283	4,150
Tokyo	2,352	3,550
London	1,215	1,050
Frankfurt	301	405
Sydney	175	240
Hong Kong	168	316
Taipei	90	180
Seoul	96	161
Kuala Lumpur	90	184
Singapore	46	135
Bangkok	60	122
Jakarta	9	42
Manila	7	37

agriculture, capital labour ratios, and natural resource endowments, CEA would still be at an early stage of development in 2002 and could potentially sustain a leadership role in growth for a long time.[4]

Table 1.2 of course can only be viewed as a rough indication of a snapshot in time for the markets concerned. It does not provide performance details, when exchange rates are adjusted. The Tokyo stock market capitalisation went up by around 75 per cent during the two year period, although its true, exchange rate adjusted growth had been far less.

But data on relative stock market returns do point to the region's detachment from the world trend. Tables 1.3 and 1.4 depict the contrast between the emerging East Asian stock markets and the recession-hit West in 1992. Similar results came from Greenwood, who used monthly data for the US and East Asia between January 1988 and August 1992 to create an efficiency frontier.[5] His Asia stock was the Morgan Stanley Capital International Combined Far East (East Asia) which excluded Japan. As expected, the frontier showed that diversifying US funds into East Asia had the potential to raise return and/or reduce risk. For example, allocating 40 per cent of a US portfolio to East Asia could lift annual return by 1.5 per cent for a given level of risk, or diverting 20 per cent could raise return by 0.75 per cent per annum while actually reducing the risk level.

The West–East stock market divergence persisted into 1993–94. *Far Eastern Economic Review (FEER)* weekly data showed that exchange rate

Table 1.3 IFC stock market index return: 1992

Country	Annual growth in US$ terms %
Malaysia	34.6
Philippines	33.7
Thailand	31.4

Source: Development Finance, International Finance Corporation, December 1992

Table 1.4 Stock market performance: 1992

	% change in US$		% change in US$
Thailand	30	USA S&P 500	5
Hong Kong	27	IFC Composite	–3
China	110	UK FT 100	–5
Malaysia	24	Japan Nikkei	–26

Source: Development Finance, International Finance Corporation, December 1992

adjusted stock market index growth between the Morgan Stanley world index and Southeast Asian stock market indices remained uncorrelated in those years. Whereas the MS index recorded about 5 per cent return in the eighteen months to September 1993, the unweighted average return for Singapore, Kuala Lumpur, Bangkok and Jakarta indices was over 20 per cent.[6]

Our tests corroborated these funds management implications for investors. Figures in Table 1.5 were derived from the same *FEER* data and show how East Asia's recent attempts at deregulating national financial markets have heightened certain markets' volatility. While these figures do not show it explicitly, much of the increased volatility had resulted directly from domestic financial market liberalisation moves. It is not surprising that the Morgan Stanley world index had shown less volatility than individual Southeast Asian markets. The implied message is that portfolio risk could be cut by spreading investments worldwide rather than concentrating funds in Southeast Asia. This message complements Greenwood's results.

Of interest are the covariances between Southeast Asian markets. They say that risk could be reduced not only by spreading investments between Southeast Asia and the rest of the world, it could also be done by allocating funds between certain Southeast Asian countries. For instance, the Bangkok SET and Kuala Lumpur indices record positive performance correlation while the SET and Jakarta Composite show negative correlation. Lack of correlation also characterises individual East Asian stock indices and Japan's Nikkei. For example, while the Hong Kong Hang Seng surged over 1991–93, the Nikkei 225 remained strapped during this period around its lows after suffering a 50 per cent+ decline from its 1990 peak.

East Asia's cyclical detachment from the rest of the world has been accompanied by further intraregional economic integration. Japan, which had initially felt reserved about the APEC (Asia–Pacific Economic

Table 1.5 Stock market volatility

Standard deviation March 1992–September 1993					
Morgan Stanley Index	Southeast Asia (unweighted aver)	Singapore ST index	KLSE composite	SE of Thailand	Jakarta SE index
4.05	4.87	6.14	5.87	11.38	6.93

Selected Markets Covariances March 1992–September 1993						
MS-SEA	ST-KLSE	ST-SET	ST-JKSE	KLSE-SET	KLSE-JKSE	SET-JKSE
−2.36	2.22	16.17	−0.09	41.36	14.77	−9.46

Source: FEER, various issues, 1992–93

Cooperation) concept, has come to embrace warmly the idea of an Asia–Pacific economy.[7] Among others, Japanese Diet member Tetsuo Kondo mooted the need for a great triangle of cooperation linking the ASEAN nations, Australia and Japan. In this vision, Japan would supply technology and capital, ASEAN natural and labour resources, and Australia both natural resources and technology.[8] Here, Kondo was talking about the region from a resource endowment perspective, a partial and quite outdated picture given the rapid rises in NIE wage rates over the past decade.

East Asia is well entranched in Western business perceptions as an Oriental El Dorado. The caricature of a region of high savings and investment returns made possible by diligent, well educated and growth driven workforces has not been too far off the mark. After a couple of postwar decades entrapped in political totalitarianism or authoritarianism, East Asia by the late 1970s had emerged bursting with energy. One billion Chinese are now on the march, not retreating deep in the hinterland as in the 1930s, but forward towards the sea of open commerce where significant expatriate Chinese capitalist economies are operating with zeal. Taiwan, Hong Kong and Singapore have accrued in just two generations the sort of foreign reserves that are the envy of the bulk of the OECD.

On the left shoulder of the Chinese heavyweight dangles South Korea, an industrial power in its own right. Korea has transformed itself into a world class exporter of raw and rolled steel, commercial tankers and luxury cars. Along China's southern flank lies Southeast Asia, the hub of non-Chinese (except for Singapore) states fragmented by history and ethnicities, yet united in modern times by a common fear of socialism and a shared yearning for economic progress.

Beyond geography, however, Southeast Asia's economies have been driven historically by the Chinese minorities.[9] Commercial development in the area has tended to go hand in hand with the establishment of the overseas Chinese migrant communities in those countries. Surveying the broader Asia–Pacific region as a contemporary economic phenomenon, it would be difficult not to remark on what indeed constitutes a salient feature of the region: the Chinese. It could equally be called 'China–Pacific'.

This generalisation, although very tempting, would run the risk of overlooking East Asia's other mosaic, the 'strategic perceptions' one. For although China and its ethnic diaspora account for a large portion of the Asia–Pacific economy, this Greater China is adequately balanced by Japan in the east and the non-Chinese Southeast Asian polities in the south. Politically, the non-Chinese carry a slightly stronger position than displayed in economic terms, part courtesy of the PRC's underdeveloped superpower diplomacy.[10] Most of the world's multilateral developments are still initiated by the seasoned West. Despite Greater China's status in landmass, population and more recently economic performance, the world's monetary lever remains firmly in the hands of the Western based Group of Seven

(G-7). This Western dominance is the more conspicuous when China's GDP is related to others through purchasing power parity estimates, which rank the PRC second only to the US.[11]

China's rise in political and diplomatic status will likely be slower than its economic performance. This is because of the strategic interests that sometimes team up East Asia's culturally diverse nations to keep subregions in check from one another. These strategic alliances are frequently overlaid on the region's economic characteristics. Japan, perhaps, views itself as aligned more with Australia than with any other country in the region. This view does not rest just on Japan's appreciation of its own stakes in a free trade world – overriding though this economic imperative is – a world that offers among other benefits Australia as a complementary trading partner endowed with resources that Japan lacks. Nor is it simply a reciprocation to Australia's national interests as a small, relatively open economy in pursuit of the GATT agenda. The alignment reflects also the new realities that developed Western nations have come to reassess since the mid-1980s: the rise of mainland China as a very real economic superpower in the next century.[12] Constrained by its ambiguous position in Asia as a result of its imperialist past, Japan is carefully playing a contributory rather than leading role in continental Asia's development. Most appropriate to its national interests, Japan is orchestrating an 'open Pacific'.

China is rising in its own way to the economic challenge of the 21st century. Its leaders have proved to be adept at identifying the strikes that count the most. GNP growth since 1979 has been phenomenal. On the non-economic side, China has also been trying hard to accommodate change although it has refused to absorb the type of institutional change that scuttled the ex-Soviet Union and parts of East Europe. Beijing allowed the existing bureaucracies to turn themselves into capitalists, rather than let a completely new class of capitalists emerge independent of the former and of the military. Certainly, the private sector in China has boomed beyond predictions, with the non state-owned share of the economy accounting for 61 per cent of China's industrial output growth in 1992, compared to virtually nil in the 1970s.[13]

But what Beijing has done is to craft (or at least permit) a metamorphosis between the state-owned and the private sectors to give birth to a class of 'red capitalists', the army of entrepreneurs cum party officials who do not seek to destabilise the political hierarchy. In return, Beijing helps them become rich and powerful. The party leadership opened China's doors without hesitation and invited foreign capital in from all corners of the globe. By 1993, just four years after Tiananmen, there were over forty countries trading with and investing in China and over twenty providing loans to the country.[14] State-owned investment enterprises were established to handle part of this foreign capital and to assist China in learning to play in overseas financial markets. CITIC (the central government-run China

International Trust and Investment Corporation) and GITIC (the Guang-dong equivalent) poured enough money into Hong Kong by 1992 to make China the largest investor source in the Territory.

The maintenance of critical bureaucratic and military loyalty has allowed Beijing to gradually implement economic policy designed to shift resources from its revolutionary era political base, the agricultural sector, to the urban industrial sector (beyond the heavy industries cherished by dictatorial regimes). The leadership has done this while fully appreciating that such a shift could lead to the rise of new non-Chinese Communist Party (CCP) élites. Even within the traditional power base, agricultural reform has been raising the peasantry's autonomy at the expense of CCP authority.[15] Main-taining this balance between the partial protection of the party machine and the rise of the private sector has been crucial in China's success in transiting to a market economy.

Other parts of Asia have replicated these political risk taking initiatives within a stabilisation framework. Structural reform agendas have been introduced in response to the domestic need for foreign capital. These reforms all have the potential to change the balance between various domestic power structures. While individual experiences differ – Taiwan and Korea 'democratising' their political system in the last five to ten years; Thailand attempting with a degree of success to dilute its military's power; and Indonesia's ruling class liberalising the country's political system in reaction to external structural factors[16] – they all point to the opening up of the domestic economy and restructuring of the political/institutional frame-work that market liberalisation usually entails. Yet, for traditional power holders inside those countries (government officials and related groups in industries, the military and religious orders), the challenge to their position has been slow and cautiously handled by the top political leadership.

Internal caution in handling change has also reflected the importance of external security. It is this external security that has so far kept both political rulers and economic élites in East Asia in agreement to allowing structural change in their own economies. The reshaping of the global and regional geopolitical environment has, for instance, led Southeast Asia to initiating some form of collective response. Like Japan, Southeast Asia looks upon China as a two-sided coin, of opportunities and concerns. It is no co-incidence that ASEAN has been deregulating its economies as fast as the political process permitted, or precipitating the inclusion of Vietnam as a member of the grouping in every way but name.

Hand in hand with the competition to raise foreign investor interest through market deregulation, Southeast Asian governments have seen eye-to-eye on one particular issue: dealing with China. Both Indonesia's and Malaysia's strategic overtures – Indonesia supporting APEC and Malaysia pushing its own conceived East Asia Economic Caucus vision – could be speculated as directed at China rather than the West, EAEC's apparent target. For Indonesia and Malaysia, containing or diluting China's diplomatic and political clout in the region may be of more importance than excluding the West. There has been great effort by ASEAN in formalising the ASEAN Free Trade Agreement (AFTA) despite the relatively short time since the idea was floated and despite the absence of a substantial reason for such an agreement.[17] APEC's Eminent Persons Group more or less cast its judgement on the formation of sub-regional economic groupings by reiterating the Asia-Pacific's central objective as becoming a totally free trade region by 2020.[18] The point of contention is not economic, since free trade ideals have not declined in the region, but political, with regard to regional security. The interesting implication is that Japan's and Southeast Asia's concerns over China's rise are providing a role for Australia to fill. Both Japan and Southeast Asia regard Australia, its small population size notwithstanding, as a valuable strategic partner on the regional stage.

East Asia ought to be viewed thus from various perspectives, all of which bear directly on its economic development policy: from the global perspective, the Triad refers to the major regions of North America, West Europe and East Asia. From a regional perspective, several Triads are detectable: the geographical split, which may differentiate the China Basin from Southeast Asia, and both of these from Japan; the ethnic split, which draws the line between the Chinese, the non-Chinese Northeast Asians and the non-Chinese Southeast Asians; and the strategic perceptions split, which may rearrange certain ethnically based sets of relations. Japan would, from a particular angle, see itself as having more in common with Australia than with continental Asia, by virtue of its economic development stage and strategic needs. By the same token, the overseas Chinese are not a homogeneous group when it comes to perceiving where the subgroups' various destinies lie.[19] In many cases, it can be said that nationalist feelings override the sense of ethnicity within these subgroups. Taiwan is developing its own national and cultural identity quite separate from mainland China,[20] Hong Kong is reverting to Chinese rule soon, while Singapore has proved to be a staunch partner of ASEAN.

THE CAPITAL NEXUS

The above perspectives are still not sufficient to fully illustrate the kaleidoscopic nature of East Asia. Superimposing the triangular segmentations are the massive flows of capital that have long become an all-embracing force in shaping the region's development. Capital integration in East Asia has been well documented.[21] The Hang Seng Bank reported some time ago that China had overtaken the US as the largest foreign direct investor in Hong Kong, injecting about US$20 billion in 1992. Industrialised countries, led by the US and Japan, used to dominate Hong Kong's sources of foreign direct investment (FDI). In that year, the US and Japan invested $8.5 billion and

$11.5 billion respectively, their combined total being more than matched by China's.

Of China's investment figure, $5 billion was invested by Chinese financial institutions, excluding loans and interbank lending. A further $1 billion was invested through listed companies and the remainder through unlisted companies. China's CITIC Pacific was the largest listed investor in the Territory, followed by China Overseas Land & Investment and China Travel International Investment.[22] Apart from these, substantial investment comes from local and provincial government bodies and municipalities. The fields of investment are broad, covering banking and finance, transport, construction, hotels, manufacturing, importing and exporting. Hong Kong's proximity to China, its ethnic Chinese background, its infrastructure and non-interventionist government have made it attractive to mainland investors. The 1992 *Directory of Enterprises with PRC Capital in Hong Kong* contains a collection of 900 such entities, a direct result, as the compilers noted, of 'reform and openness in mainland China'. Feng and Goodman similarly provided evidence of an astounding traffic in capital between China and the NIEs of Hong Kong, Singapore, South Korea and Taiwan.[23]

Weaving into this web of capital is the Chinese diaspora. Cohesive Chinese capitalism is clearly seen in Taiwan, Hong Kong and Singapore, with their Chinese majorities. Less visible are the Chinese minorities in non-Chinese states of Southeast Asia. Although their direct exercise of political power in these states may be limited, the Chinese minorities have been controlling much of the commercial life of these countries. For the minority Chinese communities, there is a common feeling of vulnerability, an awareness of national official policies, as a result of past experience and lingering present prejudices that are sometimes institutionalised. One of the guarantees for the diaspora minorities' rights lies logically with the internationalisation of national markets. The more Southeast Asia becomes dependent on the global capital market, the less the native governments will be free to apply ethnic discrimination. The diaspora's desire for greater capital integration regionally and globally, besides its economic rationality, carries political motives. This desire influences to a large extent the course of such integration.

Besides the diversity of East Asia outlined earlier, perhaps the most crucial split concerns the net ownership of capital. This aspect needs to be elaborated given the region's current distribution of that ownership, i.e. between capital surplus or deficit countries. From a theoretical perspective, capital ownership is not an issue. It matters not whether Japan or the US or China owns surplus capital, for that capital will flow to where the marginal rate of return on capital is highest, until all regions' rates are equalised. What individual countries need to focus more on is how to use capital, rather than how to own capital. Efficient utilisation of capital in an economy will, ceteris paribus, draw more capital into that economy than otherwise. If a country's labour can be employed by a foreign firm for the benefit of both, there is no reason why this arrangement cannot be applied to capital. Taken to its logical conclusion, in this framework, there need not be sleepless nights for policymakers over current account deficits and foreign debt, as long as the debt is accumulated by the private sector. Failure on the part of borrowers to satisfy the capital usage efficiency requirement would result in a shortage of capital for those particular borrowers and higher interest rates, a reasonable market feedback outcome.

Debt and direction for capital market change

Reality, however, requires adjustment to this theoretical framework due to several inherent assumptions, two of which are vital. First is clearly perfect capital mobility. The world today can be said to be characterised by sufficient capital mobility (and internationalisation of the world capital market) for debtor countries not to be overly fearful of foreign debt. The risk of a government going out on its own to direct its citizens to withdraw foreign investment from a particular foreign country for political reasons is small. Moreover, the impact on the target country of such investment sanction would be negligible. If imperfection in global capital mobility still exists, the imperfection has been continuously rectified. Deregulation and liberalisation policy has been in force across East Asia as it has across the globe.

The second condition, perfect information, is not so easily satisfied. Information is more tricky than mobility since it cannot be legislated in. Or put another way, the lack of perfect information cannot be legislated away. Tests on capital market efficiency still do not support the strong hypothesis. If so, risk differentials will continue to exist between markets for reasons other than completely unexpected events. Country risk differentials follow, and real interest rate differentials between countries reflect not just un-systematic risks but also country investors' perception of a country's makeup or any other characteristic that causes a country to appear 'more risky' than others.

Take a large economy like the US, with less than 10 per cent of its GNP accounted for by the traded sector. Take another economy like Australia, about 1/15th the size of the US, with 15 per cent of its GDP made up by the traded sector. World cyclical swings both reward and punish Australia more than the US, rewards and punishments expressed as a proportion of the respective domestic economy. Theoretically, there should be no long-term differentials between the two countries' risk assessment, and therefore no real interest rate differentials either, all things being equal. Yet, these differentials have been long lasting because of Australia's net foreign debt being much higher than that of the US, again expressed as a proportion of GDP. Why, if foreign debt, theoretically, should not be an issue?

Is it because of policy risk, as a result of Australia's inflation management record having been dismal in the 1980s? Perhaps, but Australia's inflation rate has been lower than that of the US since 1992 and has been projected by financial markets to remain very low (around 2–4 per cent) for the balance of the 1990s. Yet, real government bond yields in Australia have been at least 2.5 percentage points higher than US equivalents, a position not much improved from the 1980s. Several capital cost studies have failed to make sense of this continued wide interest rate margin between the two economies. Financial markets still talk of Australia's foreign debt risk, when the capacity to service that debt has improved significantly in the 1990s. Australia's foreign debt servicing accounted for 12.4 per cent of total exports in 1992–93, compared to 21 per cent in 1989–90. Manufacture exports have risen from 10 per cent of total exports in 1983–84 to around 20 per cent in 1992–93.[24] Even the resource commodities exporter tag does not fit the country any more.

In East Asia, data show a spread of creditor and debtor countries across the region. This capital ownership split (the net savings surplus countries versus the deficit countries) may prove to be a decisive factor in any attempt at assessing prospects for individual national development in the region. How countries stand in their capital ownership stake determine how they develop their capital markets, and how responsive they are to the world market. In Australia's experience, a nation cannot sustain high foreign debt to GDP levels without giving away a large degree of domestic policymaking autonomy. The real interest rates, which could disadvantage local industries (borrowers), will make sure of that. Responsiveness usually comes in the form of broad liberalisation of financial markets as well as change in institutional and political structures to allow for a strengthening of the regulatory framework, one of the major criteria for foreign investment attraction. In the capital market, efficient regulations require information systems capable of effecting and monitoring large volume transactions. When international information flow accelerates, domestically focused political directives lose their potency.

Table 1.6 shows that international capital does not differentiate regions, ethnicities or nationalities. What counts is capital formation, mobilisation, distribution and utilisation/management. Net creditors include the traditional powerhouses of Germany, the UK, Switzerland and Japan, as well as the NIEs of Asia. On the other side of the ledger, net debtors consist of, again, a cross-regional grouping: Italy, Canada, the US, Saudi Arabia, South Korea and most of the ASEAN economies.

The largest net debtors are also spread across regions, e.g. Canada and Australia. However, among the largest debtors, a bias towards parts of Asia can be detected. Besides New Zealand and Australia's high net foreign debt to GDP ratios, the Philippines and Indonesia both carry 60 per cent leverage, a high risk category based on conventional international rating.

Table 1.6 World's net debtors and creditors: 1993

Debtor countries	Net foreign debt (US$ bn)	Net debt as % of GNP	Yearly exports as % of net debt
US	611.5	10	73
Canada	237	43	55
Australia	112.3	39	38
Brazil	111.2	25	447.4
Italy	107	9	161
Mexico	75.7	23	335
Indonesia	73.6	60	46
India	73.5	27	274.7
China	69.3	15	125
South Korea	42.5	14	186
Thailand	37.4	35	89
New Zealand	35	87	28
Philippines	32	60	31
Pakistan	18.4	34	54.2
Malaysia	15.8	28	269
Sri Lanka	5.4	56	9.7
Saudi Arabia	16.7	27	60.8

Creditor countries:
Britain, Switzerland, Germany, Hong Kong, Taiwan, Singapore, Brunei

Sources: Key Indicators of Developing Asian and Pacific Countries, ADB, and International Financial Statistics, IMF, various issues

Sri Lanka follows closely at 56 per cent, with Pakistan and Thailand in the 30–40 per cent region, far higher than the ratios for the problem economies of Latin America, Mexico and Brazil.

The debt servicing burden can be appreciated from the countries' exports as a multiple (or proportion) of net foreign debt. In Asia, debt servicing has been heaviest for Sri Lanka, New Zealand, the Philippines and Australia, followed by Indonesia and Pakistan. Thailand ranks some levels better, and China still more comfortable. In other regions, Italy's position is 'safe' but that of Canada is not. The extent to which a country is leveraged in net terms relative to its export capacity represents a significant constraint on that country's ability to pursue domestic policy independent of the demands of the world capital market.

Other factors come into play naturally. For instance, besides the fact that the US carries a relatively small net foreign debt as a proportion of its GNP (and the country's capacity to service its debt is high), its eminent position in international finance allows it to influence world financial markets more than a smaller country in a similar debt position could. After all, inter-national funds managers have to hold some sovereign bonds in their portfolios and US government paper remains among the most attractive. For smaller economies, high net foreign debt unambiguously imposes constraints on domestic policy. These constraints to a large extent have been driving debtor countries' capital market reforms in East Asia in accommodation of the global counterpart.

A study of capital markets and economic integration in East Asia that is not merely descriptive must therefore recognise the varied domestic posi-tions within the international context. Policy decisions about capital markets and integration are made on this basis. A reasonably comprehensive approach to looking at the region's capital markets would need to apply critical analysis to the economic information available as well as cast a view on socio-political parameters. It should also hypothesise a theoretical framework within which the relationships between economic and non-economic variables could be interpreted and projected. The following chapters attempt to deal with these multiple requirements. It is hoped that the attempt does not undermine too much the coherence of the subject by admitting the plurality of views on, and factors in play in, the development of East Asia's capital markets.

NOTES

1   Ohmae, K. *Triad Power: The Coming Shape of Global Competition*, Free Press, 1985.
2   *Asian Wall Street Journal*, 18 May 1993, p. 1.
3   *Time Australia*, February 1993, p. 18.
4   Thomas, V. 'East Asia's Infrastructure and Financing', presented at the Institute for International Research's conference on Policies and Financing in the Asian Region Through the 1990s, Singapore, November 1993.
5   Greenwood, J.G. 'Portfolio Investment in Asian and Pacific Economies: Trends and Prospects', *Asian Development Review*, ADB, vol. 11 (1), pp. 122–3.
6   *Far Eastern Economic Review*, various issues, 1992–93.
7   Among others, see Garnaut, R. 'The 1990s in The Region – Economic', p. 247, in Harris and Cotton (eds), *The End of the Cold War in Northeast Asia*, Longman Cheshire-Rienner, 1991.
8   Business Asia, *The Australian*, 8 September 1993, p. 5.
9   Lever-Tracy, C. and Tracy, N. 'The Dragon and the Rising Sun: Market Integration and Economic Rivalry in East and Southeast Asia', presented at the 1992 Meeting of International Working Party on Labour Market Segmentation, Cambridge, July; and 'The Making of a New Little Dragon: The Overseas Chinese and the Transformation of Guangdong', Asia Research Centre, Murdoch University, 1993.
10   See for example Segal, G. 'The Challenges to Chinese Foreign Policy', in Harris, S. and Cotton, J. (eds), op. cit.

11   *Asiaweek,* 6 October 1993, p. 29.

12   Overholt, W. *China: The Next Superpower,* Weidenfeld and Nicolson, 1993.

13   *China Economic News,* various issues, 1992–94.

14   *Market Brief,* GK Goh Securities (Hong Kong) Ltd, May 1993.

15   Chongyi, F. 'The Peasantry and the Chinese Communist Party', Working Paper, Asia Research Centre, Murdoch University, 1993.

16   Cohen, M.J. *Taiwan at the Crossroads,* Asia Resources Centre, Washington, 1988; Hewison, K. *Bankers and Bureaucrats: Capital and State in Thailand,* Yale University Southeast Asia Monographs 34, New Haven, 1989; and Robison, R. *Indonesia: The Rise of Capital,* Allen and Unwin, 1986.

17   Akrasanee, N. a prominent Thai government adviser and member of APEC's Eminent Persons Group, offered the inside view of the acronym AFTA as 'agree first and talk after' (Busines Symposium, Conference of Economists, Perth, Western Australia, September 1993).

18   *The Australian,* 31 August 1994, p. 1.

19   Clegg, S. and Redding, S.G. (eds), *Capitalism in Contrasting Cultures,* Walter de Gruyter, Berlin, 1990.

20   Chien, F. 'A View From Taipei', Foreign Affairs, Winter 1991–92; The ROC Joins the UN, pamphlet issued by the ROC Foreign Affairs, May 1993; Zagoria, D.S. 'Taiwan and the Asia–Pacific New International Order', and Cheng, C.Y. 'The Role of the Republic of China in the World Economy', papers presented at the New International Order Conference, August 1991, Taipei.

21   *Country Economic Brief,* Asian countries series, Department of Foreign Affairs and Trade, Government Publishing Service: Canberra, 1992 and 1993; and Robison, R., Chalmers, I. and Spencer, C. *Investment Flows in East and Southeast Asia,* report to the Western Australia Department of Commerce and Trade, 1993.

22   *South China Morning Post,* 8 October 1993, p. 1.

23   Chongyi, F. and Goodman, D. 'Guangdong: Greater Hong Kong and The New Regionalist Future', paper presented at the China Deconstruct Conference, Washington DC, October 1993.

24   Australian Bureau of Statistics, *Australian Economic Indicators,* various issues.

Chapter 2

East Asia's capital market reform within the global political economic framework

Ky Cao

As a prelude to the more specific capital market studies which follow, this chapter seeks to lay out a broad political economic framework in which the development of East Asia's capital markets will likely fit. This framework is founded on a number of major strands of development in the world's political, social and economic spheres over the last decade. We will try to argue the points by drawing together evidence in recent years and the theoretical bases on which the understanding of the role of capital in political economy rests. Along the way, we will raise several questions regarding this political economic role of capital, how capital has evolved over time, and whether an analysis of the interaction between the modern global capital market and national counterparts in East Asia could help shed light on to the development path of these markets. Besides interesting theoretical implications, this analysis could also serve as a strategic outlook on capital market trends that might prove valuable for international funds managers and investors.

ECONOMIC DEVELOPMENT AND CAPITAL MARKETS

According to Rostow, there is no common thread, no single pattern or sequence, that runs through the experience of all countries' economic development history. This is particularly true, he conceded, of stimuli required for the economic take-off stage which may come in various forms, one of which is through technological revolution. This seems to conform to later, more extended views on economic growth despite Rostow's pre-occupation with the industrial revolution in his theorising.[1]

One of his outspoken critics, Kuznets, questioned the empiricism of Rostow's thesis, demanding a more detailed description of what Rostow meant by 'political, social and institutional framework . . . which exploits the impulse to expansion', a requirement for the take-off not to be aborted. Equally in need of clarification is Rostow's claim that investment be maintained at over 10 per cent of national income for the take-off stage to be sustained.[2]

Logical as Kuznets' demands are, one could sympathise with Rostow's sweeping statements about the stages of growth. From the traditional stage – where productivity is seen to be capped by the limitations of science, low mobility or social change, and great divisions of wealth – to the mass consumption stage which Rostow didn't bother to define, one could detect not so much clear-cut transitional patterns as broad manifestations of common behaviours. The stages described by Rostow are indeed filled with overlapping characteristics,[3] and East Asia's recent history has led to the inevitable conclusion that studying economic development there does require one to step above neat segmentation, beyond the realm of quantitative analysis, and to stray a little from the confines of empiricism. This is not a question of methodology. It is not even one of unreliability of data, to which Asian economies are known to be prone. It is a matter of necessity given the close correlation between politics, economics and society in Asia's policy formation.

This closeness has been made more pronounced than, say, in the case of Western societies due to the absence of a mercantilist phase, whose commercial development pioneered by private traders would have tended to decouple trade and commerce from the state (at least until the latter caught up in the form of military support for maintenance of overseas markets or institutional reform). Furthermore, as this chapter unfolds, other issues of conceptual import will emerge regarding how to treat capital markets and economic integration in their totality without having to treat first the definition of capital and the measurement of its return. This treatment obviously would need to take into account the social political environments that contribute to choices for integration, driven mainly by global technological change. All of these factors seem to make choices at domestic level both crucial (e.g., for portfolio analysis) in the medium term, and yet increasingly less relevant in the long run.

A later look at the history of economic thought on capital may assist in tracing certain development patterns for economies. By adopting the sequencing view of economic growth, one could to some extent presage the conditions necessary for East Asia's transition to the next stage of development, i.e., its prospects for capital market reform and further economic integration. The subsequent chapters do not concentrate exclusively on investment flow or ratios to GNP, but also on the process of capital formation, management and utilisation, and the institutional and regulatory environment within which this process takes place. The reform drives in various East Asian capital markets to improve transaction transparency, liquidity, and other market characteristics is just as vital as the amount of gross capital actually accumulated.

East Asia's financial take-off

In many ways, East Asia's transition towards take-off can be viewed as more or less achieved. The rise in capital formation in the region has been an integral part of real economies' expansion from predominantly agrarian production to early industrialisation. This capital formation – in the post foreign aid era – has consisted of domestic saving and foreign direct investment, facilitating the establishment of an industrial base in urban areas. Most early development economists, including Lange, Lewis and Nurkse, regarded capital accumulation as fundamental to growth. Not unlike Rostow, Lewis identified three stages of savings-driven investment for development. He quantified national savings at 12–15 per cent of national income as necessary for capital availability for investment. Then, the next step would be to channel these savings to investors, and finally the economy must be able to use the capital effectively.

In East Asia, the preconditions for higher investment to GNP ratios are established: availability of willing and innovative workforces (including entrepreneurs) and of risk capital; social acceptance of a factory-based economy with high division of labour; emergence of new social élites to substitute land-based authorities; and channelling of surplus product by the new élites from agriculture to industry, with labour responding to material incentives. East Asia has also satisfied another prerequisite for take-off: the establishment of 'leading sectors', as Rostow put it. Export oriented industries have made significant inroads into global markets, not only forcing out labour-intensive competitors but even challenging traditional capital-intensive multinationals.

In other ways, however, this transition stage has not been completed. Investment in transportation and other infrastructure has not been pronounced in East Asia. Only in recent years have governments in East Asia looked at infrastructure seriously. Thailand's roads are a shambles, and so are China's rural and interprovincial transportation systems.[4] As the following chapters reveal, financial infrastructures lag even more behind, although they have received increasing government attention in the last half decade. Capital market development has historically trailed behind real economy development, since the former requires not just the availability of capital but also the efficient distribution and management of capital. The latter is needed to improve matching needs between capital suppliers and demanders, to raise market liquidity, reduce transaction cost, spread investment risk and maximise capital return, in order to promote sustained and balanced economic growth. This efficiency relies on well developed market technology and operation, which in turn requires a high degree of institutional sophistication.

Given the size of these remaining tasks in completing the transition stage, the need for modern government and political structures has never been more pronounced. The length of this transition depends on the resources devoted to the replacement of the old order, and on the open-mindedness of political leadership, which appreciates the practical needs for political as much as economic liberalisation. Political and market systems reforms are the broad manifestations of this stage's successful completion.

In East Asia, economic growth triggered by the transition to early industrialisation has spawned material wealth across the citizenries, forming the foundation for emerging middle classes. Whether these 'new rich' correspond to the Western liberal concept of middle-classes depends on how one views these classes. While East Asia's new rich do not have a track record in consolidating institutional democracy as understood by the West, the deep changes in East Asian societies over the last decade have brought up middle class consumption behaviours indistinguishable from Western counterparts, a development corroborated by the tremendous growth in world trade. Even democratisation is clearly spreading in the region, if not in the way Western liberals would have imagined. A generational change is galloping across the continent, with the new rich urging and managing change, from political structure and industrial organisation (Taiwan, South Korea, the PRC) to corporate administration. It would, therefore, seem myopic to strain one's eyes looking for the things that remain different between East Asia's new rich and the West's older rich. These differences are social-conceptual in nature, and have very little impact on how economic and even political integration region-wide or worldwide progresses. They in fact merely symbolise market variations of the type that have driven massive intra-industry trade growth between countries.

The new rich in East Asia are now both providers of labour and consumers of increasingly elaborate manufactured products. Collectively, they are also the modern owners of capital. As the skill levels required in the labour content rise, there is increasing need for more technology in both education (for labour input efficiency) and financial sector application (for capital mobilisation and utilisation efficiency). Demand for sophisticated products will be accompanied by demand for financial arrangements that would facilitate real and financial products' transfer. This consumption trend is accompanied by saving/investment activity whereby previously simple accumulation of savings through an inflexible system of state banks will lose attractiveness, giving rise to more innovative and varied alternatives. These demands for new and flexible financial systems and services will signal the coming of age of economies that have so far been driven by capital available from traditional sources, or channelled through traditional intermediaries. Changing capital sourcing and distribution patterns, i.e. changes in the market of capital and in its management, can reveal much about the make-up and stage of development of an economy under observation. Conversely, changes in political and social stuctures provide insights into the medium term prospects for financial systems and markets reform in East Asia.

REFORM: A GLOBAL IMPERATIVE

Robison and others have argued convincingly that the success of a reform process is based largely on existing social structural factors, the sets of relationships that are reflected in state policy directions and which are subject to dynamic evolution.[5] Although their arguments are made with regard to political economic reform, i.e. a society's evolution towards democratic capitalism – with emphasis on democratic – they could also be applied to the more specific capital markets reform (and economic change, with emphasis on capitalism). By looking at these social structural relationships and their role in determining the domestic policy framework, linkages between the state picture and the global economy can be highlighted. This would allow us to appreciate the fundamental difference that has evolved between the political/social framework and the economic framework. For small (not least open) economies, this difference is bound to widen over time.

While acknowledging that social structural factors play a determining role (through policy formation) in the effectiveness of market reform in East Asia, the domestic perspective will likely be of limited significance. For when it comes to capital markets and economic change, the dictates of the global market have been so overwhelming that few national power structures have been able to withstand its impact for long. International structural factors are far more pervasive than domestic factors in pressuring national polities to change. There is little argument over the world oil price falls since the 1970s being the trigger for Indonesia's socio-economic restructuring.[6] To these, we may add structural factors that are less accidental and more technical in character, such as certain market conditions necessary for the effective transfer of capital between a country and the rest of the world. In other words, for a country to attract foreign investment, it must comply with basic rules prevailing in the global market (e.g., for credit monitoring), and structural change within an economy will have to reflect the demands of the international market in the long term.

The global economic framework has tended to take precedence over national ones, since national economic development has always been determined by access to technology and capital, the first being borderless by nature and the second having been increasingly internationalised. International capital is the weight of finance that circulates the world in search of an acceptable balance between return and risk. This capital is handled by globally focused specialists on behalf of multinational savers/investors. International capital is not concerned with nation states but with relative economic performance, whether this be between regions or countries, or between sectors within one country. If one looks at the multinational investors and savers as an exogenous and homogeneous force, the international capital market then becomes an exogenous (universal) club to which nation states could apply for membership. The degree of exogeneity depends on an economy's relative size, whether the economy is a net creditor or debtor, and the extent of its financial technology capacity. Size, long run capital surplus and advanced technology will form a formidable force in influencing the climate of the global financial club. For the large majority of economies that are neither overwhelming in size, leaders in financial technology, nor monopolies in the supply of world capital, they have basically two choices: either to join the club in a bid to attract part of this capital (and with it, technology), or not to join. Most have sensibly chosen the first alternative.

Integration and sovereignty

At the heart of the conflict between so called national sovereignty and economic growth for any country lies the ownership of capital and financial technology. While the latter is born out of advanced communication technology and institutional sophistication, the former can be accumulated with real economy progress at more primitive levels. Rising household incomes following an era of surging productivity tend to lift savings as a proportion of earnings. Depending on how long the productivity surge lasts, consumption growth will gradually regain grounds and overtake savings growth to bring savings ratios down. The lower the base from which household incomes take off, the longer this productivity surge, an experience seen in low income countries catching up with the OECD by using transplanted industrial technology.

Because of this timing in the stage of development, East Asia is in the midst of a capital accumulation phase which should ease as its economies reach capacity bottlenecks. The current phase, however, has been allowing East Asia's capital surplus countries far more room in domestic policy matters than deficit countries. The large literature on the topic of foreign debt in the US and Australia stemmed from concerns over sovereignty resulting from the rises in these countries' foreign indebtedness in the 1980s. Australia, being a small, open economy, had felt these concerns more acutely. Pressures have since been exerted on domestic policy to come up with an effective domestic savings strategy, culminating in the Fitzgerald report of 1993.[7]

Similarly, most debtor nations around the world are waging a dual struggle, one aimed at attracting foreign capital (for growth) and the other directed (against losing policy autonomy) at boosting domestic savings. Both require advanced financial sectors that will conform to the demands of the global market (foreign savers) as well as those of domestic savers. For creditor nations, the direct pressure is from domestic rather than foreign savers, although in order to satisfy domestic savers these countries need to bid for foreign users of their capital. This interaction sooner or later leads to them (surplus nations) taking account of foreign capital market conditions and rules, which are dominated by prevailing global standards. At household/business level, what counts more is not national sovereignty but return on savings, which can only be maximised by better access to more markets. There is thus an inherent tendency towards globalisation in the market for capital.

This view of the international capital market can be differentiated from the modernisation school of thought on political economy. Modernists regard joining the international (developed economy) club as a natural progression from traditional society to industrial democracy. This is done through either a transplantation of more developed countries' capitalist thoughts and institutions, or an internal process covering phases of development as outlined by Rostow and, in more recent times, New Growth theorists.[8] When certain societies failed to proceed along this relatively straight line, modernists would look to cultural factors to explain these societies' failure to railroad towards democratic capitalism.

But such a view ignores the great differences in culture among those countries that have crossed the line (and among those that have not). If one accepts that democracy has more to do with behaviour and thought than with institutional make-up, then cultural factors may not count for much. Should democracy be viewed strictly as a system that allows for competitive elections or one in which oppositional politics is internalised within a single party? One-party states are not necessarily undemocratic, if access to the political market is open to all. The economic corollary for this is the contestable monopolistic market. Further, where can we fit cultural peculiarities in the many single-party states that still dominate the culturally diverse developing world? Similarly, communism or capitalism could not be ascribed to cultural factors since one ethnic group, say, the Chinese, could excel in playing by either system's rules.

It is difficult to perceive a linear progression or cultural divide in the framework of the international capital market. Nation states have the power to choose to be or not to be part of the global system within a certain time frame. In the longer term, relative economic performance will impose change on them regardless of domestic choices. This limited time frame allows for the manifestations of what statist theorists call the value judgement based policy of governments according to the distribution of power and relationships within a society.[9] In this statist world, the government can take a partisan view and play a critical role in establishing the domestic political economic agenda. Government control can also come in many guises. The totalitarian (Leninist) approach, by which the government assumed ownership of all factors of production, prevented market determination of economic behaviour in any form; or the authoritarian world in which markets are allowed to determine prices and influence resource allocation while the state, reflected in the make-up of a particular government and sometimes personified by a political leader, plays a dominant role in the ownership of production factors (such as in Indonesia). The fundamental difference between these two statist systems is clearly the existence of the market. The latter, government-led market economy is closer to the development history of East Asia, where foreign aid had contributed critically to early industrialisation and where the lack of traditional bourgeois classes (and with it a competent private sector) had permitted the government to assume the steering role in development.

It has been documented that the current East Asian Newly Industrialised Economies (NIEs) used to receive massive amounts of US aid in the 1950s and early 1960s. During this period, government-received aid financed about 70 per cent of South Korea's total imports and 85 per cent of its current account deficit. For Taiwan, aid paid for up to 40 per cent of goods and services imports in the early 1950s. Similarly, foreign investment handled directly by government bodies constituted around 90 per cent of Singapore's gross external liabilities. Without a developed private sector capable of managing such early transfer of capital, it is no surprise that government direction had been pervasive in East Asia in those times.

This active role had sometimes transformed governments into semi-bourgeoisies, in competition against other influential classes or groups in the fight to control capital and power in national economies. This social competition has lingered to the present as seen in Malaysia and Indonesia, where governments continue to erode the influence of the religious fundamentalist groups.

How long totalitarianism could persevere is now history. Whether founded on dialectical materialism and scientific socialism of the soviet mould, or on humanist socialism along Lukacs' lines[10] – i.e. giving force to the introduction of democratic (open-election) reform in the communist movement – major non-market based regimes have ceased to exist. Certainly, remnants of totalitarianism, not least of all in socialist form, still dwell in corners around the globe. But these regimes are insignificant in any practical sense in the context of world development. With today's telecommunications technology, attempts at totalitarianising economies would seem futile, and not likely to last the distance that the Second World had managed to do.

Authoritarian regimes' longevity is higher, simply because they are shored up by the existence of the market, which feeds a degree of efficiency into inter-industry/sector resource allocation. This efficiency offsets to a large extent the inefficiency associated with intra-industry allocation, the latter caused by state ownership of a large portion of productive processes (state monopolies in closed markets). The long term tendency, however, is for these regimes to yield to global forces, to make room for a relatively stronger private sector in a competitive bidding for global capital. State monopolies distort the domestic market not only through their market position but also their reliance on political patronage. Indonesia and China represent perfect cases for the study of such monopolies. Political leaders' and government officials' ownership of production factors and business operations in these countries have made system reform extremely difficult without the all-embracing pressure exerted on them from the outside. These pressures had more or less impinged on these countries' national security. International structural changes like the falls in world prices for oil, one of Indonesia's staple export commodities, triggered the reform of the 1980s. The rapid rises in Taiwan's and Japan's GDP in the 1960s and 1970s added momentum to the PRC's dramatic philosophical somersault in 1978.

The ruling partnerhips of East Asia's underperforming economies (the non-NIEs) saw that their interests were being threatened by continued inefficiency in the general economy. These partnerships, usually comprising government and the largest state enterprises, have made attempts to reform their system under their own terms. But the experience has been that when the time for economic liberalisation could no longer be avoided, the imperative has been for governments to privatise or deregulate market structures at faster than planned pace, to encourage competition or at least introduce market contestability in order to improve international competitiveness.

Contemporary examples of the friction and fusion of domestic social factors and international structural factors riddle East Asia's economic landscape as related in the chapters that follow. This interaction has also been found in Australia in the 1980s. The long term trend decline in real commodity prices over the forty years to the mid-1980s had jolted Australia into large scale deregulation of its economy during the last decade. In the labour market, where social values and political relationships influenced employment policy, resistance to real wage falls had been mounted in a series of government-union accords between 1983 and 1989. But these accords failed to prevent two outcomes: high levels of unemployment, and a decline in the Australian real average weekly earnings during this period.[11] It is clear that domestic policy choices which reflect internal social-political relationships can be implemented in the medium term in so far as their costs are accepted. These choices in the end can only control nominal (in this case, wage) levels, not the purchasing power that those levels represent. Realisation of this distinction has made interesting impact on the spirit of the accords. They varied in tune significantly during the applicable period, from idealistic (Accord 1 in 1983 was written in strong protectionist language) to opening up the labour market (Accord 4 was about 'growth through exports', in matching, not hiding from, overseas productivity) to greater internationalisation (Accord 7 in 1989 was influenced by the Garnaut and Hughes reports recommending free trade).[12]

The long term also unveils the flaws of dependency theory, whose founding advocates were so pessimistic as to segregate countries according to their location and domestic social-political configurations.[13] The rapid economic ascendancy of East Asia within the international trading structure has imposed a revisionist dependencivist effort, whose product is the 'international division of labour' paradigm. Certainly, there may have been a logical economic stratification at the beginning of East Asia's entrance into the international trading system and capital market. As early international trade tended to revolve around comparative advantages in resource endowment, so the new entrants to the global capital market would need to go through certain rites of passage. But intra-industry trade and national expansion into export fields that are not closely related to relative resource endowment only underline the potential ease with which countries could shift their comparative advantage away from classical assumptions and, therefore, from the dependency (old or new) pigeonholes. The success of this type of shift is testament to East Asia's willingness to strike a balance in favour of integration with the international market. This has happened in full cognisance that the existing ruling partnerships' relative political autonomy will be eroded over time.

Thailand began the post-war years with a policy of agricultural exports and import substitution industrialisation. In the 1980s, however, the country switched towards export-oriented manufacturing and policies that encouraged foreign investment and freer capital flows. Thailand is now touted as one of the most promising 'new tigers' in Asia. Hong Kong has shown even more flexibility in responding to change in its short history. Its high degree of integration with the global market has engendered speedy transition from a backward trading post to a labour-intensive manufacturing economy, and then to an elaborate manufacturing and services centre against the background of the rise of labour-intensive China.[14]

Local maxima in political economy

In the medium term, therefore, domestic social structural relationships could obstruct, or facilitate, integration. In the long run, the vested interests of the eventual majority in a society would pave the way for integration, even in the face of earlier obstruction. 'Eventual' does not mean permanent, however, and can be best understood in tems of 'local', as against 'global', maxima in optimisation theory. This eventual majority is a transient one, produced in a particular period of time as a consequence of international and local development phases which have the capacity to redistribute power between groups in a society. This eventual majority is based on two observable factors: the said redistribution of social classes, and thus political power, within domestic society; and the at-times conflicting interests of a government vis-à-vis the civil society at large. The first observation relates to monumental changes that pervade national communities within a relatively short timespan and which are taken advantage of by previously unempowered classes. The industrial revolution in Britain left in its wake a significant reshuffling of power among Britain's social classes as well as those of other societies in contact with the UK. The Russian revolution sent home the message that the early industrial economic system was unsustainable and that allowance would need to be made for the emergence of labour unions and workers' rights across the Western world. The eventual majority applies to the state as much as to civil society, to government as much as the masses. Put crudely, in each development phase, there will be an increasing number of interest groups that will come to agree that change must be made in order to preserve or enhance their individual interests. When these combined interests outweigh the combined potential losses as a result of change, then change will be enacted. The trick in pinpointing when major changes occur is to estimate the net marginal benefits of the major interest groups in a society as a result of change. Although this sounds too wishful for political economic theorising, the direction of change may be able to be picked by grasping at the most vital factors at work in a society. In the late 20th century, there can be no denial that these vital factors are global capital and telecommunications technology, two forces that have been proven to operate well beyond the control of national political and social groups.

With advanced technology, the formation of 'local' eventual majorities has become more frequent and predictable than in the distant past. More extensive educational exchange has facilitated integration (internationalisation), which has historically imposed pressure on and provided strong incentives for domestic governments to take account of the masses' aspirations. National interests, similarly, have been seen as served in the long run by integration, which engenders economic growth and provides nations with the wherewithal to preserve local cultures. Those with the lowest levels of cultural autonomy have been countries (or ethnic groups) with the least access to the world capital market, and hence economic clout. Deprived of interactions with the international market, a country would thus decline in the long term, first economically (relative to others and in some cases, absolutely) and ultimately physically in the form of the collapse of the status quo, risking the disintegration of the state as witnessed in parts of the ex-communist world. At this juncture, a government would have to fall in order that the state be saved.

REFORM: A DOMESTIC PERSPECTIVE

East Asia's efforts at capital market deregulation, in various ways and at different levels of achievement, illustrate the region's willingness to proceed to completion of the transition stage. Governments have been grappling with liberalisation policies designed to open up markets without raising the risks of political chaos.

There are no universal lessons regarding the implementation of various sequences of capital market reform. The IMF has emphasised three well known aspects which are interrelated in any structural reform programme: macroeconomic stability, relative prices alignment for tradeable goods and services, and social/political support. Social/political support could only be achieved by the existing élites not feeling threatened by reform; a stable macroeconomy demands the existence of a strong institutional framework; and the realignment of domestic relative prices to world prices calls for substantial integration with the world trading system and capital market.[15]

Experience shows that market liberalisation programmes need strong institutional support since they tend to entail high inflation, as borne out in Latin American and East European economies. Much of Asia is no exception. China's periodic price surges over the past ten years, for instance, have been caused by a weak central bank unable to control credit creation and money supply; a central government fiscal structure that encourages deficit financing and thus public sector borrowings; outdated central government macroeconomic management practice; the gradual reduction in the old two-tier pricing policy and the termination of extensive government subsidies, leading to jumps in the prices of basic products; and urban pay rises for inefficient state enterprises and government organisations, which remain protected for political reasons despite a deregulating environment (the partial approach dilemma).[16]

These problems point to the need for a developed institutional framework for effective implementation of central monetary policy and supervision of financial markets activity and standards. This framework would need to be stable, removed from the vagaries of political contests – such as manifested in the PRC's regional government officials resisting central government policy directives. Stability requires the full commitment of the central government to make the framework enforceable and transparent, to make a country's sovereign risk assessable by the global capital market. In the PRC, the 1993 appointment of Vice-Premier Zhu Rongji to head of the central bank was clearly aimed at providing the institution with strength, stability and credibility. The standardisation of regulatory institutions and processes is not an indication of a global demand that national values be ignored, but a necessity if the capital market is to work effectively. Capital is a positive, not normative, good, and evaluation of its potential return must be based on objective relationships that can be compared and monitored worldwide.

While economic reform sequencing remains an unresolved issue, capital market development does carry general steps seen as necessary by the International Finance Corporation:[17]

- Deregulate interest rates and credit allocation. Competitive financial intermediation, which encompasses both the credit and securities markets, usually leads to improvement in financial institutions' services, such as in financial instruments.
- Eliminate tax disincentives against equity financing. This can be done specifically through favourable corporate tax rates for publicly listed companies; investment allowances related to the costs of plant and machinery; reduction of inheritance taxes for listed companies; tax credits for securities acquisition; taxation of interest of credit instruments being equated with the level of taxation of dividends and bond yields; exemption of securities transactions from capital gains taxes; favourable tax treatment for premiums paid on life insurance policies; and lower withholding taxes on dividends for foreign portfolio investors.
- Enforce existing regulations on financial institutions.
- Keep government interference in the operations of financial institutions in which it has an interest 'to a minimum'.
- Have the central bank develop a strategy for the appropriate use of its own support, including penalty provisions for breaching reserve ratios, capital adequacy provisions, reporting requirements, loan loss coverage, asset concentration limits, and the range of permissible banking requirements.
- Pass law to enhance the performance of financial markets, such as lending limitations on specific borrowers, insider lending provisions, allowing banks to invest in equities, capital adequacy guidelines, and provision of deposit insurance.
- Pass law to improve money and capital market operations including mandates for the regulation of primary and secondary securities markets, incentives for companies to go public, definition of key items such as securities, brokers, underwriters and public offerings.
- Improve listing and disclosure requirements and enforce accounting and auditing standards.

Capital market reform trends

Indicative of capital market pressures placed on China is the PRC government's deregulation moves in recent times. Over 1992–93, increasingly negative real deposit interest rates at home (as a result of a capped rate market) undermined China's savings stock. Unofficial records estimated capital outflow at US$30 billion in the first half 1993, or three-quarters the size of China's total foreign reserves.[18] Recognising the problem, the People's Bank of China (the central bank) lifted interest rate ceilings in July 1993 in response to earlier jumps in unofficial rates, and helped ease domestic savings outflow by establishing a tighter money environment. Similarly, moves towards a commercial banking system have been pursued in an attempt to streamline the financial environment. The government was intent on setting up specialist banks to provide 'policy' loans in order to free the big four state banks to transact commercial loans. Until 1993, such banks tended to grant commercial loans up to the limits of prudence and would then be called upon to provide low cost loans to priority state construction projects, resulting in large numbers of non-performing loans in the banks' portfolios.

China's re-engagement in the world's capital markets after a forty-year break is also broadening the country's range of funding sources. From commercial bank credits and export credits to multilevel government and corporate bonds issues in the domestic and international bond markets, as well as equity issues, these are helping China diversify from its previous over-reliance on a very few market segments. The Bank of China recently offered bonds in London and sought to list the bonds on the London Stock Exchange – the first time that Chinese bonds would be listed on the LSE.[19] Similarly, Guangdong's GITIC sold five-year floating rate bonds into the Euromarket in 1993. These bond offerings, among others, were aimed at re-establishing China's links to the global institutional investor market.

To appreciate the speed with which China has undertaken financial market reform, the foreign exchange market says it all. As late as mid 1993, official policy had been expressed as moving towards full convertibility of the renminbi in the following five years. Policy then changed to expecting a unified national swap market to operate in 1994–95. By end 1993, the renminbi had been floated, with full convertibility expected to come within two to three years.[20] Questions remain as to how the system will cope with full convertibility when it actually happens, but there is reason to believe that the transition would be smoother than expected.

Across the Straits from China, Taiwan's liberalisation of its own capital market is at a more mature stage. Taiwan's central bank has undertaken significant deregulation of four major areas: prices, market entry, operations and capital flows. Along with IMF recommendations, the interest and exchange rates markets have been liberalised to align domestic relative prices with those in the international market. According to the Banking Law and the Central Bank of China Act, the central bank is authorised to prescribe ceiling rates for bank deposits and approve the ranges of bank lending rates proposed by the Bankers' Association.[21]

But as experienced by other price regulated markets, interest rates restrictions – initially implemented with a view to promote economic growth without inflationary pressure and prevent competitive bidding for deposits by banks (which could lead to high-risk lending to satisfy higher deposit rates) – had led to the creation of an underground market. Prescribed rates at lower than market clearing levels diverted savings from the regulated financial institutions to the unregulated market, prompting credit rationing on the part of the banks and causing misallocation of funds.

As bank lending rates tended to lag the inflation rate, real bank rates became relatively high in downturn years and low in boom years, quite contrary to logical counter-cyclical policy. The central bank consequently phased out interest rate controls on bank deposits and established the money market in 1976, providing an important source of finance besides the banks and the unregulated market.

The years 1980, 1985 and 1986 marked further major decontrol steps in Taiwan. Interest rate ceilings were lifted off certificates of deposit and debentures, bank and credit cooperative discount bills, foreign currency loans, and letters of credit made by domestic banks on the basis of borrowing abroad. These deregulating rounds included the central bank's directive that all banks set prime rates, serving as further benchmarks for the lending rate range. Banks were also allowed to set their own rates on foreign currency deposits, an amendment that helped keep the rates in line with those in international financial markets and encouraged foreign exchange earners to hold foreign currency deposits.

Like other interest rate controlling regimes, Taiwan had found such control harmful during times of higher than expected growth. Low interest rates caused excess demand for funds, which in turn forced the authorities to enact credit rationing, an inefficient process amidst the lack of alternative capital allocation criteria. In this regard, decontrol is a more effective step (than attempts to raise national savings) to solving excess funds demand, since decontrol allows capital allocation to be carried out efficiently.

Other efforts in internationalising the financial sector included inviting the entry of foreign banks, which quickly became a significant force in Taiwan in the 1980s; legislating for foreign exchange market deregulation; lifting controls on trade related transactions on the current acount and allowing Taiwanese to freely hold and use foreign currencies; and encouraging foreign investment in local stocks. The Ministry of Finance lifted restrictions on the number of domestic bank branches that could be established in a given foreign city, recognising the need for local banks to step up penetration of world markets. Integration into the global framework has been underlined by Taiwan's deliberate policy of placing foreign banks on an equal footing with domestic ones. Amendments in the Banking Law have also sought to facilitate the establishment of privately owned banks to enhance the industry's efficiency and enforce stricter supervision and standards. All banks are now required to adhere to the Bank of International Settlements (BIS) endorsed capital adequacy provisions. In 1992, the futures market was legalised by the Legislative Yuan, permitting local investors to trade in hard foreign currencies directly. In 1993, the Ministry of Finance signed futures trading memoranda with the US, Singapore, the UK and France.[22]

The 'Taiwan Funds' issued abroad are targeting foreign capital for investment in domestic securities, a move constituting the first phase of a three-phase plan to permit the entry of foreign investors in the local securities market. Phase two would allow foreign institutional investors to invest directly in the domestic market, and the final phase would be total liberalisation of direct investment by both foreign individual and institutional investors.[23]

Similar changes have been seen in South Korea, where the foundation for a financial economy take-off was laid in the late 1980s. Notwithstanding its remarkable export performance, South Korea has in recent years been suffering from its own rapid growth pace, with surging imports causing external deficits to emerge. Compounding the need for capital has been the change-over from an industrial economy to a service economy. In early 1994, the government unveiled significant reform steps. To provide incentives for foreign investment in the country, Seoul has permitted offshore borrowing equal to 50 per cent of foreign equity (75 per cent for high tech firms). The government has also cut retained earnings tax from 25 per cent to 15 per cent, negotiated with OECD countries with regard to transfer pricing tax; scrapped approval required for land purchases for manufacturing, and set up relations centres to assist foreign invested firms establish themselves in the local economy. Between 1994 and 1997, according to the Ministry of Finance, the government will also cut the number of closed sectors from 224 down to 92.

In Southeast Asia, Thailand can be viewed as a window into the subregion's transformation. While foreign investment in Thailand fell in 1991 amidst the political uncertainty following a military coup, the liberalisation trend over the previous decade has provided solid support for continued growth in the capital market and economy in general. Since its establishment in 1975, the Stock Exchange of Thailand (SET) has grown to one of the emerging markets of Asia. The market capitalisation to GDP ratio rose from 3.88 per cent in 1980 to 56.65 per cent in 1992, with daily market turnover jumping from US$1.06 million to US$301.23 million over the same period.[24] The current 1992–96 Seventh National Economic and Social Development Plan emphasises government priority in mobilisation (rather than accumulation) of savings, improvement in capital market efficiency, promotion of the securities business, investment in the provinces, and internationalisation of the Thai capital market.[25]

Among revamped provisions, the Securities and Exchange Commission (the unified supervisor of the Thai capital market) places significant importance on the speed of stock and debt issue approval and the disclosure of information by issuers. Strict registration and draft prospectus requirements are exempt only under certain conditions, such as to offerings of shares to less than thirty-five persons in twelve months or with a total value of less than 20 million baht (under US$1 million), or exclusively to institutional investors. Legislation has also provided severe penalties for unfair securities trading practices including price manipulation and insider trading, both classified as criminal offences. Other legal changes include the requirement that a mutual fund now must be registered as a juristic person, and a mutual fund supervisor (equivalent to a trustee) be appointed to ensure regulatory compliance. Private fund management, a new securities business, has been opened to accommodate the need of major investors who wish to invest money in securities through the use of professionals.

In general, Thailand has been closely replicating reform moves seen in other East Asian leading as well as emerging markets. Financial policy liberalisation, reduction of withholding tax (from 25 per cent to 15 per cent since January 1992 for foreign companies' receiving capital gains and interest income, and from 20 per cent to 10 per cent for their dividend income), and introduction of a value-added tax (also since January 1992, with listed companies now paying 7 per cent VAT instead of the previous business tax rate of 9.9 per cent on gross receipts). Further, other conventional moves involved the adoption of the Bank of International Settlement standards and the establishment of Bangkok International Banking Facilities (to strengthen Bangkok's offshore financial activity). These developments highlight the trend in national market integration with the world framework discussed previously.

Along with developments in market structure and regulatory framework, technology is being applied with greater speed in the region's capital markets. In 1993, the Hong Kong Stock Exchange installed a new trading system for automatic matching of orders while South Korea's has been developing a fully integrated securities system (System 2000) to replace the existing one. China's Shenzhen and Shanghai exchanges are introducing much bigger capacity computer systems designed to support more brokers and handle a far larger transaction volume. A number of trading centres are being set up in various parts of the PRC to trade bonds and some of these have started developing their own trading systems. In April 1991, Thailand introduced 'ASSET', a floorless trading system that allows brokers to enter orders (through computers from their offices) that are routed to the mainframe computer for automated matching process. National securities trading markets are being appreciated as the next 'integrated market' in China, the Philippines and India.

The extensive application of new technologies (or new application of old technologies) has two important implications. One is the opening of national markets to the flow of world capital; and two is improved central monetary authorities' management capability. In the first case, greater capital market integration will make it harder for a government to succumb to the temptation of returning to a closed regime. In the second, it is likely that there will be a long term reduction in unsystematic risk associated with these emerging investment markets as national economic policy becomes more effective and unofficial activities are curtailed. There is no stopping the spread of modern trading and settlements systems given the availability and increasing affordability of IT technologies like satellite communication networks.[26]

Points of caution

Perhaps one of the biggest short term risks faced by some East Asian economies is that the traditional instinct of political paternalism may continue to cloud the leaderships' judgement. This risk doesn't stop at the partial sectoral deregulation problem mentioned previously, or even misplaced industry policy. It extends to a simplistic belief that a 'third way' could be found for Asia's developing world, where markets could be configured at will by government policy, a notion that capitalism can be used as a tool to achieve socialist ends. China, as discussed, is a potential economic superpower. But probably more than any other East Asian country, China seems to be considering treading this ideological tightrope. The country has opened up with remarkable speed, with individual leaders like Deng and Zhu vowing continued market liberalisation. But at the same time, growth in general government consumption in the twelve years to 1992 had consistently outstripped GNP growth, and this gap has been enlarging over the last few years. The mixed signal is that as far as government intervention in economic production is concerned, Beijing has been retreating, as seen in the rise of the private sector. The non state-owned sector of the PRC economy has raised its share of industrial output growth dramatically, from nil in the 1970s to 61 per cent in 1992 and a projected 75 per cent by 2000.[27] Thus, while realising that productive processes would be better left to the private sector, China has not come around to the view that government abuse of private sector wealth could be just as harmful as direct government assumption of economic production.

The danger for overspending regimes is that, besides fanning inflation, with government demand activity surging, an infant private sector may be deprived of resources and room for development. There lingers in parts of state bureaucracies an illusory belief that the government deserves credit for steering development successfully for the past few decades, ignoring the vital role played by external assistance through foreign aid, investment or privileged export market access. Part of the PRC's central bureaucracy, for instance, still expresses pride in the country's ability to feed a billion population, while ignoring the fact that the billion only managed to feed themselves when freed of bizarre government interventions in agriculture.[28] East Asian governments would better be aware of capital market sentiments as reflected in surveys like the 1993 Arthur Andersen-EIU one: that the large majority of senior managers in the financial sector nominated government spending as the number one potential cause for capital shortage in the Asia–Pacific region.[29]

Short to medium term obstacles to a consistent and proper programme of economic liberalisation and integration will cause individual economies to vary in their success in developing their capital markets. Without a clear cut commitment to market and institutional reform in its own right, economies run the risk of being bogged down in the transition stage as global investors bypass them in favour of other destinations. China's growth over the last few years has been drawing world porfolio investors' funds to East Asia, but this money has flowed to Hong Kong's stock market rather than China's own. Although China has received a substantial amount of direct capital over the last decade, it is Hong Kong that benefited most from world indirect capital punted on China. In terms of financial market deepening, the Territory has done extremely well, having been catapulted to second rank in Asia (after Japan) in stock market capitalisation. In other words, it is China's industrial growth that investors came to support, but it is Hong Kong that handled the transactions. Governments thus carry with them the real responsibility for system reform, by acknowledging markets and private sector activity as the primary structure and force behind the sustained development of the financial economy.

The reality of financial markets development positively affecting GDP growth has traditionally supported the hypothesis of financial liberalisation in development literature. The essence of liberalisation is to enable the economy to provide payment services, mobilise and manage savings and allocate credit efficiently; and to allow the pooling, trading and pricing of risks to improve the flow of information and to promote growth, all of which are of crucial relevance to East Asia. The structuralist critique (and the so called new view of the role of finance) has, however, questioned this financial liberalisation hypothesis by pointing to the experience of countries like South Korea, where financial system reform has been claimed to have merely shifted savings from the informal to the formal market without any concomitant gain in savings. But as Chu's chapter on Taiwan shows, there is more to financial liberalisation than mere capital shifting. Both the quality and quantity of investment have increased in Taiwan with liberalisation and formalisation of the capital market since the late 1980s.

Perhaps there is a case of apple–orange comparison between the liberationists and the structuralists. The latter's point of contention is the fear that liberalisation diverts funds from the informal to the formal market and reduces the supply of loanable funds. This potential could be a real issue in earlier times, when funds were mostly foreign aid or limited agricultural surpluses being used to lay an industrial foundation. By the time economies begin to concern themselves with where to stash away their export surpluses, the structuralist fear is no longer relevant. In fact, when services begin to play a role as vital as manufacturing, the formalisation of the capital market becomes an imperative. Some form of credit tightening is required to focus market participants' minds on efficiency, rather than availability, of capital.

For a taste of what the world capital market can do to remind national governments of their obligations, several brief foreign investor reactions in recent years prove telling. As global investors turned their eyes towards opportunities in China, Malaysia and Indonesia reported a 3 per cent and 8 per cent drop, respectively, in inward foreign investment commitment in 1992. As mentioned, Thailand suffered a fall in foreign investment in 1991 because of a military coup. China was also deserted following Tiananmen, but has since registered a 380 per cent jump in investment commitment, reaching US$57.8 billion in 1992, out of a concerted national effort to convince foreign investors of an unequivocally open China. By these external pressures, Southeast Asia has been pushing ahead with its establishment of 'growth zones' to attract high-yen driven Japanese invest-ment. By 1994, all pretences seemed to have been dropped in Indonesia when the government unveiled a sweeping deregulation programme which allows for 100 per cent foreign ownership of most sectors of the economy, even in those previously considered to be of 'national security' significance.

THE SYNTHETISATION OF ECONOMIES AND MARKETS

The first synthesis: nature of economic policy

The above discussion points to the overwhelming long term trend, amid short term divergences, of East Asian economies integrating with the world economy. This section looks at the fundamental direction in which this integration takes place. The policy battle line in the economics literature of the 1970s and 1980s had been over what role governments should play in facilitating economic growth and development. The Keynesian revolution, which brought about a degree of stability in a world of less interdependent national economies, was caught by the 1970s' oil shocks. International-isation had made national demand management policy gradually ineffectual, with business cycles replaying themselves at global level. When troubles were also seen as coming from the supply side rather than from inadequate aggregate demand – Keynes' fundamental focus – the retreat of active demand management policy became unavoidable. The rise of mone-tarism was no coincidence, since it went hand in hand with the intellectual decline of protectionism in the international trade arena. At both macro (fiscal policy) and micro (industrial tariff policy) levels, interventionist government activity had either ceased to be effective or become outright harmful.[30]

The debate over government role ought to have been settled, in Drucker's view, in the mid-1970s, his 20th-century 'great divide' period.[31]

As he noted, by 1973, 'salvation by society' no longer worked, and the misplaced hope that national governments could determine economic and social policy results should have been laid to rest. But the policy debate survived due to the extension of the arguments into far more pervasive spheres. Cultural and political constructs were called into play by those who believed that domestic factors set the relevant policy framework. A variation of this school of thought is the 'socio-cultural factor' view of development in explaining why, in some economies, central directives seem to have had a more cohesive popular response than in others. Another variant is the 'vested interests' (mainly politicians) variety that affects policy formulation and implementation. In a nutshell, these variations tend towards the statist approach to development policy, whereby the role of the government, negatively or positively, is seen as crucial. Of the vested interests variation, J. Buchanan received a Nobel prize in reward for his work on public choices theory – regarding policy formation in accord with domestic political relationships. Burstein, on the other hand, painted, in his study of Japan, an economy that is the antithesis to Western experience.[32]

The 'socio-cultural divide' school was supported by many business leaders in the US, who have used the spectre of a Japanese economic juggernaut to fan the protectionist fires at home. Wary of its inherent dangers, US administrations have resisted outright protectionist measures and resorted instead to 'breathers' in the form of voluntary export restraint (among other things) on the part of Japan. Moreover, international policy coordination with regard to exchange rates from the mid-1980s led to Western pleas for Japan to take up measures (among them fiscal expansion and a campaign to 'buy foreign') to cut its record trade surplus.[33] Trying to defuse tension, Tokyo duly obliged, and Japan's domestic demand soared across the late 1980s. Japanese import volume growth averaged over 10 per cent per year (doubling exports growth) between 1988 and 1990, cutting Japan's annual trade surplus from US$95 billion to US$63.5 billion in that period.[34] But despite Reagan's small-government rhetoric, US central government spending did not shrink in real terms during the 1980s, with nominal levels rising over 15 per cent during 1985–88. The budget deficit remained at over US$155 billion, or more than 3 per cent of GNP, at near the peak of the domestic economic cycle.

Rising Japanese foreign investment underwrote much of the US's fiscal spending (and Australia's public and private sector debt binge). The US federal government's net borrowing from foreign sources increased from US$32.6 billion in 1985 to US$66.6 billion in 1988. By the time the recession hit in full in 1991, not counting the Savings and Loans debacle, the US federal budget deficit touched US$280 billion, or about 5 per cent of GNP.[35] The debt fall-out, exacerbated by the reluctance of the Federal Reserve to loosen monetary conditions quickly, triggered the early 1990s downturn, events replicated only in other English speaking economies and which could hardly be blamed on Japan.

There have been two broad thrusts developing in the 1990s regarding the role of government in market economies. At one end, yielding to the early 1990s' re-emergence of the large-government school, political leaderships in some OECD economies were pressed to pull back, in a rhetorical sense, from the 'free market, free trade' push of that decade. Active industrial policy was brought back briefly on to some agendas, especially when seen against the background of a very effective and apparently coordinated development strategy pursued by the high profile East Asian region. Drucker's reciprocal trade, i.e., managed trade in other people's language, points to a distrust of the prevailing free trade environment, where trade has become downright adversarial instead of being complementary or even competitive.[36] Government–industry relationships have been argued as the key to successful industrial development, and the high growth rates of East Asian countries have been attributed to the top-down approach, variations of the statist or dirigiste theories of development.

At the other end of the spectrum, the success of East Asia has reinforced the free market conviction of the small-government camp. From their perspective, the best performers have been nation states with the most competitive domestic markets (the case of Japan's car and electronics industries,[37] and Hong Kong in general). The World Bank has reported that active industrial policy has been at best neutral in assisting growth in the NIEs and high flying emerging economies like Thailand and Malaysia.[38] The IMF has also concluded that the 'East Asian miracle' has been realised by people, not governments.[39] Furthermore, the much publicised US external accounts deficit – the apparent outcome of 'naive' free trade advocacy – has been more a result of large government than of trade uncompetitiveness. The merchandise trade deficits that the US had been sustaining – topping US$100 billion in seven of the ten years to 1992 – had in fact been comfortably offset by the country's not insignificant services trade surpluses, which reached US$59 billion in 1992, a fivefold increase since 1986.[40] In 1992, thus, the US suffered a US$33 billion deficit in the goods and services trade account (its merchandise trade deficit was US$92 billion), or half of one per cent of GNP. This ratio is insignificant given the dynamics of international trade and the definitional problems associated with trade statistics. The ratio is also much less than the 5–6 per cent of GNP level represented by the federal budget deficit, which had built up a steady flow of debt servicing payments, the real culprit of the US's substantial current account deficits.

In the financial sector, the 1980s' results have been looked at by the free market school as nothing special beyond the fact that a lesson in effective financial supervision has been learned. From the unforeseen liquidity growth and rising indebtedness, to the necessary clampdown on economic activity, the rash of entrepreneurial bankruptcies and bad debt explosion, a wealth of experience in market liberalisation and financial technology is thought to have been acquired. The debt binge in the US (and Australia) over the last decade had been attributed to several major factors, most of which were technical: the taxation structure that favoured borrowing rather than equity raising; the flourishing of financial derivatives; the internationalisation of domestic markets, which changed the structure of liquidity and had taken a significant degree of control from national governments' hands; and changing social attitudes to debt and savings.[41] The 1990s has been a decade in which a game of regulatory catch-up is being played out. Financial standards and reporting have been upgraded, e.g., the BIS's shifted emphasis on to the risk categories in bank assets rather than the ratios of various reserves themselves. Or the US's grappling with accounting standards which deal with the surging asset securitisation trend around the world in the last five years. The floating of exchange rates by an increasing number of countries over the last ten years has also led to translation requirement in financial reporting, just as business bankruptcies have turned today's corporate board members into ultra-conservatives in the face of tougher penalties for directorial negligence.

At the heart of the matter, the point of differentiation between the two camps is the nature of policy and new regulations. If the regulations aim broadly to limit failures in the market (e.g., through stricter reporting standards, infrastructure building, strategic relations/alliances, education and training, or R&D incentives), then free market proponents will probably support them. If new restrictions and interventions are to be applied to market structures and productive processes, the free market advocates will disapprove. The line in the sand then is not so much between small- and large-government supporters, as between supporters of government involvement in market structuring and productive processes on the one hand, and those against such interventions on the other.

In this regard, there might not be a lot of conflict between the two camps, since the interventionist camp itself has undergone a re-evaluation of what 'active' government involvement means. Would it be correct to term governmental initiatives in, say, opening up foreign markets through diplomatic bargaining and strategic alliance – something perhaps favoured by both camps – as 'industry policy' in the traditional sense of the term? While governments confine themselves to acceptable strategic activity, privatisation and corporatisation – the latter involving public sector enterprises emulating the working conditions of the private sector – will continue to form the central plank of industrial reform in East Asia. This trend is unlikely to be reversed in the foreseeable future.

Economic rationalism in globalisation

The changes affecting economic policy and behaviour across the globe can be summed up in Drucker's claim that there may not be economic theories any more, only economic theorems.[42] Rather than approaching policy from an omnipotent angle, designed to manipulate markets and steer an economy's ideological course, governments have switched their efforts towards dealing with specific issues such as labour relations, trading hours, public enterprise management, and other microeconomic matters. The emphasis on the micro foundation has seen 1980s' governments turn their focus on the nuts and bolts that make individuals and firms tick. Thatcherite Britain was a case in point, where industry issues were dealt with selectively, although within a blanket philosophy of empowering the market with the allocation of resources. Reagan's supply-side view of the world is another. Decontrol the markets (but not necessarily lowering standards) and return to workers their flexibility. Supply-side economics is an expression of faith in microeconomic efficiency, something that national governments could assist, in contrast to the recognition that the macroeconomic picture is now to a large extent in the hands of the global capital market. Economic rationalism in goverment policy is not a domestic choice but an external constraint. And due to its measurable results in raising national welfare, this constraint has been embraced by the OECD and East Asian emerging economies.

What implications for East Asian capital markets can be drawn from here? The macro nature of capital markets would make it safe to predict that liberalisation of these markets (and their standardisation to the international framework) will proceed apace. The common pattern of market deregulation in East Asia has been unmistakable. Incidences of dirgisme and paternalism at large still exist in various economies, but they are more residual problems with a short to medium term time frame than deliberate long term policy. Market liberalisation has been proved to entail transitory clashes among vested interest groups and these tensions will have to be worked through from the inside, to take their course. Externally, cross-country capital flow and their attendant technological transfer have made national governments' attempts at retaining controls on domestic markets increasingly ineffective. Governments can still own companies and industries at home and abroad – or direct the flows of foreign investment into certain sections of the domestic economy – but they have had to adhere increasingly to the rules of international business or suffer capital/technology withdrawal. This constraint is felt most acutely by debtor countries.

International business rules in capital markets refer to the regulatory framework within which capital is formed, mobilised, managed and utilised. How capital formation is realised in an economy is perhaps of secondary importance to the global capital market. How efficiency is ensured in the mobilisation, management and use of this capital – i.e., from all aspects including the effectiveness of macroeconomic policy, the banking system, taxation regime, labour's technical skills, and structure of the domestic capital market – is on the other hand of vital interest to global capital market participants. These three steps of capital usage at domestic level bear directly on the return on capital as a whole. This efficiency is assessed between countries and markets via standardised reporting processes that involve prevailing accounting and legal procedures. The more the clarity and comprehensiveness of the information flow from a particular economy, the higher the willingness of global investors to consider that economy as a potential destination for their funds. An economy in need of foreign capital, therefore, will be placed under intense scrutiny when it comes to what that economy does with the capital it attracts. Domestic policy approaches will over time have to accommodate this scrutiny by converging to the world framework as discussed.

Within East Asia, as long as creditor nations like Japan and the NIEs continue to pursue liberalisation policy, the rest of the region (assuming they are unwilling) will have to follow. This is particularly true when most developing debtor nations' foreign debt is in the government sector, i.e., of the sovereign risk type,[43] which carries far larger repercussions than private sector debt in the case of default. To diminish this sovereign risk, debtor countries will need to create and develop a private sector economy for this to take over an increasing share of national debt raising in the future; and to speed up reform of their domestic capital market to converge with the global market, so that foreign investment in the domestic economy can be encouraged to shift from debt to equity in the long run.

The leaders' adjustments

National accommodation of global market pressures is not confined to small, open economies. Even the US, despite its relatively small traded sector as a proportion of GNP, has suffered from a temporary disregard of the demands of this international marketplace. Besides the well worn example of its motor car industry of the 1980s, the US's industrial 'malaise' has been pinpointed in an in-depth analysis by an MIT team late that decade.[44] While some of its conclusions were predictable – such as, US corporate pre-occupation with short term gains; neglect of human resources; and failure of cooperation among individuals, firms and suppliers, as well as firms and government – the team's telling point is its emphasis on the need for the US real economy to respond more rapidly to changing world demand and supply patterns.

The 'parochialism' lesson that the US manufacturing sector came to learn by the late 1980s has also been applied to the other economic superpower.

Japan's bureaucracy, the much vaunted guardian of the country's macro-economic stability, got chastised occasionally. In 1992, the Ministry of Finance gloated over its 'rescue' of the stock market when it pushed through a fiscal spending programme worth yen 13 trillion (US$116 billion).[45] After more than halving in value between 1990 and 1992, however, the Nikkei 225 index had failed to regain ground over a year later despite a run of three more fiscal injections worth a total of yen 30 trillion.[46] There was indeed one difference between the Japanese and the major English speaking markets, and that is the Nikkei declined over two years compared to the overnight crashes that characterised the latter markets.

Whether this sort of 'gradual crash' is preferable is debatable. The 1987 New York crash was done and finished within a few days. While the damage was extensive, the economy adjusted to the new environment rapidly. Notwithstanding the property price boom that followed the crash as a result of US (and worldwide) monetary easing, the subsequent US downturn in 1990–91 had been less sharp than anticipated. The financial sector was expecting a depression given the collapse of the junk bond market and other high flying schemes, epitomised by the US Securities Exchange Commission's and Attorney's Office's indictment of Drexel Burnham Lambert in 1989.[47] The Savings and Loan problem added a further dimension to the public debt. Yet, the US suffered just 1 per cent contraction in real GNP, making that recession the shortest and shallowest postwar. And although the real economy experienced a couple of false starts in 1992, the recovery since has been quite traditional, with short term interest rate rises in early 1994.[48]

The relatively light US recession in the absence of government intervention – the Bush Administration maintained a 'neutral' policy stance throughout the downturn (even if he had wanted to, Bush would have found little room to manoeuvre fiscally given the large US federal budget deficit and decline in Japanese portfolio investment) – says much about the capacity and speed with which the US private sector came to terms with its own problems. US corporations slashed spending and took advantage of the Federal Reserve's accommodating monetary and regulatory policy to rebuild balance sheets. The instant feedback environment in the US financial economy – where the equity market could lose a third of its value overnight and recessions bring about rapid adjustments – has advantages despite the trauma of volatility. The system bred almost instantaneous reaction to market forces, making required adjustments highly effective. There was little superficial fiddling at corporate level, and bad debt provisions were made as much as practicable. Accounting standards were revamped and auditing systems tightened. Within two years of the 'financial crisis', the US's corporate world was back in profit,[49] its capital market sreamlined and internationalised further by the revoking of the Glass–Steagall Act – which forbids domestic banks from operating across state boundaries – and with the opening of the 144A market to attract corporate issues from medium sized foreign firms.

Japan's has been another story. In its recent history, the Japanese economy has seemed to be able to weather unexpected setbacks. The oil shocks of the 1970s only made the country more efficient in extracting more GDP out of each barrel of oil imported. The endaka (strong yen) trend of the 1980s, which saw the yen rise by 150 per cent against the US$, only taught Japanese companies to be more cost conscious and to take advantage of hedging strategies that ended up giving Japan a larger slice of US manufacturing. If the yen had to rise, then US$ prices of Japanese products could be contained by Japanese companies sourcing their inputs and supplies from US based companies themselves.[50]

This adaptability, however, hadn't been apparent in Japan's financial sector. Adopting the market share priorities of their manufacturing counterparts, Japanese financial firms expanded strongly during the 1980s, gaining a reputation for their placement power. But when Japan's urban real estate prices collapsed, share values that had been overcapitalised on property prices slid with them. Cross-shareholding prevented the type of overnight crash that New York is used to, but it had also kept the Japanese corporate sector mired in the crisis. The consensual corporate culture, the mutual assistance arrangements, all this structural system of values that had worked for the real economy were holding back Japan's financial sector. To limit corporate insolvency, the central authorities had allowed banks and companies to circumvent the bad debt provisions dilemma. By maintaining a comprehensive safety net under the financial institutions, the government was lumping together the good and the bad, absolving the latter from facing up to their shortcomings, and thereby hurting the financial sector as a whole.[51]

It had taken Japan two decades of internationalisation of its own capital market to come to terms with deregulating its interest rates at home in the late 1980s–early 1990s. Although there is still considerable support for the traditional close-knit industrial system, corporate Japan realises that this era may be over. In 1993, the country's major banks started making their largest-ever provisions for bad loans. The switch in corporate financial policy was only the beginning of a trend since the city banks had been the healthiest part of the Japanese banking system. Trillions of yen in unaddressed bad debts are still reported for the regional banks, housing loan finance companies and agricultural cooperatives. By mid-1994, James Capel Pacific still reported Sakura Bank, one of Japan's top banks, as having the weakest balance sheet, with non-performing loans equal to about six years' worth of core profits.

In a 24 March 1994 speech, the then Governor of the Bank of Japan cited US banks' quick recovery on their prompt action to deal with bad debts by discounting sales to investors, a strategy that he urged Japanese banks to follow. As he spoke, balance sheet repair at a large number of Japanese banks continued to be more cosmetic than real. They were shifting their bad debts to the Cooperative Credit Purchasing Company (CCPC), a holding company created by the government in March 1993 to buy the banks' bad loans in exchange for interest-free credit. In the six months ended 31 March 1994, the CCPC purchased loans with a face value of US$25.5 billion, at an average discount of 56 per cent. The resulting US$14.2 billion in tax write-offs flowed straight to the banks' bottom lines. So far, the CCPC has only liquidated US$290 million in bad real estate underlying debt, deferring the day of reckoning for many banks.[52]

In May 1994, the Nihon Keizai Shimbun reported the return to profitability of local brokers, with fourteen of the largest twenty-five Japanese houses registering profits in the year to end March 1994. But the news belied the continuing subsidies the authorities were handing out to firms like Dai-Ichi and Yamatane. The *Far Eastern Economic Review* believed that more than half of first section-listed brokers had seen the value of their shareholder equity decline by more than 25 per cent from their peak. In the case of Cosmo, Sanyo, Kankaku and Yamatane, this resulted in a bail-out led by the Ministry of Finance. There has been much criticism of the subsidies approach since it was seen as doing nothing for capital market liberalisation in Japan. But given the extent of financial damage to business that the halved Nikkei Index represented, these was not much else that the MOF and politically sensitive MITI could do.

Japan's attempt at meeting the bad debt dilemma in a more substantial manner in 1994 perhaps signals a new phase of internal effort in realigning itself with the global capital market. The CCPC has given the major banks some room to manoeuvre. Sakura planned to write off US$2.8 billion in bad loans in 1994 and a further $2.8 billion in 1995. Sumitomo Trust & Banking Company wanted to do the same by about US$1.1 billion in 1994, while

Table 2.1 The state of Japan's top seven securities houses

	Recurring losses of capital %	% decline in value of capital from peak
Nomura	3.2	1.2
Daiwa	5.6	6.5
Nikko	6.5	6.7
Yamaichi	7.9	14.1
New Japan	33.7	34.3
Sanyo	60.3	43.3
Kankaku	64.5	67.5

Source: Salomon Brothers

Bank of Tokyo was looking at approximately US$3.3 billion – nearly all the bad debts it had officially declared. In the 1993 fiscal year (ended March 1994), Japan's 21 biggest banks wrote off or added reserves against US$35 billion in shaky loans, compared to US$10 billion in fiscal 1992. Many banks even raised capital to pay off debts. Daiwa Bank sold US$480 million in mandated stock-convertible bonds in 1993. And banks have been rebelling against MOF regulations such as the prohibition for banks to cut dividends. On 23 March 1994, Hokkaido Takushoku Bank hinted that it would cut its dividend by nearly 30 per cent. The banks also expected that MOF prohibition of banks reporting net losses, which had made it so much harder for them to write off bad debts, would be repealed.

The second synthesis: management approach and social attitudes

A reason for the Japanese approach to policy matters being seen as uniquely successful in postwar decades has been due to a partial mis-interpretation of what had actually constituted the 'Japanese miracle'. Prewar, Japan was already an industrial power, with world class industries. The country's tight-knit industrial organisation that stemmed from an oligopolistic structure driven by zaibatsus (industrial groupings) continued to dominate the domestic business landscape until relatively recently. The dismantling of the zaibatsus immediately after World War II was only nominal, and these subsequently re-emerged as today's conglomerate groupings (keiretsus). There is little misunderstanding in modern Japanese studies literature that the country's economic miracle had in fact been in the making for well over a century.[53]

Similarly, the postwar savings rate differentials between Japan (and most Asian NIEs) on the one hand, and the US and other English speaking economies on the other, cannot be attributable to the Asian or Japanese culture (usually claimed to be dominated by Confucian thoughts). The 1980s' Japanese household savings rate of around 15 per cent (compared to the US's 6 per cent) or national savings rate of around 30 per cent of GNP (twice that of the US) does not necessarily carry cultural connotations. Prewar, the Japanese and US savings rates were roughly the same. The subsequent divergences resulted in those countries' policy choices and economic development stage (with its accompanying social attitudes *vis-à-vis* savings). Japanese authorities made a fundamental choice presented by a US Occupation Force economic adviser in 1950: Joseph Dodge's recom-mendation for tax exemption on interest earned on postal savings bank deposits of up to yen 3 million, a sum twenty-five times the annual income of the average Japanese worker at the time.[54] The plan passed through the Japanese cabinet and Diet amid protestation that it was 'regressive'. By the time this tax exemption was removed in 1988, virtually every income class Japanese household had at least one such account.

Other factors explaining the high savings rate include: the country's relatively primitive financial services, e.g., in the use of cash-substitute products, with personal cheques unknown until the early 1980s; its bonus system, where workers receive large lump-sum distributions of up to 50 per cent of their salary in annual or semi-annual payouts; Japanese male workers, most of whom live by the regular stipends provided by their wives, find most of their bonuses safely put away in the bank whenever they get them. Besides these, it has been claimed that, adjusting for definitional variances in US and Japanese savings statistics, the two countries' rates would differ by just a third of the official magnitude.[55]

Whatever policy characteristics had made Japan such a high savings country have been changing in recent years. Market regulations regarding savings, as mentioned earlier, have been reformulated and the system opened up. The maruyu (post office savings system) is losing many privileges. Under the previous rules, the system had been able to offer a slightly higher rate of interest on their accounts than the banks, together with an explicit government guarantee on those accounts that carried an unfair advantage over private banks in attracting household savings. The maruyu has been the world's largest financial institution (assets in 1989 reached US$1 trillion and by 1993, US$2.5 trillion) outside the central banks.[56] But in the light of Japan's current deregulation programme, with interest rates on time deposits and (by 1994) ordinary accounts liberalised, the maruyu is slowly but inexorably converting to the national and world framework. Similarly, the country's underwriting market is heating up as domestic banks enter the securities business, the ban on such activity having been lifted since April 1993.[57] Tax reform has also taken the OECD road, with a consumption tax introduced in 1989. (Australia is the only country in the OECD without a formal consumption tax, although its indirect tax base has been expanding.)

On the heel of Western countries' clamouring for a spendthrift Japan late last decade, the rise of a new generation of workers more aware of the 'quality of life' is reinforcing this economic transformation. The Sakura Institute of Research and the Ministry of Labour have provided evidence of social change that pervades among Japanese youth. The growing number of young workers who either change or quit their jobs and the burgeoning ranks of non-student, part time workers cannot be attributed to a declining interest in work per se. According to research, they represent an 'attitudinal shift that places heightened importance on the value and suitability of work'.[58]

On the employer side, Japan has been examining the issue of symbiosis – the challenge of living together – to the point that the concept has turned into official policy by the Keidanren (peak business council).[59] This symbiosis looks at relationships within Japan that had given the country undue mystification: the relationship between companies and consumers,

companies and local communities, and companies and their own employees. In a Keidanren survey, 90 per cent of companies said that they felt
a gap exists between their corporate principles and what society accepts to
be the norm. Anecdotes given included scandals in the securities industries,
excessive corporate involvement in money games and financial engineering, the over-specification of products, the practice of making frequent
model changes, over-packaging of products, bid-rigging, shaky transactions, and the neglect of employees' private and family life.[60] All these
issues point to a significant era (not just generational) change in Japan, a
change that appears to accommodate increasingly the less regimented
workstyle and lifestyle seen in Western economies.

The swing in the pendulum has raised other questions regarding
Japanese (East Asian) business practices and philosophy. Corporate management has turned its back on market share expansion and reverted to the
more short term 'Western' concept of profitability as a measure of corporate
performance. The driving force behind the Japanese corporate expansion
of the 1970s and 1980s was its maruyu which, together with an official
interest rate ceiling policy at home, provided Japanese firms with the lowest
cost of capital in the OECD. As the maruryu changes – together with lower
domestic market capitalisation due to the asset bubble burst – cost control
(the other side of the profit maximisation coin) is in fashion. With a
relatively weak world market over the early years of the 1990s, Japan's
corporations had found themselves unable to expand markets at rates seen
in the past to compensate for low margins. Consequently, industrial
production stagnated.[61]

The new environment has been bearing on Japan's labour market.
Lifetime employment has slowly lost its priority in an industrial landscape
forced to be more cost conscious by the changing international market. The
tight mutual support network within the Keidanren has been gradually
eroded because of the poor performance of the domestic asset markets in
1992–93. Industrial productivity is being threatened by the rising number of
unwanted workers on the payroll,[62] and the market share (size) strategy of
the last decade has left Japan with a relatively shallow financial sector. The
last point is significant in that it has made it difficult for Japan to capitalise
on, for instance, the emerging securitisation wave of the 1990s, a development that could have gone some way towards easing Japan's corporate
sector balance sheet problems earlier.

Some research evidence has added uncertainty over Japan's productivity
prospect.[63] The country's physical productivity – industrial production
index divided by labour input – has presumably ranked top in the
developed world due to the level of Japanese technology and efficiency. It
increased by about 90 per cent in the fifteen years to 1990, compared to
about 60 per cent in both the US and Germany. However, when productivity is measured from a value-added perspective, Japan drops below

the other two. Taking GDP and simply dividing it by the number of employed hours, adjusted for purchasing power parity as estimated by the OECD, Japan had consistently lagged both the US and Germany. Although the gaps had been closing over time, US and German productivity in 1990 still ranked 1.2 times and 1.15 times, respectively, that of Japan (Drucker confirms US productivity lead in manufacturing in the 1980s and in agriculture in the early 1990s).[64] The difference between the physical and value-added productivity levels is due to the mentioned Japanese practices of market share priority and of labour hoarding. When total industrial production cannot be raised rapidly (due to output market constraints, especially for Japan's efficient export industries), the only way to maintain high physical productivity growth is to improve hourly (value-added) productivity. Japanese firms, therefore, would need to consider labour shedding more seriously.

Convergence

In the 1990s, as English speaking economies respond to the Japanese challenge by cutting down on leisure time,[65] Japan is showing behaviour more closely identifiable with that in Western markets. This gradual synthesisation of values is reflected in the Japanese government's 1990 adoption of the Basic Plan for Public Investment, which was aimed at raising public spending on social overhead capital (quality of life infra-structure).[66] The international standardisation of Japanese capitalism has been made more pronounced by the seven-party alliance's taking of power

Table 2.2 GDP per employed person: 1991, in US$ (using 1990 purchasing power parity exchange rates)

Country	GDP per person	
USA	47,700	
France	46,500	
Italy	44,500	
Germany	42,000	
Japan	37,500	
Britain	35,500	
Growth in output per employed person, %		
	1990	*1991*	*1992*
Japan	5	−0.4	−4.2
USA	1.9	1.3	3.8

Source: US Bureau of Labor Statistics

Table 2.3 Manufacturing productivity (annual average growth, %)

	1970–79	*1980–89*	*1990–92*
Japan	6.4	2.9	0.6
USA	2.4	3.1	2.2
France	5.5	4.1	1.0
Germany	4.5	2.6	2.6
Britain	2.2	4.3	2.1

Value added per hour worked indexes
1989, Britain = 100

	All business	*Manufacturing*
Japan	70	130
USA	138	161
France	118	123
Germany	104	130

Sources: IMF, University of Groningen, McKinsey, James Capel, as reported in *The Economist*, 28 May 1994

in Japan in late 1993. It would have been quite inconceivable to Japan observers just a couple of years earlier that the incumbent government, a political party that had ruled since the start of the postwar economic miracle, would be voted out in favour of a jumble of minor factions. Especially when those factions' driving social force had been an international economist and management consultant. What is remarkable about Kenichi Ohmae is that he never made any secret about his perception of his own position in the world, that of a global citizen first and Japanese last.[67] For a public Japanese figure, this is indeed significant. It would be hard to imagine a US Republican political aspirant expressing such non-nationalistic sentiment out loud.

There have been some reshufflings in the Japanese political arena since. But to concentrate on the operational aspects of the Japanese political transition would risk missing the point. The new political parties had little affiliation with the bureaucracy nor the way the latter goes about its business. There would be conflict between the demands for tax cuts to the middle class, for example, by the new parties and the prudential tendency of the MOF. There was also concern over the longevity of the fragile coalition and its calls for reform of the electoral system, which in its view had caused election campaigns to be far too expensive and corruption prone. As it would later turn out, Hosokawa, the coalition's prime minister, would resign in April 1994 after eight turbulent months. But a further surprise would also follow, in the form of a veteran socialist succeeding

Hosokawa's successor, Tsutomo Hata. Murayama, the uncharacteristic socialist, is, despite his age, the symbol of a quiet revolution in Japanese society.

Reflecting this change, the MITI has been actively pursuing studies of *risotura*, the massive restructuring required of the Japanese economy. As corporate Japan was losing its competitive edge, MITI has been extensively reviewing Japan's socio-economic policy. For many Japanese firms still held back by tradition, *risotura* has come as a shock. Active labour shedding, instead of natural attrition, has become much less uncommon. Ohmae contended that most Japanese firms had roughly 30 per cent excess capacity in 1992–93, and recovery over the following few years would not be sufficient to bring Japan back to the previous cosy environment. Drastic restructuring is inevitable.

Japan's internal adjustment is throwing open the national development direction debate in many East Asian countries. There was a strong view expressed in the last decade that Japan, rather than the West, should be the lighthouse for Asian economic development policy path. The East Asia Economic Caucus concept, in a broad sense, attempts to totemise this view. But the cyclical changes, together with the rising tide of global capital flow now sweeping the region, have imposed an increasing standardisation of operational structure and regulatory framework across national boundaries. Internal social structural change, not only in Japan but also in the China Basin and Southeast Asia,[68] has added momentum to this globalisation, with the consequence that segmentation concepts (subregional or even regional) are not likely to be productive, substantive or long lasting.

Amid diplomatic manoeuvrings and political alliances that crisscross the Pacific, the underlying economic convergence is continuing its imperial course. Views propagating 'unique Asian values' have ceased to be meaningful. Arguments pointing to the variance between East Asian new rich and Western middle classes, both in sources and social impact outcomes, have turned peripheral. Go Chok Tong's Singapore has distanced itself gradually from Lee Kwan Yew's city state and moved closer to Clinton's US. George Bush's yearning for a gentler, kinder nation was reciprocated by Murayama's promise of a gentler, kinder Japan under his tenure. Asian family values are heading along 'conventional' patterns. Urbanisation takes the working-age people from villages and leaves old parents and young children behind, laying the groundwork for the decline of the agrarian economy and the inevitable emergence of some form of urban social welfare system; women's increasing participation in the workforce means higher divorce rates for families and a restructuring of family units and policy; Singapore recorded a 27 per cent rise in juvenile crime between 1992 and 1993 despite its controversial use of capital punishment. As *The Economist* observed, 'in the heartland of Confucianism, family values are falling prey to the market'.

Table 2.4 Family structure

| | Divorce rate per 1,000 pop., % | | Fertility rate, % | |
	1982	1992	1980	1991
Hong Kong	0.55	0.98	2.22	1.45
Singapore	0.81	1.41	1.77	1.77
South Korea*	5.9	11.8	3.00	1.75

Source: The Economist, 28 May 1994

Note: *Divorce rate is % of number of marriages, 1980–90

The third synthesis: towards a new capital theory of value

Marx and Engels asserted that in the case of economic profit, the classical economists had only shown its positive side. The latter had postulated conditions which regulated the exchange values of commodities, providing a cost theory of the labour value. Profit was regarded as the balance whose size would be determined by other given factors: the value of product and the value of labour power.[69]

This interpretation of profit was thought to be simplistic in early literature, since the why and wherefore of its existence as a category of income remained unexplained. In the theory of rent, the limited supply of land was pointed at as the reason for rent and rent acquisition by land-owners. Classical theory had no parallel reason for profit, or why profit should be appropriated by capitalists. What would happen if profits were taxed or eroded into wages, or if they should constantly fall for some reason? Ricardo's successors like J. S. Mill, Walker and Clark had sought to explain profit along two lines: by developing a new category of real cost, for which profit was an exchange equivalent, or by conceiving profit as a return to special productivity of capital, which was accumulated and brought to use by capitalists (just as land by landlords).

But what these theories suffered collectively, as Marx put it, was that their analysis was based on the nature of the system itself, a characteristic that earned from him the nickname of 'vulgar economics'. Marx saw the nature of profit as not inherent in the capital theory of value, but in the class structure of the existing society. He aimed his sight at the peculiarities of class relations that caused disequilibria in (not just on) capitalism's base. In contrast to equality and rights, Marx witnessed inequality of economic status; as against contractual freedom, he saw economic dependence and compulsion.

There is no mystification about Marx's view of profit. The essence of the relation between capitalists and labourers bears a major analogy to that between owners and their slaves in earlier forms of society in which owners took away the surplus product above the subsistence of their serfs. This surplus product – in a more advanced, capitalist society in which exploitation has been masked by a supposedly competitive market for exchange between equivalents – becomes surplus value. Mill drew the parallel between a slave system and capitalism, with the difference being only in the mode of purchase of labour. Marx extended the idea to a distinction between labour and labour power, the latter being detached from the worker himself. Since the worker had no alternatives but to sell labour power for subsistence, that power and the subsistence level became equal in value. As labour in action was able to realise a product of greater value than the labour power (or subsistence) itself, a profit is made for the employer, something not derived from any procreative quality of capital per se. The class structure inherited from an unequal past allowed the capitalists to appropriate this surplus value. Wages, therefore, represented not the value of the workers' produce but the cost of subsistence. The output's value thus held three components: fixed wage, fixed capital and surplus value. Allowing for a proportion of technology, an expansion path could be formulated for the capitalist economy which would lead over time to a falling rate of surplus value (profit).

This law of diminishing profit rate, which Marx expounded in Volume 1 of *Das Kapital*, would intensify class conflict and risk causing a system collapse, unless capital accumulation could be accelerated to expand the economy. Economic growth, in turn, would raise wages at the expense of profit, a situation correctible by capitalists introducing more labour-saving techniques. This capital intensification, or organic composition of capital ratio in Marx's terms, would rise as the profit rate fell, and the only way to counter this process would be to exploit (immiserise) workers further.

Increased exploitation would not necessarily stop at national borders. In his portrayal of how profit had been kept up since the first industrial revolution, Mandell painted a picture of imperialist economies exporting capital to their lower wage colonies and semi-colonies. This picture is not dissimilar to the present environment where global capital flows in search of low cost (primarily low wage) destinations.[70] But far from turning the world into a system of equalised profit rates as conjured up by Marshall, who believed in the theory of undertakers' profit in a perfectly competitive system, Mandell's capital exports would create a differential system of varying national prices of production and at the same time unified world market prices. This dual result would allow developed countries to maintain high surplus value by selling their products at prices greater than their own national production prices, but less than the buying countries' production prices. The process would intensify differential profit rates and put all the various spheres of production under the control of capitalists, making colonies and semi-colonies a permanent source of supply of profit.

The merging of capital and proletariat

Marxians' immiserisation view of the world economy has not stood up to the test of time. Capital did flow to cheap labour countries and the division of labour did materialise in all initial stages of these economies' development. But trade relationships and patterns could and have changed substantially between the capital exporters and capital receivers within a few generations. The rise of the American colonies and Australia *vis-à-vis* Britain, the most significant 19th-century capital exporter, is a clear example. The changing international trade patterns from resource endowment-determined to intra-industry based over the 20th century show that the division of international labour has been less permanent than Marxian theorists had thought. Sweezy has also proved that once technological change (quality of labour and machinery, not just processing techniques) was allowed into the production function, it would have been possible to derive an economic expansion path in which neither wages nor profits would have to fall over time.[71] Just as Rostow conceded that technological change could make or break an economy's move to take-off, this dynamism would need to be better factored into Marx's model for the latter to remain relevant.

With the modern labour theory of value, Marx's capital composition can be interpreted as inclusive of human, not just physical, capital. As this capital ratio rises, its return is reaped by workers as well as capitalists. Moreover, capital ownership can no longer be seen in terms of inheritance preserved for a small capitalist class, since the bulk of the world capital stock is now owned by households, i.e., the workers themselves.[72] Profit is thus not only taxed, or eroded into wages by an exogenous mechanism like a state's progressive income redistribution policy as speculated by critiques of the classical economists, but internalised as an integral part of workers' value and income. This fusion of the worker and capital ownership is vital in that if the capital composition ratio rises, leading to higher wages, the net profit rate will not necessarily fall if this wage increase leads to higher savings by households and a larger capital pool. An increase in capital supply will then lower the cost of capital and encourage investment, including that in research and development. Again, in complement to Sweezy, there would not necessarily be a conflict between the capital ratio and real net profit.

Marx's followers rejected the long term equalisation of global profit rate because they did not foresee the ability of less developed countries in turning surplus value into profit for both workers and capital employers. This has been achieved by raising continuously the human capital ratio in labour content and adapting to higher levels of production to participate in equal (intra-industry) trade. Nor did they fathom that intra-industry trade would be possible as a result of differential market preferences, differentials that have opened up exchange in equivalent-technology products such as most durable consumer goods today. Intra-industry trade has also been serving low income countries by helping them obtain mass production technology (used in their traded sector), and in accessing consumer goods of various technological levels, the classes of goods that they would not otherwise have been able to consume. Unlike the zero-sum game of the Marxist world, international trade introduced complementary growth in trading nations' welfare.

In surveying the political economy of capital, three problems stand out. One is that the Marxist emphasis on class structures has long been irrelevant. There is no distinction between capital on the one side and labour on the other. The view that surplus value could be realised only through labour power – even when this power embraces human capital, a factor Marx did not explicitly allow for – is completely untenable. Profit as explained by classical and neo-classical economists – i.e., as payment for entrepreneurial services rendered – still belongs to labour-related (managerial) activity. In modern capitalism, profit could be (and has been mainly) derived from non-labour related activity, such as household investment in shares and bonds. Households determine how to dispose of their after-tax income via an intertemporal evaluation of total (present and future) return. Governments decide how much to add to national savings (capital supply) and in turn create national funds such as workers' funds, pension and superannuation funds. In this regard, modern financial theory provides an insight into the troubled question of profit. Utility theory can explain income allocation, with savings mostly determined by interest rates (price of capital), whose setting in turn depends not only on capital supply/demand characteristics but also on the relative workings of financial systems in response to changes in aggregate demand at home and global levels.

The crux of the second problem lies in the Marxian and classical economists' concentration on a production function. Profit in that context is straitjacketed to physical and, at best, human capital, which is still an integral part of a production process. Again, profit in modern capitalism is to a greater extent directly related to non-productive processes. Portfolio capital flows are far larger and more significant than the monetary flows necessary for international goods and services trade (or to the real economy for that matter).[73] Portfolio return (profit) is a result of a vast array of interrelated factors that make up the investment markets' conditions worldwide, only a part of which concerns production: ethnic distribution; demographics and social attitudes which affect international and relative national savings in the short and long terms; market structure (both for output and input), which affects productive and allocative efficiency; structural change such as the shift from bank deposits to other savings vehicles; the state of the financial sector, implying technology in the financial infrastructure and in the institutional framework (advancement in political and regulatory knowledge), which affects the cost of capital through capital mobilisation and management. This list is not exhaustive.

And the third problem centres on the inadequate accounting for technological change in political economic modelling of capital and economy. The inclusion of technology must be done in a much more dynamic way than the 'proportional' approach tried by Marxian, classical and New Growth theorists. The typical inclusion of technology in economic analysis has been to factor in changes in technology at the same rate across all firms, industries or markets, of the Domar and Solow types.[74] This proportional allowance has not captured the haphazard nature of creation and development of new technology, which has periodically thrown economies into convulsions.[75] Some industries decline while others rise, some markets shrink while others expand. The lack of sectoral flexibility in modelling of this permanent structural rearrangement of economies has left a large hole in the understanding of capital and its markets. Technology is an all-encompassing influence on economic life, from the more conventional discovery and implementation of technical concepts that result in better machinery, to new and creative ways of mobilising, utilising and managing finance.

These three fundamental problems beg the question whether profit (return on capital) and surplus value (return on non-labour power) can still be considered synonymous. There clearly is a need for a rethink of how capital and labour are treated in development economics, whether the emphasis should revert to capital value rather than labour value, especially when capital is defined in a multi-dimensional sense that embodies technological change; and whether production functions should continue to be the testing ground for the treatment of the role of and return on capital; which in turn raises the issue of how to address capital in the international trade theory framework, one that focuses on goods and services rather than savings, regulatory institutions and portfolio capital. Exchange rate theory, when approached from this new perspective, would likely yield quite different policy outcomes to what is accepted in the current literature.[76]

SOME ROUND-UP REMARKS

What this chapter has set out to do is look at East Asian capital market reform within a global political economic framework, one that has sustained great changes over the last two decades driven mainly by an intensification in capital mobility. By providing a broad view of capital markets that reaches past a description of their technical and institutional processes to their very *raison d'être*, it is hoped that further research can be stimulated. This is required in order to gain a more thorough understanding of capital and its relationships to other factors of production (especially labour) and to economic life in general. The task of formulating a theoretical framework capable of treating all these linkages (not least quantitatively) that feed into the global capital market is urgently needed.

With this chapter's highlight of the major trends in the global economy, some important insights could be drawn on capital market transformation in East Asia. For instance, for a comprehensive projection of the region's national capital markets and the principles underlining the ways and means which they will probably adopt, one must appreciate:

1 the historical progression of economies that have successfully emerged to a sustainable take-off stage;
2 the capacity of economies to choose in the short to medium term not to participate in the global capital market framework, or to participate only selectively;
3 world trends in financial technology and economic thought governing the direct and indirect use of capital;
4 the distribution of capital ownership between countries and the implications for debtor countries; and
5 the ownership of capital at individual level in modern capitalism and its implications for future economic organisation.

This impressive array of subjects is not designed to distract or dishearten potential researchers. Some observable facts are clear. That economies have been reforming in accordance with structural factor demands, at international and domestic levels: price realignment, institutional reform, development of legal codes and accounting standards, to name a few.

At a more practical level, it is important to note that for (especially indirect) investors with a short to medium term time frame in East Asia, an understanding of domestic social structural relationships is vital in assessing the relative potential (unsystematic) risks and returns of various national markets. These relationships are both outcomes and determinants of particular economic development stages that economies are passing through, and whether they are more outcomes than determinants in some economies than in others should be evaluated carefully. These stages are not solely of the Rostow type since East Asia's economic development embraces experiences of vastly different national backgrounds. An example is China's and Southeast Asia's conventional move from agricultural surplus to early industrialisation, against Hong Kong's, Singapore's, Taiwan's and South Korea's leapfrogging to industrialisation via an infusion of foreign aid and capital, and early adoption of foreign capitalist thoughts, systems and technology.

The search for factors that underline economic change will likely produce positive spinoffs on research into social and political change. So far, political theory has not been able to explain how social classes and political groups are formed and redistributed. Marx took class distribution as a given. So have others. When a society changes, political scientists readjust their view of it. This effort may be futile if they continue to ignore the synthesis between a Western dominated global capital market and the real economy strength of East Asia's emerging powers. The impact of technology has obviously played a great part in the formation and redistribution of classes and power in modern society, and so has the development of the global trading and financial systems. That much is clear. The issue now, perhaps, is establishing a 'formula' that could pinpoint the particular threshhold where a society reinvents itself, a point in time when its existing class structure mutates. A relevant socio-political theoretical framework should be able to fuse these internal and external pressures on economies and predict outcomes based on this fusion. Which social classes will emerge or disappear; what state/governmental structure will be capable of handling the domestic changes amid intense globalisation?

Besides the broad interest that such findings would generate, grasping at the fundamental economic and social forces at play in each economy would be of valuable assistance to the construction of investment portfolios. In the meantime, tracking these economic and socio-political prospects through a 'tatonement' process remains the prerogative of investors. To this end, the following chapters will provide a complementary exposition of the institutional, regulatory and activity development of national capital markets.

For longer term investors, besides taking account of domestic changes, the broad trend that can be kept in mind is that of East Asia's gradual conversion to the synthesised global picture, where transparency of transactions and the establishment of effective regulatory systems as recommended or demanded by international bodies will lower unsystematic risk over time. There is little doubt that national capital markets will continue to flourish with further deregulation aimed at raising allocative and operational efficiency. The difference between the Chinese way of doing business – in decentralised units, a mode which has been influenced historically by the Chinese diaspora in the region – and that of the Japanese and Koreans whereby large conglomerates operate closely together (or not so closely, in the Korean case), will become less significant over time as to how capital markets will be developed and economic integration effected. Similarly, strategic perceptions regarding governmental relationships and business alliances (of the trade in goods and services nature) will have limited impact on capital markets since financial technology has already overtaken directorial policy at national level. What the states can do is to facilitate this integration via policy that is aimed at capitalising on the skills offered by the global market in order to develop the domestic ones.

Another factor impacting on risk assessment of East Asia in the long run is the distribution of capital ownership. This distribution will probably determine almost all the risks, systematic and unsystematic, associated with capital formation and return in various economies. Debtor countries will be less able to determine policy based on sovereign wants, and therefore the risk of them reverting to a closed regime is small while that concerning debt servicing is high. It is no coincidence that Latin America, the debtor region, has been reforming its markets fastest and in closest consultation with world institutions like the World Bank and the IMF; and that Japan or the East Asian NIEs (a creditor group) have taken their time in their compliance with conventions and guidelines established by world bodies. This variety of sovereignty will be seen applied within East Asia, for instance between China and Southeast Asia excluding Singapore (debtor group) and the NIEs and Japan (creditors).

Investors would also need to monitor closely the world's major regions' economic cycles for portfolio structuring purposes. For even in the context of the long run, the global standardisation of structures will not overshadow the cyclical divergences that have begun to affect East Asia as a region within the world economy. These dissynchronised growth patterns are not an aberration in the world economy's expansion path, but will most probably constitute an enduring feature of the 1990s and beyond.

NOTES

1 Rostow, W. *The Stages of Economic Growth*, Cambridge University Press, 1960. Rostow's thesis, based on the industrial revolution in 18th–19th century England, is quite compatible with Jones' view, for instance, on growth spurts throughout history (Jones, E.L. *Growth Recurring: Economic Change in World History*, Oxford University Press, NY, 1988). Among the major themes argued is that of the tendency to growth in organised society, capped mainly by political reactionary forces. Jones cautions against 'take-off' notions and steers attention towards gradualism and connective phases in economic growth, such as between the Tokugawa and Meiji eras. He also nearly dismisses the importance of the steam engine and limits modern science's role in explaining growth as a general theory. But placed together with Rostow's trajectory for growth, Jones' own does not seem to differ fundamentally. Does it matter if growth in earlier times had not depended on a particular set of factors (advanced scientific knowledge and development being one) similar to those of industrialising England or emerging East Asia? Both Rostow and Jones seem to view sustained economic growth in the same vein, i.e. based on a conducive political economic environment for such growth.

2 Kuznets, S. *Economic Growth and Structure*, London: Heinemann, 1965.

3 Cairncross, A. 'Essays in Bibliography and Criticism, XLV: The Stages of Economic Growth', *Economic History Review*, April 1961.

4 Jiyuan, C. *et al.*, *Changes and Development in Rural China*, Guangdong Higher Education Publishing House, 1992, p. 122.

5 Robison, R., Hewison, K. and Rodan, G. (eds), *Southeast Asia in the 1990s: Authoritarianism, Democracy and Capitalism*, Allen & Unwin, 1993.

6 Robison, R. *Indonesia: The Rise of Capital*, Allen & Unwin, 1986.

7 Fitzgerald, V.W. *National Saving: A Report to the Treasurer*, Commonwealth of Australia, AGPS, Canberra, 1993.

8 Almond, G. and Coleman, J. *The Politics of Developing Areas*, Princeton

University Press, Princeton, 1960; Almond, G. 'Capitalism and Democracy', *PS: Political Science and Politics*, vol. 24, 3, 1991, pp. 467–74; Weiner, M. and Huntington, S. (eds), *Understanding Political Development*, The Free Press, NY, 1987.

9 Skocpol, T. 'Bringing the State Back In: Strategies of Analysis in Current Research', in Evans, P.B. *et al.* (eds), *Bringing the State Back In*, Cambridge University Press, Cambridge, 1985; and Timberger, E. 'State Power and Modes of Production: Implications of Japanese Transition to Capitalism', *The Insurgent Sociologist*, vol. 7, Spring, pp. 85–98.

10 Lukacs, G. *History and Class Consciousness*, W.O. Graham, 1923.

11 *Labour Force Australia, Average Weekly Earnings* and *Consumer Price Index*, various issues, Australian Bureau of Statistics, Canberra.

12 Hodgkinson, A. 'An Industry Policy Debate for the 1990s – What Lessons From the USA?', *Economic Papers*, Economic Society of Australia, September 1993, pp. 81–96.

13 For example, Elliot, D. 'The Socio-Economic Formation of Modern Thailand', *Journal of Contemporary Asia*, vol. 8, 1, pp. 21–50.

14 Krueger A, 'Pacific Growth and Macroeconomic Performance', in Ariff, M. (ed.), *The Pacific Economy: Growth and External Stability*, Allen & Unwin, 1991. Country studies that rejected dependency include Hewison (1986) and Robison (1986).

15 'Financial Development and Economic Performance', *IMF Survey*, January 1993.

16 Zhang, J. 'Inflation in China: A Necessary Evil', Working Paper, Asia Research Centre, Murdoch University, 1993.

17 *Development Finance*, International Finance Corporation, December 1992, p. 10.

18 *Market Brief*, GK Goh Securities (Hong Kong) Ltd, May 1993.

19 As Guangdong contains Shenzhen, one of China's SEZs and the seat of one of China's stock exchanges, some international fund managers have gone as far as calling this SEZ a 'sovereign entity' (*South China Morning Post*, 8 October 1993, p. 1).

20 Policy expressed in early 1993 was for full convertibility by 1998. At the end of 1993, the renminbi was floated with full convertibility projected to be brought forward to 1995 or 1996 (*SCMP*, 23 November 1993).

21 Chang, C.C. 'Financial Liberalisation in the Republic of China', in Rhee and Chang (eds), *Pacific Basin Capital Markets Research*, North Holland: Elsevier Science Publishers BV, 1990.

22 Cheng, T. 'The Development of the Futures Market in Taiwan', paper presented at the International Securities Institute (ISI) conference on Developing Capital Markets, Hong Kong, 17–18 March 1993.

23 Chang, op. cit.

24 Stock Exchange of Thailand.

25 Sahasakul, C. 'An Analysis of the Rapid Evolution of the Thai Market, Its Regulatory Framework and Automation', paper presented at the Second Annual ISI Securities Conference, Hong Kong, March 1993.

26 Tsoi, D. 'An Introduction to the Technologies and its Impact on Market Development', and Scott, N. 'Impact on Market Development and Profitability: The Cost of Technology', ISI conference, Hong Kong, March 1993.

27 *China Economic News*, 21 February 1994.

28 Wu, J. *The Chinese Peasantry and the Agricultural Modernization*, Zhongynan Peasant Publishing House, 1990; and Chen, J. *et al.*, *Change and Development in the Chinese Countryside: Retrospect and Prospect*, Guangdong Higher Education Publishing House, 1992

29 Andersen, Arthur and EIU, *Asia–Pacific Capital Markets: A Vision of Change*, 1993, e.g., pp. 27–30.
30 Moderating arguments to this general view of Keynesianism are provided in Blinder, A.S. 'The Fall and Rise of Keynesian Economics', *The Economic Record*, vol. 64, 187, December 1988, pp. 278–94. Topical discussions on industry policy of various countries include Krugman, P. 'Targeted Industrial Policies: Theory and Evidence', paper presented at the 1983 Industrial Change and Public Policy Symposium, Bank of Kansas City, Jackson Hall, pp. 123–56. The Asian Development Bank made its points regarding the non-importance of industry policy in fostering growth in its *Asian Development Outlook 1991*.
31 Drucker, P. *The New Realities*, Mandarin, 1989, chap. 1–3.
32 Burstein, D. *Yen!*, Bantam–Schwartz, 1989.
33 The Group of Five industrialised nations (the US, Japan, West Germany, France and Britain) met at New York's Plaza Hotel in September 1985 to launch this new exchange rate policy coordination programme in response to the US$ appreciation (and US current account deterioration) through the first half of the 1980s. This meeting subsequently caused a slide in the US$ to such an extent that, by February 1987, the G–6 (now including Canada) had to reconvene in Paris to send a messsage to the international market to support the dollar (the Louvre Accord). By 1990, however, it became clear that even the top G–7 (with Italy joining the club) governments could not influence exchange rates that much as further deregulation of national capital markets around the world had allowed capital to flow freely, impacting on exchange rates along the way.
34 *1991/92 OECD Economic Survey: Japan*, OECD, Paris, 1992, p. 27.
35 *International Financial Statistics*, IMF, Washington DC, October 1992, pp. 542–45.
36 Drucker (1989), pp. 123–25.
37 Porter, M. *Competitive Advantage of Nations*, Harvard University Press, 1991.
38 *East – The Asian Miracle*, World Bank Report, 1993.
39 *IMF Survey*, November 1993.
40 US Department of Commerce.
41 Kaufman, H. 'Debt: The Threat to Economic and Financial Stability', paper presented at the Federal Reserve Bank of Kansas City Symposium, Jackson, Wyoming, 28 August 1986.
42 Drucker (1989), p. 150.
43 Pitchford, J. *Australia's Foreign Debt: Myths and Realities*, Allen & Unwin, Sydney, 1990.
44 Dertouzos, M., Lester, R.K., Solow, R. and the MIT Commission on Industrial Productivity, *Made in America: Regaining the Productive Edge*, MIT Press, 1989.
45 *The Economist*, 1 May 1993, p. 3. The Y10.7 trillion package in the 1992 budget (2.3 per cent of GNP as reported in the *1991/92 OECD Economic Survey: Japan*, p. 67) was followed by a Y2 trillion supplementary package in the same year.
46 *1992/93 OECD Economic Survey: Japan*, Paris, November 1993, pp. 44–46.
47 Stewart, J.B. *Den of Thieves*, Simon & Schuster, 1992.
48 *Quarterly National Accounts*, OECD, 4, Paris, 1992, p. 33; *International Financial Statistics*, IMF, various issues, 1992–94.
49 *Comments on Credit, International Market Roundup* and *Bond Market Monitor*, Salomon Brothers, various issues, 1992–93.
50 A brief account of how Japan dealt with endaka is contained in Burstein, D. (1989) op. cit. and Ohmae, K. *The Borderless World*, Fontana, 1990.
51 Corporate Japan's oscillation in dealing with bad debts had caused Japan's Big Four securities firms to lose the fight against Western houses even in Japan's backyard. The *Asian Wall Street Journal* (25 May 1993) reported that after years of selling Japanese shares to Japan's neighbours, the four firms – Daiwa,

Yamaichi, Nikko and Nomura – now wanted to underwrite the neighbours' top shares to the world. But while the Japanese had been in Asia for more than fifteen years, they'd been laggard in appreciating that the tide had turned, with more Asian companies seeking to raise capital by going public. Japanese firms found themselves faced with the same shortage of connections and experience in the changed environment as newly arrived Western counterparts. The only US firm's office in China in 1993 was opened in March by Merrill Lynch & Company but had acquired a name for quality operations in the local market.

52 *Australian Financial Review*, 29 October 1993, p. 40

53 Concerning Japan's prewar industrial power, see Kennedy, P. *The Rise and Fall of The Great Powers*, Vintage Books, 1989, e.g., pp. 288–9. For reference to Japan's long standing industrialisation effort, see Jones, E. op. cit. The 'economic miracle' in fact sprouted from over a century of modernisation effort dating back to Tokugawa times (prior to Meiji).

54 Drucker, P. *Managing for the Future*, Butterworth–Heinemann, 1993, p. 57.

55 Ohmae, K. *The Borderless World*, Fontana, 1990, pp. 181–3.

56 *AFR*, 28 October 1993, p. 14.

57 AWSJ, 3 June 1993, p. 9. Nomura Securities had been cutting its fees charged in underwriting corporate issues. In June 1993, the company was lead manager of domestic straight bonds offered by Tokyo Electric Power, Honda Motor and Hitachi Metals. It reduced the underwriting fee for each issue by 0.05 yen for every 100 yen from the previous commission. The move was triggered by the recent change in the primary corporate bond market with regard to pricing methods and fee structures, to entice Japanese issuers away from the cheaper and more liberal European bond market.

58 In its *Monthly Review: May 1992*, Sakura Bank reported that the job separation for 15–29-year-olds had been on a long term uptrend although it had declined for women in their twenties (largely because fewer of that age bracket quit their jobs once married). Of workers in the 15–29 age group who quit their jobs in 1990, part timers accounted for 16 per cent of men and 21 per cent of women, up from the comparable 9.6 per cent and 12.5 per cent in 1980. The Ministry of Labour's *Survey on Employment Trends, 1993* shows similar results. It defined two age groups, those up to 29 and those above. The Ministry then compared the 1980 and 1990 percentages of workers in the two groups who cited one of three specific reasons for quitting their jobs. Inadequate wages accounted for 10 per cent of the total for both years, and there was no significant difference between the two groups. Work conditions (work hours and time off, etc.) accounted for a high percentage of the younger age group in both 1980 and 1990. Both age groups' shares had climbed significantly over the ten year period. Finally, not only did a relatively high share of the younger age group cite lack of interest in their particular work as the reason to quit in both 1980 and 1990, this younger age group share had surged away from the older age group's share who cited such reasons. This younger generation's behaviour was picked up by another Ministry of Labour survey, *Young People's Attitudes to Work, 1990*. In that survey, a majority of young workers dissatisfied with their jobs cited an inability to apply their own capabilities as the key reason for their dissatisfaction.

59 'Special Survey on Japan', *The Australian*, 10-11 July 1993.

60 In addition, respondents were concerned with problems that were threatening to undermine the quality of life, such as the practice of long office hours, long term assignments from home, or not taking holidays; problems associated with business' lack of interest in community affairs, illegal waste disposal, continued deterioration in commuting, housing and traffic conditions. Some respondents

felt that individuals' lives had been neglected and that companies needed to deal more openly with consumers and households by upgrading levels of communication and disclosure.

61 *Economic and Industrial Trends in Japan, Monthly Report*, Industrial Bank of Japan, various issues, 1993.

62 Japan's job offers/seekers ratio fell steadily from 1.4 in 1991 to about 0.9 in 1992 (*1992/93 OECD Economic Surveys: Japan*) and 0.8 in 1993 (IBJ *Monthly Report*).

63 *Monthly Review*, Mitsubishi Bank, July 1992.

64 Drucker (1993), p. 80.

65 See, for example, Schor, J. *The Overworked American: The Unexpected Decline in Leisure*, 1992.

66 *1991/92 OECD Economic Surveys: Japan*, p. 60.

67 Ohmae (1990), p. 268

68 Goodman, D. 'China's Coming Revolution: Political Perspectives on Social and Economic Change', Working Paper, Asia Research Centre, Murdoch University, August 1993; and 'China as Number One', paper presented at the China as a Great Power in the Asia–Pacific: Myths and Realities workshop, Australian National University, 2–3 December 1993. Also, Robison (1986) and Robison *et al.* (1993).

69 The first explanation came with 'undertaking', an activity compounded out of the three services of labour, land and capital, with the addition of risk bearing. This was the view of J.S. Mill, who regarded profit as a payment (interest, insurance and wage) to superintendence, in reward for abstinence, risk and exertion. This didn't answer the question of how large a profit should be at any given time (business cycle implication). Walker suggested the Marshallian concept of 'marginal undertaker'. As Walker saw it, undertakers, like land allotments, carried various degrees of efficiency and productiveness. If the undertaker received a reward greater than he could get separately as an investor or a salaried manager, this must have been due to the special advantages he gained from the composition of functions of an undertaker. The marginal undertaker then would be the person whose special advantages were so small that he was on the balance of choice between becoming an undertaker and hiring himself out for a salary and loaning his capital at interest. Profit would then be the supra-marginal person's productivity and that of his fellows who tightened their belts at the margin.

This marginal undertaker concept didn't help set the levels of margin for various professions or different situations, nor explain the relationships between these. The margin is not a determining factor but one that is determined by the scarcity of supply of superior units. In the case of land, a margin is understood as a restriction imposed by nature, while in the case of superior undertakers things are not that clear-cut and visible.

Clark's 'dynamic theory' took over this question of margin with a twist. His profit was seen as payment for a pioneer who took temporary advantage of a monopoly situation as he effected changes in the economic organisation and adapted resources to them. Profit was the excess earning based on change, over the alternative interest on capital and wage as a manager. Once the monopoly position passed, competition would resume as other businesses caught up, and profit would tend to disappear into the wider community either via decreased prices or increased wages. However, it is unknown whether changes can be foreseen by some but not by others. Further, are natural obstacles the only things to be overcome before resources could be moved from one use to another?

It seems that the more attempts were made at explaining profit, the more they were distanced from the basic question posed by Marx. Implied in the theories of profit outlined is the capacity to earn return on capital. In any one business in any one time, with a given amount of undertakers' capital, the income of undertakers would be mainly governed in the same way as income of the passive shareholders, i.e. the receipt of interest payments on capital. Therefore, the possibility of gains through increases in capital value would be of particular importance as capital became central to a theory of profit. In today's corporations, the common stock is seen as undertakers' capital, the yield on it as profit, and changes in its value as the capital increment which is part of the gains of undertaking.

70 Mandell, E. *Late Capitalism*, London, 1975.
71 Sweezy, P. *Theory of Capitalist Development*, London, Dobson, 1962.
72 Drucker (1989) claims that the great bulk of capital in the developed world is held by households. If all the 'super rich' of the developed countries were to disappear suddenly, 'the world economy would not even notice it' (p. 173).
73 Ohmae (1990, p. 196) reports that in 1988, the total *annual* flow of economic activity within the world's major three regions (the Triad) amounted to US$600 billion. This was equal to the *daily* volume in foreign exchange trading. Drucker (1993, p. 6) notes that every day, the London Interbank market turned over 15 times the amount of Eurodollars, Euroyen and Euromarks needed to finance world trade.
74 Domar, E. *Essays in the Theory of Economic Growth*, Oxford University Press, Fair Lawn, NJ, 1957, pp. 70–82; and Solow, R. 'A Contribution to the Theory of Economic Growth', *Quarterly Journal of Economics*, February 1956, pp. 65–94.
75 Pasinetti, L. 'Technical Progress and Structural Change', 1993 R.C. Mills Lecture, *Economic Papers*, Economic Society of Australia, vol. 12, 3, September 1993.
76 Nguyen, T. 'The Dynamic Effect of Devaluation on the Balance of Payments of a Small Debt Ridden Open Economy', *The Economic Record*, September 1993, pp. 275–85.

Chapter 3

Emerging Asian equity markets development

A historical perspective

Catherine Roc

Equity markets have not been a major driving force in the development process of Asia's emerging economies. While established early this century, they only gained importance recently. Over the past five years, some of these markets reached the level of development (measured by the ratio of market capitalisation to GDP) achieved by mature markets in the US, Japan and Europe (see Figure 3.1 below). Most of them, however, still lack breadth and depth.

Little is known about emerging Asian equity market development in general, or about the factors that governed this development. Academic studies that specifically examine equity markets in emerging Asian economies are not numerous. Most literature relates to these markets only in the

Table 3.1 Market capitalisation

Market	% of nominal GDP
Hong Kong	151
Malaysia	126
Tokyo	90
Singapore	86
London	80
Taiwan	75
Mexico	49
Thailand	39
Korea	38
Germany	22
Philippines	16
Indonesia	14
Brazil	11

Source: Data derived from tables in Appendix 1, pp. 110–16

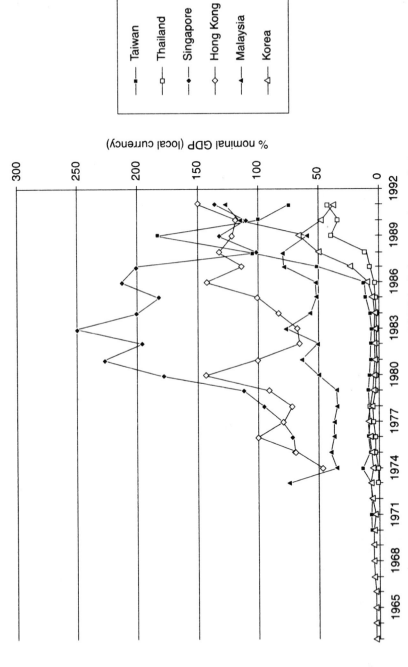

Figure 3.1 Time-series of market capitalisation as a per cent of GDP in Asian emerging markets

Sources: Information derived from Appendix Tables (3)A1.1 to (3)A1.7

context of the development of a specific country's financial system.[1] Other studies[2] provide a static analysis of these markets and their problems at a specific date. Except for general discussions on policies that may lead to stock market development in developing countries,[3] including Calderón-Rossell's recent general model of stock market growth,[4] the dynamics of the Southeast and East Asian emerging equity markets over the past three decades has not been comprehensively examined, a gap which this study attempts to fill.

The purpose of this chapter is to examine the structures and dimensions of eight Asian equity markets (Korea, Hong Kong, Singapore, Taiwan, Malaysia, Thailand, Indonesia and the Philippines), and to analyse the changes that took place between 1960 and 1992, in order to identify the major determinants of their development and their 'mini-boom' between 1987 and 1990. It is yet uncertain whether the emergence of equity markets in different economies at a particular stage is inherent to a country's financial and economic evolution, or whether it is mainly the outcome of specific government policies or the particular behaviour of economic agents in different regions. After assessing the role of economic progress in the comparative development process of each of the Asian emerging stock markets surveyed since the 1960s, a comprehensive review of the different obstacles (regulatory, political, historical and sociological) that have hampered the demand, and especially the supply of equities in Asian stock markets, is presented. This will allow us to demonstrate that in addition to the necessary precondition of strong economic performance, the removal of these obstacles through the parallel trends of deregulation and improved surveillance[5] has been critical in the recent rapid development of the equity markets in Asia.

CHARACTERISTICS OF ASIAN STOCK MARKETS

An early start

Share transactions started early in this century in many Asian countries[6] and the institutionalisation of stock trading has been effective in most of these countries since the 1960s. The trading of shares started in 1860 in Hong Kong and the Hong Kong Stock Exchange (HKSE) was founded in 1914, representing mainly British interests. After sharebroking had become a significant activity in Singapore and Malaysia, supported by the rubber boom in the 1910s, ten Singapore firms and nine firms from Kuala Lumpur, Penang and Ipoh formed the Malayan Stock Exchange in 1960. It was first renamed the Stock Exchange of Malaysia when Singapore joined the Federation of Malaysia in 1963, then became the Stock Exchange of Singapore and Malaysia after the separation of Singapore from Malaysia. The common stock exchange of the two countries separated in 1973 and the Stock Exchange of Singapore (SES) was incorporated in 1974. In 1912, the Vereniging voor de Effectenhandel (an association of stockbrokers) was established in Jakarta, effectively laying the foundation for Indonesia's first stock exchange. Closed during World War II, it re-opened in 1952 after national independence, but unstable economic and political conditions, in particular the policy of confrontation with the Netherlands which resulted in the prohibition against trading Dutch securities, forced the Jakarta Stock Exchange (JSE) to close in 1968. It opened again in 1977 mainly in order for foreign-owned companies to transfer a majority of their shares to Indonesian nationals. Taiwan started the development of a securities market in 1954 when the 'land to the tiller' programme was initiated, whereby large landowners could obtain bonds and shares of the largest government-owned enterprises in exchange for their lands, which were then allocated to the tenant farmers. There was no formal stock exchange at the time, but the Securities and Exchange Commission was established in 1960 to govern securities transactions and to supervise all aspects of the securities market. The Taiwan Stock Exchange (TSE) was formed a year later. In 1956, the Daehan Stock Exchange was established as a predecessor of the Korea Stock Exchange (KSE). It remained essentially a market for government bonds without an institutional structure until the early 1960s, when the government decided to foster capital market development as a means of bolstering domestic savings. A massive collapse of stock prices towards the end of 1962 brought about the shut-down of the market for three months. The exchange reopened in 1963 with significant control by the government. The Manila Stock Exchange was founded in the Philippines in 1927 while a second exchange, the Makati Stock Exchange, started trading in 1965.

Underdevelopment until the late 1980s

Asian emerging equity markets (except Singapore and Hong Kong) remained comparatively small in terms of market capitalisation, turnover and number of listed companies until the second half of the 1980s. These markets have suffered from the classical defects of bank-dominated economies: shortage of equity, lack of liquidity, absence of institutional investors and the subsequent domination by individuals and speculators. After two decades of rather subdued growth, market capitalisation grew rapidly over the 1980s (see Appendix Tables (3)A1.1–1.7). Between 1985 and 1990, Asian emerging markets development accelerated, with annual average growth rates of market capitalisation ranging between 2 per cent in Singapore (which after rising fast until the early 1980s, felt the blow of the Pan-Electric crisis),[7] and more than 70 per cent in Korea, Taiwan and Thailand. It is worth noting that in 1989 alone, Indonesia's market capitalisation rose 823 per cent. Care must be taken, however, in interpreting market capitalisation data: the important weight of inactive shares in the market (discussed below) tends to distort market capitalisation figures upwards.

Market capitalisation rose both because of rising prices, and because of an increasing number of listings and issues. After two decades of generally sluggish growth, new listings have risen rapidly over the past five years, especially in Korea, Taiwan, Thailand and Indonesia (see Figure 3.2). However, with fast rising foreign and domestic demand, the major problem in these markets remains the limited supply of equities.

The low liquidity which characterised most Asian emerging stock markets was followed by a surge in trading volume and value turnover, a subsequent increase in liquidity (Table 3.1), and sharp increases in prices and price-earning ratios. Trading values and volumes have surged since the mid-1980s (Figure 3.3, and Appendix Tables (3)A1.1–1.7) in all stock exchanges. In 1980, the annual turnover volume in most Asian emerging economies was comparatively small, ranging from 1.6 million shares in Indonesia to 11 billion shares in Taiwan. As a comparison, in 1992 volume turnover ranged from 29 billion shares in Taiwan to 0.8 billion shares in Thailand. Value turnover reached US$220 billion in Taiwan in 1992, US$121 billion in Korea, US$11 billion in Malaysia and US$31 million in Thailand.

Prices on the markets have followed the turnover pattern, reflecting the strong increase in the demand for equity. In general, prices started rising sharply in 1988, and culminated in the late 1980s before retreating slightly in 1992. The Stock Exchange of Thailand (SET) index in December 1989 stood at 879.2, more than double the 386.7 level recorded at the end of 1988. On the Korea Stock Exchange (KSE), the Stock Exchange Composite reached an average of 873 in 1990, after having hovered around an average level of 100 for the previous fifteen years. In Singapore, after showing stable and slow growth in the 1970s, the Straits Times Index has been rising rapidly since 1980, albeit recording slower growth in the past two years than most other Asian emerging markets. The rises in indices were price-driven rather than volume-driven.

The rapid growth experienced in the 1980s by Asian emerging equity markets is impressive when compared with the developments observed in more mature stock markets during the same period. Although total world market capitalisation growth between 1981 and 1987 reached just above an average of 16 per cent per annum, Asian markets (including Japan's) rose approximately 30 per cent per annum and grew from 17.4 per cent of total world market capitalisation in 1981 to 38 per cent in 1987. This may be distorted, however, by the speculative bubble recorded in Japan in this period. Nevertheless, Asian emerging markets' share of total emerging markets capitalisation rose from 20 per cent to 41 per cent in this period[8] and continued to improve until the end of the decade.

More importantly, most Asian emerging markets have increased their

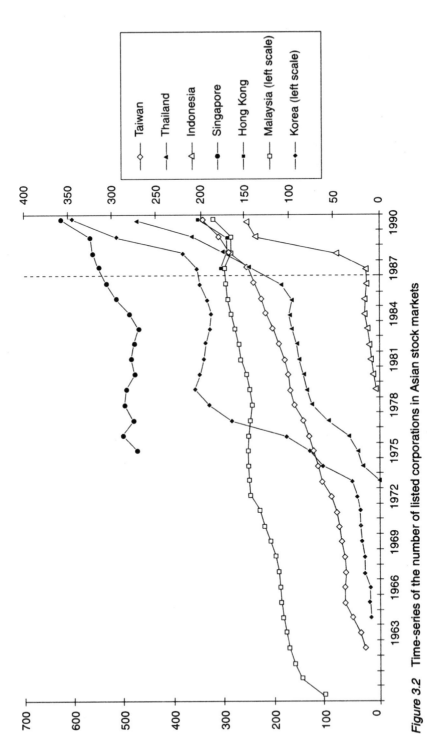

Figure 3.2 Time-series of the number of listed corporations in Asian stock markets

Sources: Information derived from Appendix Tables (3)A1.1 to (3)A1.7

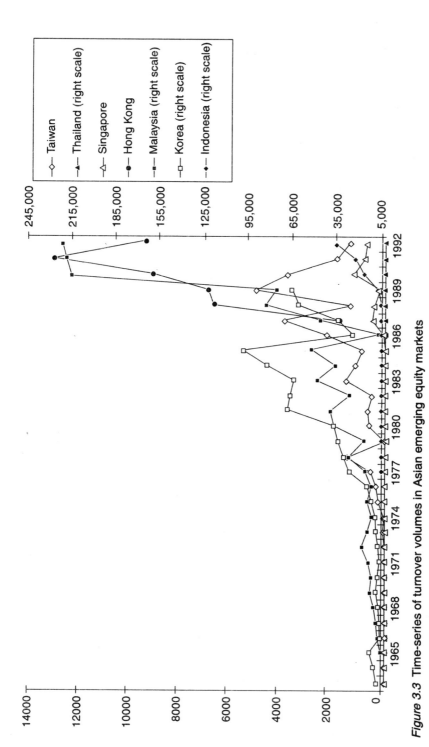

Figure 3.3 Time-series of turnover volumes in Asian emerging equity markets

Sources: SG Warburg Securities; Thorn (1988); Bank of Korea Annual Reports (various issues); Bank of Thailand Quarterly Bulletin (various issues)

contribution to economic activities during the 1980s. The ratios of market capitalisation relative to GDP[9] remained under 50 per cent in Korea, Taiwan, Thailand and Malaysia, before surging in the past five years (see Table 3.1 and Figure 3.1). Only in Hong Kong has the ratio weakened since the beginning of the 1980s. On average, in the Asian countries surveyed, private consumption has fallen to less than 50 per cent of GDP while the ratios of Gross National Savings (GNS) to GDP rose to an average 30.1 per cent between 1981–90 (from about 19 per cent in 1961–70), and the ratio of Gross Domestic Capital Formation (GDCF) to GDP rose to an average 28.8 per cent (from an approximate average of 20 per cent in 1961–70), contributing to the rapid financial growth of the regions. However, a higher share of capital expenditure has not been financed through accrued equity issues and, until very recently, Asian emerging markets had not been a stable source of long-term funds for capital formation. In fact, Appendix Table (3)A2.1 shows that the ratio of funds raised through equity issues as a percentage of GDCF remained relatively subdued as well as highly volatile. On average, capital raised through new issues, new listings, rights issues and placements remained below 5 per cent of total nominal gross domestic capital formation in all Asian emerging markets until the mid-1980s. After 1986, this ratio rose to higher levels with a maximum of 36.8 per cent recorded in Hong Kong in 1987. Reflecting depressed economic conditions and correspondingly lower share prices, these ratios have tended to slacken slightly over the past two years. Further, the distribution of listed stocks still does not reflect the economic structures of the countries surveyed. Although manufacturing provided the main boost to the different emerging Asian economies in general (for example in Malaysia it still accounts for approximately 75 per cent of total investment), funds raised in the equity market through the issue of securities of manufacturing companies have been relatively small.

The main problem: lack of supply

By and large, the 'main obstacle to large-scale and rapid development of securities markets is the chronic deficiency in the supply of securities',[10] and it has been a greater obstacle to Asian equity market development than the deficiency of demand.[11] The large subscription to new issues observed in most of the markets surveyed since their institutionalisation gives an account of the absorptive capacity of the markets and reveals that companies would have experienced in general little or no difficulty in funding capital through the primary market. For instance, while oversubscription was already observable in Malaysia in the late 1960s,[12] it has also been observed in most Asian emerging markets[13] and became more important in the beginning of the 1990s.[14] Nevertheless, whilst the scarcity of shares discouraged potential investors, the level of demand (albeit higher than

Table 3.2 Liquidity ratios

	1970	1975	1980	1985	1991
Hong Kong	n.a.	0.19	0.16	0.32	0.29
Korea	0.43	0.36	0.45	0.55	0.88
Singapore	0.13*	0.13	0.15	0.09	0.36
Taiwan	0.84	2.61	0.91	0.47	3.74
Malaysia	0.22*	0.15	0.21	0.15	0.19
Thailand	n.a.	0.4	3.20	0.34	0.86
Indonesia	n.a.	n.a.	0.15	0.04	0.35
Philippines	n.a.	n.a.	1.52	0.54	–

Notes: * = Estimates

supply) remained insufficient to promote large trading volume and liquidity. Subsequently, the lack of a deep and active secondary market also proved to be a negative factor for the supply of securities.

THE ROLE OF ECONOMIC GROWTH

Relative development of Asian emerging equity markets, relative economic growth and relative increases in income

The relatively recent speeding up of Asian economic development, and with it of the modernisation and development of the financial system, have been cited as factors which have governed the emergence of stock markets in Asia.[15] Ayling argues that the 'size of financial markets in Less Developed Countries (LDCs) is likely to remain small unless economic growth in these countries can catch up with the rest of the world'.[16] In fact, Calderón-Rossell's partial equilibrium model of stock market growth in a world-wide perspective shows that 'in general, economic progress in all regions, with a few exceptions, was the fundamental force behind stock market growth'[17] and that 'the markets' growth rates of the 1980s mainly reflect the different growth patterns of the economies and market liquidity in the different regions . . . Asian stock markets grew mainly as a result of economic growth'.[18]

However, it is not clear whether the Asian emerging stock markets growth is actually and directly related to the pace of economic activity. In the context of Calderón-Rossells' econometric model of world stock market growth,[19] four problems support the uncertainty of this causal relationship.

- The application of Calderón-Rossell's model does not show conclusive results when extended to the period 1960 to 1992. The problem may result from the author looking at two sets of markets: 'Asian markets', which include the large Japanese market, or 'emerging markets', which include South American, European and African markets as well as Asian markets. The inclusion of other countries is likely to distort the observation for Asian emerging markets.

- Calderón-Rossell's model, based on data from 1980 to 1987, cannot explain why rapid economic growth in Asia in the 1970s did not translate into more rapid equity market developments as observed in the late 1980s, and cannot provide a convincing explanation for the sudden surges in market development in the past five years.
- As a partial equilibrium model, it fails to take into account the potential effect of government policies.
- This is a generalised model which cannot be applied to the analysis of the different patterns of each stock market growth within Asian emerging economies.

A review of the data available in Appendix Table(3)A3.1 indicates that the relative development of the Asian emerging equity markets seems to be correlated with the relative economic growth observed in this region. For example, between 1965 and 1970, Korea showed both the highest average annual rate of economic growth and the highest average annual growth rate of market capitalisation. Later, between 1970 and 1975, Taiwan and Korea led the economic growth of the Southeast and East Asian regions, and their equity markets development measured by the growth rate of market capitalisation, surged compared with that of the slower developing economies. Between 1975 and 1980, in addition to Taiwan and Korea, Singapore and Hong Kong emerged as fast developing countries with rapidly growing stock markets. Later again, when nominal GDP growth rates accelerated during 1985–90 in Thailand to an average of 13 per cent per annum and in Malaysia to 6 per cent per annum, they triggered a surge in the average annual growth rates of market capitalisation to 74 per cent and 32 per cent, respectively. In addition, over the same period, renewed economic growth in Korea and Taiwan (with a real growth rate at 17 per cent (annual average) for Korea and 11 per cent for Taiwan) brought about sharp increases (above 70 per cent per annum) in their respective market capitalisations. It is worth noting that this pattern can also be found when comparing market capitalisation data with real GDP numbers, which are better indicators of economic activity.

The role of increased wealth and economic development in allowing more people in Asia to invest in corporate shares is visible in the data shown in Appendix Table (3)A3.1. The general tendency of markets to grow with increases in income per capita (which is an indication of the level of economic development and individual wealth) suggests that the rates of growth of income also affect stock market growth. Examining the relative growth rates of GDP per capita and of market capitalisation per capita in Asia's emerging economies, it appears that the relative growth of Asian equity markets corresponds to the relative income gains by individuals in the countries studied. Strong growth in income per capita between 1975 and 1980 in the Newly Industrialised Countries (NICs)[20] corresponds to sharp growth in market capitalisation per capita, while a rise in the growth of per capita income later in 1985–90 in the ASEAN countries corresponds to a surge in the growth of their market capitalisation per capita.

However, income gain is not the only relevant factor. The level of income per capita is most important. Large income gains, if realised from a low base, will be largely directed towards higher consumption, and thus will not significantly affect investment. A high level of GDP per capita will be followed by not only a higher savings rate, but also by a relatively higher share of invested savings, as well as several other factors favourable to the demand for equity investments (e.g. in general, a higher level of education). Confirming this relationship, amongst the markets surveyed, market capitalisation per capita was the highest in Singapore and Hong Kong between 1970 and 1992, where average nominal and real income per capita were also the highest. The growing middle class that resulted from increased social spending after the independence of Singapore increased the number of individual participants in the share market.[21] Korea, showing the lowest nominal GDP per capita of the NICs at the beginning of the 1990s, is also the NIC with the lowest average market capitalisation. The comparative under-development of the Philippine equity markets can be partly attributed to the relatively low level of income per capita.

A 'wave pattern'

Following the relationship detailed above between relative economic growth and the relative growth rate of market capitalisation, the pattern of economic growth in East Asia explains the 'wave pattern' apparent in the development of the region's stock markets whereby foreign direct investment (FDI) triggered rapid economic growth in some Asian countries, which itself led to the development of the equity markets.

Roughly, while Singapore and Hong Kong showed the highest growth rate of market capitalisation between 1975 and 1980, Korea and Taiwan were the leading markets between 1985 and 1990. The next five-year period (1990–95) has been witnessing a surge of newer markets such as Thailand and Indonesia. Large foreign direct investments (FDI) from Japan to Korea, Taiwan, Hong Kong and Singapore resulted in a surge in economic growth[22] in these countries in the 1960s. FDI flows subsequently triggered an increase in the relative growth of the market capitalisation recorded in these countries compared with other Asian countries, as the

number of potential investors increased and corporate investments accelerated sharply. In fact, the data collected show that the growth rate of market
capitalisation measured on a per capita basis started to surge in Korea and
Taiwan between 1965 and 1975. The average annual growth rate of market
capitalisation per capita, measured in local currency, rose to about 47 per
cent in Korea, and 54 per cent in Taiwan in this period. Between 1975 and
1980, the 'leading' stock markets were Hong Kong, Thailand and Singapore, followed by Taiwan, Korea and Malaysia.

The NICs (supported by strong Japanese direct investments) started to
climb the comparative advantage ladder as rapid growth produced acute
labour shortages and steeply rising wages. This shift in comparative
advantage obliged the NICs to repeat in lower advantage countries the
pro-trade investment pattern previously initiated by Japan.[23] They started
investing in less developed Asian countries in the beginning of the 1980s,
as they were losing their initial comparative advantage in labour intensive
industries. By the mid-1980s, the Asian NICs had become capital exporters.
The subsequent economic growth recorded in the recipient countries,
mostly Malaysia and Thailand at this stage, stimulated a surge in the two
countries' stock markets. Between 1980 and 1985, Malaysia's market
capitalisation growth rate reached 13 per cent, Thailand's rose to 16 per
cent, and Indonesia's 23 per cent, more than the annual market capitalisation growth rates recorded in Singapore and Hong Kong. The same
pattern is apparent in Indonesia from the mid-1980s,[24] and especially since
1990. Thus, the patterns of intra-Asian foreign direct investments helps to
explain the wave pattern observed in the development of Asian stock
markets because of the strong boost that Japanese (first) and intra-East
Asian (later) FDI gave to the regions' economic growth.

BEYOND ECONOMIC GROWTH

No direct link

Economic growth alone, however, does not adequately explain the rapid
growth of stock market activities observed concurrently in all the countries
surveyed at the end of the 1980s. The period 1985–90 was a period of
exceptional growth for all markets (except Singapore, and to a lesser extent
Hong Kong) with average annual market capitalisation growth rates of
approximately 74 per cent in Thailand, 75 per cent in Korea, and 70 per
cent in Taiwan. The stock markets of Hong Kong and Singapore, which
remained comparatively subdued until the end of the 1980s, grew 52 per
cent and 16 per cent, respectively, between 1990 and 1992 (Appendix Table
(3)A3.1). Further, while renewed investments in Indonesia and the following economic recovery could possibly provide an explanation for
increasing stock trading and listings, they are unlikely to explain the boom

of the stock market in 1989 and 1990. A more rigorous analysis of the data suggests that there are limitations to the model of Asian emerging equity markets development based on the general relationship between stock market and economic activity. In effect, economic growth was a necessary, but not sufficient, condition for stock market growth.

In general, Asian stock markets grew faster than their economies with the differentials between market capitalisation growth rates and GDP growth rates widening in recent years. Appendix Table (3)A3.1 shows that the ratio of market capitalisation to nominal GDP rose in all the countries studied. During 1970–75, the average ratio of market capitalisation to GDP was 46 per cent in Hong Kong, 7 per cent in Korea, 15 per cent in Singapore, 11 per cent in Taiwan, 29 per cent in Malaysia and 0.3 per cent in Thailand. The ratios between 1985 and 1990 were, respectively, 125 per cent, 41 per cent, 147 per cent, 86 per cent, 78 per cent and 20 per cent. This may suggest that with a relatively higher level of economic development as well as an already relatively high level of market capitalisation, further development of the latter would be easier. In other words, there could be a 'multiplier' effect between economic growth and stock market growth, i.e. the higher is per capita wealth, the more economic agents will invest, the higher the liquidity generated by higher demand, the more demand is encouraged and the more (with the consequent rise in prices) companies are likely to have their shares listed and raise investment funds through new issues.

However, there are some indications that Asian emerging stock market development is not directly responding to economic growth. Appendix Table (3)A3.1 shows also that Asian stock markets did not grow uniformly faster than GDP growth. The differentials between the growth rate of market capitalisation and that of nominal GDP between 1985 and 1990 in the ASEAN countries are larger than in the NICs between 1975 and 1980, periods when both groups showed comparable average levels of market capitalisation. For example, between 1985 and 1990, Malaysia's annual GDP growth rate averaged 8.6 per cent while stock market growth was as high as 35 per cent. In Thailand, the rates were 15 per cent and 77 per cent, respectively. In contrast, between 1975 and 1980, the average nominal GDP growth rates recorded in Hong Kong, Korea and Taiwan were between 20 per cent and 28 per cent, while their market capitalisation growth rates were between 30 per cent and 46 per cent. Given that ASEAN countries recorded a slightly lower level of real income per capita, this suggests that at the end of the 1980s, in the ASEAN countries, either economic activities were more 'efficient' in triggering stock market development than they had been in the NICs (except Singapore) ten years earlier, or other factors contributed to boost the stock markets.

Another indication of the existence of possible non-economic factors is the fact that absolute market capitalisation per capita is not proportional to absolute income per capita (see Appendix Table (3)A3.1). The role of income per capita has not been obvious in recent years, since average real GDP per capita between 1985 and 1992 in Malaysia, Thailand and Indonesia was still lower than that for the NICs between 1975 and 1980 with equivalent levels of market capitalisation. Korea's average nominal income per capita between 1975 and 1980 was 24 per cent of that of Hong Kong in the same period, but its market capitalisation per capita was less than 3 per cent of Hong Kong's. Between 1970 and 1975, these average ratios were 19.2 per cent and 1.8 per cent, respectively. In 1991, the ratio of income per capita in Korea to that of Hong Kong almost doubled from the average recorded in the 1975–80 period to 46 per cent, but the ratio of market capitalisation rose more than fourfold to reach 8.7 per cent. Indonesia's market capitalisation per capita in 1990–92 was just above that of Taiwan for the period 1970–75, but Indonesia's GDP per capita was much lower than Taiwan's for the corresponding period. As a further example, Thailand recorded a market capitalisation per capita of about US$808 in 1991, which was double that of Taiwan in 1980–85. However, Thailand's real income per capita was half that of Taiwan for the corresponding period.[25] Therefore, it is clear that higher wealth and higher levels of economic development do not flow through proportionally to a higher level of stock market development.[26] Several additional and 'non-economic' factors influence the supply and demand for corporate shares which breaks a possibly direct relationship between economic growth, economic development, and growth in individual wealth on the one hand, and stock market development on the other.

Further, although the current average real and nominal rates of economic growth recorded in the region are not higher than those observed in the 1970s, market capitalisation levels in all countries have surged very rapidly in the second half of the 1980s. This cannot be completely explained by the fast growth in incomes per capita, since this was on average not higher than in the previous period, and would have been unlikely to trigger a comparable rise for all countries, given that they exhibited widely varying levels of income per capita. For example, market capitalisation grew by an annual average of approximately 70 per cent in Korea, Taiwan and Thailand between 1985 and 1990, despite varying levels of income per capita.[27]

In short, if economic progress is the underlying force behind stock market growth, it cannot solely and accurately account for the pace of equity market developments recorded in the Asian emerging economies. A linear relationship between the level of per capita income and the level of market capitalisation per capita, and between the growth rate of GDP and the growth rate of market capitalisation, cannot be established. Neither the long underdevelopment of the markets nor the recent 'equity boom' observed in these countries can be fully attributed to the growth in economic activities.

Stock market development and the structure of the economy

The structure of the economy, including income inequalities, and the structure of the industrial base, may have partly contributed to weaken the link and the possible multiplier between economic growth and equity market development.

The colonial era certainly contributed to hamper stock market development in Asia by failing to generate an indigenous bourgeoisie.[28] By the end of the colonial era, the Indonesian bourgeoisie, including the Chinese, was still relatively poorly developed. After the 1930s non-Dutch foreign capital (essentially US and UK) rose with increasing investment in petroleum, tin and large scale manufacturing. Estate crops remained dominated by Dutch and other foreign corporations. After 1949 and the end of the colonial era, Chinese capital accumulation accelerated but the expansion of indigenous capital was largely that of state capital.[29] While the importance of the Chinese capital and its influence on stock market development will be discussed below, it is clear that lack of significant capital accumulation and investment by Indonesian nationals contributed to limiting the potential for stock market development. Furthermore, foreign companies did not wish to invest locally and profits were reinvested in Europe. The same historical pattern can be observed in Malaysia and the Philippines, and to some extent in Thailand.

The distribution of national wealth explains partly the combination of a comparatively low level of market capitalisation per capita with a relatively higher level of economic development (as measured by GDP per capita). With a large share of the population living at the subsistence level,[30] savings, and subsequently investment, were not significant amongst the indigenous population. One of the problems arising from the Southeast and East Asian pattern of growth is the region's tendency to adopt capital-intensive growth strategies, creating small pockets of highly paid workers, leaving the rural or traditional sector behind.[31] It is clear that this prolongation of the economic dualism created during the colonial era has been negative for the development of stock markets – most of the population continues to be economically unable to participate in the stock market. In fact, within the Asian countries surveyed, the income distribution pattern may explain some of the differences recorded when comparing stock market development given the same levels of economic development. During the 1970s, Malaysia, for example, was still primarily an agricultural country that relied heavily on the output of rubber, rice, palm oil and coconut products, and where people employed in agriculture accounted for about half of the total working population. However, in Singapore, Hong Kong and Taiwan, already significant industrialisation may have created an improved distribution of income in these countries which could help explain their comparatively high level of stock market development in the 1960s and 1970s.

However, while wealth distribution characteristics may provide a partial explanation for the late development of stock markets in ASEAN countries (excluding Singapore), this factor cannot explain the sudden stock market 'boom' achieved by all these countries in the past five years: no significant improvement towards reduced income inequalities has been achieved over the past five years. Further, this explanation for the divergence in equity market development and economic development implies that the marginal equity investment that could be undertaken by a minority of very wealthy people following a rise in income would not compensate for the potential rise in equity investment resulting from the same income increase spread between a majority of poorer people, but this is debatable.

The structure of the industrial base has been a further impediment. The governments of most Asian economies have played a predominant role in the development of the industrial sector, particularly in Indonesia, Singapore and Korea. As a result, large and medium scale industrial enterprises in these countries have generally been public enterprises. In 1985, the public sector accounted for more than 50 per cent of large and medium scale industrial activities in Indonesia, Korea and the Philippines.[32] Public enterprises have not been encouraged to raise funds of their own. Instead, they have received funding directly from the government or/and have benefited from low interest loans from state-owned banks, or from borrowing abroad with government guarantees. Listings and share issues have been made redundant by these 'easiest' sources of funds. Growth is thus driven by relatively few unlisted state-controlled companies. In Taiwan, for example, only one state-controlled company, China Steel Corporation, is listed.

The majority of private sector companies have tended to be relatively small, and consequently their needs for investment funds have been modest with comparatively larger requirements for working capital. Thus, they have been able to generate sufficient funding from personal loans, retained earnings, short-term facilities with commercial banks which can be rolled over if necessary, and loans from the kerb markets. In addition, family ties and relationships between corporate businesses and banks in some cases helped secure the necessary loans.

While the privatisation wave started in the past three years and the subsequent inflow of equity began to correct this defect, the 'equity boom' took place before any major change in the industrial structures and cannot be fully explained by the latter.

Thus, it appears that other (non economic) factors may be at the root of the rapid stock market development observed lately in Asia, and the increased speed by which the ASEAN equity market activities reacted to stronger economic growth in recent years, and more specifically since 1985.

THE EFFECTS OF SOCIOLOGICAL AND INSTITUTIONAL FACTORS IN HAMPERING AN EARLIER DEVELOPMENT OF ASIAN EQUITY MARKETS

Lack of confidence

One of the most important demand obstacles to equity market development in Asian emerging economies is the lack of confidence prevalent in these markets, and thus is related to supervisory and regulatory issues. The lack of confidence stems from 'exogenous' factors to the stock market, such as political instability, cultural habits and beliefs and lack of education; and 'endogenous' factors, such as additional risks triggered by an inadequate regulatory environment. In fact, most studies have favoured deregulation and strengthened supervision to foster equity market growth.[33]

A limited public comprehension has discouraged the public from participating in the capital markets. It is clear that the propensity to invest in shares rises with the level of education: a high level of education increases confidence in the markets by contributing to a higher level of knowledge of financial activities. The level of adult literacy in Asia remains lower than that of developed countries, although it has been rising rapidly. Large disparities also remain. While the adult literacy in Korea stands at 97 per cent, Indonesia and Malaysia had ratios below 80 per cent. In 1960, with the exceptions of the Philippines and South Korea, the ratio was below 70 per cent.[34] South Korea, Hong Kong and Singapore achieved universal primary education approximately two decades ago, and this could have been a significant positive factor in the development of their financial markets. By contrast, the comparatively poor performance of Indonesia in adult literacy contributes to explaining the underdevelopment of the Jakarta Stock Exchange: Indonesian shareholders represented only 0.02 per cent of the total Indonesian population at the end of the 1980s. It remains that assessing the sole influence of the level of education of shareholders on their involvement in stock markets is difficult because the education level and the income level of an individual are closely related. Still, high educational levels increase the probability of above average income levels, as well as relatively higher knowledge of and confidence in stock market activities and higher confidence in equity investments.

Political instability has certainly negatively affected the development of the equity markets of East Asia. Political risks influence stock investment[35] in two main ways: restrictions on the repatriation of funds, and expropriation. Furthermore, political instability hampers economic growth, and thus dampens stock attractiveness. It encourages alternative forms of savings, as well as 'capital flight'. The magnitude of the negative impact of political risks on equity market behaviour is, however, difficult to assess. Although a correlation can be found between changes in the level of domestic political risk and changes in the systematic risks of the stock market, no causation between the two observations has been demonstrated.[36] As for education, it is difficult to differentiate between the direct impact of political instability on investor confidence, and the indirect impact through poor economic performance which usually results from unsettled political conditions.

Nevertheless, it is most likely that emerging Asian stock markets, especially in Southeast Asia, have suffered from a lack of confidence resulting from the unsettled political conditions present in almost every Asian country in the 1960s and 1970s. In Hong Kong, the political crisis triggered by the communist demonstration of May 1967 dampened market confidence, with the most important factor in the recovery of the Hong Kong stock market at the end of the 1960s being the general recovery of confidence in the colony's economic future after the disturbances.[37] The uncertainty over Hong Kong's future in the beginning of the 1980s was a significant factor in the weakening of turnover performance in the HKSE. Most recently, stock prices plummeted in Hong Kong during 1992 over the crisis set by Chris Patten and the uncertainty about Hong Kong's future continues to maintain a high level of systematic risk in the Hong Kong market.[38] The conflict in Indochina is most likely to have been one of the main factors which paralysed the equity market in Thailand up to the end of the 1970s. In 1979, during a period of fast rising economic growth in Malaysia, the KLSE fell to just above the 1978 level, due mostly to the deterioration of the political situation at the border of Thailand and Cambodia, the US–Iran crisis and political unrest in Afghanistan.[39] The same pattern was observable on the Stock Exchange of Singapore (SES). The Philippines were subject to martial law between 1972 and 1983, stifling the country's equity market. Later foreign investors pulled out of the Manila Stock Market in 1984–85 with the deterioration of the political situation following the murder of Ninoy Aquino.[40] In Indonesia during the late 1950s, the Sukarno government nationalised all Dutch businesses following the struggle to liberate Irian Jaya, with Dutch capital subsequently taking flight. Following economic chaos, high inflation, radical political events and the 1965 aborted communist *coup d'état* stifled the development of the capital market.

Poor quality and limited available information has contributed largely to weakening investor confidence. Uncertainty resulting from poor information (unqualifiable risks) is a major disincentive to investment. While the lack of adequate information is a commonly used argument to explain the weakness of Asian emerging stock markets, it is unclear as to the source of this information deficiency. Five main reasons explain the poor quality and quantity of information available:

1 The lack of a competent stockbroking industry has certainly contributed

to limit available research on stocks and markets. Central to the risk assessment process, information and research on equity markets and individual stocks are very important for institutional investors whose investment decisions are very much research-driven.[41] In fact, at the opening of the Korean stock market in January 1992, foreign investors have mainly bought and sold Korean shares on the basis of available research and accurate financial information on individual firms,[42] and the prospectus of the June 1992 Jardine Fleming Asia Pacific Funds underlines the poor quality of research as one of the main problems discouraging many foreign institutional investors from Asian emerging markets.

2 Poor information on particular stocks or on equity markets in general has been reinforced by inadequate telecommunication infrastructures.[43] Most stock exchanges did not have reliable information systems. Stock price indices, when they existed, suffered from averaging and thin trading, included non-traded securities, and were not adjusted for cash dividend.[44] Information on stock prices has been limited until recently, with the exception of Hong Kong (since 1969 the Hang Seng Bank has compiled an index of 33 active shares representing at least 90 per cent of both turnover and market value of stock traded, and from 1970, the HKSE has published several weekly and daily reports on share prices). Finally, regulations such as price variation limits have contributed to the distortion of price information because when new information requires a price change larger than the allowable price range, trading limits delay the determination of the equilibrium price.

3 The lack of standard, tight and effective disclosure requirements has contributed to keeping information supply at minimum levels. Although studies are still divided on the potential negative impact of poor disclosure frameworks,[45] several examples of market failure (e.g. insider trading scandals) indicate that Asian market regulations have not been sufficient to ensure orderly trading. The negative effects of limited disclosure rules have been reinforced by the poor quality of the information effectively disclosed. In Malaysia and Singapore 'one of the important factors stimulating a rising volume of stock purchases has been the mandatory disclosure of information required by the stock exchange from newly listed companies. The information which is passed on to the public by the Exchange, plus daily stock quotations and the publication of monthly financial data, have helped to encourage an expansion in stock trading and investment.'[46] However, this development has been limited to Malaysia and Singapore. Most other Asian countries did not have standard disclosure requirements until very recently. Although Thailand and Indonesia have both since 1983 implemented a relatively extended degree of financial disclosure requirements, in practice these various disclosure standards have not been successful

due to lax enforcement.[47] Indonesia is an extreme but also typical example of these problems, and as of 1992 'there is no single regulation, old or new, which explicitly mentions the obligation of the listed companies to make full disclosure to the public'.[48] And when disclosure, already very limited, was revealed to be incorrect in Indonesia, there were no provisions in law establishing the rights of affected investors.[49] As a recent example of the inadequacy of disclosure requirements and the effects on the market, in August 1992, Argos Pantes, an Indonesian textile company with a market capitalisation of US$238 million (Rp27.8bn) projected annual earnings of US$1.36 million. This was unexpected since as part of its initial public offering (IPO) in the previous month, the company had projected earnings of Rp87.2bn. The 68 per cent downward revision looked very much like a case of the company deliberately misinforming a number of brokers and investors. Investor confidence consequently slipped sharply after such a blue chip company misled the market and the stock index fell to 220 from a peak of 645 in July 1990. It is worth noting that the issue of listing requirements is a difficult one in Asia: while the demand for equity and subsequently the market liquidity would benefit from tougher disclosure requirements, the supply of equity (especially from Chinese companies) would suffer from such requirements as we will discuss below.

4 Contributing to the low quality of information available, accounting standards have been (and are still) non-existent in most Asian emerging equity markets. According and auditing practices have not been thorough enough to ensure proper financial reporting,[50] especially for Chinese companies. In fact, the lack of consolidated accounts allows for large conglomerates, like the Korean chaebols, to move money from company to company without reporting it to the public. In the 1970s in Hong Kong, there were an insufficient number of auditing firms in the colony to make a proper review of the listed companies. Most formal accounts, balance sheets, and profit and loss accounts were archaic in form and deficient in content[51] and 'revealed the minimum that the law requires, but withholding much that is necessary for a shareholder to know if he is to evaluate the management's performance adequately'.[52]

5 Finally, another factor which may have negatively influenced the supply of information is the fact that the demand for equities has outstripped supply, albeit at very low levels. Modern agency cost theory[53] suggests that in order to raise funds in a competitive market, in which many firms are seeking to raise funds, companies would have to establish reputations for the wise use of funds and would have to issue adequate information. However, in most Asian emerging markets, with demand far outstripping supply of equity, the market was not competitive, and subsequently firms were not obliged to provide extensive information in order to place their shares.

Insufficient audits and financial reports, and inaccurate financial information have certainly contributed to keep potential investors at bay. Korea's early measures in the 1970s to protect investors through the creation of the Securities Supervisory Board in 1977 and requiring auditing of listed companies by certified accountants were at least partly responsible for the significant early development of the Korean Stock Exchange. Prices rose rapidly in the 1970s, although the supply of equities was increased by stronger measures to encourage companies to go public under the 1972 Corporate Inducement Law.[54] However, most Asian countries did not benefit from governmental direction in auditing and accounting matters until the late 1980s.

Apart from the indirect effect on the supply of equity through a lower demand for corporate shares, the deficiency of financial information available has also resulted more directly in subduing the supply of equity. In general, only large firms have been able to issue shares due to the lack of information for potential buyers. Larger companies are the only ones well-known enough to reassure investors when official information is limited.[55] But these firms also have prime access to bank loans, and since bank loans are often a cheaper form of capital (as we will discuss below) they frequently choose bank loans over equity raising. Smaller firms, without reliable information on their business, can only issue securities with a high risk premium, i.e. at discounted issue prices, and thus at a high cost of capital or when investors are willing to take significant risks.

However, the negative impact on the Asian emerging stock markets of inadequate information should not be overestimated. Low accounting standards have certainly affected potential foreign investment, but their impact on domestic investment may have been much more subtle. Foreign investors' reluctance to invest in Asia is not the single most significant factor which has undermined the development of Asian markets. First, foreigners were in many cases prevented from investing in these markets by a myriad of regulations. Second, foreign investors, when allowed to participate in the equity markets, have represented until recently only a very small share of total investment. A low grade of accounting standards and information requirements may not necessarily be responsible for the lack of domestic investors' confidence because the information needs of each country are determined by different environments and cultural values.[56] No research has been done on whether the available accounting information can be used efficiently for decision making by the indigenous individual. Each country adopts appropriate accounting standards which are applicable to their own unique environment. This means that the potential negative impact of poor accounting methods and information has to be put in context – the rather poor level of information by Western standards may be considered adequate by Asian investors (who in some cases have access to informal information through family and other networks). One problem may be that most developing countries acquired their accounting systems from their former colonisers, and therefore the system in use may have been inappropriate for their needs. Dickie and Layman[57] also argue that while in the US disclosure is the primary mechanism for protecting investors, disclosure is inadequate in most Asian countries to protect and attract small investors – the typical small investor is unable to understand a financial statement.

Inadequate legal measures have reinforced the lack of confidence already stemming from the low level of education, political instability and information deficiencies. Although excessive regulations can stifle securities markets,[58] the existence of legal infrastructure is an essential element in the development of securities markets.[59] Emerging markets in Asia have been characterised by over-regulation in areas where the free market forces should have been prevalent, and under-regulation where a normal regulatory and supervisory body would have been useful to support market confidence. Inadequate regulations[60] have contributed to increasing the risk of investing in equities.

Most of the regulatory problems stem from the prime objective behind the creation of these stock markets: a vehicle to localise foreign firms, privatise state-owned companies and spread ownership, particularly in Indonesia, Malaysia, Thailand and Korea. The policy of developing stock markets and pushing foreign companies to issue publicly traded shares to permit indigenisation of foreign firms (and the spread of wealth) is part of the larger pattern whereby since the 1960s, many Third World countries have sought to reduce the level of foreign (Chinese as well as Western) influence over their economies.[61] Assuring an efficient stock market and attracting more capital and more investors in order to provide for an efficient means of channelling savings to productive investments, was secondary to the goals set for equity markets in these countries. Regulation on the stock markets was thus of the 'public choice' type[62] and has not protected the rights of minority shareholders.

Since shares, as transferable obligations, represent contractual relationships, they are most sensitive to the structure of legal rights and their enforcement. The legal structures and the mechanisms to enforce legal decisions are in general very poor[63] in the stock markets surveyed, and shareholders' rights are very limited. In the absence of enforced contractual rights for small individual investors, firms are not forced to act in accordance with investors' interests. In such a context, funds for investment are most likely to be forthcoming only for institutions with an ability to enforce claims, offering a partial explanation to the preference for bank deposits in Asian economies.

These rights were already jeopardised by the concentration of share-ownership (see below) generally observable in Asian stock markets. One of the problems which stem from this concentrated ownership structure is that there is an agency problem between the dominant shareholder on the one hand, and the small shareholders on the other hand. As there is no mechanism for checking the power of the dominant shareholder, important decisions, including the use of retained earnings, are solely at the dominant shareholder's discretion. In such a situation, the dominant shareholder has an incentive to expropriate the firm's earnings for his own use since the cost of using them is shared by others.[64] In Korea, corporate management has been dominated by the government and could not be trusted to report honestly to minority shareholders.[65] In Malaysia, Gomez[66] reported that the implementation of the NEP and the creation of Pernas[67] have contributed to a minority obtaining control and ownership of a large segment of the corporate sector while squeezing numerous small shareholders. In Indonesia the existing Company Law contains no protection for minority shareholders other than the right to vote and participate in shareholder meetings.[68]

A major consequence of these ambiguous legal frameworks is the stifling of the development of equity markets. The lack of adequate protection for small investors is reflected in an unequal distribution of gains between small and large shareholders. This in turn results in minimal participation by small investors, leading to a lower demand for securities and ultimately to thin trading and poor liquidity.[69]

Further, with inadequate regulations stock market crashes due to insider trading scandals or stock market manipulations have been numerous, and have resulted in weaker market confidence. For example, market confidence was weak in Malaysia between 1985 and 1986 due to the impact of the collapse of Pan-Electric industries at the end of 1985, and turnover and market capitalisation slackened significantly. The growth rate of market capitalisation fell by over 10 per cent in Malaysia and Singapore in 1985 compared to the previous year. Although this fall in market capitalisation was reinforced by negative rates of economic growth, market capitalisation fell much faster than the decline registered in GDP growth. The Taiwan stock market was shaken in 1992 by a crisis involving the powerful 'big hands'.[70] The speculative tactics of Lei Po-Lung and Oung Ta-Ming, were responsible for more than 50 per cent of turnover on some trading days.[71] It is most likely that public confidence was seriously affected by such manipulations, and in 1992, the growth of market capitalisation was negative while real and nominal economic growth was above 7 per cent. The alternation of boom and bust periods in Hong Kong[72] has also contributed to undermining confidence.[73] In addition, differing rules and regulations between the various markets tended to confuse investors and complicate regulatory enforcement before the merger in 1981 of the four stock exchanges (Hong Kong Stock Exchange, Kan Ngan Stock Exchange, Far East Stock Exchange and Kowloon Stock Exchange). The Thai market experienced heavy volume turnover and a major speculative boom in prices in 1977, then crashed and slid until the early 1980s (Appendix Table (3)A1.4). The Bank of Thailand argues[74] that, due to the subsequent loss of confi- dence, savings in the forms of equities as a percentage of total savings fell in the period 1977–80 to 9.35 per cent, compared with 12.52 per cent during the period 1972–76. Market capitalisation annual growth rate fell from a peak of 171 per cent in 1977, to three consecutive negative years below –8 per cent in 1979, and 1981. In contrast, economic growth during this period was on average a real 4 per cent per annum.

The adverse impact of an inadequate legal framework

As for the possible negative impact of inadequate accounting standards on investors' confidence in Asian emerging markets, it is difficult to assess to what extent the differences in regulatory environments were negative for each country. Rozeff[75] argues that in regulatory matters, imitation of another country's regulatory system and laws is not sufficient justification, even if the country being cited has more advanced capital markets. Imitation does not necessarily represent a step taken to serve the public interest. Thus, the adequacy of regulations in Asian emerging stock markets has to be assessed in light of the outcome and failures of the market, and not in comparing the regulatory environment to those of other more mature markets.

Until the late 1980s, restrictions were placed on foreign investment (Table 3.3) in most economies surveyed, deriving from the governments' goal to spread wealth ownership within the country through share issues by major companies. Foreign investors, when permitted to invest, were heavily taxed. Therefore, despite the creation of a few mutual funds for foreign investors in the Far East, developing countries' markets had been virtually untapped by foreign portfolio investors until the mid-1980s.[76] Lack of confidence in these markets has certainly not encouraged foreign investors, but in any case, in most countries they were restricted in their investments in these markets. It is worth noting that where foreign invest- ment (mostly through mutual funds) was allowed, the market illiquidity and the lack of equity supplied, kept institutional foreign investors at bay. For instance, in Indonesia, between 1984 and 1989, there were no new listings, and foreign mutual funds had great difficulty building up portfolios because of the lack of Indonesian shares available.

Rhee[77] provide a classification of the Asian emerging markets depending upon the degree of government control over foreign exchange and foreign ownership in 1987. However, prior to 1987, some changes had already taken place so this classification has been extrapolated back to the begin- ning of the 1980s (see Table 3.3 below). Our estimations for 1992 of the extent of openness to foreign investment will assist in understanding the changes that have taken place in Asian emerging stock markets over the past five years (this will be discussed in detail below).

Table 3.3 Barriers to foreign investment in the Asian equity markets[78]

	1980	1987	1992
Hong Kong	1	1	1
Korea	5	4	3
Singapore	3	2	2
Taiwan	5	4	4
Malaysia	4	3	3
Thailand	4	3	2
Indonesia	5	4	2
Philippines	4	4	2

Source: Ghan Ree, S., 'Securities Markets and Systemic Risks in Dynamic Asian Economies', OECD, Paris, 1992

Notes: (1) Laissez faire economy, where neither exchange controls nor any limitation regarding foreign ownership of domestic firms by foreign investors exist.
(2) Capital markets are fully liberalised except for restrictions on selective industries and/or firms in 'national interest'.
(3) Capital markets are substantially open but not completely liberalised. Usually foreign exchange controls do not exist or they are minimal for normal investment activities. However, foreign ownership of domestic firms is limited to a fixed percentage of the shares outstanding or of voting rights.
(4) Capital markets are in the process of being opened. Foreign exchange controls exist and foreign investors do not have direct access to local equity markets.
(5) Totally closed, not even investment through mutual funds allowed.
* Regulatory changes concerning foreign portfolio investments underlying this table are presented in Appendix (3)4.

In addition, the tax structure has contributed to render equity investment unattractive. Most Asian governments have encouraged investment in domestic government securities in order to finance large infrastructure expenditure. Subsequently, the tax structures have been biased in favour of investment in long term government securities. For example, Singapore Post Office Savings Bank (POSB) deposit earnings are tax free, while dividend income is subject to income tax. In Taiwan, interest income has been subject to a lower withholding tax than has dividend income, while in Indonesia, savings accounts were favoured by a high 15 per cent withholding tax on all dividend receipts.

Further, regulations on share price movements have also been an additional important factor in constraining (foreign and domestic) investment. Share price variation limits were introduced in several countries (Taiwan 7 per cent, Indonesia 4 per cent (removed in 1987), Thailand 10 per cent, Malaysia 30 per cent, but also in Korea and the Philippines) in order to improve confidence by limiting the downside risk associated with speculation. Instead it had the effect of discouraging investors from investing in the stock market since it effectively prevented them from achieving large immediate trading profits. Further, as price change limits prevented stock returns from following a random walk, they allowed for arbitrage opportunities, and subsequently manipulation.[79] Empirical evidence shows that the benefits of the price limit system in the KSE in reducing volatility have not offset the costs of the market inefficiency caused by the limits.[80] Price fluctuation limits have also encouraged investors to demand high dividends because these measures limit the scope for capital gains, and thus contributed to the low supply of equity.

The limited role of institutional investors

Mutual funds, pension funds and insurance companies have not played a decisive role in the accumulation of funds in Asian emerging economies, and on the rare occasion in which they did, they have failed to channel these funds to the equity markets. Korea, where institutional investors held over 54 per cent of listed shares in 1977 and helped the market's early developments, is an exception. Some Asian pension funds have played a significant role in mobilising savings for long term finance, but regulations have prevented them from being significant institutional investors in equity markets. Furthermore, most of these institutions have crowded out potential individual investment in the equity markets. Thus, pension funds in Asia (primarily in Malaysia, Singapore and the Philippines) have had a substitution effect *vis-à-vis* voluntary savings and a forced saving effect. Both of these effects have resulted in available investment funds being diverted from the stock markets.

Voluntary savings usually have been small in pension funds, but some have gathered very high levels of compulsory savings. Data are scarce, but studies by Emery and Lee and Jao[81] indicate that savings through pension funds in Taiwan, Indonesia, Thailand and Hong Kong have been negligible. In contrast, pension funds have been more important in Singapore via the Central Provident Fund (CPF) and in Malaysia via the Malaysian Employee Provident Fund (EPF). The CPF and the EPF have mobilised a large share of respective domestic savings since their creation in 1952.[82] The two largest insurers and pension funds in the Philippines, the Government Service Insurance System and the Social Security System, which provide pension and social benefits to government workers and private sector employees, respectively, have also been significant potential sources of long term finance.

The majority of the pension funds accumulated, however, are captive investment – they have to be directed to government securities. Of the S$26.8bn of members' balance accumulated through the CPF in 1986, S$13.6bn (51 per cent) was invested in government bonds, and the remainder was deposited by the Monetary Authority of Singapore (MAS) for future subscription to government bond issues. In fact, Singapore government securities have been principally created to absorb the CPF surplus and about 70 per cent of total Singapore government stocks are held by the CPF. Under the First Malaysian Development Plan (1966–70), the EPF was expected to bring a third of the internally-sourced funds required by the M$910 million public development expenditure. In 1991 the EPF still invested 68 per cent in Malaysian government securities and only 6 per cent in corporate securities.[83]

'Compulsory' investments in pension funds have crowded out private investment in other insurance and pension schemes as well as direct investment in equities. In Singapore and Malaysia, the rising levels of savings and the subsequent potential larger equity investment pool have been offset by the relatively faster growth in contributions to the CPF and EPF. The diversion of savings from the equity markets that resulted from the high compulsory savings through the CPF, is best shown by the result of the 1978 Investment Scheme in Singapore. When in 1987, contributions to the CPF were made available for members to invest in shares of the Singapore Bus Service Limited (SBS), S$18.8 million were withdrawn from the funds, or 94 per cent of the value of the total 20 million shares offered for public subscription by SBS. The substitution effect of the compulsory pension savings schemes away from equity investment is an additional factor explaining why income per capita and market capitalisation per capita have not grown proportionally, and in essence why rising saving rates have not translated proportionally into rising equity investments.

Government restrictions have also prevented other savings institutions from playing a significant role in the stock market. For instance, in Singapore the Post Office Savings Bank (POSB) mobilises a large share of private sector savings not invested in the CPF, since the POSB interest earnings are tax free (unlike dividends from equities). The level of POSB deposits rose from 3.4 per cent of total savings deposits in 1974 to 23.4 per cent in 1986, and the POSB's total assets grew at a phenomenal annual compound rate of 36.2 per cent from 1974 to 1986, which testifies to its success in competing with other investment alternatives. With a large share of its assets being mandatorily invested in long term government bonds, the POSB, like the EPF and CPF, has diverted potential investment away from the equity markets.

Over the past decade, personal investment in the US, as well as in Europe, has been increasingly skewed towards investment in mutual funds.[84] Although mutual funds have existed since the 1950s in the majority of the countries surveyed in this study, they have not played a significant role as institutional investors in Asian emerging equity markets. Lack of investor protection as well as poor knowledge of financial markets have discouraged investors from saving through mutual funds and only Malaysia and Singapore have had some success.[85] They have not been significant as a source of institutional investment in equities[86] until the late 1990s. One of the impediments facing mutual funds and to a lesser extent pension funds and insurances in Asia's emerging markets is tightly linked with the lack of equity supply and liquidity in the market. The more desirable stocks are often closely held by the owners (see below) who are reluctant to part with them. Thus, the institutions have had to satisfy themselves with less attractive shares. This has been a problem especially for mutual funds as returns have been less attractive for potential members. In addition, with a high degree of illiquidity in the market, large investments in equity have been difficult to pursue without influencing share prices significantly (at least in the short term).

The policies of the insurance industry with respect to the purchase and sale of various classes of assets have been, and continue to be, very important factors in the underdevelopment of the Asian equity markets surveyed. Data on the insurance business in Asia is scarce,[87] but as examples, Thailand's life insurance industry was a minor component of the financial market in the 1970s with only about 0.5 per cent of gross household savings.[88] Korea's represented about 0.6 per cent. While the low levels of economic development and average income per capita explain partly the low levels of funds gathered by insurance companies until recently, their continued small investment in equities are mostly due to inadequate regulatory measures.

Very low insurance premium per capita and the very small number of policy holders[89] in Indonesia, for example, most likely reflect the importance of traditional agriculture in the economy as opposed to commerce. One of the main constraints on contractual savings institutions is the need for contributors with a steady and regular source of income. The modern sectors often represent a minority share of the total population. The very low levels of income that characterised the large population of farmers, as well as insurance offices concentrated in the cities, have contributed to prevent a significant development of the insurance industry. Lack of confidence has also been important for the insurance industry due to loosely implemented regulations and inefficiency.[90] Cultural habits and beliefs also prevent Chinese people, often the wealthier people in the Asian countries and thus the most likely to take up insurance policies, from doing so.[91] The late transformation of most Asian economies from traditional to modern societies which took place in the 1960s is an additional reason that can explain the underdevelopment of the insurance business until recent years. In short, the economic structures have been the major factors behind the lack of funds gathered by insurances in the 1960s and 1970s and their consequent absence as meaningful institutional investors in the local stock market during these two decades.

The investment funds of life insurances grew significantly from the mid-1970s to the mid-1980s, reflecting the growth in income and wealth of the policy holders, as well as the acceptance of modern, as opposed to traditional, business practices. In Indonesia, the coverage value of the twelve life insurances increased from US$271.1 million in 1974 to US$1.8bn in 1978[92] (564 per cent increase). The total assets of the Malaysian life insurances rose from M$700 million in 1975 to M$3,646 million in 1985 (420 per cent increase). In Singapore, total assets of life insurance doubled between 1981 and 1985, while in Taiwan assets rose from NT$6,785 million in 1975 to NT$87,720 million in 1985 (1,193 per cent increase). In Korea, assets represented W6,582 billion in 1985, up from W105 billion in 1975 (6,169 per cent increase). In Thailand, the total sum insured increased eight fold between 1974 and 1983, from B3,901 million to B30,260 million.[93]

However, the increasing amount of savings invested through life insurance has not been sufficient to significantly raise the amount of funds invested in equities markets. First, the amount of savings mobilised remains limited. For example, in Thailand, the ratio of total savings to savings invested in life insurances grew only slowly between 1967 and 1988.[94] Second, the insurances' investments in the equity market increased more slowly than their total assets. Loans and real estate investments were more profitable instruments for insurance investments. In fact, in 1984, most of the invested funds of Indonesian life insurance companies were held in state commercial banks as time deposits.[95] Further, the initial and still large domination of the life insurance industry by foreign companies was not conducive to the development of the local stock exchanges. Foreign insurance companies were not inclined to invest in the local equity markets and were not likely either to get listed on the domestic stock markets given that they were able to raise funds in their country of incorporation. Moreover, investment in shares was discouraged by regulations obliging insurance companies to invest a large percentage of their funds in Government securities. In South Korea for instance, insurances were encouraged to make large direct loans to industrial companies in the Government designated priority sectors, rather than invest directly in the stock market.[96] The ADB[97] notes that in 1984 loans to such customers represented 65 per cent of total Korean insurance companies assets.

The effect of inadequate regulations and sociological factors on the supply of equity

The lack of confidence, inadequate regulations and the absence of meaningful potential institutional investors explain the weak demand for equity. The subsequent negative impact on share prices contributed to hampering the supply of equity. In addition, the inadequate legal and institutional framework combined with sociological factors to limit directly the number of shares effectively available to investors.

In Korea, between 1984 and 1988 the stock market experienced tremendous growth in both market capitalisation and prices. The Korea Composite Index rose from 143 to 907 over this period. Such an explosive increase in stock prices is normally associated with a declining cost of capital, and thus rising investment opportunities and funds requirements. However, despite the availability of low cost capital and the need to finance the growth of the real sector, companies did not rush to the equity market with initial listings or new issues[98] (see Appendix Table (3)A1.1). The rationale behind this was that the before-tax cost of debt had been kept artificially low by ceilings on interest rates and loan guarantees, low interest rates for targeted industries, and the frequent bail-outs of large corporations by the Government. A favourable tax treatment of debt versus equity accentuated this pattern. New listings in Korea picked up only from 1988, encouraged at least partially by strong Government incentives and pressures. A comparatively small number of new listings was also observable in Indonesia, Malaysia and Taiwan until 1987 (see Figure 3.3). However, in those cases, rather than artificially low interest rates, it was too high dividends, controlled IPO prices and the importance of Chinese businesses that kept the supply of equity subdued.

Due to a lack of confidence by the investing public, and the distortion in the taxation structure favouring interest income over dividend income, listed firms must offer dividend rates that are comparable to after-tax bank interest rates in order to offer competitive investments. To meet investors' demand for high returns, many companies have had a payout ratio in excess of 100 per cent.[99] This situation aggravated their financial positions and further discouraged them from issuing more shares. In Indonesia, in 1984, the ADB[100] noted that four out of the twelve listed companies were paying cash dividends higher than their net profit after tax. Governments in both Korea and Indonesia have reinforced this problem by giving companies 'informal' guidance on dividends expected.[101]

In addition, consistent with their goal of improving wealth distribution through shareholding, some governments have attempted to negotiate a low price for shares offered in the primary markets in the hope that the prices would appreciate in the secondary market, providing favourable returns for primary investors, and stimulating the demand for more shares. A significant amount of underpricing in Korea[102] for example, seems largely due to the Korean tradition of setting the initial offering price at the par value, because of the Korean Securities and Exchange Commission's reluctance to grant autonomy to the issuers and underwriter in determining offer prices. The Korean regulators fear that unusual price behaviour may impose substantial capital losses on new shareholders, and make the investing public lose confidence in the market. A minimum of 50 per cent of new shares issued in Indonesia had to be offered to PT Danareksa.[103] While this was intended to permit wider share distribution through Danareksa's unit trust vehicles, it had the effect of depressing share prices in the initial share offering. The systematic underpricing of shares is an added cost because it forces the issuing firm to offer a larger number of shares in order to raise a desired level of capital. This in turn dilutes further the original owners' control (which is most likely to discourage even further the supply of shares, as we will discuss below) and places additional burdens on the company in future years since the additional shares have the effects of diluting future earnings per share.

The nature of the original equity ownership is also an important determinant in the supply of equity. In Asia the importance of this factor is particularly pronounced as the characteristics of Chinese businesses play a significant role in constraining the supply of equities. The conglomerates that emerged in the 1970s, and especially the 1980s in Southeast Asia, were predominantly Chinese-owned.[104] The proportion of Southeast Asian capital in Chinese hands is disproportionately high[105] in relation to the number of Chinese in the total population of Southeast Asia. Therefore, the attitudes of the Chinese towards equity is particularly relevant to understanding the reluctance of companies to raise funds through share issues. The importance of the overseas Chinese in Southeast and East Asian business is reflected by the impact that their business behaviour has on stock market activities. Being the main business force in the region, their reluctance to raise funds through equity issues is obviously significant for the supply of equity.

Some characteristics of a typical Chinese business summarised by Goldberg[106] will assist in understanding why Chinese entrepreneurs are wary of equity issues: centralised decision making with one key and dominant person, strong family control via the occupancy of key positions,[107] and generally autocratic leadership style, are some of the relevant characteristics. The clear implication of these characteristics is that issuing equity is not a favoured method of raising finance because of the potential dilution of control it brings. In addition, the traditional fusion of family and firm encourages emphasis on organisational security, restrictions of access to information, and employment and advancement of persons whose trustworthiness is guaranteed by kinship, prior personal bonds, recommendation and/or loyalty. Therefore, 'business activities are above all interpersonal interactions;[108] and 'what is relevant is not the dichotomy between kin and non-kin, but between personal and non-personal, for the Chinese have a strong antipathy to impersonal contacts as a basis for business dealings'.[109] This interpersonal trustworthiness and a preference for personal rather than institutional ties is uniquely important to the neo-Confucian culture area. Subsequently, while the operating decisions of larger companies are often delegated to lower-level management, Chinese managers rely on highly centralised financial decision making and on personnel practices which enhance trust and control.[110] Such concerns are naturally not consistent with a stock exchange listing which would create institutional and legal ties rather than personal ties between shareholders and owners. Centralisation of control presents also the advantage of dramatically reducing the likelihood of hostile acquisition. Centralisation of control does not allow for the information disclosure required by listing procedures. The associated information diffusion and lack of secrecy as well as the implementation of income reporting, tax collection and auditing procedures are serious problems for Chinese-owned businesses. Many owners of private enterprises consider that going public, and thus being forced to disclose their financial condition to the public, would make the tax liabilities more open. By contrast, banks, especially when owned by Chinese families, often do not demand that borrowers should disclose their financial affairs beyond the confines of the bank manager's office.[111]

The problem of disclosure requirements is particularly significant in the countries (e.g. Indonesia, Malaysia, Thailand and the Philippines) where the ethnic Chinese dominate the national economy, controlling the majority of the private companies, but constitute a politically vulnerable minority of the population. Private companies tend to retain a private status due to the desire of the Chinese owners to avoid divulging the extent of their holdings. Where Chinese economic influence is not contentious (e.g. Singapore, Hong Kong and Taiwan), their companies are frequently public and their shares are traded on the stock exchange.[112] In Malaysia and Indonesia objections to Chinese business have been particularly strong. In fact, the renewal of violence against the Chinese which culminated in the 1969 riots in Malaysia and the 1973 and 1974 riots in Bandung and Jakarta may have contributed to stifling the development of both stock markets at a time when they could have developed more rapidly.

In addition, the preference by Chinese for personal relationships has contributed to limiting the need for fund raising through equity since kin and social networks give the Chinese access to large pools of credit and capital. The funds involved in Chinese networks are believed to be 'ubiquitous, readily accessible to those whose personal trust and credit-worthiness are well established,[113] available in large amounts and efficiently transferred'.[114] Furthermore, the reliance on trust and networks in external business relationships and its consequent impact on equity supply is reinforced by another specific feature of Asian Chinese businesses: their strong banking ties.[115] This characteristic favours bank loans or informal loans in preference to equity, especially so given that several major Asian banks are Chinese-owned or Chinese-managed.[116] In fact, one of the important factors in the rise of the Indonesian groups Astra and Liem was that they were able to gain access to networks of credit from overseas Chinese. When their financing needs became too large for the domestic market, they chose to raise finance internationally mostly through US bank loans. Yoshihara[117] argues that capitalism in the region is dominated by Chinese entrepreneurs whose capitalism is not integrated to the rest of the economy because Chinese companies and capital remain within a Chinese sphere.

It is clear that the preponderance of Chinese corporations in the Asian economies surveyed has limited the number of firms going public, and restricted the supply of equity. As many family businesses have grown into conglomerates with complex shareholding structures and alliances, conservatism of management has contributed to keeping the effective supply of equity small. For instance, only ten of the about two hundred companies of the Charoen Pokhand group in Thailand are listed.[118] A majority of the Chinese business empires are still not represented on the HKSE. In Taiwan, typically only 10 per cent of a company is sold to the public on listing.

When the company is listed, shares are often dormant.[119] In Hong Kong, shares in around 200 of the 260 listed companies are dormant.[120] All the major Taiwanese groups, with the exception of Asia Polymer BTR Nylex, are family controlled even if it is not always obvious from the complex shareholding structures of these Taiwanese companies. An estimate of the proportion of stocks actually held by the controlling family in Taiwan would rarely be less than 60 per cent to 70 per cent.[121] Stakes are distributed to family retainers, or held by charitable institutions (hospitals and schools) sponsored by the family.

Chinese companies are not, however, the only firms in Asia reluctant to raise equity funds. In the Philippines, the number of listings of commercial and industrial stocks does not reflect the importance of the industrial and commercial sectors in the economy. This is chiefly attributable to the ownership structure of most manufacturing/trading companies in the country. With the exception of a few major companies like San Miguel Engineering Equipment Inc. PLDT, most of the commercial industrial firms are privately-owned family corporations whose shares are only traded within the family. In South Korea, founder families are the dominant owners of the largest enterprises and control the management. In case of the 'chaebol group', the owner maintains his control through a combination of direct shareholding and cross-holding amongst affiliated firms. At the end of 1986, in Korea, the main shareholder and persons related to him together held on average 35 per cent to 62 per cent of a company's total outstanding shares.[122] More importantly, the founder owners in general holds far more shares than necessary for maintaining control. The proportion of South Korean firms under managerial control is extremely low (less than 2 per cent at the end of 1986). Due to cross-holding between the chaebols the effective floating supply may be around 20 per cent of the total listed shares. Hence, of the approximate 8,300 million shares theoretically tradable on the KSE by 345 listed companies in 1987, the effective number available for investors is probably only in the order of 1,660 million. Consequently, there were (and still are) few quality stocks available for investors on the KSE because most businesses were closely held by families.[123] In addition, the supply of equity is further reduced by the practice of interlocking directorates in financial institutions with the chaebols. For example, more than three quarters of all short term finance companies are controlled by the chaebols. A number of conglomerates exercise effective control over banks through a variety of associated companies: Hyundai is a major shareholder in three of the big Korean banks.

However, the aversion of Chinese business to equity issues is showing signs of loosening. Financial difficulties (after the financial collapse of Indonesia's Bank Summa, the Astra groups sold stakes in its groups to repay the debt of Summa) and the large size of the conglomerates, combined with a new generation of managers educated in Western universities, and the recognition that going public would not significantly reduce the control of the owner family since the controlling group often keep a majority at stake,[124] have pushed Chinese-owned companies to raise equity finance more and more via share issues. The ratio of annual turnover to market capitalisation can be interpreted as an indication of the liquidity, and indirectly, of the weight of inactive shares in the market. Table 3.2 shows that Taiwan and Korea had the highest ratios in 1991, but also that the ratio has been rising in all markets.

To survive in a more competitive and international environment, Chinese family firms may have to modernise their management practices (only a handful of the biggest Chinese family firms in the early twentieth century still flourish in the 1980s in Southeast Asia). Southeast Asian countries will soon face the same challenges which drove foreign investors out of their Chinese home location in the first place, high costs, scarce land and labour. It will strike first in Malaysia and last in Indonesia.[125] Southeast Asian countries will have to transform themselves towards higher technology, professionally managed corporations. Relocation could take place in favour of Indochinese countries. The spread of domestic and foreign Chinese businesses throughout the East Asian economies may 'portend the dissolution of many of the ethnic characteristics of Chinese business and the transformation of the more successful of these companies into truly global corporations'[126] because 'to become global players in specific industries, Chinese companies must transcend their present location specific advantages and develop instead non-cultural firm specific advantages that can be exploited around the world. In so doing, Chinese businesses will form strategic alliances with non-Chinese businesses, further diluting their ethnic characters'.[127]

In addition, political pressures are at work against the tight family control of some large companies. For example, since 1970, ownership structures have evolved in Malaysia and Thailand in the 1980s towards family-owner members holding no more than enough shares to maintain control.[128] Further, with the growing importance of Chinese capital flows in Southeast Asia, and the increasing need for capital of these countries, relaxation of anti-Chinese policies is expected. Governments are in fact playing the cultural card to attract Chinese capital.[129] This could also encourage Chinese owners to divulge more information and thus remove some of the disincentives to issue shares. In Malaysia, with the relaxation of the NEP guidelines which used to favour Malay business, Chinese business may have been encouraged to divulge their affairs somewhat more. In addition, increasingly though slowly, Southeast Asian Chinese are identifying as Thais, Indonesians or Malaysians[130] and this should help lower racial tensions towards Chinese business.

The risks are that the large flows of overseas Chinese investment will stir anti-Chinese feelings and subsequently contribute to keeping the number of new listings subdued, and that the influx of foreign Chinese investors will reinforce the Chinese cultural pattern of doing business.[131] In relocating operations to Southeast Asia, Chinese firms can continue to cling to their traditional ethnic business practices which have become outmoded or uncompetitive in their more competitive home location. Thus moving to locations where they are a minority preserves the Chineseness of the Chinese business operations. This could have an adverse impact on the development of Asian emerging stock markets. However, Lim[132] argues that the 'de-sinifying' consequences of internationalisation could counter the 're-sinifying' effects of the large influx of foreign Chinese investments. As for now, while it is clear that Southeast and East Asian conglomerates are going global, it is not clear whether they have effectively started to lose their ethnic characteristics. In fact, they largely remain tightly family run.[133] For example, Charoen Pokhand of Thailand, controlled by the Chearavanant family, is deriving 50 per cent of its assets outside Thailand and has only listed 60 of its 200 companies. Lippor of Indonesia, controlled by the Riady family, has 40 per cent of its assets outside Indonesia but remains largely family-held, and in Indonesia, up to now no real move towards modern business practices is observed (except in Astra due to its financial difficulties).

TOWARDS MORE EFFICIENT EQUITY MARKETS: DEREGULATION AND IMPROVED LEGISLATION

The surge in emerging Asian equity markets development over the last five years, inadequately explained solely by economic factors, stems largely from the recognition by governments of the need for efficient equity markets, and the subsequent necessity for a new institutional framework. The 'mini-boom' observed at the end of the 1980s and the beginning of the 1990s has coincided with moves destined to remedy some of the problems highlighted earlier, therefore suggesting this recent 'boom' was mostly triggered by new regulations designed to improve the allocative efficiency of these markets.

Improved regulations: towards a new role for stock markets

Four of the Asian countries surveyed (Indonesia, Malaysia, Thailand and the Philippines) opened, or re-opened, equity markets during the 1960s and 1970s in order to spread national wealth through a wider distribution of shares. Regulations were often inadequate to ensure proper trading because the initial motivation behind the creation of a stock market was simply to provide people with opportunities to buy shares, rather than to ensure an efficient allocation of national savings to productive investments (as discussed in previous sections). Hence, the efficient allocation of longer term funds was only of secondary importance.[134] During the past few years, however, the increased need for capital investments has dictated a move towards more efficient equity markets. Subsequently, in the 1980s, and particularly since the beginning of the 1990s, equity markets in Asia have been liberalised significantly with the easing of legislative and administrative barriers in order to improve market efficiency, while tougher regulations were adopted to boost investor confidence.

Although savings rates have usually been comparatively high in Asia, the financing of economic development in Asian countries has relied heavily on foreign financial resources. Foreign direct investment (FDI), international loans, and aid have been the major sources of investment finance. Seven significant features have emerged concerning the financing of economic development in the Asian developing countries and are of significant importance in understanding the move towards more efficient equity markets:

1 Infrastructure development has not kept pace with economic growth in the Asian NICs and the ASEAN members. These infrastructure constraints will be critical if economic growth is to be sustained.[135]
2 Some Asian LDCs have borrowed heavily to finance their development efforts, and large foreign loans have led to heavy debt service burdens. The fall in foreign exchange earnings associated with the decline in commodities prices have aggravated the debt problem. This is particularly valid for primary products exporting countries like Indonesia, the Philippines and Malaysia (although manufactures are increasingly important for export earnings).
3 There has been a steady erosion of public sector resources available for development financing. Recurring balance of payment constraints, and rising budget deficits since the mid-1980s have forced Malaysia, Indonesia and the Philippines to rely on alternative forms of domestic finance or on foreign inflows, including international aid.
4 Foreign direct investments have been slowing due to the global economic slowdown in the past few years. Further, with the main aid donors in recession, official development assistance has also been weakening, and on the back of the international debt crisis, international loans to less developed countries have been curtailed.

5 Authorities have started to recognise the importance of the securities markets as an instrument to overcome the mounting problem of over-reliance on debt financing by the private sector. In a context of slowing world growth and subsequent weaker net exports, heavily geared balance sheets have begun to be regarded as posing further threats to the stability of economic growth.[136]

6 The planned and/or implemented privatisation of government-owned enterprises which accompanied the liberalisation of economies initiated in the mid-1980s has also reinforced the need for efficient equity markets. In the future, more privatisations are planned, with Singapore, Malaysia, Indonesia and Thailand leading the way. To finance these developments, securities markets must be further developed, modernised, liberalised, and opened to foreign investors. The reform of the CPF in Singapore in 1993 was directly motivated by the demands of the stock market implied by planned privatisations.[137]

7 In addition, Singapore and Hong Kong have regarded their respective developments as international financial centres as central elements of their economic growth. One of the chief objectives of Singapore's privatisation is to add depth and breadth to the local stock exchange.

In short, with the rise in oil prices after the second oil shock, stiffer terms on foreign loans in the 1980s, and the fall in non-oil commodities prices, foreign liabilities have risen. The high cost of debt servicing, and the associated constraints that it places on economic growth, emphasised the need to develop alternative sources of capital from the local private sector and the nation's savings pools. At the same time, the availability of international financial resources was reduced when large infrastructure expenditures were becoming imperative. Household savings have become a central issue of policy discussion in recent years and, to a large extent, the development of capital markets has been seen as the key to assist private sector financing and thereby continued strong economic growth.[138] Subsequently, Asian policy makers took both demand-following measures and supply-leading measures during the second half of the 1980s to mobilise savings and channel them towards stock markets.

Broadly, the various 'regulatory' measures undertaken[139] have been designed to improve investor confidence through tougher and more effective regulations on information, improve the attractiveness of share investment through redesigning the taxation structures, attract domestic institutional investors, open equity markets to foreign individuals and institutional investors, develop and reinforce the stockbroking industry. Share issues and listings have been fostered mostly through the creation of unlisted or second-board markets with less stringent listing requirements, and tax incentives.

Towards liberalised foreign portfolio investments

Since 1987, most Asian stock markets have opened up to foreign portfolio investments although some remaining regulations continue to limit their scope (Table 3.3). By opening the markets to foreign institutional investors, the governments hoped to cool the markets' speculative tendencies, and introduce a more mature approach to investment. The first development which stimulated foreign interest and made foreign equity investment easier in emerging Asian markets was the introduction of 'Far East funds' allowing foreigners to invest in widely diversified portfolios of Asian stocks. Most Asian governments created their own foreign funds to encourage investment in their equity markets without having to open their markets to direct foreign individual interests, which they feared could stimulate speculation or endanger ownership of domestic assets. For example, in 1986, the Thai authorities tried to boost foreign investment with the creation of two foreign funds, the Bangkok Fund and the Thai Fund. Foreign investment in Thailand was further promoted from 1987 through the establishment of onshore foreign funds with the provision of tax incentives for foreign investors. In 1990, three closed-end mutual funds to mobilise foreign capital were approved with a capitalisation value of US$69 million, US$75 million and US$75 million, respectively. Further, in 1992 the Bank of Thailand issued nine licences to privately-run mutual funds management firms. Foreign investment funds invested in the SET rose from US$69 million in 1989 to US$553 million in 1990 (700 per cent). Privately-run funds have also been established to garner potential funds for investment in Asian equity markets. Foreign funds investment began to be important in the late 1980s, with Korea, Thailand and Taiwan being the first investment locations for these funds.

In Thailand, with the first liberation measures, foreign investors' purchases on the stock market rose from 5.5 per cent of the turnover of the SET in 1984 to 10–15 per cent by late 1986.[140] In 1992, foreigners were reported to account for as much as 40 per cent of trading volume on some days.[141] The surge in foreign portfolio investment recorded in Thailand since 1985 has coincided with the expansion of the SET measured in terms of turnover and market capitalisation (Appendix Table (3)A1.6). While foreigners held only slightly more than 11 per cent of all publicly traded shares in 1988, almost solely in the form of shares especially designed to trade on a foreigner-only board (the 'alien board'), foreigners account for approximately 20 per cent of the total traded shares in 1993, with the majority comprising shares listed on the local board and held through nominees.

The KLSE is currently considering the possibility of allowing international investors to subscribe to new privatisation issues which are too big to be absorbed by the local market, for example the upcoming flotation of the National Electricity Board (TEN) which should be much larger than Malaysia Telekom, currently the largest capitalised stock on the exchange with a market capitalisation of M$26,844 million.[142] In March 1992, for the first time foreigners were allowed to participate in a new Malaysian issue. Out of the 685 million shares on offer for Tenaga National (TEN), 60 million (or 9 per cent of the total shares offered) were tendered for by foreigners. However, the market is not yet open to direct foreign participation in new issue.

The government of Taiwan opened the TSE to direct foreign institutional investment at the end of 1990. A compelling reason for further opening the market to foreign investment could be the weak performance of the Taipei Stock Exchange over the past year. However, many restrictions such as allowing repatriation of capital gains only one day each year continue to limit foreign investment. Hence, although share purchases have been accelerating slowly, total international investments reached only US$1.37 billion by 1992. The Security and Exchange Commission (SEC), the TSE's regulatory agency, said that it would allow foreign banks that are listed among the world's 1,000 largest to invest in its domestic market. This is a relaxation of the original requirement for them to be in the top 500 list, and it could help boost foreign portfolio investment in the TSE.

In 1989, the Korean government allowed foreigners holding convertible bonds floated overseas by Korean companies to acquire domestic shares within certain limits if they wished to convert the bonds into shares. A further step towards liberalisation was taken in 1992 with the opening of the stock market to foreign individual investors. However, procedures that govern foreign investor activity on the KSE remain complex and restrictive.[143] Matters such as taxation and repatriation of funds remain unclarified. Furthermore, the availability of shares to foreign investors remain obviously restricted as 80 listed companies had already hit the 10 per cent ceiling on foreign ownership as of May 1993.[144] Nevertheless, between 3 January 1992 and 20 February 1992, foreign capital of US$570 million flowed into the Seoul bourse and more than 700 foreign investors registered with the Securities Supervisory Board. The additional investment, however, accounted for only 0.54 per cent of market capitalisation.[145] Still, foreign investors now own about 3 per cent listed shares, and 5 per cent if the indirect ownership through funds is included. In 1992, foreigners were reported to have been instrumental in forcing Korean share prices higher.

In 1989, foreign investors were permitted to invest in Indonesian equities through direct share purchases on the JSE,[146] and in 1992 the Indonesian government allowed foreign investors to hold 100 per cent ownership of new companies in Indonesia. In addition, new laws will permit foreign investors to purchase up to 49 per cent of state banks listed on the stock exchange.[147] (The banking sector is currently the sole remaining category of equities from which foreign investors are barred.)

While the importance of 'Asian' fund investments in Asian markets should not be overestimated, (they represented in 1992 only between a minimum of 0.5 per cent in Malaysia, and a maximum of 4 per cent of total market capitalisation in Thailand[148]), their role in driving prices higher by their investments, but also through encouraging foreign and domestic individuals to invest, is significant. The establishment of onshore and offshore country funds by private mutual funds or by the Asian governments have contributed to channelling foreign funds to the stock market.

Increased interest by foreign investors (especially from US financial institutions) since the beginning of the 1980s has combined with the concurrent liberalisation of these stock markets to boost the demand for equities in Asian emerging markets. The well-documented weak correlation between developing countries' stock market prices and those of Western stock markets[149] has provided for risk diversification and sparked interest in the Asian emerging markets. Foreign investors were further encouraged by prospects of high returns due to the countries' high economic growth rates and the presence of some of the world's leading corporations.

The fresh wave of US pension fund investments has also certainly provided a significant stimulus to the mini-boom observed in the Asian emerging equity market.[150] A recent Salomon Brothers study showed that in the 1986–88 period, US investors invested a cumulative US$0.7 billion in global equities. Between 1989 and 1991, their purchases totalled around US$60 billion, a near 100-fold increase. Unfortunately, no breakdown of their investments channelled towards Asian securities is available. However, even under the conservative assumption that the share of their total funds invested in Asian equities did not increase, the absolute level of funds directed to Asian equity markets would still have increased very significantly.

Furthermore, US mutual funds have almost certainly shifted a large share of their funds destined to risky investment in emerging markets from Latin America to Asia, after the Latin American debt crisis which began in 1982, and most probably also a large share of the funds formerly destined to the Japanese share market when it collapsed. The Latin American debt payment crisis in the early 1980s, the subsequent shortage of development funds and international loans, and the resulting economic recession in most Central and South American countries, contributed to a sharp drop in confidence by equity investors, and weakening stock prices. Looking at the International Finance Corporation (IFC) composite indices of stock prices in the different emerging South American and Asian equity markets, one can observe a somewhat inverse relationship between Asian emerging market stock prices and Latin American emerging market stock prices. It is clear that prices in Asian emerging stock markets rose in the second half of the 1980s while stock prices in Brazil, Chile, Mexico and Argentina remained flat. It is worth noting that in the early 1990s, the reverse pattern is observable. While data on mutual funds investment are not available, we can assume that foreign funds pulled out of Latin American markets were shifted towards Asian equities, thereby helping prices to rise in Asia. This possible shift was certainly made easier by the reforms undertaken by the Asian emerging markets from the beginning of the 1980s. As an example, Baring Asset Management's emerging markets fund is reported to have shifted large amounts of money from Latin America to Asia and is now heavily weighted towards South Korea, Malaysia and Thailand.[151]

In summary, as shown by Table 3.3, Asian emerging stock markets have become more accessible to foreign investors, particularly to institutional investors. Subsequently, individual and institutional foreign investors have been increasing their participation in the local markets to significant levels, especially in Indonesia and Thailand. The lack of clarity of most of these liberalisation measures, remaining impediments to foreign portfolio investments, but also prevalent share market condition, have limited the impact of the opening to foreign investments, especially in Korea and Taiwan. Their role thus remains very limited, representing in general less than 5 per cent of equity investors compared with 9.7 per cent in the US, 24.9 per cent in the UK, 28.6 per cent in France, 14.6 per cent in Germany, 38.2 per cent in Australia, and 8.1 per cent in Japan. For instance, foreign institutional investment (the only form of equity investment permitted) in Taiwan is only just below US$2.2 billion, or about 1.5 per cent of market capitalisation in 1993 including investments through country funds.[152] Only in Indonesia can foreign investments (10 per cent of market capitalisation in 1990) account for most of the 'equity boom' between 1989 and 1991. Still, in Malaysia, Thailand and particularly Indonesia, foreign investments have helped fuel the price rises recorded in the stock markets and subsequently encouraged the increases in listed issues. The impact on volume turnover has not been insignificant and has also indirectly encouraged domestic investors' interest and additional equity supply.

Improved confidence and increased incentives

Since the mid-1980s, in parallel with the partial liberalisation of Asian emerging stock markets and their limited opening to foreign investment, equity investment was also made more attractive through more stringent regulations and numerous incentives. Although Asian emerging stock markets' regulatory agencies have shown a willingness to come to grips with the main regulatory deficiencies, regulations are not yet sufficient: the main failings are the lack of measures available to 'punish' malpractices, and the lack of implementation of these measures. Insider trading rules are good examples of these failings. In Malaysia, for instance, while there are laws against insider trading, to date there have been few investigations or prosecutions of investors suspected of trading in securities based on inside information.[153] Nevertheless, the timing of these measures coincides closely with improved liquidity, and thus allows us to posit the existence of a direct causal relationship between conscious government policies in favour of equity investment, and the growth of the stock markets.

New legal frameworks have certainly helped to attract rising levels of domestic savings into the stock markets. The implementation of adequate regulatory bodies and stricter information disclosure requirements contributed to restored public confidence. The protection of investors has been enhanced in most Asian countries although the new regulatory settings are still far from offering the same level of protection and transparency as in the US (which may not be necessary). More effective supervision and control of the securities industry and of trading practices have been implemented. Supervisory bodies were established in Hong Kong in 1987 and in Thailand in 1992 while a revision of the legal environment took place in 1983 in Malaysia and in 1986 in Singapore. Several reform packages implemented between 1987 and 1992 reinforced the controls over the Indonesian equity market. In addition, to ensure wider investor confidence compensation funds have been created in Malaysia, Hong Kong and the Philippines.

Improved availability and quality of information through stricter disclosure requirements have also played an important role in enhancing interest in stock investments. Regulations have in general been implemented in favour of accurate financial reporting and more transparent information.[154] New rules have been established to improve accountancy standards. For example, since 1991 moves have been made in the direction of generally accepted accountancy standards in the Indonesian markets and BAPEPAM[155] now obliges companies to release financial results and interim figures to two designated major local newspapers while quarterly reports have to be submitted to the supervisory agency. For the first time a system of fines has been established to limit late reporting.

In addition, more accurate stock indices in Hong Kong, Malaysia, Singapore and Indonesia, with more comprehensive compilation rules, have contributed to improving available information on stock performance.

Further, as a result of the liberalisation process in the Asian equity markets, financial reporting and research have also improved in the past five years. Rising competition for overseas investors' funds, and the opening of the stockbroking industry to foreign stockbrokers, has pushed local securities companies to improve the information and research available. With the growing importance of foreign stockbrokers and foreign institutional investors, companies have had to improve disclosure. In common with developments in major financial centres, particularly in London, the corporatisation of the stockbroking industry is another policy initiative which helped bring new expertise in research, fund management techniques and technology. Subsequently, market information, such as price indices, graphs and short term market commentaries are now becoming increasingly available in regional magazines and newspapers.

Rules limiting directly or indirectly local institutional investments on the domestic stork markets have also been modified. In addition, the most obviously distorting tax dispositions in favour of government bond or commercial lending have been removed to enhance market activities. For instance, in 1987 in Thailand, the income tax structure was modified to reduce the differential tax treatment of earnings from interest or dividends payment. As a further example, in Indonesia the attractiveness of equity investment has been enhanced through the imposition of a tax on bank term deposits which have been absorbing almost all Indonesia's domestic savings.[156]

New investment instruments have been made available to attract domestic and foreign investment. For example, to attract Singapore investors with interest in buying Malaysian shares after the 1990 split, Singapore developed in Central Limit Order Book trading system, or CLOB International which is an OTC market allowing investors to trade in a number of listed international securities. Presently, CLOB International securities consist of Hong Kong, Malaysia, and Philippines stocks. Of the 129 companies listed on CLOB, 118 are Malaysian. In March 1988, the installation of NASDAQ-Link in Singapore enabled investors in the Asian time zone to transact in 33 internationally known NASDAQ stocks.

Thai authorities approved the setting up of 95 rural securities offices to promote investment in the SET in the beginning of the 1990s. Indonesia's equity market received a boost with the opening in 1989 of the Surabaya Stock Exchange with the resulting decentralisation of equity trading stimulating interest from investors outside of the capital city.

To attract more foreign investors in the companies listed in the Asian emerging markets, Hong Kong, Singapore, Malaysia and Thailand have implemented, or plan to, futures exchanges in order to provide investors with hedging possibilities. In Hong Kong, a futures contract based on the Hang Seng index was launched in May 1985, which had become the most successful and most actively traded contract on the exchange. Towards the end of summer 1987 volumes exceeded 25,000 contracts daily. However, volumes dried up after the October 1987 crash. In January 1993, Hong Kong introduced an option on the index, and by the end of 1993 introduced options on individual stocks.

Since the end of the 1980s, Malaysia, Singapore, Hong Kong, Taiwan, Korea and Thailand have all expanded the capacities of their securities markets through automated trading systems. This enhances market efficiency through timely dissemination of relevant information, improves market surveillance by alerting the exchanges and regulatory bodies of unusual movement in prices, and increases trading volume through computerised order routeing, matching price determination, clearing and settlements. For instance, in 1984, Malaysia implemented a 'Securities Clearing Automated Network Service' (or SCANS) and in 1990 improved its clearing settlement system with the implementation of the 'Fixed Delivery and Settlement System' to control script movements and provide stock-broking firms with improved management of their cash flows. Malaysia switched to automated trading in June 1992, using SCORE (System on Computerised Order Routing and Execution). This system enables the KLSE to handle a greater volume than previously, which was a significant development in overcoming the primitive nature of some of the KLSE's operations (for example, in March 1991, millions of US dollars in shares certificates were reported lost).

Supply-leading measures

Increased demand, and subsequently rising share prices, combined with economic growth and larger investment needs, have been the major factors behind the increasing number of listings. However, improved legal infra-structures and incentives were necessary to ensure sustainable stock market growth; liberalisation and improved regulation of the underwriting and stock-broking industry, relaxation of listing rules and the creation of 'second board' exchanges have contributed to bring new companies to list.

In line with developments in securities markets around the world, the corporatisation of the stockbroking industry in Asian countries improved the financial strength of the industry, as well as upgraded the level of technical expertise and professionalism of the industry. Governments in Taiwan, Indonesia, Malaysia and Singapore opened up the industry to well known foreign brokers and investment houses, which promoted the development of stock market expertise and raised the standard of research, marketing and client servicing, as discussed above. This encouraged a larger number of companies to seek a listing on the stock exchanges. A natural development following the corporatisation process, and in favour of increased share supply, has been the shift from fixed commission to negotiated commission. Where, as in Korea, commissions are determined by negotiation between the underwriters and the sellers, the primary markets are generally more active than in countries such as Taiwan and Indonesia that place legal limits on commissions.[157]

Since the mid-1980s some listing rules have been relaxed and 'second board' exchanges or/and OTC markets (to encourage smaller companies to raise equity finance) have been established in Thailand, Singapore, Indonesia, Malaysia and Korea to match the rising demand and to provide the Asian stock markets with some breadth. The creation of second-board stock exchanges have provided an alternative for the growing number of small and medium sized companies to raise funds. Easier listing requirements are attractive for tightly held family companies, especially in a context of toughening rules for main board listings. For instance, a new 'parallel bourse' was opened in Indonesia in 1987 with less stringent requirements to enable over the counter trading of new public share offerings by smaller companies. This was a welcome improvement on the previous state of affairs: until 1987, there had been no locally-owned private companies listed, as only a few relatively unattractive companies had sought to go public but Danareksa had refused to support their issue. In addition, one of the major achievements of the JSE was to end the restriction requiring a minimum of 50 per cent of all new share issues to be offered to PT Danareksa which had previously had the effect of depressing prices of initial share offerings. Under the new system, Danareksa may still take up shares in a new offering but is not automatically required to take a commanding 50 per cent block.

Further, new tax rules have been introduced, or old ones amended, to encourage companies to go public, particularly in Indonesia and Thailand.

In summary, a broad range of supply-leading measures have been implemented since the mid-1980s. Coincidentally, equity raising has become more important as a source of investment (Appendix Table (3)A2.1). A significant number of companies in diversified sectors have listed. For example, the Hong Kong stock market, which had been generally dominated by property companies, financial institutions, trading houses and utilities in broadening to encompass large manufacturing and industrial companies. While the respective impact on the number of listings of higher prices, accelerating economic growth and specific incentives are difficult to assess, it is clear that the improvements brought to regulatory environment in favour of equity raising have contributed to the surge in the number of companies seeking a listing on the stock exchanges observed in most Southeast and East Asian emerging economies since 1986 (see Figure 3.3).

According to Calderón-Rossell's model of world stock market growth, between 1980 and 1987 prices were the main determinant in the growth of listings. However, Asian companies may respond faster to regulatory incentives, and particularly to 'easier' disclosure requirements and creation of second board exchanges, than to share price increases because of the strong influence of sociological factors such as the desire to keep the company within the control of the family. These factors, still difficult to correct through government policies in favour of stock exchange development, may explain why in Asian emerging markets the demand for equities is still largely outstripping the supply and why liquidity has not increased at faster rates.

The role of privatisation

Privatisation started at the end of the 1980s as Asian emerging stock markets achieved impressive price performance in general. In Thailand in

1988 the supply of securities was increased by the approval for certain state corporations to be listed on the SET. The Krung Thai Bank was the first to be floated. With rising demand for equity, publicly listed companies took advantage of the high liquidity in the economy to improve their debt/equity ratio by substituting equity capital for bank borrowing. The privatisation of government companies has contributed to the increase in the range of corporate stocks available on the stock markets and has stimulated foreign and domestic investors' interest. For example, the privatisation process in Malaysia and Thailand helped alleviate the scarcity of shares, and also contributed to boost turnovers and market capitalisations. Further, as we already mentioned, these privatisations encouraged the relaxation of previous laws limiting foreign investment and also promoted the development of more efficient stock markets. Opening to foreign investors averted the risk that stock market liquidity would dry up because of the large volume of shares issued, and more efficient markets assured governments of high prices for their privatisation issues.

The privatisation programmes initiated to date contributed to boost the stock markets' turnovers and in the longer term they will contribute to the further development of the Asian equity markets. Large scale privatisations are expected, such as the Electrical Authority of Thailand, Thai Oil, Bangchak Petroleum and the Petroleum Authority of Thailand in Thailand. Several large IMF-influenced privatisations may also come to the Philippines market, like Philippines Airlines, Manila Electric Company and Philippine National Bank.[158] In Taiwan, schedules to sell shares of the twenty-two Government companies and list them on the stock market were announced but subsequently withdrawn because of the weakness of the stock market. However, China Steel has already sold part of its shares and the goal is to privatise it completely by the year 2000. In 1986 Singapore established the Public Sector Divestment Committee to set up the guidelines for the privatisation of twenty-three Government linked companies. An estimated S$590 million worth of shares will be released over the next decade.[159] The government has announced that it will be publicly listing several heavily capitalised government-linked companies (GLCs). It is expected to begin with Singapore Technologies Industrial Corporation (STIC). In September 1993 the Telecoms listing was expected to be capitalised at between S$12 and S$20 billion. While those listings represented a major boost for the Singapore market capitalisation, it also provided ground for further demand-enhancing measures in order to avoid the risk of a shortage of available funds. One of the main liberalisation measures directly related to the privatisation programme is the CPF liberalisation, with the relaxation of existing rules to release up to S$31 billion for re-deployment across a broad range of permitted investments, including stocks. The further CPF liberalisation is likely to boost stock market capitalisation and local fund management.

CONCLUSION

While economic growth provided the underlying stimulus for the development of Asian emerging equity markets, the particular paces of development of each of these equity markets and the equity 'boom' recently observed in these countries after about thirty years of sluggish stock market activities can be fully explained neither by the level of economic development nor by the pace of economic growth. The timing of the stock market liberalisation and of the new legal measures adopted in Asian equity markets coincides with the improved liquidity and the rapid growth of market capitalisation observed in the past five years. This suggests the existence of a causal relationship between conscious government policies in favour of equity investment, and the growth of the stock markets.

Improved confidence through more efficient regulations and increased incentives for investors have been a positive scenario for an extended number of participants, strong price performance and rising liquidity in the Asian emerging stock markets since the mid-1980s. In addition, the measures undertaken have had the effect of improving stock trading environments and systems which have further resulted in increased trading and turnover at stock exchanges. At the same time, supply-leading measures, although more difficult to implement and therefore less effective, have contributed to bringing new companies to list. This, in turn, has further increased investment opportunity for large institutional investors which previously had been limited by the market's illiquidity.

Sustained high growth rates, improving regulations towards international standards, privatisation and continued liberalisation to foreign investment should combine with growing interest in the region by large foreign institutional investors and a rising pool of domestic funds available for equity investment to keep the development of Asian emerging equity markets on fast track.

Appendix 1
Asian emerging equity market statistics

Table (3)A1.1 Korea Stock Exchange

	List of corporations	Market capitalisation (won bn)	Turnover volume (mio unit)	Turnover value (bn won)	GDP nominal (won bn)	Market capitalisation (% GDP)
1993	–	112,635	–	163,740	241,000*	47
1992	688	84,711	6,979	90,624	229,939	37
1991	686	70,470	4,051	62,565	207,517	34
1990	669	78,070	3,128	53,454	172,725	54.6
1989	626	95,477	3,398	81,200	143,001	66.8
1988	502	64,544	3,038	58,121	127,963	50.4
1987	389	26,172	1,656	20,494	99,790	26.2
1986	355	11,994	993	9,598	86,511	13.8
1985	342	6,570	5,564	3,621	80,847	8.1
1984	336	5,149	4,350	3,118	67,126	7.7
1983	328	3,490	2,751	1,753	59,604	5.8
1982	334	3,301	2,872	1,974	52,879	6.2
1981	343	2,959	3,075	2,534	46,798	6.3
1980	350	2,527	1,645	1,134	37,831	7
1979	355	2,609	1,561	1,328	29,357	8.9
1978	356	2,893	1,369	1,425	23,030	12.6
1977	323	2,351	1,218	1,375	17,123	13.7
1976	274	1,436	598	629	13,357	10.7
1975	189	916	310	334	9,952	9.2
1974	128	533	157	180	7,398	7.2
1973	104	426	1,230	160	5,276	8.1
1972	66	246	84	70	4,044	6.1
1971	50	109	50	34	3,298	3.3
1970	48	98	78	42	2,672	3.7
1969	42	87	98	42	2,130	4.1
1968	34	64	76	20	1,630	3.9
1967	24	39	72	25	1,260	3.1
1966	24	19	49	11	1,024	1.9
1965	17	15	431	9	798	1.8
1964	17	17	317	27	712	2.4
1963	15	10	242	26	499	2

Sources: Bank of Korea, *Monthly Economic Statistics*, various issues; SG Warburg Securities; J.P. Morgan Economic database; *Economic Statistics Yearbook*, 1990, Bank of Korea; *Stock Monthly*, January 1993, Korea Stock Exchange, Seoul

Note: * = estimates

Table (3)A1.2 Kuala Lumpur Stock Exchange

	List of corporations	Market capitalisation (M$ bn)	Turnover volume (mln units)	Turnover value (M$ mln)	GDP nominal (M$ mln)	Market capitalisation (% GDP M$)
1993	–	618	–	–	159,000*	398
1992	–	238	12,493	96,000	140,300	170
1991	324	161	12,349	30,097	128,000	125.8
1990	285	132	12,130	29,522	114,616	114.9
1989	280	61	4,138	20,000	101,463	60.1
1988	280	74	4,631	15,000	90,861	81.2
1987	280	65	2,343	10,078	79,625	81
1986	287	39	88	3,369	71,594	54.4
1985	284	42	2,870	6,181	77,547	53.5
1984	281	46	1,852	5,714	79,550	57.7
1983	271	53	2,275	7,934	69,941	76
1982	261	33	1,066	3,252	62,579	51.9
1981	253	37	1,636	8,059	57,613	63.6
1980	250	27	1,482	5,600	53,308	50.3
1979	253	16	638	1,641	46,424	33.9
1978	253	12	1,107	2,539	37,886	31.7
1977	256	11	598	1,047	32,340	34
1976	264	10	432	1,011	28,085	35.6
1975	268	9	617	1,306	22,332	40.3
1974	264	8	391	722	22,858	35.3
1973	–	13	596	2,300	18,723	70.9
1972	–	n/a	938	2,155	14,220	–
1971	–	n/a	579	934	12,955	–
1970	–	n/a	454	746	12,155	–
1969	–	n/a	587	1,139	11,629	–
1968	–	n/a	472	859	10,160	–
1967	188	n/a	260	420	9,774	–
1966	–	n/a	169	226	9,394	–
1965	–	n/a	54.4	n/a	9,937	–
1964	–	n/a	n/a	n/a	8,056	–
1963	160	n/a	n/a	n/a	7,515	–
1962	158	n/a	n/a	n/a	7,056	–
1961	138	n/a	n/a	n/a	6,696	–
1960	93	n/a	n/a	n/a	6,837	–

Sources: Market capitalisation: *BZW Equity Working List* (Quarterly), published by BZW Research Department, various issues; SG Warburg Securities, *Malaysia Report*, various issues; *Ng Beoy Kui* (1989), see Note 1, p. 122; Turnover data in million units: *Datastream-IFC statistics*, 1986–93

Note: * = estimates

Table (3)A1.3 Taiwan Stock Exchange

	List of corporations	Market capitalisation (NT$ bn)	Turnover volume (bn unit)	Turnover value (NT$ bn)	GDP nominal (NT$ bn)	Market capitalisation (% GDP-NT$)
1993	–	5,223	–	9,320	5,600*	93
1992	256	3,105	26	8,756	5,301	59
1991	221	3,184	33.9	11,919	4,222	75.4
1990	199	2,681	67.7	21,400	3,878	96.1
1989	181	6,174	88.5	25,700	3,497	176.6
1988	163	3,383	27.2	7,920	3,223	105
1987	141	1,544	76.9	2,670	2,855	47.9
1986	130	583	39	676	2,473	20.4
1985	127	414	15	195	2,343	16.7
1984	123	305	18	325	2,100	13
1983	119	203	24	364	1,900	9.7
1982	113	201	10	134	1,773	10.6
1981	107	219	13	209	1,491	12.3
1980	102	178	16	162	1,195	11.9
1979	96	153	13	206	991	12.8
1978	87	120	24	362	829	12.1
1977	82	94	11	172	707	11.3
1976	77	73	7	146	589	10.3
1975	68	50	7	130	549	8.5
1974	64	85	3	44	410	15.5
1973	62	30	4	87	316	7.3
1972	49	20	2	54	263	6.3
1971	45	17	1	24	226	6.4
1970	42	13	1	11	228	5.7
1969	42	10	0.4	4	–	–
1968	40	9	0.7	8	–	–
1967	38	18	0.8	5	–	–
1966	38	27	0.7	5	–	–
1965	37	25	0.5	11	–	–
1964	31	19	0.7	36	–	–.
1963	23	7	0.2	10	–	–
1962	18	n/a	–0.05	0.4	–	–

Sources: The Central Bank of China, *Economic Statistics*, various issues; Turnover in volume: China and Johnson (1990), p. 294, and SG Warburg Securities, *Taiwan Weekly Bulletin*, 15 January 1993; Turnover value: *Datastream-IFC statistics*, 1987–92, and Chou and Johnson (1990), p. 294 for 1962 to 1987; SG Warburg Securities

Note: * = estimates

Table (3)A1.4 Stock Exchange of Thailand

	Listed corporations	Annual turnover (baht bn)	Turnover volume (min units)	Market capitalisation (baht bn)	Nominal GDP (baht bn)	Market capitalisation (% GDP)
1993	–	2,054	–	3,312	3,700*	90
1992	305	1,896	–	1,438	3,440*	55
1991	276	769	793	897	2,316	38.7
1990	213	585	627	613	2,051	29.9
1989	175	368	377	659	1,776	37.1
1988	141	253	156	223	1,507	14.8
1987	109	123	122	138	1,253	11
1986	92	30	153	75	1,095	6.8
1985	95	17	99	49	1,014	4.8
1984	93	–	83	47	973	4.8
1983	85	–	71	34	910	3.7
1982	78	–	61	29	820	3.5
1981	76	–	30	23	760	3
1980	72	–	58	25	658	3.8
1979	65	–	97	28	558	5
1978	57	57	178	33	488	6.8
1977	36	27	97	19	403	4.7
1976	22	–	5	7	346	2
1975	16	2	3	5	303	1.6

Sources: Bank of Thailand *Annual Report*, various issues; SG Warburg-Phatra Thanakit, Thailand, *Equity Market Earning Guide*, February 1993

Note: * = estimates

Table (3)A1.5 Jakarta Stock Market

	Listed corporations	Stock issued (mln units)	Turnover volume (mln)	Turnover value (mln Rp)	Market capitalisation (mln Rp)	Nominal GDP (Rp bn)	Market capitalisation (% GDP)
1993	–	–	–	18,000,000	69,465,357	273,000*	25
1992	162	1,778	1,706.7	7,959,450	24,839,450	256,508	9.7
1991	146	1,182	1,007.92	5,778,250	16,438,000	227,163	14.1
1990	132	969	702.59	7,311,290	12,440,150	196,919	11.6
1989	57	294	95.79	964,270	4,358,500	167,185	4.7
1988	24	64	6.94	30,590	481,560	142,105	0.6
1987	24	58	2.52	5,180	112,080	124,817	0.1
1986	24	58	1.43	1,820	94,230	102,683	0.1
1985	24	57	1.89	3,210	89,330	96,997	0.1
1984	24	57	1.22	3,240	94,946	89,885	0.1
1983	17	48	3.51	10,107	100,743	77,623	0.1
1982	13	40	5.01	12,624	99,507	62,476	0.2
1981	9	20	2.89	7,651	47,874	58,127	0.1
1980	6	14	1.66	5,733	39,520	45,446	0.1
1979	3	7	0.12	1,333	23,930	32,025	0.1
1978	1	0.3	0.02	218	4,050	22,746	0.02
1977	1	0.3	0.01	153	2,730	19,011	0.02

Sources: Turnover value and volume 1977–83: ADB (1984); ADB (1985), Table 2, 'The Capital Market in 1993', Business News, Jakarta, 12 February 1993; 'A guide to Asian stock markets', Robert Lloyd George, Longman, Hong Kong, 1991

Table (3)A1.6 Stock Exchange of Singapore

	Turnover value (S$ mn)	Turnover volume (mn shares)	Market capitalisation (S$ min)	Nominal GDP (S$ min)	Market capitalisation (% GDP)
1993	–	–	214,774	89,007	241.3
1992	18,700	16,018	80,704	74,975	107.6
1991	12,600	17,360	82,944	60,960	136.1
1990	15,800	23,039	62,548	57,133	109.5
1989	23,600	6,970	70,200	52,821	132.9
1988	–	10,168	48,288	48,273	100
1987	22,478	9,757	85,408	43,433	196.6
1986	7,906	3,764	85,289	39,683	214.9
1985	6,274	2,937	70,619	38,924	181.4
1984	8,108	2,890	79,332	39,615	200.3
1983	11,620	3,359	91,446	36,576	250
1982	5,105	1,550	65,859	33,808	194.8
1981	13,419	2,734	71,279	31,636	225.3
1980	7,806	2,184	51,106	28,863	177.1
1979	2,309	963	29,371	26,313	111.6
1978	3,383	1,489	22,696	24,071	94.3
1977	1,158	640	18,218	22,166	82.2
1976	1,928	708	15,130	20,571	73.6
1975	1,830	800	13,668	19,140	71.4
1974	1,140	534	7,000	18,389	38
1973	3,104	702	–	17,291	–
1972	2,163	931	15,000	15,504	96.7

Sources: Turnover 1965–72: Stock Exchange of Malaysia and Singapore, Bank Negara Malaysia; SG Warburg Securities, Singapore, July 1992, p. 7; Turnover in volume: *Datastream-IFC statistics*, 1986–93

Table (3)A1.7 Hong Kong Stock Market

	Market capitalisation (HK$ mln)	Turnover value (HK$ bn)	Nominal GDP (US$ mln)	Market capitalisation (% GDP)
1993	2,637,924	–	102,000*	300*
1992	1,356,822	346	96,560	181.5
1991	949,172	273	81,650	150.4
1990	650,410	280	71,361	117.1
1989	607,725	207	64,000	121.2
1988	580,378	364	55,560	133.2
1987	419,800	132	47,140	114.6
1986	413,000	54	38,255	138.6
1985	–	33	33,500	–
1984	203,000	29	31,811	81.7
1983	–	43	28,575	–
1982	127,000	106	30,692	68.4
1981	–	105	29,522	–
1980	189,000	30	27,552	137.9
1979	–	30	21,387	–
1978	61,000	6	17,336	75
1977	–	13	14,801	–
1976	59,000	11	12,090	99.3
1975	–	1	9,422	–
1974	20,000	–	8,863	45.1
1973	–	193	7,597	–
1972	56,410	–	5,389	185.6

Sources: SG Warburg Securities, Hong Kong, October 1991, p. 11; Market capitalisation in US$: Bruno Solnik (1990), p. 310; Turnover in value and volume: *Datastream-IFC statistics*

Note: * = estimates

Appendix 2

Table (3)A2.1 Capital raised through new issues, right issues and placements

	Hong Kong (US$ mn)	(%)	Korea (Won bn)	(%)	Singapore (US$ mn)	(%)	Malaysia (M$ mn)	(%)	Thailand (US$ mn)	(%)	Indonesia (RP bn)	(%)
1992	2,924	11.00	–	–	873	4.60	–	–	1,102	2.5	694	0.74
1991	2,222	9.77	2,687	3.41	641	4.03	4,392	14.00	3,088	10.84	4,040	5.60
1990	970	5.11	2,917	4.63	1,724	13.16	8,649	23.07	2,391	11.16	10,332	17.5
1989	997	6.28	14,669	29.86	799	7.59	2,508	8.34	1,295	13.63	3,085	6.88
1988	1,218	8.66	7,771	32.41	366	4.25	–	–	670	5.82	24	0.06
1987	4,450	36.77	1,899	6.10	720	10	1,385	7.58	670	7.38	0.4	0.0
1986	1,140	11.4	840	3.23	–	–	189	1	88	0.99	0.8	–
1985	316	3.47	295	1.29	227	3	632	2.73	164	1.62	–	0.0
1984	214	2.46	479	2.28	378	4.35	1,990	7.54	260	2.74	0.3	0.15
1983	215	2.45	463	2.48	501	6.12	1,317	5.22	60	0.72	35.5	0.1
1982	1,255	12.25	277	1.79	393	5.35	603	2.65	88	1.02	20.6	0.21
1981	711	7.11	306	2.30	499	8.36	900	4.34	44	0.54	37.9	0.05
1980	135	1.37	171	1.39	1,025*	4.75	137	0.83	–	–	8.8	0.26
1979	78	1.02	217	2.05	1,038*	6.45	211	1.72	–	–	25.1	–
1978	167	2.52	285	5.59	1,054*	7.62	99	1.06	–	–	–	0.05
1977	156	3.13	141	4.19	1,103*	8.89	120	1.6	–	–	2.4	–
1976	–	–	102	3.63	1,183*	9.17	51	0.83	–	–	–	–
1975	–	–	83	5.46	–	–	–	–	–	–	–	–
1974	–	–	32	4.07	–	–	–	–	–	–	–	–
1973	–	–	30	2.38	–	–	–	–	–	–	–	–
1972	–	–	14	1.68	–	–	–	–	–	–	–	–
1971	–	–	2	0.27	–	–	–	–	–	–	–	–
1970	–	–	5	0.79	–	–	–	–	–	–	–	–
1969	–	–	6	–	–	–	–	–	–	–	–	–
1968	–	–	20	–	–	–	–	–	–	–	–	–

Sources: B2W Working List (various issues), B2W Research Department; *Annual Report* (various years), Bank Negara Malaysia; *Economic Statistics Yearbook* (various issues), Bank of Korea; SG Warburg Securities database; Cole and Park (1983), Table 21, p. 203

Note: * = estimates derived from Ng Beoy Kui

Appendix 3

Table (3)A3.1 Equity markets and economic growth

	1990–2 %	1985–90 %	1980–85 %	1975–80 %	1970–75 %	1965–70 %	1960–65 %
Average annual growth rate of market capitalisation (local currency)							
Hong Kong	52	18.9	11.9	46.8	−1.2	n/a	n/a
Korea	5.2	75.4	21.9	26.1	61.4	48.9	11.6
Singapore	15.7	2.1	9.3	31.4	0.0	n/a	n/a
Taiwan	8.1	70.1	20.4	29.2	48.1	−6.8	40.6
Malaysia	34.9	34.9	13.0	26.5	−5.2	n/a	n/a
Thailand	55.9	77.4	15.6	51.8	n/a	n/a	n/a
Indonesia	41.6	269.1	22.7	14.2	n/a	n/a	n/a
Average annual growth rate of nominal GDP (local currency)							
Hong Kong	7.1	16.4	13.9	24.5	16.2	n/a	n/a
Korea	10.1	16.6	13.2	28.5	32.4	26.4	29.1
Singapore	26.2	10.2	6.3	8.6	9.6	12.9	5.8
Taiwan	4.4	10.7	10.7	20.4	21.5	n/a	n/a
Malaysia	5.6	8.6	7.9	19.3	13.7	4.2	7.8
Thailand	6.5	15.2	9.1	16.8	16.0	n/a	n/a
Indonesia	7.7	17.2	12.3	30.6	34.2	75.6	358.6
Average market capitalisation as % of GDP (nominal – local currency)							
Hong Kong	150.7	125.2	30	62.6	46.4	n/a	n/a
Korea	38.0	40.5	6.8	10.5	6.8	3.3	1.2
Singapore	136.3	146.7	210.1	107.3	14.7	n/a	n/a
Taiwan	75.0	85.7	13.8	14.1	10.9	n/a	n/a
Malaysia	126	78.4	60.4	37.5	28.8	n/a	n/a
Thailand	39	19.9	4.0	4.5	0.3	n/a	n/a
Indonesia	7.0	1.9	0.1	0.0	n/a	n/a	n/a

	1990–2 %	1985–90 %	1980–85 %	1975–80 %	1970–75 %
Average annual real GDP growth rate (US$)					
Hong Kong	4.9	6.6	4.1	9.2	4.7
Korea	7.7	9.8	6.9	5.6	6.4
Singapore	11.4	4.7	4.9	7.2	7.7
Taiwan	6.7	7.6	5.4	8.7	6.2
Malaysia	7.0	4.2	2.4	5.5	4.6
Thailand	7.4	8.1	4.0	n/a	n/a
Indonesia	3.8	4.6	2.5	6	5.4
Philippines	−0.1	2.8	−4.2	3.4	3.7

Market capitalisation per capita growth rate (local currency)					
1990–2	1985–90	1980–85	1975–80	1970–75	1965–70
%	%	%	%	%	%

	1990–2 %	1985–90 %	1980–85 %	1975–80 %	1970–75 %	1965–70 %
Hong Kong	52.7	17.5	31.9	41.8	–16.4	n/a
Korea	4.0	73.7	14.1	38.9	46.7	40.1
Singapore	21.55	–0.7	25.0	n/a	n/a	n/a
Taiwan	7.6	68.0	14.6	15.6	53.7	n/a
Malaysia	33	31.6	25.8	11.9	–8.1	n/a
Thailand	54.9	74.5	12.3	n/a	n/a	n/a
Indonesia	38.9	262.8	20.8	n/a	n/a	n/a

Nominal GDP per capita average growth rate (local currency)

	1990–2 %	1985–90 %	1980–85 %	1975–80 %	1970–75 %	1965–70 %
Hong Kong	n/a	14.9	12.2	21.1	14.1	n/a
Korea	n/a	15.5	14.9	28.6	27.9	24.1
Singapore	n/a	6.8	5.0	7.2	7.7	n/a
Taiwan	n/a	9.0	13	15	n/a	n/a
Malaysia	n/a	6.0	5.0	16	10.6	1.8
Thailand	n/a	13.3	6.9	0.0	n/a	n/a
Indonesia	n/a	13.4	14.1	27.2	28.5	306.4
Philippines	n/a	9.3	n/a	n/a	n/a	n/a

Average nominal GPD per capita (US$)

	1991 %	1985–90 %	1980–85 %	1975–80 %	1970–75 %	1965–70 %
Hong Kong	14,200	9,703.6	5,780.4	3,880.4	1,652.6	n/a
Korea	6,540	3,443.4	1,731.6	931.4	318.2	54.6
Singapore	12,782	8,921	6,741.6	4,544.2	2,546.8	n/a
Taiwan	7,663	5,674.2	3,147.4	1,970	845	165.6
Malaysia	2,539	2,045.2	1,971.6	1,315	626.4	76.4
Thailand	1,429	955.6	748.8	n/a	n/a	n/a
Indonesia	623	503.8	566.4	367	142.2	15.4

Average real GPD per capita (US$)

	1990–2 %	1985–90 %	1980–85 %	1975–80 %	1970–75 %	1965–70 %
Hong Kong	9,761	8,430	6,246	4,736	3,326	567
Korea	3,932	3,027	1,929	1,534	1,084	179
Singapore	9,252	7,205	5,854	4,187	3,102	475
Taiwan	4,822	3,936	2,713	2,056	1,437	231
Malaysia	2,695	2,178	1,967	1,625	1,283	219
Thailand	1,372	1,042	780	138	n/a	n/a
Indonesia	725	629	534	444	334	57
Philippines	609	582	630	632	527	95

	Average market capitalisation per capita in US$					
	1990–2	1985–90	1980–85	1975–80	1970–75	1965–70
	%	%	%	%	%	%
Hong Kong	25,591	12,042	4,404	4,316	1,677	n/a
Korea	2,229	1,945	139	126	30	1.86
Singapore	17,120	10,725	12,805	5,145	2,001	n/a
Taiwan	7,299	5,194	411	247	86	5.48
Malaysia	4,119	1,692	1,194	502	218	n/a
Thailand	808	303	38	n/a	n/a	n/a
Indonesia	58	11	0.63	0.08	n/a	n/a
Philippines	231	79	n/a	n/a	n/a	n/a

Sources: Data derived from Tables (3)A1.1–1.7

Appendix 4
OVERVIEW OF REGULATORY CHANGES

1980
Hong Kong
• Unification of the stock exchanges into the Hong Kong Stock Exchange

1982
Singapore
• Computerised trading system is introduced
• Installation of SESCOMS, a system for instantaneous transmission of information from trading room to broking firms
Thailand
• Businesses are exempted of tax on sales of securities in the SET

1983
Malaysia
• Securities Industry (Amendment) Act replaces the new legislation with new provisions on enforcement and investigations to protect the public
Taiwan
• CSEC starts to upgrade quality of financial reporting

1984
Malaysia
• Creation of the Securities Clearing Automated Network Services and MASA, a real time

information reporting system
• Relaxation of the guidelines on commercial banks lending for shares purchases
Singapore
• Amendment of the listing manual to encourage more foreign and domestic companies to seek listing on the SES
• Introduction of the All-Share Price Index
Thailand
• Securities Exchange Amendment Act which defines the transferability of stocks and introduced penalties for stock manipulation and insider trading

1985
Singapore
• Corporatisation of the stockbroking industry
Hong Kong
• A stock index future contract was launched in Hong Kong based on the Hang Seng Index
Thailand
• Implementation of tax rates in favour of listed businesses
Taiwan
• Computer assisted trading system (CATS)

1986
Malaysia
- Corporatisation of the stockbroking industry Introduction of the KLSE Composite Index

Singapore
- Securities Industry Act 1986

1987
Korea
- Creation of an OTC market

Hong Kong
- Creation of the Securities and Futures Commission

Indonesia
- 'Pakto' and 'Pakdes' measures in favour of liberalisation in the JSE
- Opening of 'Bursa Parallel'

Malaysia
- Installation of AWAS

Singapore
- Launching of SESDAQ
- Tax concessions for trading in international securities

Taiwan
- Creation of the OTC market
- The Accounting Research and Development Foundation issues accounting/auditing standards

Thailand
- Modification of income tax in favour of shares investment
- Creation of a second board
- Establishment of stock trading place for non-residents

1988
Korea
- Automated trading system (SMATS)

Malaysia
- Reduction of the appropriate debt/equity ratio for companies seeking listing from not less than 1 to not less than 0.5 on industrial, property, tourism and plantations
- The KLSE set up a second board for companies with paid-up capital of less than M$5 million

Philippines
- Commission for the capital market development

Singapore
- Establishment of NASDAQ-Link
- Introduction of negotiable commission rates

Taiwan
- Brokerage licences are liberalised

1989
Korea
- Foreigners holding convertible bonds of Korean companies can acquire domestic shares

Hong Kong
- Revised listing rules in Hong Kong aimed at strengthening the protection of investors by increasing the efficiency of dissemination of price-sensitive information by listed companies

Indonesia
- Opening of the Surabaya Stock Exchange
- Overseas brokerage house can open joint venture

Singapore
- Introduction of floorless trading system CLOB
- DBF (CPF) index to monitor CPF trustee stocks

Indonesia
- Opening to foreign investors
- End of the limitation on share price movements

1990
Hong Kong
- New merger and takeover code

Indonesia
- Privatisation of the JSE
- New set of laws for the equity market
- Reform package to prepare for privatisation of JSE
- Introduction of the BT Jakarta Index

Malaysia
- Improvement of the clearing settlement procedure
- Setting up of Broker Depository System and Central Depository System
- Splitting of the KLSE and SES
- Paid-up capital for member

brokerage companies is raised
to M$20 million from M$5 million
Singapore
- Development of CLOB
  International
Thailand
- Deregulation of exchange
  control permitting foreigners to
  remit proceeds from the sale of
  stocks up to certain limits
- Beginning of privatisation
1991
Hong Kong
- Creation of the Hang Seng Sub
  Index Indonesia
- New rules for public offerings
  and regulation of share price
  movements. BAPEPAM obliges
  companies to improve the
  publication of financial results
Korea
- Foreign securities companies
  may open branch offices
Malaysia
- Opening of its second board
- Introduction of EMS Index and
  Second Board Index
- Creation of KLOFFE (option and
  futures market)

Singapore
- A scripless system is
  implemented
Thailand
- Setting up of 95 securities office
  in the country
- Computerised trading with ASSET
- Extention of trading house and
  unification of board lots
1992
Indonesia
- Foreign investors can buy shares
  of state banks listed on the JSE
Korea
- Foreign investors may, within
  certain limits, invest in stocks
  listed on the KSE
Malaysia
- Automated trading using SCORE
Singapore
- Foreign brokers can acquire full
  ownership of member companies
Thailand
- Adoption of the Securities and
  Exchange Act which set up a
  Security and Exchange
  Commission

NOTES

1 Emery, R.F., *The Financial Institutions in Southeast Asia*, Praeger, New York (1970); Kitchen, R.L., *Finance in Developing Countries*, Wiley and Sons, London (1986); Khoury, S., *The Deregulation of the World Financial Markets*, Quorum Books, New York (1990); Ng Beoy Kui, *The Development of Capital Markets in the SEACEN Countries*, SAECEN, Kuala Lumpur (1989); Ariff, M. and Johnson, L., *Securities Markets and Stock Pricing: The Case of Singapore*, Longman, Singapore (1990); Skully, M., *ASEAN Financial Cooperation in Banking, Finance and Insurance*, Macmillan, London (1985); Ho and Ho (1991), Cole, D. and Park, Y.C., *Financial Development in Korea*, Harvard University Press, Cambridge MA (1983); and Lee, S.Y. and Jao, Y.C., *Financial Structures and Monetary Policies in Southeast Asia*, Macmillan, Hong Kong (1982).

2 Patrick, H.T. and Wai, U.T., *Stock and Bond Issues in LDC's Capital Markets*, IMF Staff Papers 20 (1973); Drake, P.J., 'Securities Markets in Less Developed Countries', *Journal of Development Studies*, 13 (2) (1977), Drake, P.J., 'The Development of Equity and Bond Markets in the Pacific Region' in Tan, A. and Kapur, B., *Pacific Growth and Financial Interdependence*, Allen and Unwin, Sydney (1986); Saw Swee-Hock, *Investment Management in Singapore*, Longman, Singapore (1989); Saw Swee Hoch, *Securities Market in Singapore*, Singapore Securities Research Institute, (1985); Rowley, A., 'Asian Stockmarkets: The Inside Story', *Far Eastern Economic Review*, Hong Kong, (1987), Ghon Rhee,

S., *Securities Markets and Systemic Risks in Dynamic Asian Economies*, OECD (1992), *Pacific Basin Capital Markets Research*, ed. by Ghon Rhee and Chang Rosita, Vol. 1 and Vol. 2, North Holland, Amsterdam (1990 and 1991).

3 Patrick and Wai (1973), *op. cit.*; Drake (1977), *op. cit.*

4 Calderón-Rossell (1990), *op. cit.* and Calderón-Rossell, 'The Determinants of Stock Markets Growth: A Worldwide Perspective', in Ghon Rhee and Chang, (1991), *op. ci.*

5 Because of information limitations in several markets and possible inconsistencies of data due to the large number of sources utilised, statistics presented in this paper should be considered indicative of trends. Information on regulatory changes are not systematically and officially compiled, and thus cannot be treated as exhaustive. These details come from the various issues of the annual reports of the Bank of Thailand, the Bank Negara Malaysia, the Bank of China (Taiwan), the Bank of Korea, as well as reports from several stockbroking institutions (SG Warburg, Barings Securities, Thornton Management, Jardine Fleming) and investment bank J.P. Morgan. Useful information is also provided by issues of the *Asian Wall Street Journal*, the *International Financial Review*, the *Far Eastern Economic Review*, *Fortune*, *Euromoney*, *Asia Finance* and the *Jakarta Post*, amongst others.

6 for additional information on this brief history of Asian stock exchanges, see Ng Beoy Kui (1989), *op. cit.*; Tan Pheng Theng, 'The development of the securities industry', *The Securities Industry Review*, Vol. 4, n. 1, April 1978, Chia, Uzman, Gondokusumo, Cheong, *Globalisation of the Jakarta Stock Exchange*, Prentice Hall, Singapore (1991) and Lie, C.J. and Fung, H.G., 'Stock Market and Economic Activities: A Causal Analysis', in Ghon Rhee and Chang (1991), *op. cit.*; Cole and Park (1983), *op. cit.*

7 In 1985, Pan-Electric Industries Ltd, a public listed company, defaulted on a $7.5 millions loan repayment as a consequence of its having incurred losses estimated to be $40 million on forward contacts. It came to light at the time when several stockbrokers were heavily involved with Pan-El group of companies in respect of forward share contract estimated to total $140 million out of the estimated $600 million exposure on forward contract of all companies. The total estimated capital funds of all stock broking companies was about $350 millions. The spectre of insolvency for the stockbrokers was imminent and the SES subsequently suspended all trading operations from 2–4 December 1985. For additional information, see Pillai, Philip, N. 'Singapore Securities Market: A Watershed in Regulations and Development', in *Current Development in International Securities, Commodities and Financial Futures Markets*, ed. Koh Kheng Lia, National University of Singapore, Butterworths, 1991.

8 Calderón-Rossell, J.R., (1990), *op. cit.*, p. 115–17.

9 GDP data are nominal, in order to be comparable with market capitalisation data, which are nominal.

10 Drake (1986), *op. cit.*, p. 99.

11 Dickie, R.B. (1981), *op. cit.*, Drake (1986), *op. cit.*

12 Emery (1970), *op. cit.*

13 Ng Beoy Kui (1989), *op. cit.*

14 For example, in February 1993, the initial public offering (IPO) of Denway Investments, a holding company for state-owned automotive assets in Guangdong on the HKSE was oversubscribed 657 times, a record for Hong Kong market.

15 Ariff and Johnson (1990), *op. cit.*

16 Ayling, I.E., *Internationalisation of Stock Markets: The Trend Towards Greater Foreign Borrowing and Investment*, Gower, Aldershot, (1986).

17 Calderón-Rossell, (1990), *op. cit.*, p. 128.
18 Calderón-Rossell, (1991), *op. cit.*, p. 537.
19 Calderón-Rossell, (1991), *ibid.*
20 Singapore, Korea, Taiwan, and Hong Kong.
21 Neoh Soon Kean (1989), *op. cit.*
22 Lim, Linda and Pang, En Fong, *Foreign Direct Investment and Industrialisation in Malaysia*, Singapore, Taiwan, Thailand, OECD, Paris, 1991.
23 Numerous studies have documented the shift in comparative advantages and the wave pattern observable in FDI in Asia: Rana, Pradumna B., 'Recent Trends and Issues on Foreign Direct Investment in Asian and Pacific Developing Countries', *Asian Development Bank Economic Staff Paper*, No. 41, March (1988); Rana, Pradumna and Dowling, Malcolm, 'Foreign Capital and Asian Economic Growth', *Asian Development Review*, Vol. 8, No. 2 (1990); Riedel, James, 'Intra-Asian Trade and Foreign Direct Investment', *Journal of Southeast Asian Studies* (1991), Naya, S., 'Direct Foreign Investment and Trade in East and southeast Asia', in R.W. Jones and A.O. Krueger, *The Political Economy of International Trade*, Oxford, Basil Blackwell; King, Timothy and Roc, Catherine, 'Intra-Asian Foreign Direct Investment: Southeast and East Asia Climbing the Comparative Advantage Ladder', *Asian Economies*, No. 80, March 1992, Lim, L. and Fong, P.E. (1991) *op. cit.*
24 To reduce is dependence on crude oil exports revenues, Indonesia liberalised foreign direct investment between 1986 and 1988. As a result, FDI soared to US$5bn in 1990 from US$2.5bn in 1986.
25 As a further example, the market capitalisation per capita in Malaysia for 1990–92 stands at US$4,119, which is just below the double of Korea's US$2,229. However, Malaysia's real and nominal income per capita is much lower than Korea's. This points to other factors helping the Malaysian equity market or hampering the KSE. Malaysia may have benefited from a common market with Singapore.
26 Calderón-Rossell reached the same conclusion in its world stock market growth model, comparing broadly 'developed' markets and 'underdeveloped' markets.
27 Measured in US$ terms, average nominal GDP per capita in Korea, Taiwan and Thailand were approximately US$3,443, US$5,674 and US$956, respectively.
28 Robison, R., *Indonesia: The Rise of Capital*, Allen and Unwin, Sydney, 1986.
29 Robison (1986), *ibid.*
30 Myint, H., *The Economies of Developing Countries*, Hutchinson, London, 1980.
31 Doner, Richard F., 'Approaches to the Politics of Economic Growth in Southeast Asia', *Journal of Asian Studies*, 50, No. 4, November 1991.
32 ADB (1985), *op. cit.*
33 Patrick and Wai (1973), *op. cit.*; Drake (1977), *op. cit.*; Kitchen (1985), *op. cit.*; Emery (1970), *op. cit.*; Ng Beoy Kui (1989), *op. cit.*; Khoury (1990), *op. cit.*; Rowley (1987), *op. cit.*
34 Tilak, J., 'Development of Education in Asia', *Asian Economies*, March 1992, No. 80, Seoul.
35 Errunza, V.R. and Rosenberg, B., 'Investment in Developed and Less Developed Countries', *Journal of Financial and Quantitative Analysis*, Vol. 17, No. 5 (1982) and Hong, L.L., *Political Uncertainty and Portfolio Diversification: A Study of the Hong Kong Stock Market 1977–84*, Accounting Research Study No. 9, AFM (1986).
36 Hong L.L. (1986), *ibid.*
37 Emery (1970), *op. cit.*, p. 130.
38 Hong (1986), *op. cit.*
39 Ng Beoy Kui (1989), *op. cit.*

40 However, in this case it is here very difficult to differentiate between the impact on the equity market of the political uncertainty on confidence and the resultant disastrous economic performance with the real GDP growth rate plunging 11.2 per cent in 1984 and 8.5 per cent in 1985.

41 Prospectus of Jardine Fleming Asia Pacific Funds, June 1992; Smith New Court Far East, 'A Quantum Leap', Hong Kong, November 1992.

42 'Korea's stock market shows stability after opening', KOTRA, Vol. 10, No. 5, p. 22.

43 Anecdotal evidence is given by Chia (1991), p. 165; For example, Indonesian investors have found it difficult to contact their brokers on the trading floor to buy and sell shares because of the existence of only one inter-house telephone connecting the gallery and the brokers' desk.

44 Errunza, V.R., 'Emerging Markets: A New Opportunity for Improving Global Portfolio Performance', *Financial Analysts Journal*, Vol. 39, No. 5, (1983).

45 While Benston's cost-benefit analysis of mandatory financial disclosure (within the US market) is in favour of strict disclosure requirements that tend to improve resource allocation and provide for investors' protection Rozeff argues that 'the economic rationales for mandatory disclosure are surprisingly weak . . . and one cannot assume that mandatory disclosure administered through a government bureau is a cost effective way of reducing securities fraud'. Disclosure requirements are unnecessary since the market's response to earnings announcements is very small. Investors seem to use other alternative sources to form expectations of cash flows in the price formation process. Control is not evidently required as the theory of market efficiency suggests that investors are protected by the tendency of prices to reflect unbiased estimates of underlying values.

46 Emery (1970), *op. cit.*, p. 553.

47 Asian Development Bank (ADB), *Capital Market Development in Selected Member Countries*, Manila, 1985.

48 'Existing stock market rules not conducive to fair business', *Jakarta Post*, 2 May 1991.

49 Dickie (1981), *op. cit.*

50 ADB (1985), *op. cit.*

51 Ferris, G. (1970), *op. cit.*; ADB (1985), *ibid.*

52 Chan and Lam (1968), *op. cit.*, p. 10.

53 Jensen, Michael and Meckling, William, (1976), pp. 305–60.

54 For additional information on measures taken by the KSE in the 1970s, see Cole and Park (1983), *op. cit.*, p. 93.

55 Patrick and Wai (1973), *op. cit.*

56 Harrison and McKinnon (1986).

57 Dickie and Layman (1988), *op. cit.*

58 McKinnon, R., *Money and Capital in Economic Development*, Brookings Institution, Washington, 1972; Shaw, E., *Financial Deepening in Economic Development*, Oxford University Press, 1973.

59 Modigliani, F. and Perotti, E. 'The Rules of the Game and the Development of Securities Markets', in Ghon Rhee and Chang (1991), *op. cit.*

60 We will adopt Modigliani and Perotti's definition of inadequate legal rules: 'Legal inadequacy is the consequence of a regime of intervention which is at the same time excessive and insufficient: excessive because executive and administrative discretion is too pervasive and ends up fostering corruption and opportunism rather than supervision; and insufficient because the legal rule is intentionally left lacking clarity, completeness, or even more simply enforcement' (Modigliani and Perotti, 1991, *op. cit.*, p. 60).

61 Dickie, R. and Layman, T., *Foreign Investment and Government Policy in The Third World*, St Martin's Press, New York, 1988.

62 Phillips and Zecher have described two theories of regulation: the public choice theories whereby the regulatory programmes are the outcomes of political and economic processes in which various people and groups maximize their own private welfare, and serve private interests rather than public interests. This is opposed to the market failure theory which suggests that regulation of stock markets arise to cure several failings of these markets, such as fraud, insider trading, price manipulation. Phillips, Susan and Zecher, Richard, *The SEC and the public interest*, MIT Press, Boston, 1981.

63 See for example, Ferris, G., *A Study of the Securities Market in Singapore and Malaysia*, International Executive Service Corps Project No. 2067, 1970.

64 Lee, K. and Lee, C.H., 'Sustaining Economic Development in Korea: Lessons from Japan', *The Pacific Review*, Oxford University Press, Vol. 5, No. 1, (1991).

65 Cole and Park (1983), *op. cit.* However, in Korea, the problem of concentrated ownership for investor confidence may be only recent and the fact this problem did not appear until recently may have contributed to the comparatively early development of the KSE. Lee and Lee show that the origins of the concentrated ownership in an owner manager system can be found in the conditions prevailing in the initial stage of the Korean industrialisation. Capital was scarce, technological capacity rudimentary and the firms had to rely on the government for credit and trade quota allocation. Thus what mattered most was the ability of the manager to manage relations with the authorities. Consequently, the shareholders did not contest the centralisation of management.

66 Gomez, Edmund T., 'Politics in Business: UMNO's corporate investments', *Forum*, Kuala Lumpur, (1990).

67 Pernas is a large government-owned business conglomerate which played a significant role in acquiring investment in key sectors to be held in trust for the ethnic Malays.

68 Dickie (1981), *op. cit.*

69 Modigliani and Perotti (1991), *op. cit.*, p. 57.

70 Wealthy investors who control the movement of vasts amount of capital, and whose influence extends into politics.

71 *Asian Wall Street Journal*, 22 September 1992, p. 14.

72 Market capitalisation fell sharply in 1974, 1982 and 1987.

73 Lee and Jao (1982), *op. cit.*

74 Bank of Thailand, *Annual Report*, 1990.

75 Rozeff, Michael S. (1991), *op. cit.*, p. 420.

76 Errunza and Agtmael (1982), *op. cit.*

77 Ghon Rhee (1991), *op. cit.*

78 Compared to the classification made by Rhee for 1987, I downgraded the Philippines from a 3 to a 4. The Philippines, although appearing to have a comparatively liberalised financial system with no foreign exchange control, was practically less open. Foreigners were virtually barred from getting money out of the Philippines. In theory, remittances were permitted but in practice the central bank was simply not processing permissions especially after the 1984 political crisis.

79 Chu, Liluan Eric, 'Market-based accounting research: international comparison and new evidence', PhD thesis, New York University, Graduate School of Business Administration, (1991).

80 Chung, U.C., 'Capital Liberalisation in Korea', Pacific Focus, *Inha Journal of International Studies*, Vol. 3, No. 1, Spring 1988.

81 Emery (1970), *op. cit.* and Lee and Jao (1982), *op. cit.*

82 In 1992, the national savings rate of Singapore reached 46 per cent of GDP and net inflows to the CPF made a significant contribution (just short of five percentage points). Already in the late 1960s, Malaysia's savings through provident and pension schemes as a share of GNP were amongst the highest in the world, and the growth rate of CPF savings has been on average constantly higher than private sector savings.

83 In 1984, with 97.1 per cent of its resources in invested in Government securities, the EPF provided the bulk of long term financing to the Government for its long term programme (Bank Negara Malaysia Annual Report, 1991). Separately constituted private provident funds and pension funds in Malaysia invested a higher proportion of their assets in corporate securities. In 1974, this was estimated at 31 per cent. However, the total sum of these assets was just above M$430 million and therefore not sufficient to make these funds significant investors in the equity market. In 1991, the ratio had only reached 34 per cent. Bank Negara Malaysia Annual Report, 1991.

84 Schwarz, R.A., *Equity Markets*, Harper and Row, New York, (1988), p. 9. In 1985, 23 per cent of US individual investors were equity shareholders through large mutual funds, and in 1992, they owned US$280bn of equities through these funds.

85 Emery (1970), *op. cit.*

86 There is little quantitative information on Hong Kong's mutual fund industry because like all financial institutions in Hong Kong, these funds are not required by regulatory authorities to publish their financial accounts. However, Lee and Jao argue that unit trusts have played a relatively minor role in Hong Kong financial markets while Emery does not mention them in his comprehensive review of Hong Kong's financial institutions. In Thailand, since 1963, the domestic mutual funds industry has been limited to a single company, the Mutual Fund Co. which in 1970 had only 150 shareholders. The degree of taxation and withholding tax imposed on purchasers of mutual funds were reportedly burdensome and discouraging. Mutual funds are not mentioned in the literature on financial institutions in Singapore. In Malaysia, mutual fund shares, although they have been offered to the public since 1959 have not been very successful. Six mutual trusts were listed in 1967, but they were virtually unknown. From 1957 on, four funds were incorporated in the Philippines but subsequent falling equity prices and bad management practices in the 1960s led to a widespread disillusion which lasted through the 1970s. Lee and Jao (1982) do not mention them. We will see in chapter 4, that increased investment through mutual funds in the 1980s were instrumental to the Asian stock market 'boom'.

87 Various issues of the annual reports of the Bank of Korea, Bank of China in Taiwan, Bank Negara Malaysia, as well as the quarterly bulletin of the Bank of Thailand and Datastream, provide some recent data on the insurance industry. It is difficult to find quantitative data for Hong Kong since they are not required to publish financial statements. Studies on Asian financial systems provide some general highlights on their activities. Emery (1970), *op. cit.*; Lee and Jao (1982), *op. cit.*, Tan Chwee Huat (1989), *op. cit.*, Skully (1987), *op. cit.*

88 Rozental, A.A., *Finance and Development in Thailand*, Preager, New York (1970).

89 The Indonesian Insurance Council reports that there were 2.2 million life insurance policy holders in 1982, or about 1 per cent of the population. *Indonesian Development News*, National Development Information Office, April 1983.

90 Emery (1970), *op. cit.*

91 Skully (1985), *op. cit.*

92 Indonesia Development News, *op. cit.*

93 Bank of Thailand, *Annual Reports*, various issues.

94 ADB and Nomura Research Institute, *Indonesia: A Capital Market Study*, July (1984), p. 19.

95 ADB (1984), *ibid.*

96 This had the further effect of limiting the supply of securities, as cheap loans were made easily available to fast growing exporting companies which were the most likely to need funds to expand.

97 ADB (1985), *op. cit.*

98 Han Kim and Lee, Y.K., 'Issuing Stocks in Korea', in Ghon Rhee and Chang (1990), *op. cit.*

99 Companies have paid out in dividends more than they had earned.

100 ADB (1985), *op. cit.*

101 In Korea, to make corporate shares more attractive to investors, private stockholders of government-controlled companies were entitled to claim dividends up to a specified level which equalled the level of interest in one-year time deposits. Non-government-controlled companies had also to follow the practice. ADB (1985), *op. cit.*; Cole and Park (1983), *op. cit.*; Dickie and Layman, (1992), *op. cit.*

102 Han and Lee (1990), *op. cit.*

103 PT Danareeksa is a government-controlled fund which issues funds certificates which are secured by shares and bonds it purchases in the market.

104 Mackie (1992), *op. cit.*

105 Wu, Y.L. and Wu, C.H., *Economic Development in Southeast Asia: The Chinese Dimension*, Stanford, Hoover Institution, (1980). The only industry in Thailand, for example, in which Thai ethnic Chinese firms are not significant is primary activities. In manufacturing and commercial ventures, Chinese dominate, owning about 90 per cent of capital They represent only 50 per cent of capital in banking and finance because of massive Government involvement to limit the control of Chinese owned banks. Sino-Thai have played a predominant role in the economic development of Thailand since the mid-nineteenth century. Of the ninety families controlling most of the groups and firms in Thailand, most of them are Sino-Thai. Indonesia's Chinese minority, only about 5 per cent of the total population, controls an estimated 75 per cent of corporate assets.

106 See also *The Economist*, 16 November 1991.

107 In Taiwan, the majority of listed companies is over 60 per cent controlled by a single family (SGW).

108 Goldberg, M., *The Chinese Connection*, UCB Press, Vancouver, (1985), p. 20.

109 Mackie (1992), *op. cit.*

110 Deyo, F., 'Chinese Management Practices and Work Commitment in Comparative Perspective', in *The Chinese in Southeast Asia*, ed. by Lim, Linda and Gosling, Peter, Maruzen Asia, Singapore, (1983).

111 Rowley (1987), *op. cit.*

112 Drake (1986), *op. cit.*

113 Robison (1986), *op. cit.*

114 Park and Cole (1983), p. 57.

115 Goldberg (1985), *op. cit.* ADB (1985), *op. cit.* The ADB (1985) notes that in Thailand and the Philippines, particularly some businesses have had close relationships with commercial banks.

116 Yoshihara, K., *The rise of Ersatz Capitalism*, Oxford University Press, Singapore (1988), argues that capitalism in the region is dominated by Chinese

entrepreneurs whose capitalism is not integrated to the rest of the economy because Chinese companies and capital remain within a Chinese sphere.

117 Yoshira (1988), *op. cit.*
118 *The Economist*, 'Southeast Asia's Octopuses', 17 July 1993, pp. 61–62.
119 Cheong, Sally, *Corporate Groupings in the KLSE*, Modern Law Publishers, Selangor, 1990.
120 Rowley (1987), *op. cit.*
121 SG Warburg Securities, *Keeping it in the Family: A Guide to Taiwan's Equity Market*, April 1991.
122 Lee and Lee (1992), *op. cit.*
123 Rowley (1987), *op. cit.*; Cole and Park (1983), *op. cit.*
124 So far in Indonesia, for example, most flotations have seen the divestment of no more than 20 per cent of the existing holding, thereby leaving full control in the hands of the original owners, and as most listings involved only one or two business components of Indonesian conglomerates, these listings did not entail the management of the companies floated.
125 Lim (1991), *op. cit.*
126 Lim (1991), *ibid.*, p. 27.
127 Lim (1991), *ibid.*
128 Mackie (1992), *op. cit.*
129 Lim (1991), *op. cit.*
130 Mackie (1992), *op. cit.*
131 Lim (1991), *op. cit.*
132 Lim (1991), *ibid.*
133 *The Economist*, 17 July 1993, *op. cit.*
134 Dickie (1981), *op. cit.*
135 Asian Development Bank, *Asian Development Outlook 1991*, pp. 19–49.
136 Although Modigliani and Miller showed that high debt-equity ratios were not always negative for the value of the firm.
137 J.P. Morgan Singapore, Economic Research Note, *CP Rules and the Stock Market*, 14 May 1993.
138 A causal relationship from financial development to real economic growth has been very difficult to establish by empirical studies. Calderón-Rossell suggests that, similarly to the concept of dual economies applied to developing countries, stock markets may also represent a set of economic agents that are more wealthy, sophisticated, and technologically efficient than the rest of the economic agents that do not participate in the equity markets. As a result, he argues that the significance of stock markets regarding economic activities may be questionable and lower than anticipated. Furthermore, in Asian emerging markets, the small number of listed companies up to now their concentration in property and their comparatively smaller contribution to economic output, also suggest a more limited relevance of stock markets in the economies.
139 A table summarising all the major regulatory changes is presented in the Appendix 4.
140 Rowley (1987), *op. cit.*, p. 216.
141 'Thai stock plunge lures bargain hunters', *The Asian Wall Street Journal*, 10 March 1993, p. 9.
142 SG Warburg Securities (Far East), *Singapore/Malaysia, Quarterly Market Review*, July (1992).
143 KOTRA, 'Initial Assessment of Korea's Stock Market Liberalisation', *Korea Trade and Business*, May (1992).
144 'Better than billed', *The Economist*, 8 May 1993, pp. 82–84.

145 KOTRA, May 1992, *op. cit.*

146 'Financial deregulation spurs capital market growth', *Indonesia Quarterly Development News*, National Development Information Office, Vol. 12, No. 4, March/April 1989.

147 'Full foreign ownership allowed in priority zones', *Indonesia Quarterly Development News*, National Development Information Office, Vol. 15, No. 3, Spring 1992.

148 Derived from SG Warburg Securities, *Far East Emerging Markets Funds and Trusts*, London, December 1992. Total fund capitalisation as a share of total market capitalisation in 1992 was 2.6 per cent in Indonesia, 1.1 per cent in Korea, 0.5 per cent in Malaysia, 0.7 per cent in Taiwan, and 4 per cent in Thailand.

149 Solnik, Bruno, 'Pacific Basin Stock Markets and International Diversification', in Ghon Rhee and Chang (1991), *op. cit.*; Brown, S. and Otsuki, T., *Risk Premia in Pacific-Run Capital Markets*, New York University Working Paper, May 1992.

150 The decline in US short term interest rates in the second half of the 1980s coincided with a substantial outflow from cash into equity mutual funds and added one source of support to the domestic market and also to foreign equity markets, *US Markets*, JP Morgan Research, 8 December 1992.

151 *The Economist*, 'Attractive Dragons', 19 December 1992, p. 71.

152 Estimates of SG Warburg Securities.

153 Tan Chwee Huat, (1989), *op. cit.*, p. 207.

154 Chou, S.R. and Johnson, K., 'An empirical analysis of stock market anomalies', in Ghon Rhee and Chang, (1990), *op. cit.*

155 BAPEPAM is Indonesia's Capital Market Executive Agency. It used to promote, supervise and manage the securities market. In 1990, the Capital Market Decree transformed BAPEPAM into a SEC-type 'watchdog' with larger supervisory responsibilities, while the responsibility for the administration of the stock exchange was transferred to the private sector.

156 'Financial deregulation spurs capital market growth', *Indonesia Quarterly Development News*, National Development Information Office, Jan/Feb 1990, 8.

157 Dickie (1981), *op. cit.*, p. 190.

158 Hargrove (1991).

159 SEACEN (1989), *op. cit.*, p. 23.

Chapter 4

China's stock markets

Jane Brooks

INTRODUCTION

The People's Republic of China (PRC) has been one of the most fashionable investment themes in Asia over the past few years. As international investors sought to gain access to the world's fastest growing economy, China's GDP growth reached 13.5 per cent in 1993 and an estimated 10 per cent in 1994, with industrial production continuing to surge by an annualised 16 per cent in value added terms in the first half of 1994.[1] The China stocks listed in Hong Kong and other exchanges like Shanghai and Shenzhen present an attractive opportunity to investors wanting to participate in the modernisation of the country's economy in the longer term. The PRC's stock markets are developing rapidly and the number of listed companies is set to expand substantially in the coming years. In the short term, however, China's own stock markets will remain relatively small and illiquid for an economy of its size. They will also experience many problems, some common to other emerging markets and some peculiar to China. This chapter provides an overview of the development of the China stock markets over the past decade, from their origins in 'curb' markets in employee stock to the increasingly sophisticated markets in Shanghai and Shenzhen today. It also discusses the evolution of Hong Kong as a 'China market' through the H share listing programme and offers some speculation over the prospects of both mainland's and Hong Kong's stock markets.

The early years

The original securities markets in China were established in the 1890s. During the 1930s and 1940s, Shanghai was home to Asia's most vibrant stock markets. Trading reached its zenith during the Japanese occupation of the city. In 1948, due to the hyper-inflation experienced under the Kuomingtang government, the markets were suspended. The following year saw the markets officially closed with the gaining of power of the Chinese Communist Party (CCP). The CCP viewed stock markets as one of the ultimate symbols of capitalism, unfit for China's new economic development path. Under Mao Zedong, this path was guided through state planning as the market approach was firmly rejected. Treasury bonds continued to be issued from 1950 to 1958 to fund budget deficits, but thereafter until 1978, the government renounced the use of all forms of securities.

By the time Mao died in 1976, China's experiment with socialism had left the country well behind other Asian nations in the economic growth stakes. This slippage was most notable vis-à-vis East Asia's market based Newly Industrialised Economies. China's industries were still using plants and processes introduced by Soviet advisers in the 1950s, with some dating back to the 1920s. In an endeavour to catch up, in 1978 China opened its doors to the world and embarked upon an ambitious programme of economic reform. Since then, the country has gradually reduced the role of the state plan in favour of a more market oriented approach. This has been crucial in achieving its fast pace of growth in the last fifteen years.

Besides the severe structural problems in the economy such as misallocation of resources, abysmal labour and capital productivity and monstrous bureaucratisation, another serious constraint facing the PRC when it started reform was a severe shortage of capital. Among the government's earliest tasks were therefore the seeking out of new sources of funds as well as introduction of modern means of public financing. In 1981, China recommenced domestic bond issues. Exclusion from international organisations between 1949 and the mid 1970s had previously inhibited China's borrowing overseas, but in 1982 the PRC returned to the international capital markets.

Nevertheless, debt issues alone were insufficient to fund the rapid take-off of the economy following the extension of reforms from the countryside into urban areas in 1984. Rural–urban migration exacerbated city unemployment in addition to the surfacing problem of massive underemployment in state-owned enterprises, which still commanded the bulk of state bank lending. Smaller enterprises, collectives and the new private enterprises that sprung up around the nation as a result of reform had to tap into other capital sources such as private savings and corporate spare cash in the informal market. The new private and collective enterprises were concentrated in the service sector and processing industries, and operated outside the formal state structure. They were often supported by other enterprises and local authorities but were of low priority for state bank loans.

To finance expansion, private and collective enterprises also resorted to selling shares to their own employees and occasionally to those of other enterprises. These shares were the first 'stock' issues in China since 1949, although they were more akin to corporate bonds or preference shares than ordinary shares. Commonly, employees were guaranteed a rate of return, usually higher (even double) than that available from the large state banks for savings deposits. As an inducement to investors accustomed to rationing, enterprises often paid dividends in kind. Over the balance of the 1980s, these experimentations with securities issues remained confined to the non-state sector. Not until recent years did these practices become widespread with the advance of the private sector, which by then was accounting for more than half of the annual growth in national industrial production.

DEVELOPMENT SINCE 1990

In line with prevailing development theory and after years of debate over the securities markets' role in a self-styled communist country, the PRC government has come to accept these markets as a cornerstone of modernisation. The government envisages that the securities markets should target two main sources of funds, namely the 'under the mattress' money belonging to individuals and households in China, the corporate spare cash and the 'no-strings attached' institutional funds from overseas. The other essential risk hedging role of the securities markets in economic management is much less understood and is barely discussed among the monetary authorities.

However, China's reformers increasingly recognised the value of the securities markets in reorganising state enterprises into joint stock companies that were subsequently listed on the stock exchanges. These have been encouraged to seek funding for plant modernisation or debt reduction in the equities markets both at home and overseas, and an official programme of listings was sanctioned. The restructuring of state enterprises to improve profit incentives and reduce their welfare burden has been a key government objective.

Concerned over the potential loss of state control over key industries as well as a sell-off of state assets at deep discount, the government has at no stage discussed a full fledged privatisation programme. The CCP is in fact unwilling to consider such far reaching ideological questions, for fear of negative implications to its claim to power. As a result, the government continues to hold a majority stake in most of the listed enterprises, with China's forthcoming new Securities Law expected to restrict the joint holdings of overseas investors in listed companies to no more than 35 per cent of the share capital. But the lack of funds which has already inhibited the state shareholders from participating in rights issues is looming large as a major complication for the new law and may force a revision in due course.

In most other aspects of state enterprise reform, however, the government has stood firm. Corporatisation of state enterprises is underway nationwide and the worst performing entities are being allowed to go bankrupt, while other salvageable ones will be auctioned to the highest bidder or merged with other enterprises. Despite its reluctance, the government is being forced to address in practical terms the questions of what constitutes state property, who actually owns it, how to value it and, as important, how it can be best used to society's advantage. Together with these issues are those emerging from the impact of enterprise rationalisation such as the need for and provision of a welfare system. It remains to be seen how these issues will be resolved and the impact the solutions will have on the development of various securities markets. It is however quite clear that, as the government gradually winds down its role in the management and direct ownership of enterprises, hundreds more of these will seek to raise funds and list on China's fledgling stock markets over the balance of this decade. The scope for such an increase can only be described as tremendous, with as many as 60,000 companies being eligible for listing within the next ten years. In the meantime, greater appreciation of the importance of property ownership has led to a scramble to claim title to enterprises and other property.

THE SHANGHAI AND SHENZHEN STOCK MARKETS

Between 1984 and 1988 over 3,000 enterprises issued shares. As time went by, the owners inevitably began to trade such issues to other buyers who had no direct connection to the enterprise that issued the shares. As trading grew, informal 'curb' markets for both stocks and treasury bonds evolved in China's major cities. The first over-the-counter (OTC) market began operating in Shenyang (in China's northeast) as early as 1986. It was quickly followed by another in Shanghai and by 1988, virtually all of China's large cities had OTC markets. The most active trading at that time was in treasury bonds as state employees were forced to purchase these through compulsory deductions from their pay and were keen to sell them.

Trading in the embryonic markets was anarchic. There were no trading rules, let alone shareholders' registers or adequate publication of prices. Nevertheless, trading was brisk. Participants began to consider means of building on the initial success of the stock markets. By early 1989, Shanghai and Shenzhen were planning to establish centralised trading floors. Shenzhen was also looking forward to its first stock issues to overseas investors. These developments were delayed by the events of June 1989 and the austerity programme thereafter. Eventually, Shenzhen opened a unified trading floor on 1 December 1990, ahead of the opening of the Shanghai Exchange by three weeks. The Shenzhen market's official inauguration had to wait until July 1991. Most of the companies listed on either exchange were small private or collective enterprises that had traded in the OTC market and whose early share issues were unofficial. In 1991,

Table 4.1 The development of China's securities markets

Date	Development
1982	The first corporate bond issues in China since 1949 China's first overseas sovereign issues since 1949
1984	China's first securitised company registered in Beijing: Tianqiao Department Store The first public share issue since 1949 completed by Feilo Acoustics
1986	Corporate bond issues become widespread. Over-the-counter trading starts in Shenyang and Shanghai
1987	Trading spreads nation-wide Shenzhen companies begin public share issues
1988	Official markets established for trading of state bonds in Shenyang, Tianjing, Shanghai, Wuhan, Guangzhou and Shenzhen
1990	Shanghai Securities Exchange celebrated its official opening on 19 December, but not before, Shenzhen, which opened the PRC's first centralised trading floor three weeks earlier
1991	Shenzhen Stock Exchange was officially opened on 3 July
1992	Shanghai Vacuum Electron Device was listed on 21 February as China's first B share, available to, overseas investors. By year end, 18 B share issues had been listed in Shanghai and Shenzhen
1993	January: the China Securities Commission was established July: Tsingdao Brewery became the first PRC incorporated company to be listed in Hong Kong August: Shanghai Petrochemical became the first PRC American Depositary Receipts (ADR)

Source: Hu Yebui, *China's Capital Market*, The Chinese University Press, 1993

other companies quickly joined the markets. Unlike the previous issues by non-state enterprises, the new issues had several separate share classes. The 'A' shares for domestic shareholders were themselves divided into three types: states shares, legal person shares that could be held by other enterprises, and individual investor shares. These divisions continue to exist at the time of writing. In theory, each type of shares can only be held by a specified group of investors although in practice trading takes place across the boundaries. The state shares remain unlisted. Voting rights and dividends are equal for all categories of shares.

Overseas participation in the PRC stock markets was delayed for another year until 1992. It was decided that because of the inconvertibility of China's currency, the renminbi, a separate class of shares, would be established for non-PRC investors. Hence, the 'B' share market was born, with Shanghai trading them in US dollars while Shenzhen used Hong Kong dollars. B shares supposedly can only be held by overseas investors, but in practice, domestic investors with access to foreign exchange have been participating in this market and provided much of the liquidity. This situation may eventually be formalised. In February 1992, Shanghai Vacuum Electron Device was the first company to list B shares in Shanghai. Shortly afterwards, Southern Glass became the first to do so in Shenzhen. Such was the initial enthusiasm of international investors that the latter company was able to win overseas investors with only an A share prospectus containing accounts to PRC rather than international disclosure standards.

A flurry of activity in mid 1992 brought 17 other B shares to market in Shanghai and Shenzhen. An initial enthusiastic response from overseas institutions meant that the first issues were heavily over-subscribed. As the novelty wore off later that year, investors became more rigorous in their demand for information in relation to subsequent issues. The standards of information provided by B share issuing enterprises rose accordingly. Turnover in the Shanghai and Shenzhen markets increased in 1993 as nation-wide telecommunications links and computer systems were upgraded, trading and settlement practices improved and new brokers started trading. During that year, overseas brokers were for the first time allowed to trade directly in the stock markets.

Individual investors have largely been precluded from initial participation in B share offers as most of these have been done through private placement instead of as open public offers. To date, just one company's prospectus, that of Shanghai Outer Gaoqiao, has managed to reach the standard required to obtain approval from the Hong Kong authorities for a public offer in the Territory. Unfortunately, due to poor sentiment at the time of the SOG issue in June 1993, the offer was well under-subscribed and no other company has since opted for this route to listing. Foreigners' honeymoon period with the PRC markets drew closer to an end as inadequate disclosure and other problems associated with these markets came to the fore. Investors gradually shifted attention to other avenues for investment in China stocks as these became increasingly available, leading to more realistic valuations (i.e., lower pricing) of new issues. Sensing the trend, many PRC companies have allied themselves with Hong Kong vehicles to access funds in the Hong Kong market.

Throughout 1993, more B shares were listed in Shenzhen and Shanghai but these markets have remained orientated primarily to domestic investors. A network of brokers has recently been unfolding across China. At the end of the year, China had thirty-six specialist securities firms covering virtually all of the country's main cities. Securities services are also offered by 1,200 banks and investment companies, domestic and foreign,[2] and their offices are linked by satellite into the Shanghai and Shenzhen exchanges. Other cities have also lobbied the government for their own stock exchange but so far the central authorities have been reluctant to consider the establishment of more markets given the difficulties faced by the existing ones.

Trading also takes place on two other markets in China: the Securities Trading Automated Quotations Service (STAQ) and the National Electronic Trading System (NETS). Even compared to the Shanghai and Shenzhen markets, the number of issues and turnover have been minimal on the STAQ and NETS. Rules governing trading in shares are almost non-existent. The STAQ market accounted for 58 per cent of the RMB7.5 billion nation-wide turnover in corporate bonds in 1993. NETS is a national network that trades in a few shares of companies that have issued shares to other corporate shareholders but have not usually issued a prospectus or shares to individual investors. In theory, such shares cannot be bought by the other types of investors although in practice such a barrier remains unclear. NETS also trades corporate bonds, accounting for 42 per cent of national turnover in 1993. Trading on a trial basis started in mid 1992 via a computer network based in Beijing.[3] Hectic trading in the previous summer pushed prices sharply higher but China's Securities Commission stopped new listings of corporate shares in late 1993 until new rules governing trading were in place. Trading in existing shares has since been lacklustre.

Table 4.2 The PRC securities markets: December 1993

No. of companies	Type of company
13,000 shareholding companies, 9,440 more than 1992	
	Of the new companies, there were:
	2,968 joint stock companies
	6,472 limited liability companies
	1,776 had issued stock to employees
	There were over 25 million shareholders in China.

Market	Turnover
Shanghai	
101 A shares	RMB238 billion (US$27.6 billion)
22 B shares	RMB3.7 billion (US$430.2 million)
Shenzhen	
73 A shares	RMB180.7 billion (US$21 billion)
19 B shares	RMB31 million (US$3.6 million)
Hong Kong	
6 H shares	HK$102 million (US$13.6 million)
STAQ and NETS	
17 corporate bonds	RMB7.5 billion (US$872 million)

Sources: 'China Securities News', *China Daily*, 9 February 1994; *South China Morning Post*, 11 March 1994

The reorganisation of companies and listing of A shares is continuing apace. Since 1993, enterprises from outside Shanghai and Shenzhen have also been allowed to issue shares and list on either of the two stock markets although they have remained a minority. Outside China, stock exchanges normally approve listing candidates immediately prior to an initial public offer or share placement. Ahead of this time, companies are free to work with financial advisers of their own choosing towards a listing. By contrast, China's Securities Regulatory Commission (CSRC) determines which enterprises have the right to list, where at and the total number of shares that can be offered for each type of share. An upper annual limit for the number of share issues is also set. In 1994, the CSRC approved the issue of RMB5.5 billion worth of shares to domestic investors, similar to the number issued in 1993. The value is based on the par value of a share, usually RMB1.[4]

THE OUTLOOK FOR THE SHANGHAI AND SHENZHEN MARKETS

The PRC stock markets are here to stay as China cannot afford to dismiss them as a means of funding the modernisation of its industry and infrastructure. The inhibition for these markets is the volatility characteristic of all emerging markets in the East Asian region. This high volatility relative to more established stock markets of the OECD could only be reduced over time when the risks (and their management) are better understood by local participants and trading and disclosure rules improved. In the absence of deep financial markets skills and a satisfactory regulatory framework, large institutional investors will continue to stay away and the liquidity of China's markets will remain thin. Another issue is that the local markets and those for foreign investors have remained separate from and moved independently of each other. PRC investors continue to pay little heed to stock fundamentals and movements in the A share markets are largely driven by rumour. This situation might not be ameliorated significantly until the renminbi becomes a fully convertible currency, thereby facilitating the merger of the A and B share markets. This would then allow the participation of a larger number of PRC and foreign institutional investors that would take greater notice of market fundamentals and rely less on speculative impulses.

Initially, PRC investors viewed the markets as a no-lose game. There were plenty of takers for new issues due to abundant spare corporate cash, growing incomes accompanied by high domestic savings rates, and low (often negative) real rates of return on bank savings accounts. Throughout 1992–93, A shares were typically issued at and had maintained a premium over their equivalent B shares. At their height, some A shares traded above 100 times annual earnings. Several of the largest A shares are the counterparts of H shares listed in Hong Kong. Many companies issuing A shares have not issued B shares, especially if they have had no need for foreign exchange to import overseas produced equipment or to make non-renminbi debt repayments. As a consequence, B share issues have been out-numbered by A shares, although for much of 1994 the situation has been somewhat reversed, with B shares being traded at a premium to A shares.

In the two years to early 1994, the lure of investing in the world's fastest growing economy drove up the prices of those China stocks which foreigners had access to. The multiples reached very high levels, with those of H shares going well in excess of the rest of the Hong Kong market during the second half of 1993. These unrealistic valuations were more a reflection of the scarcity of means to place portfolio investment in China than of the shares' actual value. The considerable risks of investing in Shanghai and Shenzhen or in 'China plays' in Hong Kong were not addressed until the first half of 1994. Earlier in the year, the initial excitement dissipated as H share prices (as well as prices of the B shares on China's two stock exchanges) took a plunge from their highs. The A share market also collapsed, caused largely by investors' (both domestic and international) increasing recognition of the difficulties facing the markets and the overall Chinese economy. Domestic investors in particular were concerned about the volume of new issues. Indeed, Shenzhen authorities had to postpone the 1994 listing programme after share price declines led to demonstrations by individual shareholders in the city. This has since been followed by a decision by the CSRC to delay all new A share listings until 1995.

Foreign investors' greatest complaints concerning the Shanghai and Shenzhen markets remain poor liquidity, excessive share price volatility and insufficient shareholder protection. The paucity of corporate disclosure has been exacerbated by the immaturity of market practice and the fact that information is available only in Chinese. Overall, Shenzhen is regarded as the poorer of the two domestic markets. The use of listing proceeds by a number of companies for diversification into new businesses, often into the overheated property market or non-related companies, has increased disenchantment among overseas investors.

To be fair, the regulatory environment in general has improved greatly since 1992. Admittedly, as in other parts of the PRC legal system, it is likely that the development of formal regulations will continue to lag and lead market practice in account of the feedback process between lawmakers and market practitioners. But indications are that things have been changing for the better. Established at the start of 1993, China's Securities Regulatory Commission took over responsibility for China's stock markets from the People's Bank of China (the central bank) and the Ministry of Finance. Since then, the CSRC has worked closely with the two stock markets and their listed clients to improve regulations and raise the standard of market practice. A draft securities code, *Tentative Rules on the Issuance and Administration of Stocks*, was promulgated in May 1993 for the A share market and the law is likely to be finalised by early 1995. Meanwhile, a company law has been approved by the National People's Congress meeting in March 1994 but which covers only joint stock companies and not the other types of enterprises.

Some far reaching tax and financial system reforms were initiated on 1 January 1994. In the longer term these should reduce bureaucratic interference in business and encourage PRC enterprises to behave more like companies elsewhere. The tax changes were instituted without much advance notice. Implementation to date has been confusing and subject to local officials' interpretation. In response to protests, some measures have been scrapped or postponed indefinitely. For example, a proposed stock trading levy will now not be imposed and introduction of a capital gains tax will probably not include gains in the stock market, after the authorities had taken stock of the deteriorating market sentiment in the first half of 1994 as a result of the tax change confusion.

Improved auditing requirements were introduced in July 1993 for all PRC enterprises, although PRC accounting practice continues to differ materially from the International Accounting Standards. Companies issuing H shares must publish results according to both sets of regulations and state where they differ. Companies with B shares listed in Shanghai or Shenzhen have been encouraged to issue accounts to international standards though they are not bound to do so. A number of companies are reluctant to bear the additional costs involved. Accounts prepared according to PRC accounting standards are used to decide the tax liabilities of the company and the level of dividends to be paid. Enforcement remains a problem largely due to insufficient staff, inexperience and inadequate supervision. The authorities are attempting to educate companies and domestic investors about the opportunity and obligation as well as risks in raising and investing funds in the stock market. Many domestic investors remain ignorant of the workings of the equity market despite the poor performance of the A share market in 1993–94. The early 1994 price falls came as a big surprise to many of the local participants, who blamed the CSRC for opening the listing gate too wide too fast. Prices of the A shares soared in July that year as soon as the 1994 A share listing programme was halted by the Commission and other measures to boost the market were suggested, such as allowing foreigners to invest in A shares through the investment funds. A positive trend is that many of China's daily newspapers now carry reports on activity in the securities markets while several specialist publications are becoming widely read. The local media also runs increasingly sophisticated commentaries on the stock markets.

The flexibility of Shenzhen as a special economic zone (SEZ) meant that in the initial phases of development, the city's stock market was able to develop more rapidly than its counterpart in Shanghai. However, Shenzhen stock market's development was stalled by the riots that occurred during a lottery to decide the allocation of A shares in August 1992, diminishing the clout of Shenzhen relative to the other city. Since then, Shenzhen has fallen further behind its rival, which has emerged as the preferred choice of PRC enterprises for listing and has become significantly larger. Indeed, some Shenzhen companies are believed to be considering obtaining secondary listings in Shanghai and overseas exchanges.

New issues will dominate China's stock markets in the next few years. The number of listed companies will increase rapidly, probably at a pace faster than the markets are able to digest. Recent initial stock issues, especially for companies outside Shanghai and Shenzhen, continue to draw investors. Once listed (mostly in 1994), however, many such stocks have performed poorly. Over-supply (due to bottlenecks in the exchanges' capacity to handle new listings) is likely to constrain market growth for some time, although government measures to rebuild confidence in the A share market have produced some positive results in the second half of 1994. New issues are being offered at a discount similar to stocks that are already listed, have large capitalisations and offer exposure to a wider cross-section of the Chinese economy. As a result, the extreme valuations that characterised China's markets in the early 1990s have been declining recently. In the domestic markets, a credit squeeze since mid 1993 and bond sales are depriving the markets of liquidity at a time when other domestic investors, disappointed by declining performance, are cutting back on their activity. At the time of writing, 1994's quota of A share listings, after repeated delays, has finally been postponed until 1995.

Nevertheless, expectations on the part of Chinese companies and under-writers remain high. The regulators in Shanghai and Shenzhen are concerned at moves by the better Chinese enterprises to obtain listing elsewhere and are taking advice to improve market practices. However, the preference of many international investors including China funds, for the greater transparency, better regulation and higher liquidity in other markets, will continue to encourage Chinese companies to list overseas.

Other PRC cities are lobbying hard for approval to establish China's third stock exchange. Wuhan, Tianjin, Shenyang and Hainan all have active OTC markets. The first three all justify their claim as being far away from the boom towns of the south and thus will be able to channel investor funds to state enterprises in China's hinterland. Wuhan is the centre of the PRC's inter-bank market and has the largest share of the domestic bond market, while Tianjin was the site of one of China's pre-1949 markets. For the time being, however, it is unlikely that the CSRC will allow the appearance of more stock markets when both Shanghai and Shenzhen are struggling to establish themselves. The Commissions' efforts are being directed towards improving the standards of the existing markets, especially Shanghai, the potentially best bet as a domestic financial centre capable of linking up with and competing against the major centres in the region. China's principal goal is to raise funding for enterprises, many of whom have expressed desire to access overseas markets. Listings by PRC companies will also be sought by several of the world's major markets including New York and London as these are keen to attract their own direct China plays. Even Sydney is playing host to a dozen PRC listings in 1994 and 1995, a notable potential member being China International Trust and Investment Corporation's Australian arm.

The extent to which Chinese enterprises will go overseas (i.e., the Western markets) for listing is difficult to pinpoint. But it can be speculated that once initial enthusiasm dissipates, Hong Kong and Shanghai will remain the PRC's principal stock markets: Hong Kong for its developed financial markets capable of linking Chinese enterprises to Western markets, as well as for the lack of PRC sophistication in convincing foreign investors of Chinese investor protection law; and Shanghai for the fact that Beijing clearly desires a centre in China's east, for political as well as nostalgic reasons.

HONG KONG AS A NATURAL CHINA MARKET

The development of the Hong Kong stock exchange as a major market for China stocks was a logical corollary to its growing economic ties with China as well as to the development of the B share markets in Shanghai and Shenzhen. Hong Kong and China are increasingly interwoven in terms of capital and trade flows. Over 55 per cent of all direct investment in China emanates from the Territory, while Hong Kong's manufacturers employ upwards of 3 million people in their factories in China. Major companies have increasingly become involved through consulting or joint ventures in China while others have sought PRC backed entities as major shareholders. Hong Kong's commercial banks have a well established role in servicing China and PRC entities have set up trading offices in the Territory in recent years, being active in Hong Kong's equity and property markets. PRC backed entities increasingly raise funds through the HKSE by listing holding companies incorporated in Hong Kong or by acquiring 'backdoor' listings via takeovers of Hong Kong companies.

In December 1992, the Hong Kong and PRC authorities signed an agreement that allowed the listing of PRC enterprises as 'H' shares in Hong Kong. The initial agreement was subsequently formalised in a memorandum signed in June 1993. In the following month, Tsingtao Brewery became the first PRC incorporated company to list in Hong Kong. It was followed by six other companies before the close of the year. Hong Kong's regulators were anxious that its listing rules not be compromised by the listing of these PRC entities. The PRC-Hong Kong memorandum adapts as far as possible Hong Kong stock market practice to cover PRC incorporated companies listed in the Territory, but operating under a different legal and accounting system and business environment in China. In order to comply with Hong Kong listing requirements and affirm shareholders' protection in the absence of a comprehensive Company Law in China, PRC companies are required to adopt articles of association that are more stringent than normal in Hong Kong. The H share companies are also required to retain a Hong Kong financial adviser for three years instead of the normal six months after listing. A joint Hong Kong-PRC arbitration committee has been set up to settle potential disputes. This arrangement has allowed Chinese enterprises to raise substantial funds and enabled a wider pool of international investors to place capital in PRC enterprises than possible at present due to the nature of China's domestic markets. Many more H share listings in Hong Kong are expected to follow over the next few years.

The H share listing programme and growing involvement by other listed companies in China that have been funded through equity issues means that Hong Kong had become the world's sixth largest stock market by the end of 1993. This development will accelerate as its role as a financial centre for China gathers momentum. The H share listings have also broadened the composition of the HKSE client base. No companies involved in heavy industries such as steel making and chemicals were listed previously. The coming on board of these large PRC enterprises will likely have an attraction effect on other PRC entities still looking for a place to list. This secondary effect will further boost the Hong Kong market's capitalisation significantly over the rest of the 1990s.

In advance of the listings, adherence to Hong Kong listing rules by PRC companies was expected to be problematic given the differing business practices in Hong Kong and the PRC. Listing has required substantial restructuring for large PRC state enterprises coming to market in Hong Kong. Frequently, the structure of these enterprises bore a greater resemblance to bureaucracies and municipal councils than companies as known conventionally outside China. This has been typically resolved through listing only the most profitable parts of the huge enterprises and hiving off their subsidiaries and welfare responsibilities. Enterprises are required to provide three years of accounts to International Accounting Standards to assist international investors in following their progress. This process of restructuring and auditing has proved one of the most difficult of the various stages to listing in Hong Kong. It is hindered by China's lack of internationally experienced auditing staff and by inconsistent valuation practices. On the other hand, overseas accounting firms are still relatively new to working in China and suffer from a shortage of Mandarin speakers willing and able to bridge the information gap.

There has been no major infringement of Hong Kong's listing rules by an H share company although analysts encounter a degree of difficulty in following the stocks. This is partly because some of the industries are new to the market and the distances to visit the companies are greater. Those

Table 4.3 Conditions for PRC companies listing in Hong Kong

Conditions

Listing requirements

Demonstrate a three-year track record

Issue a full prospectus and accountants' report

Sign a listing agreement with the Hong Kong Stock Exchange including a general disclosure obligation

Maintain sufficient Hong Kong listed securities in public hands to ensure an open market

Appoint two independent non-executive directors

Retain a sponsor for three years

Accounting standards

Adhere to PRC Accounting Standards

Adopt Hong Kong or International Accounting Standards for accountants' reports and annual accounts

Present both sets of figures in the required reports showing the material differences

Pay dividends to H shareholders in hard currencies

Investor protection

Comply with the Standard Opinion on Joint Stock Companies and supplementary documents

Hong Kong Companies Ordinance

Extended Articles of Association

Choice of arbitration in either PRC or Hong Kong

Memorandum between PRC and Hong Kong authorities

Risks Declaration in Prospectus

Source: Hong Kong Stock Exchange

companies that have some form of dual listing, whether in China or as American Depositary Receipts (ADRs) in New York, have also to abide by the requirements of these markets, some markedly different to Hong Kong practice.

Despite the initial rocky reception of Shanghai Petrochemical, the first six PRC incorporated companies brought to market in Hong Kong had performed spectacularly well in 1993. The extremely high valuations of H shares at the end of 1993 clearly registered a combination of high demand and low supply: the strong investor interest in PRC-backed companies and the limited choice of investment vehicles for China stocks. Since then, the performance of H shares has been disappointing due to the prospect of new H share listings as well as to investor concerns over the PRC economy's medium term prospects.

International investors' experience in other emerging markets such as Taiwan, South Korea and Thailand in recent years has shortened their learning curve *vis-à-vis* China. Even many China funds, with an estimated US$3 billion under management in 1993, remain under-invested. And rather than being risked in Shanghai or Shenzhen, much of the money has gone into Hong Kong's 'China concept' stocks.

New issues of H shares will continue to act as a magnet to international investors, provided China's economic growth is not disrupted by political or social instability. Besides the three companies left from the first batch of H share listings – Yizheng Chemical Fibre, Tianjin Bohai Chemical and Dongfeng Electric – a new group of twenty-two companies offering exposure to a diverse selection of Chinese industries is coming to market in 1994–95 in Hong Kong and New York. The list, selected by the CSRC, includes some of the best companies in the PRC government's priority sectors for modernisation, namely heavy industry such as steel and chemicals, infrastructural projects, transport and power plants. PRC enterprises in these areas have enormous financing needs to upgrade plant and equipment or repay a heavy foreign exchange debt burden. Some of the new listings will be as large as, if not larger than, Shanghai Petrochemical and Maanshan Iron & Steel, the largest in 1993. The new issues are expected to be offered at a substantial discount compared to those listed in 1993. Finally, unlike the H share programme that year, not all PRC companies coming to market overseas in 1994-95 will be issuing A shares due to the government's postponement of new A share issues until at least early 1995.

Hong Kong remains the most natural China market and is unlikely to be displaced from its role as a major financial centre and principal conduit for

Table 4.4 Performance of H shares since listing

	Price 31.1.94 HK$	% change since listing
Beiren Printing	4.67	+65
Guangzhou Shipyard	4.45	+114
Kunming Machinery	4.57	+131
Maanshan Iron & Steel	3.80	+67
Shanghai Petrochemical	2.87	+82
Tsingtao Brewery	7.90	+243

Source: Datastream

foreign equity investment in China. The Territory is also the nearest market that can raise substantial sums of foreign capital for China. It is the best able of the world's major markets to provide both sufficient liquidity and understanding among its financial community of the risks inherent in investing in China. In the medium term, neither Shanghai nor Shenzhen (nor any other regional centre for that matter) seems capable of challenging this role.

Table 4.5 Overseas listings in 1994–95

1994 listings	*Sector*
Yizheng Chemical Fibre	Polyester polymer
Tianjin Bohai Chemical	Alkali chemicals
Dongfeng Electric	Power generating equipment
Luoyang Glass	Sheet glass manufacturing
Qingling Motors	Vehicle manufacturing
To be listed	
Chengdu Cable	Cable manufacturing
Dongbei Electricity Transmission	Transmission equipment, transformation equipment
Foshan Ceramics	Ceramics manufacturing
Guangzhou Shenzhen Railway	Rail
Harbin Power Plant Equipment	Power generating equipment
Panda Electronics	TV and video manufacturing
Shanxi Jingwei Textile Machinery	Textile machinery
Shandong Zhouzian Power	Power supply
Xi'an Aircraft Manufacturing	Aircraft manufacturing
Wuhan Iron & Steel	Steel making
Jilin Chemical Industrial	Petrochemicals
China Eastern Airlines	Aviation
China Southern Airlines	Aviation
Huaneng International Power	Power supply
Huaneng Power (Shandong)	Power supply
Dongfeng Motors	Vehicle manufacturing
Datong Power	Power supply
Tianjin Steel Tubes	Steel tube manufacturing
Shanghai Haixing Shipping	Shipping
Zhenhai Petrochemical	Petrochemicals

Source: CSRC

Other forms of listing

In addition to the formal listing programme for PRC incorporated companies, a number of PRC backed companies acquired listings in Hong Kong and Singapore in 1993. These came to market through holding companies incorporated in the Territory or by way of 'back door' listing. The CSRC's concern that such listings may detract from the official programme has led to the Commission attempting on several occasions to curtail such listings. The CSRC is insisting on the right to approve all PRC entities seeking listing wherever that may be and has reportedly been instrumental in deferring many proposed Hong Kong listings by PRC-backed companies. Nevertheless, a number of companies are believed to have been approved for listing through holding companies incorporated in the Territory. Meanwhile, large PRC institutions are continuing to build stakes in Hong Kong listed companies with an eye for back door listing.

Back door listings have slowed down partly because there are few affordable shell companies still available in Hong Kong. Tight credit conditions in China in 1993–94 and more stringent controls over the foreign exchange earnings of PRC enterprises have reinforced the trend. Hence, PRC entities have been forced to consider other means of obtaining funds, reflected in the higher number of PRC concerns seeking mezzanine financing from overseas investors or joint venture partners. It is difficult not to assume that, as time goes by, Chinese capital seekers and providers will progress down the path of financial technique sophistication seen in Western markets in the 1980s. Whether or not this emerging era of financial engineering in China will repeat the mistakes of the Anglo-Saxon markets is hard to say. One could only observe that, since financial markets exist for reason of capital mobilisation and management, each disaster of the past has played a crucial role in upgrading the trading and regulatory systems of the next cycle, but without improving the markets' ability to control the cycle's pattern. In this context, it is hoped that China players will have the strategic sense and financial techniques to minimise volatility or its impact on their portfolios once the China stock markets turn sour. As to when and how these markets might hit the next trough, one could only speculate.

NOTES

1 The assistance of data and sources available to G. H. Goh Securities (H.K.) Ltd, where the author works, are gratefully acknowledged. Any opinions expressed herein are the author's own. Macroeconomic data on China are from the State Statistical Bureau.
2 Reuters, 15 January 1994; *Jingji Ribao*, various issues.
3 *Business Weekly*, 30 May 1993; and *China Daily*, 9 February 1994.
4 *China Daily*, 5 February 1994.

Chapter 5

China's capital market and its prudential framework

Joe H. Zhang and Joan X. Zheng

INTRODUCTION

China's economic liberalisation has broadened the avenues of finance for its business sector. Apart from traditional bank borrowing (indirect finance), companies can also raise funds by issuing shares and bonds to the public (direct finance) under certain conditions. With China's capital market gaining sophistication, prudential supervision has become a prominent issue. Further development of the capital market will depend critically on the setting and, more importantly, the enforcement of proper prudential standards.

The term 'capital market' is normally used to refer to the equity market and the market for securities at the longer end of the maturity spectrum. However, this chapter has to use the term in a broader sense to cover the whole financial market only excluding the inter-bank market. This definition is adopted because most of China's equity investments are not through the securities market. The distinction between capital markets and short-term money markets is extremely blurred in China due to the legacy of old centralised credit allocation.

The capital market in China has experienced a transition in the past ten years; and the transition is still under way. The austerity programme launched in June 1993 should be seen as a milestone in the history of China's capital market development and a starting point for a new phase. The Chinese government aimed to consolidate the achievements of the past ten years in capital market liberalisation through cleaning up the market environment, including its legal framework, and alleviating the economic and social side-effects of liberalisation. The success of the austerity programme eventually hinged on the healthy growth of the capital market.

This chapter aims to examine the evolution of the Chinese government's regulation of various segments of the capital market, the realities of the business sector and the macroeconomic policy implications of the current regulatory framework. Some of the questions that will be addressed include: why does the Chinese government encourage direct finance? What is the rationale of the policy? And why does the government try so hard to control it at the same time?

The chapter is organised as follows. The following section surveys major players in China's capital markets, their main activities and the industry structure. The third section discusses the Chinese government's regulations of the capital markets, and the fourth section examines the operations of various segments of the capital market (how credit is channelled through the capital market).

THE MAJOR PLAYERS OF THE CAPITAL MARKET AND THE INDUSTRY STRUCTURE

The People's Bank of China is China's central bank. It is the central government's agent for the conduct of monetary policy and prudential supervision. The People's Bank was the main commercial bank as well as the central bank until late 1983, when it was split into two: the current People's Bank and the Industrial & Commercial Bank of China (ICB). The Agriculture Bank (formerly a division of the People's Bank) was also made independent at this time. Prior to 1984, the Bank of China focused its business on overseas markets, particularly in Hong Kong, London and New York. Only since 1984 has it started to expand to areas outside capital cities in China. Its status was then changed from a de facto subsidiary of the People's Bank to an independent bank. The Construction Bank was also made independent of the Ministry of Finance in the early 1980s.

Banks

China's capital market is dominated by four major banks: the Bank of China, the ICB Bank, the Agriculture Bank and the Construction Bank. They are all owned by the central government. As of June 1993, their combined assets accounted for about 82.3 per cent of the total assets of the financial sector (including banks and non-bank financial institutions, but conventionally excluding the central bank).

The four major banks' respective total assets, as of the end of June 1993 were as follows:

Table 5.1 Asset size of the four major banks

Bank	Asset size
Bank of China	US$300 billion (A$447 billion)
Industrial & Commercial Bank	US$220 billion (A$310 billion)
Agriculture Bank*	US$200 billion (A$298.5 billion)
Construction Bank	US$200 billion (A$298.5 billion)

Sources: Kaye (1993); PBC (1993)
Note: *The figure for the Agriculture Bank does not include the assets of the rural credit unions under its management

The Bank of China and the ICB Bank were recently rated by *Euromoney* (Kaye 1993) as the world's eleventh and twelfth largest banks respectively in terms of shareholders' equity. However, it is the authors' view that shareholders' equity may be a poor representation of the Chinese banks' true financial position. This is because a bank's shareholders' equity is the balance of total assets and total liabilities, i.e., it is a residual item. If the bank's assets are not regularly 'marked to the market', then they can deviate significantly from their book value. This problem exists for banks in every country, but it is of particular relevance to the Chinese banks.

In China, there is no requirement for banks and other companies to revalue their assets regularly. A practical reason is that there is no active market for most assets, therefore, revaluation lacks a benchmark. There have been two nation-wide asset censuses in China's history which resemble the asset revaluation of the West: one in 1957 and the other in 1979 (Zhang and Zheng 1993b). Other than the two censuses, bad debts are not required to be written off. Instead, it is an applauded practice to reschedule, extend new loans, or to capitalise non-performing loans. In the past forty years, the government's intervention in banks' investment decisions and the banks' own mismanagement have generated a significant portion of non-performing loans, the magnitude of which cannot be ascertained.

Given the above reasons, *Euromoney*'s ranking is problematic. Nevertheless, within China's capital market, the four major banks' dominance is evident. Each of the four has an extensive branch network around the country and their activities determine the funds flows of the overall capital market. Also, they control about half of the non-bank financial institutions sector through sole or partial ownership.

Bank of China has branches and subsidiaries in major industrial countries and some developing countries. The other three major banks are also establishing a presence in the world's major financial centres.

In addition to the four major banks, there are a few regionally operating banks. They are either owned by the central government or jointly owned by the central and regional government authorities. The larger ones are the Investment Bank, the Communications Bank, China International Trust and Investment Corporation (CITIC), Industrial Bank, Guangdong Development Bank, Shenzhen Merchant Bank, Shengyan Co-operative Bank and Shaoxing Yuecheng Co-operative Bank.

The main business activities of banks in China are taking deposits from both institutional and individual customers, executing payments, lending to government and the business sector. Officially, the banking industry in China does not provide consumers with credit (for example, to finance purchase of durable consumer goods or property). However, it is not uncommon for small businesses or self-employed people to use bank loans for consumption because of the lender's inadequate monitoring, or as a result of informal understandings between the bank manager and the borrower. Also, in some cities, experimentation is occurring with consumer mortgage finance with strong incentives being offered by the government via interest rate subsidies.

In the narrow sense of the capital market, banks also play a major role. They issue bonds (called financial bonds) to finance their lending and investment; arrange and underwrite corporate shares and bonds; and act as traders and brokers in the secondary market (in over-the-counter markets as well as organised exchanges).

The four major national banks are over-burdened by 'social obligations' imposed on them by the government. For example, they are required to recruit unnecessary new staff each year to help alleviate unemployment; to provide cheap finance to priority projects such as exports and infrastructure; to contribute to the balancing of the government budget; and to exercise interest rate restraints. This has not only undermined the banks' efficient management, but also distorted proper monitoring and assessment of their performance. In a bid to rid the major banks of non-commercial activities (or 'social obligations'), the Chinese government has decided to establish two state banks: the Import & Export Bank and the Long-Term Development Bank (*Australian Financial Review* 1993). These two banks will act as the government's conduits for investing in projects which have social (or political) returns but low direct financial returns.

Non-bank financial institutions

The non-bank financial sector is composed of insurance companies, trust and investment corporations, rural and urban credit unions, securities companies, and finance and leasing companies.

Insurance companies

There is only one large insurance company in China, the People's Insurance Company, with a few wholly owned subsidiaries and an extensive branch network nation-wide. It almost monopolises the entire insurance market. The Communications Bank has a small insurance subsidiary, Pacific Insurance. Several overseas insurers also have a presence in China, but they are restricted to coastal cities and their market share is negligible.

The People's Insurance Company is a major institutional investor in the capital market (particularly Treasury Bonds and infrastructure investments). The insurance industry is supervised by the People's Bank.

Trust and investment companies

The main, if not the sole, difference between a bank and a trust and investment company is their source of finance. Banks source most of their finance through the retail network, while trust and investment companies rely on corporate deposits and purchased funds.

The China International Trust and Investment Corporation (CITIC) is the largest player in this sector, with total assets of over 70 billion yuan (A$15 billion). However, CITIC's high profile owes more to its political status. When it was founded in the early 1980s, its then chairman and managing director secured a 'ministerial rank' for it. The chairman's personal influence in China's top political circles has also enabled CITIC to gain preferential treatment in various aspects of business (Zhang and Zheng 1993b). In terms of its relationships with the People's Bank, it was outside the central bank's prudential control until very recently.

CITIC has expanded aggressively into foreign markets, particularly Hong Kong and the USA. To a large extent, its expansion has been underwritten by the political force of Beijing and the Chinese government's financial support which other large government companies cannot possibly command.

Apart from CITIC, there are hundreds of other national and regional trust and investment companies and trust and investment divisions within banks. The total number of institutions of this type is unknown because many are unauthorised and are therefore not recorded in the official registry. Some provincial and local governments also disregard the People's Bank and issue licences. These licensees are not always registered with the People's Bank. Furthermore, the People's Bank has a multi-tier branch network and every tier of office has the power to issue licences under a certain threshold. It is not uncommon for the Bank's regional offices to exceed their power due to the Bank's inadequate internal control.

Trust and investment companies are supervised by the People's Bank and are active in the capital market through project finance, corporate securities and property investment.

Credit unions

There are two types of credit unions: rural and urban. Their difference is not only that of their geographic location. In fact, this difference is gradually disappearing due to their cross expansion. They are different mainly because of their history and resultant corporate status.

Rural credit unions have existed for over forty years. Currently there are more than 60,000 institutions in this class with 340,000 branches and agencies around the country (PBC 1992). They are symbolically co-operative organisations, but in essence they are the Agriculture Bank's wholly-owned subsidiaries. The original union members have been totally cut off from the unions. From a financial point of view, the credit unions' profits are taxed in the same way as that of a bank, and their after-tax profits are either handed over to the Agriculture Bank, or retained for business expansion. The Agriculture Bank also covers the losses of many unions.

The first urban credit unions were established in the early 1980s. Currently there are 4,000 of them. Most credit unions are owned and directly supervised by the ICB, while many others are owned by companies, or government authorities and directly supervised by the People's Bank. The ownership of these institutions is clear and the owners share dividends. They are profit-oriented mutual entities.

Credit unions provide equity as well as debt finance to rural and small private businesses. They are not prevented from taking equity positions in non-financial business, investing in property or issuing shares and bonds. They can even be licensed as securities brokers or dealers.

Unlike their counterparts in Western countries, credit unions in China do not receive preferential taxation treatment for their co-operative status.

Securities companies

The first securities companies in China were licensed in 1987. Initially the bulk of these companies' business was corporate lending, since there were few securities for them to trade; the market was very inactive (bond holders were not accustomed to trading); and also banks could handle the transactions more cost-effectively through their branch networks. It was clear that the prime objective of those who set up the securities companies (with government funds) was to create new and better jobs for themselves, their relatives and loyal subordinates.

Since 1988 the government bonds' secondary market has been gradually opened up, and the push for the establishment of more securities companies has received a robust boost. Under pressure from banks and other government bodies, the People's Bank registered many new securities companies. However, the old problem of lack of genuine securities business remained. There are three factors behind this. First, few companies had been allowed to issue securities, and of those outstanding corporate securities only a fraction were allowed to be traded (few securities were standardised and fit for trading). Second, the Treasury Bonds market was a small market, and the government only opened up part of it to secondary trading (initially only those issued in 1985 and 1986). Third, the Bond price control imposed by the Ministry of Finance has made the trading one-way (more sale than purchase). All securities companies' funds were quickly tied up in Treasury Bonds.

Since 1988, some securities companies have been set up without a licence; and all other financial institutions have established securities divisions or desks. According to official statistics (PBC 1992b), as of October 1992, there were sixty-seven securities companies and 'hundreds' of securities divisions within financial institutions. These figures do not include those not registered by the government. These securities companies are mainly associated with regional governments or government agencies. Currently, all provinces and major cities have their own securities firms.

The People's Bank started to rationalise the securities industry in late 1992 by creating three mega companies, in an effort to bring all the existing small and regional securities companies under their empires through 'moral suasion'. The three companies are called Huaxia, Guotai and Nanfang, headquartered in Beijing, Shanghai and Shenzhen, respectively (PBC 1992b).

The objective for this rationalisation is to facilitate the government's control, because the government believes that the smaller the number of institutions the easier it will be to control. The government and the general public also blame the rising number of financial institutions and in par- ticular the non-bank financial institutions for excessive growth of credit aggregates and deterioration of market discipline. This line of reasoning excludes the view that market competition (with the participation of a large number of players) can bring discipline to the market. Instead, proponents of this argument see highly centralised control and a small number of players as an important condition for market discipline. This theory is also evident in the Chinese government's approach to regulation of the insur- ance industry.

It is generally agreed that the People's Bank will not achieve the stated objective through 'moral suasion' because often the existing securities companies' hidden agenda is precisely to avoid central control in order to take advantage of windfall opportunities created by government interven- tion and other market distortions. Macroeconomic control and operational efficiency through economies of scale are not their objectives.

The effort of the People's Bank to rationalise the securities industry suffered a severe blow when other government ministries raised the issue of conflict of interest in these three companies' ownership. Currently, these three companies are jointly owned by the People's Bank, the Ministry of Finance and the State Planning Commission, with minor equity injections from other government bodies. The State Council has endorsed the criticism and has demanded that the government authorities divest their equity participation. But the divestment will undermine the political clout and market profile of these three companies. Therefore, China's securities industry will continue to be made up of a large number of small regional players, at least in the short to medium term.

Finance companies and others

In every practical sense, finance companies and other similar institutions (such as investment companies and leasing companies) are no different from trust and investment companies and securities companies. Their popularity arises from the relative ease of obtaining a licence and the more lenient regulation. Their operations in the capital market have so far been based on the People's Bank's ad hoc circulars.

So far, the People's Bank has explicitly opposed establishing any private financial institution. Major institutions are exclusively owned and (partially) controlled by the government. However, individuals can become minority shareholders in small institutions. Furthermore, some newly established 'co-operative' financial institutions are, in essence, private mutual firms.

THE REGULATORY FRAMEWORK FOR THE CAPITAL MARKET

The regulatory framework should be looked at from two different perspectives: the regulatory agencies and the regulations. While regulatory functions are divided among regulatory agencies, there are considerable overlaps, ambiguities and even inconsistencies. Given that the capital market prudential framework is still at its formative stage, and that regulatory agencies have substantial discretion over regulation to suit their needs and to meet changing market conditions, this section will examine the matter only from the institutional perspective.

The People's Bank is the main regulator of China's capital market and the finance industry. However, other authorities also play important roles. They include the Ministry of Finance, the State Planning Commission, the State Commission for Economic Restructuring, the State Council Securities Commission and provincial and regional governments. There is no legislation specifying the division of responsibilities among these authorities, therefore, the central government's discretion, ad hoc assignments, the department heads' personal interests and the political struggle between authorities are all important determinants in the changing regulatory structure.

The regulations discussed here are only applicable to domestic banks and non-bank financial institutions. The sixty-five foreign banks operating in China are subject to a different set of rules (Zhang and Zheng 1993b).

The People's Bank

The People's Bank is a government ministry, just like the Ministries of Finance, Defence or Agriculture. Prior to 1984, it was a mere division of the Ministry of Finance. The Bank's elevation in the political hierarchy is attributable to the economic transition which favours more indirect measures of macroeconomic management than direct control. Since 1987, the successive governors of the Bank have always been in the 'inner circle' of the cabinet (the State Council). In June 1993, one of the deputy prime ministers, Zhu Rongji took over the governorship to reinforce the central bank's power.

The People's Bank has a total staff of over 166,400, with more than 2,300 working in its head office. The other staff are located in its three tiers of regional offices: 30 provincial, 330 prefecture (city) and 2,060 county-level offices. These offices reflect the government's administrative structure.

The internal structure of each regional office is the same as that of the head office (with the exception of the international function which is controlled by the head office and the thirty first-tier regional offices). The major supervisory divisions of the Bank are:

1 Financial Administration Division. It is in charge of authorising domestic banks and most non-bank financial institutions; authorising securities issues by financial institutions (financial bonds); setting, in conjunction with the State Planning Commission, the aggregate 'ceiling' for securities issued each year; authorising, in conjunction with the State Commission for Economic Restructuring, the issues and the secondary market trading of corporate securities.

2 Interest Rates and Savings Division. It has the power to set various interest rates and monitor compliance by the market.

3 Funds Management Division. It is in charge of allocating the central bank's credit to commercial banks and non-bank financial institutions. It also manages the Bank's statutory reserves.

4 International Division. It authorises the entry of foreign financial institutions and supervises their operations.

5 The State Bureau of Foreign Exchange Control (also known as the State Exchange Administration). It controls exchange rates, international capital flows and other areas related to foreign exchange and foreign debt. While this Bureau does not have the power to authorise foreign institutions, it supervises part of the business of authorised foreign institutions.

6 Accounting Division. It sets accounting rules for the capital market and financial institutions in accordance with the general rules set by the Ministry of Finance.

7 Auditing Division. It audits all financial institutions on a regular but mainly ad hoc basis (when abnormality surfaces or allegations are made).

Other divisions of the Bank do not have direct regulatory roles in the capital market.

The regulatory power of the People's Bank is divided between the head office and its regional offices. The power of these regional offices has seriously undermined the effectiveness of the central bank's prudential supervision and monetary policy, as has been noted by the World Bank (*Business Australian* 1993). The regional offices were traditionally controlled by both the head office and regional governments (and Communist Party machines). The conflict between national interest and regional interest often compromises the operations of these regional offices.

In terms of prudential measures, all depository institutions in China (domestic and foreign banks and credit unions) have to lodge statutory reserve deposits with the People's Bank. Judging from the way the reserve ratio adjustment is made, it is more of a monetary policy measure than a prudential device. When the People's Bank wants to reduce the growth rate of the credit aggregate, it can raise the reserve ratio. The People's Bank in fact used it several times in the past to fight inflation. Unfortunately, it does not seem to achieve any prudential objective.

Other prudential measures used in the Western capital markets, such as ownership diversification, large credit exposure limit, capital adequacy control and liquidity management have so far not been recognised as important issues by the Chinese regulators.

Most Chinese financial institutions are 100 per cent owned by the central government, while some others are jointly owned by government authorities and commercial entities. The diversification of banking ownership and control will not be an issue in the short to medium term, since the prospects of private financial institutions being established are limited.

Large credit exposure limits are used by Western country regulators to prevent banks from being heavily exposed to single borrowers and to avoid subsequent failure of the borrowers threatening the bank's viability. This issue has not been brought to the attention of Chinese regulators. Given the major banks' size, few single exposures (loans, equity positioning or underwriting of bond issues) would be too significant. More importantly, large projects tend to be government initiatives, and the prospect of bankruptcy is not high.

However, as the governments at various levels are often unable to bail out government entities due to budget constraints, all banks have a large amount of non-performing loans, loans that have been rescheduled many times, and bad loans with no mechanism for writting them off. While all banks have internal control systems of one form or another, on lending thresholds and credit limits to minimise this type of exposure, this is often ignored by managers or over-ruled by the head office.

Risk-adjusted capital adequacy guidelines were introduced by the Bank for International Settlements (BIS) in 1988 to ensure commercial banks in developed countries had adequate capital to support their operations. Member country supervisors (including the Reserve Bank of Australia) have since phased in the guidelines. China is not a member of the BIS, therefore it is not bound by the guidelines. However, under the influence of international financial institutions (particularly the International Monetary Fund and the World Bank) and in recognition of the need to strengthen the prudential standards of commercial banks, the People's Bank of China has since 1990 attempted to gradually phase in a similar system. But the effort has been thwarted by inconsistent responses to day-to-day policy pressures and by entrenched institutional inertia.

Commercial banks' liquidity management is an issue for banks themselves. However, to ensure prudence, Western country regulators impose minimum standards. For example, in Australia, banks have to observe the 6 per cent prime asset ratio, that is, at least 6 per cent of their assets must be in the form of prime assets defined by the Reserve Bank as highly liquid, and high quality assets such as cash, Treasury bonds and deposits with the Reserve Bank. The 6 per cent prime assets do not include the 1 per cent non-callable deposits with the Reserve Bank (RBA 1990). The People's Bank of China does not impose such restrictions. Commercial banks with liquidity difficulties often resort to short term loans from the People's Bank and, failing that, to abrupt recall of loans from borrowers. On several occasions, they even closed doors for some days until the liquidity crisis ended (Zhang and Zheng 1993a). Because the banks are owned by the government, this practice has not prompted runs on the banks and collapse of confidence.

The Ministry of Finance

The Ministry of Finance was once the most important macroeconomic manager of the country, controlling the budget, taxation, incomes policy and monetary policy. With economic decentralisation, the Ministry's power has been reduced, but it is still one of the most prominent authorities. It manages government finance, determines the issues and the secondary market trading of Treasury Bonds.

Since 1979, the government has issued Treasury Bonds each year. But until 1992, the government made purchase of these bonds compulsory for government organisations and public sector employees. Although the interest rates on Treasury Bonds were slightly higher than bank deposit rates, Treasury Bonds had very low liquidity and long maturity (five years). The compulsory sales approach has caused much resentment. As a result, Treasury Bonds were illegally used as a substitute for money or illegally traded at a significant discount of up to 60 per cent. Compulsory sales became increasingly difficult as public resistance mounted.

When the government was forced to open up the secondary market of Treasury Bonds in 1988, it feared a dramatic fall in Bonds price and the resultant humiliation of the government. To experiment, the government only opened a fraction of the Treasury Bonds to secondary market trading (those issued in 1985 and 1986) and also maintained price control.

A Treasury Bond issued on 1 July 1985 (face value of 100 yuan and a simple annual interest rate at 10 per cent) should have an intrinsic value (that is, principal plus interest accrued in the three years) of about 130 yuan on 1 July 1988. But the bad reputation of the Treasury Bonds and the ignorance and irrationality of the public have pushed the 'black market' price down to 70–80 yuan. When the government decided to partially open the Treasury Bonds market, it set the trading price at 110 yuan (lower than the intrinsic value but higher than the black market price). This has created more sales than purchases. The low bond price has meant the *effective* rate of return on Treasury Bonds was as high as 30 per cent (while the bank deposit rate was only 8 per cent and bank lending rate around 12 per cent). This has enabled many securities companies to hold risk-free securities to obtain high rates of return. Many wealthy and/or well-connected and well-informed individuals have made excessive profits from buying and holding Treasury Bonds until maturity (redemption). Some have used bank loans to increase the size of their holding.

It took almost two years for the market to correct the irrational trading in Treasury Bonds and bring down the effective interest rates on Treasury Bonds to bank lending rates. Now compulsory sale of Treasury Bonds has been replaced by voluntary underwriting by securities companies.

The Ministry of Finance is also in charge of accounting standards for all government and private organisations, although other ministries can adapt the standards to suit the specific circumstances of the industry they control. The new accounting standards being phased in from 1 July 1993 will converge to Western counterparts. But this transition will take decades to complete.

Auditing was traditionally a function of the Ministry of Finance, the Communist Party organisations, the police and various ad hoc task forces. The government's effort in the past decade to institutionalise regular auditing has so far achieved little. The basic issues such as 'what should be audited?', 'how should audits be conducted?' and 'who should audit what?' still have not been resolved.

The Ministry of Finance controls accounting firms which can conduct auditing, while a separate Ministry of Auditing has been in existence for over ten years. Many other authorities also conduct auditing. While capital market auditing is mainly the jurisdiction of the People's Bank, other authorities can also intervene.

The Ministry of Finance was also the taxation policy maker and tax collector until June 1993 when the State Taxation Bureau became an independent bureau under the central government. Existing taxes on capital market operations include stamp duty, income tax and other levies applicable to non-financial institutions, such as construction levies and environment levies.

The State Planning Commission

The State Planning Commission is the chief coordinator of the central government's economic policies. Under the old central planning system, the Commission's control was so exhaustive that it even specified the total output of various products by government firms. In the past decade, the

Commission has dropped most of its control measures and has retained a policy coordinating role. At present, the Commission's responsibilities in the capital market are limited to the following areas:

1 Coordination with the Ministry of Finance to determine major parameters of the government budget (including Treasury Bonds); and
2 Coordination with the People's Bank to determine the maximum amount of securities issued each year.

The power of the Commission has diminished in the past decade along with economic decentralisation. To arrest this trend, the Commission set up in 1989 six large investment companies to manage the infrastructure investments financed by the central government budget. These six companies specialise in investments in energy, chemicals, electricity, transport, communication and non-ferrous metals, respectively. Their major source of finance is the government budget and bank loans. They also have the priority to obtain a quota to issue bonds if they choose to finance through the market.

Other ministries have sharply criticised these companies for inefficiency and argued that the companies should be abolished and their investment functions transferred to the Construction Bank which previously performed investment functions.

The State Commission for Economic Restructuring

The State Commission for Economic Restructuring was set up in the early 1980s to research and advise the central government on economic restructuring. It had a small staff. But its power and profile have quickly increased. Today it even drafts laws and issues administrative (or regulatory) circulars to government bodies and private organisations. Its role in the capital market lies with its responsibility to determine the policy on corporatisation of government-owned enterprises; select specific enterprises to corporatise; decide on the forms of corporatisation (float or sale); determine, jointly with the People's Bank, corporate securities issues and secondary market trading.

As a new organisation with simple internal structure, the Commission has attracted many ambitious, aggressive and dynamic staff. This feature has contributed to the Commission's profile and its success in power grabbing. This is more evident in an even newer organisation, the State Council Securities Commission.

The State Council Securities Supervisory Commission

The State Council Securities Supervisory Commission grew from a division of the State Commission for the Economic Restructuring which was involved with capital market research. It is now answerable to the State Council Securities Committee which is composed of senior politicians. The establishment of this Commission was influenced by the system in countries such as the USA and Australia, where a separate authority exists to supervise the securities market. More importantly, this Commission offers a unique vehicle to take over power from the People's Bank and other authorities and create many senior posts. The Commission was established in November 1992 and has a staff of under forty. Most staff are graduates from the Graduate School of the People's Bank with at least a Master's degree, and some have further overseas tertiary qualifications. They are young (aged 25–40), ambitious and are equipped with some years of work experience in other ministries and some knowledge of capital markets in foreign countries. The Commission's simple bureaucratic structure also offers the staff maximum flexibility to work effectively.

At present, the Commission has no capacity to conduct daily supervision of the capital market. Its main function is to monitor the capital market, conduct policy research and draft securities legislation. It has taken over some of the power from the People's Bank in supervising the two stock exchanges in Shanghai and Shenzhen. Any new stock exchange will have to obtain authorisation from the Commission.

If the trend continues, the Commission may eventually take over from the People's Bank most of the supervisory function of the securities market.

The provincial and regional governments

Provincial and regional governments have no formal power in regulation of the capital market. However, since they own and control a large proportion of government enterprises, and they also command considerable influence over the regional offices of the People's Bank, their role in the capital market should not be overlooked.

Their frequent intervention in the capital market takes the form of issuing circulars, statements and orders. They even pass legislation on capital market issues. In most cases, these circulars or legislation are either reiteration or interpretation of the rules put in place by the ministries of the central government. In some cases, they initiate new rules. Because the supervisory responsibilities among various regulators are ambiguous, there is ample scope for different interpretation and 'territorial' dispute among the different actors. The central government authorities do not usually challenge the validity of the provincial and regional governments' intervention unless the intervention seriously contradicts the existing rules. The central government authorities and even the State Council often have to accommodate the aggressiveness or ignorance of the provincial and regional governments.

The (undisputed) responsibility of these governments is the supervision and corporatisation of financial and non-financial institutions owned by them. But these governments' own debt issues have to be approved by the People's Bank and Ministry of Finance.

In summary, the regulatory structure of China's capital market is still at its formative stage and supervisory responsibilities are not clearly defined among various government authorities. Therefore, opportunistic behaviour and demarcation disputes among regulators are typical features of capital market development. This creates much uncertainty for the business sector as to what to comply with and what to expect next. Their action in the capital market is thus based on seeking short-term and quick returns. This situation is not conducive to the development of a clear regulatory framework for the capital market (e.g., capital market practice, ethics, standards, communication and clearing systems).

THE OPERATIONS OF THE CAPITAL MARKET

Bank loans market

The bank loans market is by far the most important part of China's capital market. It not only provides the business sector with working capital, but also long-term debt and even equity capital. China's business sector has a short history of capital accumulation, therefore, it relies heavily on bank finance. Typically, China's business sector has very high gearing ratios, and there is no regulation preventing banks from taking direct equity positions in non-financial business. In this respect, China's rules are similar to those of Japan and Germany and different from those of Australia and the USA.

To understand how the business sector accesses bank finance, it is necessary to examine how the banking industry operates.

Rationing credit to banks

China's credit rationing process is made up of two stages: funds flow from the central bank to financial institutions, and then from the financial institutions to the business sector. The first stage of credit rationing works as follows.

At the beginning of each year, the People's Bank will come up with projections of total credit of the banking and finance sector, net cash injection into circulation, total cash in circulation (M_0) and broad money (M_1 and M_2) as at the end of the year.[1] These projections are based on the projections by the State Planning Commission of economic growth, inflation and other macroeconomic parameters. The Planning Commission's projections are often significantly altered by senior politicians and then are used by the People's Bank as given.

The flaws with this are two-fold. First, due to the strong interrelationship between the monetary and macroeconomic variables, these variables should be projected simultaneously or projected through a general equilibrium model rather than being projected separately. Second, political manipulation of these variables make them more arbitrary and subjective.

Next, the Central Bank will 'fine-tune' its projections, particularly that of net cash injection into circulation, the most sensitive parameter.[2] The fine-tuning is based on experience, common sense and political consideration.

The third step is that the moderated target of credit aggregate will be allocated by the People's Bank to the four major banks and major non-bank financial institutions. This process of allocation is based on past experience and possible changes to the situation of various banks' clientele. For example, the Agriculture Bank bears more of the impact of changes in the agriculture sector, thus its share in the credit aggregate should be related to expected changes in the agriculture sector.

The People's Bank's allocation of credit aggregate is also based on the major banks' projection of their balance sheets as at the end of the year. Naturally, their projection will be considered overly expansionary by the People's Bank which has to go through intense negotiations with individual banks to reach a compromise.

Finally, the People's Bank will estimate various banks' own market capacity to generate funds to meet the growth of balance sheets. The estimated shortfall will be met by the People's Bank through a loan via the lender of last resort facility. (This facility comprises two types of loans which are the most important tools of conducting monetary policy, as shown below.)

Various banks have strong incentives to overestimate their clientele's financing requirement and underestimate their own capacity to raise funds in the market, because in doing so they can secure more loans from the People's Bank. This will not only make financing easier in the year, but also give the bank a larger market share. Thus, the final decision on the various banks' funding shares depends on this bargaining process.

The quota of the People's Bank direct loans determined through the above process is called 'long-term' loans. The banks can use them on an automatically revolving basis. Put differently, banks can legitimately use these funds permanently.

Once the quota is determined, the Central Bank will schedule its lending to the banks. But each bank will push hard to get the loans in full as soon as possible because the quota each bank obtains is the up limit of outstanding balance of the People's Bank direct loans as at the end of the year; and also the cost of using the People's Bank credit is significantly lower than the cost of finance in the retail or wholesale market.

In 1991, for example, the interest rate on People's Bank's direct loan was 7.2 per cent per annum, while the interest rate for retail deposits was 7.92

per cent and 8.28 per cent for 2-year and 3-year deposits. Further, banks were allowed to float the interest rates by 50 per cent (i.e. 3.96 percentage points on 2-year deposits). Banks did float by the maximum margin in fierce competition for funds. Also, retail deposits incur higher transaction costs than the lump sum loans from the People's Bank.

In the wholesale market, the ceiling the People's Bank imposed on interbank lending rates in 1991 was 9.072 per cent, but the actual rates were higher because there was shortage of funds and both borrowing and lending banks were willing to circumvent the ceiling. At the same time, the interest rates on certificates of deposits were controlled by the People's Bank at 8.5 per cent, 9.2 per cent and 10 per cent for 1-, 2- and 3-year deposits respectively (PBC 1992).

In addition to the 'long-term' loans, the People's Bank also extends 'short-term' loans to meet commercial banks' unexpected funding needs. The commercial banks, after exhausting their 'long-term' loan quota, will turn to the People's Bank for further loans; and the People's Bank is susceptible to their pressure. The establishment of the 'short-term' loan facility is a recognition of the central bank's weakness. Further, the existence of the facility has legitimised and encouraged the commercial banks to exploit the facility.

'Short-term' loans are designed to meet banks' temporary liquidity difficulties (the duration of these loans was to be ten to sixty days). But because there is no restriction on the amount of these loans, and more importantly, the People's Bank is unable to enforce repayment of the loans, this facility has become another form of permanent loans. Although the short-term loans carry 'penalty interest rates' (compared with the rates on the scheduled long-term loans), they are still too low. Furthermore, it is the *availability* not the *cost* of finance that matters.

Allocating credit to the business sector

As mentioned earlier, the second stage of the credit allocation system involves providing funds to the business sector. Officially, each organis-ation (business or non-profit) in China is allowed to deal with one bank. Until recently, this bank was assigned by the authorities (normally the People's Bank's regional offices and regional governments). In recent years, organisations have been allowed to change their banking relationships if they are not satisfied with their existing bank. The government hopes thereby to introduce competition and greater efficiency into the banking sector; and second, to reduce the business sector's reliance on the govern-ment for finance. Under the old system, the government was under constant pressure to meet the financing needs of the business sector. That system was becoming increasingly difficult to sustain.

Under the reformed system of credit allocation, except for government priority projects, the vast majority of businesses have no guaranteed finance. They have to compete for funds. The priority projects include large infrastructure investments initiated by the central (and perhaps provincial) government, such as airports and power stations; significant industrial greenfield projects (such as iron and steel plants and shipyards); and major expansion or technological upgrading of existing firms of 'strategic importance'. The number of this type of projects and the proportion of funds in the credit aggregate have been steadily declining in the past ten years.

China's business sector is composed of a dominant government sector and a burgeoning private sector. The government firms' credit demand is very interest inelastic because they are less constrained by the interest cost, profitability, and even their capacity to repay debt. The corporate reform has improved the situation but the fundamental flaws exist due in part to the government ownership and the difficulties in performance assessment.

The private sector's credit demand is also expanded by poor enforcement of loan repayment. Soft constraints on both the government enterprises and the private sector to repay loans, coupled with officially controlled interest rates have meant excessive credit demand. Even the rapid growth in credit aggregate is not enough to meet the demand. From 1985 to 1992, while the real growth rate of GNP was around 8–9 per cent on average, and the credit aggregate grew by 28 per cent per annum on a compounding basis, credit was still very difficult to obtain.

The government is of the view that higher (or market-determined) interest rates will not reduce the total demand for credit because the fundamental problem is property rights and legal enforcement of loan repayment. But establishing a new market order and morality takes time and the government's effort to achieve the goal is not without conflict with the entrenched communist ideology and philosophy.

A practical constraint faced by the government in lifting interest rate control is the rising cost of financing government budget deficits and financial viability of the government enterprises. The government aims to ration the limited financial resources efficiently while interest rate controls are maintained.

The government sets credit rationing policies and revises them in accordance with changing economic conditions. However, two factors are critical to the success of credit rationing. One is whether the exhaustive priority list is consistent with the efficient allocation of finance. The other is whether the government's rationing policy can be implemented in a steadfast manner.

For banks, their interest is best served by circumventing the government's instructions on lending priority. First, the financial returns on most priority projects are lower than others because of the absence of a 'user pays' system. Second, the government's interest rate control is in favour of priority projects, that is, the banks are not allowed to charge floated interest rates.

For non-priority projects, a common rationing device used by banks is to cut across the board the amount applied for by a fixed proportion, since the banks often do not have the resources, expertise and strong incentives to carefully assess all applications. When this approach is known by the business sector, they respond by deliberately overstating their credit requirements and leaving some room for arbitrary cuts. This simply increases the extent of credit rationing.

Some companies adopt a different strategy. They understate their loan requirement to get an easy approval. Once a project is off the ground the bank becomes the captive of the project. It is not that the bank is really concerned about the total loss of loans already made, but that the project managers will be able to use the started projects to mobilise the government departments they are answerable to and then force the bank to inject new loans.

A second way of rationing is 'first-come-first-served'. Bank managers may not be able to reject (or do not want to antagonise) any firm or government department. So this rationing device is to protect bank managers themselves. Getting a loan is easier in the early months of the year right after banks receive a fresh injection of direct loans from the central bank. Many poor quality projects get loans because they are early in the queue or have previously been rejected several times.

The securities market

Companies started issuing shares and bonds in the early 1980s. Today, this market still accounts for a marginal share of the total capital market.

China's regulation of the securities market is both primitive and restrictive. It is primitive because the regulation does not adequately address many fundamental issues such as sufficient and reliable disclosure of issuers' financial information and even the legal status of the issuers. It is restrictive because the government tightly controls the number of companies that can issue bonds and shares in any particular year; and it also controls the total amount of funds that can be raised through issues of bonds and shares.

Why are businesses keen to issue bonds and shares? First, they hope to have their credit demand met outside the banking system. In the existing situation, their demand is either rationed out or rationed down. When bank interest rates are controlled at far below the market rates, those companies that are allowed to issue shares and bonds have competitive advantages in financing. For them, again, the *availability* of capital is more important than the *cost* of capital.

Second, even if the existing business does not need added finance, corporate managers may have a strong desire to build a larger corporate empire. This will not only bring them prestige and power, but will also help them to solve some of the practical problems. For prestige, a larger organisation is more likely to be upgraded in political status or 'rank' which is associated with salaries, housing, cars and travel standards. Business managers also have to face problems such as creating employment for the children of their employees. For a larger business it will be easier to accommodate this internally. Moreover, a larger business may have more negotiating power with the government and other organisations in solving this problem.

Third, companies want to diversify their financing and not be controlled by banks. This motive may have its commercial merit, and may also result from managers' egoism.

Fourth, managers and their companies can gain publicity in the process of issuing shares and bonds. So far, direct finance is still a new phenomenon, most managers want to capture the limelight for themselves and perhaps for their companies even if there is no commercial justification for playing the securities market.

Fifth, there are direct financial benefits to the companies, employees and particularly managers. The current income tax for stock-owned firms is 33 per cent while the figure is 55 per cent for other firms. This will be partially translated into better pay and employment conditions for employees. Most companies have also managed to give substantial financial benefits to their employees and particularly their managers by rewarding them with free (or below market price) shares and bonds.

The government encourages direct finance but at the same time tightly controls the maximum securities issued each year and screens out most companies through tough eligibility tests. The criteria include: the industry the company belongs to; the company's financial performance in the past; its asset size; and its strategic importance to other companies (externalities). The rationale is to prevent the securities market from undermining the banking industry ('disintermediation') while banks still have to operate under stringent interest rate control. The government also sees the development of the securities market as a potential challenge to the existing macroeconomic control, such as monetary targets and inflation. It is also concerned about its inexperience to supervise a sophisticated securities market.

Legislation for the securities market, prepared by the State Council Securities Supervisory Commission, was passed in 1994. Until then, the market had been governed by several tentative regulatory documents issued by various government authorities.

CONCLUSION

Capital market development in China has exposed weaknesses in the government's regulatory structure: it lacks in strategic design and co-ordination between regulatory agencies. The overlaps and ambiguities in the definition of responsibilities between regulatory agencies stem from the government's inexperience and its complex bureaucratic structure. This creates uncertainty for market participants and retards infrastructure development for the market.

The Chinese government seems to encourage securities market development because of the perceived ineffectiveness of credit rationing in the bank loans market. This explains why tight control is maintained at the same time.

If the 1993 austerity programme in China can streamline the regulatory framework, and lift the prudential standards, then the potential for further development of the capital market will be realised.

Specifically, the overlap in the regulatory framework should be reduced to avoid prevalent opportunistic power grabbing and inconsistency. All banking activities should be supervised by the People's Bank; securities market and corporate sector by the Securities Supervisory Commission (with similar functions taken away from several other departments); accounting rules set by the Ministry of Finance; auditing done by independent accounting firms and the Ministry of Auditing. A restructured framework should resemble that in Australia, except that there are no counterparts to Australia's Insurance and Superannuation Commission and Australian Financial Institutions Commission.

NOTES

1 The People's Bank of China defines M_1 as the sum of M_0 and cheque account deposits and M_2 as the sum of M_1 and other deposits. See Zhang and Zheng (1993a)
2 The sensitivity of cash injection has a historical reason: it has been used as a monetary target since 1949 although its significance has fallen to some extent.

REFERENCES

Australian Financial Review, 1993. 'State Banks for China', 20 August.
Business Australian, 1993. 'World Bank report urges China to rein in economy', p. 19, 27 August.
Kaye, T., 1993. 'Our banks lose top rankings', *Australian Financial Review*, 22 June.
PBC (the People's Bank of China), 1993. *China Finance*, various issues. Beijing.
——, 1992a. *Almanac of China's banking and finance*, Beijing.
——, 1992b, 'Developing and assisting our securities market', *China Finance*, October, Beijing.
RBA (Reserve Bank of Australia), 1990, *Prudential Supervision of Banks*, Sydney.

Zhang, J.H. and Zheng, J.X. 1993a, 'Monetary targeting in China: its effectiveness and paternalism', in *Trade, investment and economic prospects in China's three economies*, Australian National University.

Zhang, J.H. and Zheng, J.X. 1993b, 'Foreign banks in China: challenges and opportunities', ARC Policy Paper, Murdoch University.

Chapter 6

Taiwan: a new regional centre in the making

J.J. Chu

Since 1989, when the banking law was revised in order to promote liberalisation and internationalisation of Taiwan's financial system, the focus of the government has been on turning Taipei into a regional financial centre. Several factors stimulated this ambition. Taiwan's continuously growing economic strength (by the end of 1992 Taiwan's foreign reserves had grown to US$82 billion and the per capita GNP was US$10,202) was one major factor. At a more psychological level, the newly emerged desire to forge an internationally acknowledged national identity, separated from the issue of its relationship to the Chinese mainland, also worked as a catalyst to strengthen this ambition. Moreover, the increasing coalescence of the global economic system into three regional groups (North America, West Europe and East Asia) has also reinforced this vision.

With an understanding of this ambition and the distinctive geopolitical location of Taiwan in the Asia-Pacific region, this chapter adopts a historical approach to illustrate the dynamism of post-1980 Taiwanese financial liberalisation. First, it attempts to give a brief description of Taiwan's financial structure. Then it illuminates the various factors in the 1980s which drove the government in Taiwan towards financial deregulation. The third section focuses on the key policies implemented by the government to accelerate the process of financial liberalisation and internationalisation. Last, the specific effect of the post-1980 financial deregulation, i.e., massive Taiwanese capital outflow and its domestic and external consequences, will be discussed.

TAIWAN'S PRE-1980s FINANCIAL SYSTEM

The foundation of the financial infrastructure of Taiwan was laid down in the 1940s and 1950s, and was expanded in the 1960s and 1970s. Several new financial institutions were established, including the Overseas Chinese Bank (OCB) in 1961, the City Bank of Taipei (CBT) in 1969 and the United World Chinese Commercial Bank (UWCCB) in 1975. Though the 1975 New

Bank Act had certainly made several innovative financial regulatory initiatives, by the time of the financial reforms of the late 1980s however, the Act appeared not only outdated but was found to also act as a straitjacket which allowed little room for private financial agencies to participate in the system. Since the 1989 financial reform was aimed at revamping the 1975 New Bank Act on privatisation and liberalisation, a better understanding of the pre-1980s financial structure may well enable one to appreciate the significance of the reforms in the last decade. In this context, this section serves two purposes. It provides a brief introduction to Taiwan's financial system up to the late-1980s and describes the activities prevailing in Taiwan's informal financial market.

The formal financial sector

The Ministry of Finance (MOF) and the Central Bank of China (CBC) are at the top of the financial system and responsible for regulation and supervision of the organised financial institutions. Before 1961, the Bank of Taiwan performed most of the functions in relation to central banking on behalf of the Central Bank of China. Those functions included the issuing of the New Taiwan currency, the exchange and remittance business with respect to exports and imports, and the acceptance of reserve deposits from other banks. When a New Bank Act was promulgated in 1975, the regulatory strength of the CBC was increased.

Before the 1989 banking laws reform, Taiwan's financial system was composed of government-run banks, cooperatives, and credit unions. Among them, four specialised banks had been well geared to Taiwan's economic development: the Chiao Tung Bank (for providing industrial credit), the Export–Import Bank of China (for providing export and import credit), the Farmers' Bank of China (for providing rural credit), and the Land Bank of Taiwan (for financing hire-purchase of properties). Furthermore, the medium and small business banks (for financing medium and small enterprises) had also played a part.

There were only four private banks in Taiwan: the International Commercial Bank of China (ICBC), the Overseas Chinese Bank (OCB), Shanghai Commercial and Savings Bank (SCSB) and United World Chinese Commercial Bank (UWCCB). The Overseas Chinese Bank was founded by overseas Chinese in March 1961. However, after it was stricken by a crisis in 1984 and government capital was injected to rescue it, the bank relinquished 18 per cent of its share capital to the government and lost its authority to appoint the general manager. The establishment of the United World Chinese Commercial Bank in 1975 came as a spinoff of a worldwide recession which brought overseas Chinese capital back to Taiwan.

Credit cooperatives were and still are principally regional institutions. The credit departments of Farmers' Associations and those of the Fishermen's

Associations provide the base for rural credit in Taiwan. The critical element that distinguished the credit departments of Farmers' and Fishermen's Associations from commercial bank credit departments lay in the less strict enforcement of collateral requirements demanded by Farmers' and Fishermen's Associations, so that the small borrowers had easier access to loans. The Farmers' Associations contributed especially to the success of agricultural reform in the 1950s.

Apart from the monetary financial institutions, three types of non-bank institutions are prevalent in Taiwan: the Postal Savings (PS) system, the investment and trust companies, and the insurance companies. The Postal Savings system has played the most active role in the formal financial system in collecting savings deposits. The Postal Savings system was established in 1930 on the mainland and resumed full operation in 1962 in Taiwan. The PS system has long been a major financial competitor to the domestic banks and the interest rates it offered have also been slightly higher than those offered by the banks. The PS system has been involved in both financial and non-financial activities. Apart from accepting savings deposits through its post offices, it also works as a government agency to issue retirement pension payments for military and public service personnel and teachers.[1]

There are eight investment and trust companies with thirty offices throughout Taiwan.[2] The earliest one, China Developmental Corporation, was established in 1959. Another four were established in 1971. They were Taiwan First Investment and Trust Company, China Investment and Trust Company, Overseas Trust Corporation, and China United Trust and Investment Corporation. In 1972, Taiwan Development and Trust Corporation, Cathay Investment and Trust Company, and Asia Trust and Investment Corporation, joined the camp.

In the insurance business, there are fourteen fire and marine insurance companies and eight life insurance companies.[3] In 1968, the Central Reinsurance Corporation was established and worked under the supervision of the Ministry of Finance to exercise two functions: the compilation of insurance statistics and the examination of the financial conditions, management and general operation of life and property insurance companies.

Banks and non-bank financial institutions have participated intimately in the development of Taiwan's financial markets, which include the money market and the capital market. Financial products in the money market include treasury bills, commercial paper, bankers' acceptances and negotiable certificates of deposits. Those in the capital market include stocks, government bonds, corporate bonds and bank debentures.

Three bill finance companies were established after the promulgation of the Regulations Governing the Dealers of Short-term Negotiable Instruments in 1975. They are Chung Hsing Bill Finance Company, established by the Bank of Taiwan in 1976, International Bill Finance Company, established by the International Commercial Bank of China in 1977, and Chung Hua Bill Finance Company, established by the Bank of Communication in 1978. The Stock Exchange of Taiwan was incorporated in 1961 and started operations in 1962, a significant step forward towards the formation of a formal capital market.

The stipulation of the New Bank Act in 1975 was alleged to be a watershed in the history of Taiwan's financial system because it transformed the Chiao Tung Bank into a development bank, which assisted the development of the money market and new financial instruments. Furthermore, the official money market was established in 1976 under a set of restrictive banking regulations, which not only prohibited the minimum lending interest rate from exceeding the maximum deposit rate, but also overstretched the role of the Central Bank of China. For instance, the CBC was given the decisive power to prescribe the maximum rates for different kinds of deposits and to enforce the range of interest rates on different kinds of loans proposed by the Banks' Association. These restrictions considerably hampered the capacity of the financial system to operate in accordance with market forces.

The informal financial sector

It has been pointed out by several scholars (Lee, 1990; Semkow, 1992; Yang, 1993) that Taiwan's financial system is a dual system, in which a formal, organised, regulated, financial system co-exists with an informal, unorganised and unregulated financial system. The formal system mainly served the interests of the state-run industries and the big private enterprises, while a considerable number of small to medium sized businesses could not help but rely on the informal market for funds. In 1986, 30 per cent of domestic funds borrowed by business enterprises, public and private, came from the informal money market. The share from banks and financial institutions was about 47 per cent. Funds raised directly in the money market came to 7 per cent, and from the capital market 14 per cent (Lee, 1990). Lee showed that public enterprises borrowed less from the informal money market than private enterprises, because the former, being government-owned, had the strong support of government banks. A longitudinal record concerning the disparity of borrowing from the private sector by government-run and private enterprises is provided in Tables 6.1 and 6.2.

The informal financial system in Taiwan has long played an indispensable role in meeting the needs of the private industrial sector for funds. Little research has looked into the actual size of the underground financial economy of Taiwan, except for some estimation of the underground economy, which is closely associated with the informal money market, being around 14 per cent of Taiwan's GNP (Lee, 1990, p.37).

The presence of a robust informal sector can be explained by several factors. First, most of the big banks have been government-owned, and are therefore inclined to have a conservative attitude in dealing with loan applications. Government banks have to remit their profits to the Treasury, a structural characteristic that has prevented them from accumulating surpluses for future business plans like private banks usually do. In addition, small enterprises normally did not have audited accounts. They were unable to offer adequate information or collateral to the banks, hurting their borrowing effectiveness and thus leaving them with few options but to seek loans at higher interest rates from the informal money market.

Taiwan has about 70,000 exporting and importing firms, large and small, competing in the product market. Moreover, in an attempt to evade taxes and other government regulations, a considerable number of small trading and manufacturing firms did not register at all with the government. Consequently, unregistered firms, small firms and those unable to obtain credit from banks, could only turn to the informal money market for finance.

The informal sector is made up of underground investment houses and informal credit suppliers. Wang (1991) estimated that there were more than two hundred underground investment houses, of which about 30–40 firms controlled over NT$100 billion (US$3.9 billion) of capital. Since these underground investment houses were able to offer interest rates as high as 7–8 per cent *a month*, they usually attracted a substantial number of investors (ibid. p. 71).

As small/medium-sized enterprises are a main pillar of Taiwan's economy, the measures used most frequently by them to acquire sufficient production and investment finance are worth investigation. Apart from the underground investment houses, a large share of Taiwan's informal financial capital market has consisted of relatives and friends of the private money lenders. A significant segment of the market involves informal credit suppliers which cater for the borrowing of, and accept deposits from, a circle of acquaintances and relations as well as from firms that are not authorised to handle public funds. In the corporate sector, several practices have also been dissociating savings from the formal financial market, in the form of companies accepting deposits from employees, thus reducing the companies' need to borrow from banks. Interest rates for these de facto unsecured loans have understandably been higher than those for loans in the formal market, consequently attracting employees towards lending to their own companies.

Semkow (1992) pointed out that by employing 'matching' and 'bucketing', two fraudulent practices, the underground financial firms could extract easy profits from local investors. Matching involves an underground firm doing just that, matching buy and sell orders in Taiwan on the basis of the prices derived from Reuters and Telerate, but not actually placing the orders on the foreign exchanges. In this way, the broker would pocket the forex clearing fee. With bucketing, a firm would withhold investors' orders and execute them at the wrong time.

Like in many other Asian countries, one of the most efficient and common methods for individuals to raise funds in Taiwan has been to run a so-called rotating credit association, which has inevitably become a key institution in the informal money market. Groups involved in this type of fund-raising are also known as the mutual aid associations or the bidding

Table 6.1 Sources of borrowings of government-run enterprises (in NT$ million)

Year	Formal financial institutions		Borrowing from private sector						Total
	NT$	%	Non-profit organisations		Cross-borrowings between enterprises		Subtotal		
			NT$	%	NT$	%	NT$	%	
1964	5,592	99.45	–	0.00	31	0.55	31	0.55	5,623
1965	5,717	99.17	–	0.00	48	0.83	48	0.83	5,765
1966	6,215	99.27	–	0.00	46	0.73	46	0.73	6,261
1967	7,300	99.25	–	0.00	55	0.75	55	0.75	7,355
1968	7,899	94.83	–	0.00	431	5.17	431	5.17	8,330
1969	9,828	94.89	–	0.00	529	5.11	529	5.11	10,357
1970	12,261	98.24	–	0.00	220	1.76	220	1.76	12,481
1971	16,263	98.31	–	0.00	280	1.69	280	1.69	16,543
1972	18,354	98.82	–	0.00	219	1.18	219	1.18	18,573
1973	22,719	98.47	–	0.00	353	1.53	353	1.53	23,072
1974	40,287	99.85	–	0.00	62	0.15	62	0.15	40,349
1975	58,415	99.87	–	0.00	76	0.13	76	0.13	58,491
1976	68,108	99.80	–	0.00	136	0.20	136	0.20	68,244
1977	79,965	99.82	–	0.00	141	0.18	141	0.18	80,106
1978	89,917	99.87	–	0.00	121	0.13	121	0.13	90,038
1979	119,195	99.84	–	0.00	190	0.16	190	0.16	119,385
1980	174,769	97.85	–	1.12	1,829	1.02	3,838	2.15	178,607
1981	210,581	96.81	–	2.91	607	0.28	6,939	3.19	217,520
1982	247,236	95.25	–	4.36	1,024	0.39	12,341	4.75	259,577
1983	249,118	95.53	–	3.69	2,036	0.78	11,651	4.47	260,769
1984	233,432	96.20	–	2.29	3,659	1.51	9,224	3.80	242,656
1985	217,103	96.47	–	2.02	3,410	1.52	7,953	3.53	225,056
1986	214,126	96.93	–	1.66	3,106	1.41	6,784	3.07	220,910
Average	–	98.03	–	0.79	–	1.18	–	1.97	–

Source: The Central Bank of China, *Financial Statistics Monthly*, Taiwan District, ROC

clubs. A rotating credit association is usually initiated by those who have an urgent need for capital, so the organiser or initiator tends to be the leader of the association. The size of the association depends on the number of members the organiser can recruit. A rotating credit association disbands when each member gains his or her bid. The normal duration of a bidding club is the product of the number of members multiplied by the time interval between the bids. In general, a bidding club with more members in need of finance will yield better returns for those who can wait until the end. On the other hand, one with more passive bidders will offer a lower interest rate, but which is still generally higher than that offered by the banks. Bidding clubs' interest rates range from 15 to 50 per cent per annum. To what extent the 1980s financial liberalisation will undermine the vitality of these bidding clubs remains to be seen.

The positive role of the informal market lies in its capacity to supplement the formal financial market. However, as functional as this informal market has been in facilitating Taiwan's economic development, its continued existence would necessarily obstruct the maturing of the formal financial system, especially weakening the latter's intermediary function. By providing higher interest rates to lenders or depositors, the informal market draws money away from the formal market, eroding the effectiveness of the monetary authorities in their conduct of macroeconomic policy. The other side of high interest rates is the perceived high risks associated with small and medium size businesses. Allowing this situation to remain would perpetuate distortions in the capital market, where large state-owned businesses are subsidised at the expense of small/medium businesses. Those who benefit from a dichotomous capital market include private lenders to underground investment houses, as they collect high deposit returns from partially perceived high risk ventures. Besides the regressive income redistribution effect, such distortions constrain the potential development of the small/medium business sector by siphoning non-economic profits to better-off households (who can afford more savings) and thus to less productive and more speculative activities such as residential property accumulation.

CATALYSTS FOR FINANCIAL DEREGULATION IN THE 1980s

The critical factors in the late 1980s that prompted the government to deregulate the financial system were excessive hot money circulation, rampant speculative activities and a deteriorating investment environment. Two factors, with fortuitous timing, jointly contributed to the unexpected occurrence of large money surpluses in the 1980s. One was the depreciation of the New Taiwan Dollar in the early 1980s, which coincided with the start of the booming consumption decade in the West, the destination for most of Taiwan's exports; and the other was the rapid appreciation of

Table 6.2 Sources of borrowings of private enterprises (in NT$ million)

Year	Formal financial institutions		Borrowing from private sector						Total
			Non-profit organisations		Cross-borrowings between enterprises		Subtotal		
	Amount	%	Amount	%	Amount	%	Amount	%	
1964	8,116	51.89	7,175	45.88	349	2.23	7,524	48.11	15,640
1965	11,223	55.84	8,515	42.37	359	1.79	8,874	44.16	20,097
1966	14,674	54.34	11,962	44.30	369	1.37	12,331	45.66	27,005
1967	18,187	57.10	13,045	40.96	620	1.95	13,665	42.90	31,852
1968	29,122	65.01	12,776	28.52	2,895	6.49	15,671	34.99	44,793
1969	37,762	66.39	15,957	28.06	3,157	5.55	19,114	33.61	56,876
1970	36,625	62.42	18,587	31.68	3,460	5.90	22,047	37.58	58,672
1971	47,155	65.89	20,883	29.18	3,531	4.93	24,414	34.11	71,672
1972	76,784	68.31	30,952	27.54	4,671	4.16	35,623	31.69	112,407
1973	119,013	78.28	27,077	17.81	5,944	3.91	33,021	21.72	152,034
1974	135,024	69.91	54,998	28.47	3,128	1.62	58,126	30.09	193,150
1975	159,628	72.47	56,772	25.78	3,858	1.75	60,630	27.53	220,258
1976	184,128	67.68	80,986	29.77	6,928	2.55	87,914	32.32	272,042
1977	204,821	67.66	89,049	29.42	8,838	2.92	97,887	32.34	302,708
1978	242,781	63.13	133,158	34.63	8,625	2.24	141,783	36.87	384,564
1979	302,957	61.38	179,509	36.37	11,132	2.26	190,641	38.62	493,598
1980	379,492	63.77	198,875	33.42	16,761	2.82	215,636	36.23	595,128
1981	452,134	58.47	302,457	39.12	18,636	2.41	321,093	41.53	773,227
1982	473,970	60.47	289,810	36.98	19,973	2.55	309,783	39.53	783,753
1983	567,650	64.02	294,356	33.20	24,646	2.78	319,002	35.98	886,652
1984	645,811	65.76	303,917	30.95	32,303	3.29	336,220	34.24	982,031
1985	669,707	62.34	355,321	33.07	49,304	4.59	404,626	37.66	1,074,332
1986	775,568	55.23	585,436	41.69	43,338	3.09	628,774	44.77	1,404,342
Average	–	63.38	–	33.44	–	3.18	–	36.62	–

Source: The Central Bank of China, *Financial Statistics Monthly*, Taiwan District, ROC

the New Taiwan dollar since the mid-1980s, which helped raise Taiwan's nominal external surpluses (i.e., foreign reserves) in US$ terms. This timing explains much of Taiwan's burgeoning trade surplus with the United States, which has accounted for the bulk of Taiwan's external surpluses.

The presence of massive money surpluses

Between 1981 and 1986, a large export surplus with the United States was generated, exacerbated by an initial undervaluation of the NT dollar. In 1978, the NT dollar was revalued to the exchange rate of NT$36: US$1, but then underwent a steady depreciation to NT$38:US$1 in 1981 and NT$40:US$1 in 1982. In the following three years, the NT dollar stayed low, reaching a nadir of NT$40.40:US$1 in the third quarter of 1985. Coinciding with US domestic economic policy at the time that encouraged consumer spending and household/corporate borrowing activities – as mentioned in Chapter 2 of this volume – the NT$ depreciation led to a remarkable growth in Taiwan's annual trade surplus, from US$1,412 million in 1981 to US$10,621 million in 1985.

The impact of the subsequent appreciation of the NT$ was to be overwhelming. The demand for the revaluation of the NT$ came at the end of 1985. In September 1985, joint intervention by the G-7 countries (the United States, Japan, the United Kingdom, West Germany, France, Italy and Canada) in the international foreign exchange market forced a depreciation of the US$ against other currencies. As a result, in the two years from 1985 to 1987, the NT$:US$ exchange rate rose from 39.82:1 to 28.5:1. By the end of 1991, the NT$ reached 25.75:1, a rise of 5.3 per cent in that year and 38 per cent since the end of 1986.

Table 6.3 Some economic indicators: 1980–92

Year	Foreign reserves (US$ million)	NT$-US$ exchange rates	Economic growth rate, %	Per capita GNP (US$)
1980	2,205	36.01	7.1	2,344
1981	7,235	37.84	5.8	2,669
1982	8,532	39.91	4.1	2,653
1983	11,859	40.27	8.7	2,823
1984	15,664	39.47	11.6	3,167
1985	22,556	39.85	5.6	3,297
1986	46,310	35.50	12.6	3,993
1987	76,748	28.55	11.9	5,275
1988	73,897	28.17	7.8	6,333
1989	73,224	26.17	7.3	7,512
1990	72,441	27.11	5.0	7,954
1991	82,405	25.75	7.2	8,788
1992	82,306	25.40	6.0	10,202

Source: Industry of Free China LXXXI(2), Council for Economic Planning and Development, Executive Yuan, ROC, 1994

The key factor in the rapid appreciation of the NT dollar was the consistent trade surpluses with the United States. Assisted by the trade preferences offered by the US, Taiwan started to enjoy trade surpluses from the beginning of the 1970s. The country had been able to rapidly accumulate large amounts of foreign reserves. By 1985, its trade surpluses with the US had reached US$10 billion, more than twice the value of its imports from that country. Since Taiwan's exports enjoyed US$3.2 billion worth of duty-free access to US markets, Taiwan decided to make concessions to US requests for an appreciation of the NT$, as described above. Surprisingly, Taiwan's trade surplus did not suffer as a result. On the contrary, in 1987, the surplus rose to US$18.2 billion, or 18.9 per cent of GNP, despite a 24.6 per cent appreciation of the NT$ against the US$.

This phenomenon of dual increase in the domestic currency and external surplus has been explained in a number of studies, especially in relation to Japan's own established creditor status in the 1980s as a world manufacturing exporter (again, see Chapter 2 for a summary). For Taiwan, the same dynamics appear to have been at work at the time. The disadvantage generated by the increased prices of Taiwanese products was partly offset by an increase in the purchasing power of the NT$. Moreover, Taiwan's competitors such as Japan, Germany and South Korea encountered a similar currency appreciation, so that Taiwan's exports to the US, Japan, the European Economic Community and other overseas markets were not the only ones to suffer from a price squeeze. Third, the increased productivity of Taiwan's manufacturing sector (no doubt brought about to a large extent by the pressure of currency appreciation) also mitigated the loss of nominal price competitiveness caused by the appreciation of the NT$. Fourth, the desire of export-oriented factories to maintain their market shares led them to accept lower profit margins. And last, the futures exchange contracts offered by the Central Bank of China possibly alleviated the pressure of the rising NT$ to many firms.

Rampant speculative activities

The rapid appreciation of the NT dollar resulted in an abrupt monetary expansion. The rise in the NT$ was not sufficient to counter the capital inflow, at least in the early stage of such appreciation since Taiwan had to experience the so-called 'inverse J-curve'. Excess capital supply gave rise to rampant speculative activities, two of which prevailed in Taiwan in the 1980s: the rural lottery mania and the urban asset speculative binges.

On the one hand, most people in rural areas were obsessed with lotteries. It was estimated that during 1986 and 1987, as much as NT$30 billion, or roughly 20 per cent of the currency in active circulation, was devoted to the Da-Jia-Le lottery (Hsieh, 1993, p.28). On the other hand, the urban middle classes (including house-spouses and university students)

Table 6.4 Foreign trade: 1986–92

Year	Imports	Exports		Balance
		Total	% to the US	
1986	24,181.5	39,861.5	47.73	15,680.0
1987	34,983.4	53,678.7	44.20	18,695.4
1988	49,672.8	60,667.4	38.69	10,994.6
1989	52,265.3	66.304.0	36.23	14,038.6
1990	54,716.0	67,214.4	32.34	12,498.4
1991	62,860.5	76,178.3	29.29	13,317.8
1992	71,976.6	81,470.3	28.93	9,493.7

Source: Industry of Free China LXXXI(2), Council for Economic Planning and Development, Executive Yuan, ROC, 1994

plunged into short-term speculation on the stock market. Official statistics (from the Securities and Exchange Commission and the Ministry of Finance, 1989) indicate that there were about 2.5 million registered accounts at Taiwan's brokerage houses, which means that one in every ten local citizens was involved in stock investment. In 1988, the excessive indulgence in stock market activities reached such a frenzy that a group of small stock investors launched a movement to protest against the inability of the government to stabilise the market.

The pursuit of short-term benefits and over-ascribing of investors to speculative activities underpinned the fragility and volatility of Taiwan's

Table 6.5 Taiwan Stock Exchange trading volumes and values

	1985	1986	1987	1988	1989	1990	1991
Total volume (million of shares)	14,533	39,041	76,857	101,350	220,558	232,307	175,941
Daily average volume (millions of shares)	50	137	267	350	768	817	615
Volume turnover ratio	0.68	1.62	2.68	2.95	5.24	5.06	3.22
Total value (billion NT$)	195	676	2,669	7,868	25,408	19,031	9,683
Daily average value (billion NT$)	0.68	2.37	9.27	27.22	88.53	67.01	33.86

Source: *Fact Book 1992*, Taiwan Stock Exchange Corporation

equity market. The best illustration of these characteristics was the fourteen-fold rise in the weighted index of the Taiwan Stock Exchange between 1986 and 1990, from a low of 880 to a peak of 12,495 in February, and the subsequent dramatic fall of over 80 per cent from that peak to a low of 2,560.47 in October 1990. Even more unnerving was the collapse within the space of just over one month (September to November 1990) of the Taiwan Stock Exchange transaction volumes, which plunged from US$1.75 billion to US$36.5 million. Nearly 54 per cent of Taipei investors were reported to have suffered losses in that collapse.

Compounding the non-productive bias discussed earlier in relation to the informal financial market, lottery and stock speculation also enticed workers away from committing themselves to productive investment in manufacturing.

The deterioration of the domestic investment environment

It is necessary, in order to view Taiwan's financial system and market change in its totality, to digress a little from the discussions centring on the markets themselves and to survey the socio–political circumstances which had assisted in bringing about that change. Among the central issues had been the weakening enthusiasm for domestic investments.

In comparison with gross national savings, the share of investments in

Table 6.6 Total market capitalisation and trading volume of listed companies in Taiwan Stock Exchange

Year	Number of listed companies	Number of listed securities	Total market value of listed stock (billion NT$)	Capitalisation/ GNP turnover %	Total trading volume of listed stock (billion NT$)	Trading volume/GNP turnover %
1981	107	114	201.3	11.3	209.2	11.8
1982	113	117	203.1	10.7	133.9	7.0
1983	119	123	306.0	14.6	363.8	17.3
1984	123	127	390.3	16.7	324.5	13.8
1985	127	130	415.7	16.8	195.2	7.9
1986	130	133	548.4	19.2	675.7	23.7
1987	141	145	1,386.1	43.0	2,668.6	82.8
1988	163	171	3,383.3	96.7	7,868.0	225.0
1989	181	190	6,174.2	159.1	25,408.0	655.0
1990	199	213	2,681.9	63.2	19,031.3	448.5
1991	221	234	3,184.0	66.3	9,682.7	202.0

Source: *Fact Book 1992*, Taiwan Stock Exchange Corporation

GNP in the 1980s had evidently been in decline. While the share of gross domestic savings in GNP maintained a steady growth from 15 per cent in 1951–60 to 33 per cent in 1981–90, that of investments dropped to 22 per cent in 1981–90 from its 1971–80 peak of 30 per cent.

The deterioration of the domestic investment environment, namely the diminishing willingness to invest domestically, came from two fronts. On the political front, the momentum gathered since the lifting of martial law in 1987 by both independent unionists (to safeguard the rights and interests of the working class as listed in the Labour Standard Law – LSL)[4] and environmentalists (to protect a better quality of life) has squeezed the interests of many small/medium sized firms, which now found it less enticing to conduct domestic investment.

Before 1986, the political system that promoted Taiwan's accelerated economic development was a variant of the one-party system governed by the ruling Nationalist Party, the Kuomintang (KMT). However, the formation of the opposition Democratic Progressive Party (DPP) in 1986 and the lifting of martial law in 1987 brought a complete change to that picture. The new environment encouraged many marginal and subordinate groups to voice their previously ignored interests. Among the most influential of these groups have been the environmentalists and the independent union activists.

Environmental pollution started to aggravate in Taiwan in the 1970s. Nevertheless, not until the late 1980s did local victims organise anti-pollution protests and demonstrations. In many cases, local protesters even confronted, with violence, the factories which caused pollution. In early 1988, local residents near the newly designated plant site organised an Anti-Fourth Nuclear Plant Committee, with support from environmental activists, to wage a hunger strike for their cause in front of the Taipower headquarters. The ramification of this rising environmental awareness has been enterprises' putting off their plans to invest in new plants.

Table 6.7 Savings and investment: 1951–90

Year	Gross savings as % of GNP	Gross investment as % of GNP	Excess savings as % of GNP
1951–60	14.91	16.08	−1.17
1961–70	21.07	21.87	−0.80
1971–80	31.85	30.48	1.38
1981–90	33.21	22.35	10.80

Source: Table 1, 'Taiwan's Trade and the Financial System', Ya-hwei Yang. Paper presented at the conference on Taiwan's Economic Success: Trade, Finance and Foreign Exchange, p. 2, Monash University, Australia, 1993

Parallel with this socio–political change was the transformation of Taiwan's economic and employment structures in the late 1980s. In the three years to 1989, employment in the industrial sector and service sector increased by 58,000 and 337,000 workers respectively. Significantly, in 1988, total service sector employment overtook that in the industrial sector for the first time. Between 1987 and 1989, a net 236,000 people entered the labour market. The breakdown for this figure was: 161,000 leaving the agricultural sector, 60,000 entering the industrial sector and 337,000 joining the service sector. The average annual growth rate of employment in the industrial sector during this period was about 0.6 per cent, with a considerable portion of that increased labour force made up of foreign guest workers, especially from Southeast Asia.

Labour shortages in the manufacturing and construction sectors had been material in causing soaring labour costs, the most serious obstacle to date to the maintenance of Taiwan's labour-intensive export development. Some figures for labour shortages, provided by the Statistics Department in the Executive Yuan (January 1989) indicated a vacancy of 265,000 jobs in the industrial sector and 56,000 jobs in the service sector. It was said that the real situation might be much more devastating in the medium and small enterprises, the backbone of Taiwan's economy. From mid-1986 onwards, the number of low-skilled workers from Southeast Asia coming into Taiwan's construction and manufacturing sectors was officially put at around 10,000 to 30,000, although media estimates ran as high as 100,000 to 300,000. Most guest workers were scattered from Taipei to Kaohsiung in western Taiwan. Their wages were about two-thirds of local workers' and they endured long working hours, frequently more than ten hours a day. Their employment contracts were usually fixed-term and not protected by the minimum provisions of the Labour Standard Law.

Facing the impact of the LSL, environmentalism, labour shortages and guest workers, the relatively protracted labour peace was breaking down in the late 1980s. Nineteen eighty-eight and 1989 were saturated with strikes and street protests, among the more notorious being those by the Hsinchu factory workers of the Far Eastern Textile company, the County and City bus drivers in Taoyuan, Kaohsiung, Ilan and Miaoli, and by the railway workers (Chu, 1993a). Most of the key disputes had something to do with the LSL. Since the LSL requires employers to pay retirement pensions to their workers, whether the retirement is voluntary or compulsory, it struck at the heart of Taiwan's informal and flexible entrepreneurial culture based on which the SMEs (and their labour-intensive advantage to create Taiwan's export-led economic miracle) had been built. Since the majority of firms in Taiwan had never practised any pension or severance programmes and had long benefited from ignoring such costs, LSL enforcement was apparently depriving them of most of their profit margins and causing them to raise prices, losing their international competitiveness. As workers took strike action for their new rights, employers gradually closed down their operations and moved them offshore, strengthening the late 1980s' capital outflow trend.

CONSTRUCTING A FINANCIAL FREEWAY: 1980s LIBERALISATION AND BEYOND

In concomitant response to financial and socio–political pressures arising throughout the 1980s, the Taiwanese government had come to realise that no less than a complete transformation of the financial infrastructure was required. Developments in the labour market had begun to shift local manufacturing businesses, already burdened by the cost of capital available in the informal financial market, offshore. The emergence of the pension funds added a new dimension to the capital market. The rise of a 'new middle class', which was not only concerned with economic security but also 'life choices', put enormous pressure on the financial status quo. Not being content with just jobs, citizens were now demanding diversity of institutions and products. In this regard, the fortunate ballooning of Taiwan's foreign surpluses, which led to a booming service sector to offset the relative decline in the domestic manufacturing workforce, played a vital role in enforcing financial reform and in providing the means to do so in Taiwan.

Deregulation of the financial sector became a predominant issue in the 1980s. The policy was implemented to serve at least three basic objectives. First, it was directed at increasing the efficiency of the established financial system. Second, it was formulated to induce the flow of funds away from the informal speculative market to the formal banking system. Third, a more ambitious aim was to erect a solid financial infrastructure, through internationalisation of the financial markets, that would allow Taiwan to replace Hong Kong, if opportunities emerged, as the regional financial centre after Hong Kong reverts to China in 1997.

The call for the liberalisation of the financial system culminated in the 1989 Banking Law. The Law lifted the ban on the establishment of new banks, provided a legal basis for the privatisation of existing government-run banks, and removed the limits on lending and deposit interest rates.

Deregulation of Taiwan's financial institutions

Bank privatisation was one of the major reforms in Taiwan's financial history. Deregulation of private banks was instituted in the 1989 Banking Law. Although private banking did not gain full legitimacy until then, four private banks did exist before then: three of them (the Overseas Chinese Commercial Bank, the Shanghai Commercial and Savings Bank and the United World Chinese Commercial Bank) were owned by overseas Chinese, and one (the International Commercial Bank of China) was a private recast from the public Bank of China for political reasons in 1971. After private banking was legalised, the three major commercial banks (the First Commercial Bank, the Chang Hwa Commercial Bank and Hua Nan Commercial Bank) attempted to sell their share of government-owned stock to the public in 1990. With the domestic stock market in recession at the time, however, the proposal to sell shares was consequently delayed.

Measures for the establishment of new private banks were implemented and a list of approved applications were announced in 1991. By June 1993, sixteen new private banks had been licensed, intensifying interbank competition (Table 6.8). At the same time, the details of the first-stage partial privatisation of three government-run banks were being formulated. These two developments, together with the lifting of restrictions on interest rates, were expected to enhance competitiveness in the banking industry and make it a great deal more responsive to the needs of individuals and businesses, large and small, alike. It was also expected that a broad range of new financial products would be introduced as a result of financial deregulation, with the aim of drawing informal market activities to the formal sector.

Table 6.8 Sixteen newly-licensed private banks in Taiwan

		NT$ billion			
Rank	Bank	Deposits	Loans	Income before tax	Loans as % deposits
1	Chinese Bank	29.4	25.2	0.23	85
2	Cosmos Bank	27.0	25.9	0.19	84
3	Fu Bon Bank	26.9	23.3	0.25	86
4	Asia Pacific Bank	26.6	24.6	0.34	92
5	Chung Shing Bank	26.3	20.6	0.31	78
6	E Sun Bank	25.8	24.3	0.22	94
7	Bank Sino Pac	25.5	22.6	0.22	88
8	Tai Shin Bank	25.4	24.9	0.21	96
9	Pan Asian Bank	24.9	27.5	0.34	110
10	Our Bank	24.6	24.0	0.24	97
11	Union Bank	24.1	23.5	0.21	97
12	Grand Bank	23.3	24.8	0.19	106
13	Bao Dao Bank	21.9	19.2	0.08	87
14	Dahan Bank	21.0	24.0	0.22	114
15	Far Eastern Bank	17.5	19.0	0.26	108
16	En Tie Bank	7.6	5.8	0.20	76
Average		23.9	22.4	0.23	94

Source: Economic Situations and Leading Indicators on Taiwan, ROC, United World Chinese Commercial Bank, 25 July 1993

In 1988, the government lifted restrictions on domestic banks establishing overseas branches, and many of them wasted little time in doing so. By June 1993, thirteen domestic banks – United World Chinese Commercial Bank (UWCCB), the Export–Import Bank of China (EIBC), the International Commercial Bank of China (ICBC), the Chiao Tung Bank (CTB), the Bank of Taiwan (BT), First Commercial Bank (FCB), Hua Nan Commercial Bank (HNCB), Chang Hwa Commercial Bank (CHCB), Farmers' Bank of China (FBC), the Taipei Bank (TB), the Medium Business Bank of Taiwan (MBBT), China Trust Bank (CTB) and United Taiwan Bank (UTB) – had established a total of 63 overseas agencies. Among the 63 overseas branches/representatives/subsidiaries, 22 were in North America (21 in the USA, 1 in Canada), 19 in Europe, 9 in East Asia (5 in Japan, 4 in Hong Kong), 6 in Southeast Asia (2 in Indonesia, 2 in Singapore, 1 in the Philippines, 1 in Thailand, and 1 in Malaysia), 1 in South Africa, 2 in the Middle East (1 in Saudi Arabia and 1 in Bahrain), 3 in South America (1 in Mexico, 2 in Panama), and 1 in Australia.

In addition, the 1989 Banking Law also authorised foreign banks to undertake financial services which used to be restricted to the domestic banks. By June 1993, a total of 53 foreign bank branches and 31 representative offices had conducted business transactions in Taipei. Of all the foreign bank branches, 2 were Hong Kong-based, 18 American, 6 Canadian,

Table 6.9 Distribution of overseas branches of Taiwan's domestic banks

Bank/ Area	North America	Europe	East Asia	Southeast Asia	Middle East	Africa	South America	Australia	Total
UWCCB	1	0	0	0	0	0	0	0	1
EIBA	0	1	0	1	0	0	1	0	3
ICBC	6	3	2	2	2	0	2	1	18
CTB	2	1	0	1	0	0	0	0	4
BT	2	4	1	0	0	1	0	0	8
FCB	3	2	2	1	0	0	0	0	8
HNCB	2	2	2	0	0	0	0	0	6
CHCB	2	3	2	0	0	0	0	0	7
FBC	1	0	0	0	0	0	0	0	1
TB	2	0	0	0	0	0	0	0	2
MBBT	0	1	0	0	0	0	0	0	1
CTB	1	1	0	1	0	0	0	0	3
UTB	0	1	0	0	0	0	0	0	1
Total	22	19	9	6	2	1	3	1	63

Source: Economic Situations and Leading Indicators of Taiwan, ROC, United World Chinese Commercial Bank, 25 July 1993

15 European, 3 Japanese, 5 Southeast Asian, 3 Australian, and 1 South African.

The development of offshore banking units (OBUs) was also a priority. Generally speaking, the OBUs are expected to perform three functions:

1 trading and remitting foreign currency;
2 handling foreign exchange deposits for and foreign currency loans to individuals, legal entities, government agencies, or financial institutions outside the territory of Taiwan;
3 raising and managing funds in international financial markets.

Therefore, the policy to develop effective offshore banking services is meant to achieve three critical goals. The first is to facilitate the pace of international- isation of financial service activities in Taiwan; the second is to seek to establish and promote Taiwan as an Asian financial centre, and the third is to direct foreign and domestic banking branches to operate within the logic of the OBUs (Semkow 1992). On 12 December 1983, the Central Bank of China promulgated the Offshore Banking Act to promote offshore banking services. In 1984, Taiwan established an offshore banking centre and the ICBC set up Taiwan's first OBU. Four other domestic banks and two foreign banks followed suit. Between 1984 and 1989, 20 OBUs were established. By March 1992, a total of 32 banks had been authorised to established OBUs. Of these, 16 banks were domestic and the other half foreign.

Taiwan's offshore banking system, with 32 member OBUs, fell far behind its Japanese and Singaporean counterparts, which in 1993 had more than 100 OBUs. Nevertheless, Taiwan's systems asset base grew rather rapidly: at an annual growth rate of 31 per cent in 1989, 25 per cent in 1990, and 13 per cent in 1991, when it reached $US23.5 billion. More importantly, with respect to the distribution of the assets and liabilities of the OBUs – 84 per cent of deposits coming from, and 89 per cent of the loans going to, Asian nations (Semkow, 1992, p. 147) – Taiwan appears not too far from becoming a working regional financial centre.

The introduction of new financial products

Studies such as Semkow's (1992, p. 174) have attributed the widespread post-1980 fervour in buying and selling stocks for short-term benefits partly to the lack of domestic and foreign investment channels to absorb excess capital. A broad range of derivative financial products was seen as vital in dampening wild swings in speculative profits and helping market partici-pants hedge their risks and construct portfolios to their preferences.

The co-existence of, say, a stock market and a futures and options market increases the means to hedge against adverse price fluctuations in investors' stock holdings. Therefore, had Taiwan developed derivative financial markets earlier, local investors could probably have avoided to some extent the heavy losses associated with some earlier stock market bubbles and minimised detrimental social repercussions in their conduct of speculative activities. This generalisation can even be propounded despite the experiences of the more mature markets of the West, which have suffered just as frequent calamities. The difference is that, while mature markets do crash, the magnitudes of the crashes have become less ravaging compared to earlier times. Furthermore, earlier effort in establishing a derivatives market could have prepared for the internationalisation of Taiwan's financial system. As it stands at present, with this market only emerging, Taipei's aspiration to be a regional financial centre faces much work to be done and some tough competition.

Acknowledging this, the government has been pushing hard ahead. Since 1989, a series of legislation relating to the introduction of new financial products has been passed. On 1 February 1990, the government approved laws allowing the establishment of local futures brokerages and the entry of foreign futures brokers. In March 1991, Merrill Lynch and Shearson Lehman Brothers were authorised to establish branches in Taipei to execute trades on offshore portfolio investment. As a result, local investors have had the opportunity to trade in securities listed on the stock exchanges of New York, London, and Tokyo through these two foreign-based securities firms. More notable has been the case of about US$100 million worth of Dragon Bonds issued in Taiwan by the Asian Development Bank in December 1991, inaugurating the trend for foreign currency bonds directly issued there. On 19 June 1992, the Legislative Yuan passed the Foreign Futures Trading Law (FFTL). This legislation has been seen to be providing the groundwork for the rectification of the fraudulent practices of the underground futures industry in Taiwan and for the introduction of derivative financial products.

One of the more pressing market segments to be developed, however, has been more or less omitted by the authorities so far: the government bond futures and options market. For the efficient operation of a physical fixed interest market, its futures and options counterparts must be not only working but working smoothly. Well overdue (the bond market had been scheduled to be operative in fiscal 1993), the bond derivatives market had been expected to grow rapidly once the central bank started issuing deficit bonds to finance the NT$81 trillion infrastructure investment programme under the Six Year Plan of 1991–96. The value of central government bonds issued for this period was estimated to range from NT$1.1 trillion to NT$4.0 trillion, depending on the growth of tax revenues (Semkow 1992, p. 219). Unfortunately, this projection has had to be scaled down due to the lack of parallel development in the futures and options market.

Deregulating financial markets

The performance of a financial market is assessed by its capacity to allocate capital efficiently to maximise investment opportunities. In terms of lifting financial market regulations, three fundamental measures have been taken in Taiwan: liberalisation of domestic interest rates, of foreign exchange rates, and the establishment of the foreign currency call loan market.

Briefly recapping, the 1980s saw two stages of domestic financial market liberalisation. The first stage started early in the decade in response to the 1979 oil crisis and the resultant international financial turmoil. The second was prompted by rapid growth in the country's foreign reserves and thus in money supply, given the NT$'s fixed or pegged exchange rates. The first deregulating step was in interest rates. Its basic objective was to produce a price mechanism reflecting real market forces. In November 1980, the Central Bank of China promulgated the Essentials of Interest Rate Adjustment, which allowed for a wide range of loan rates and permitted the free setting of interest rates on certificates of deposit. Several positive effects of this liberalisation programme resulted, including the expansion of the money market – the ratio of money market outstanding loans to total banking loans doubled between 1981 and 1982, from 8.6 per cent to 15.6 per cent, with bankers' acceptances being most popular among short-term instruments, followed by certificates of deposits and commercial paper. Official interest rates were made more adjustable to the market-determined money market rate.

In 1985, the government undertook further steps in easing restrictions on the minimum loan rate. Banks were now allowed to announce their own interest rates on loans (prime rate) within the prescribed ceiling and floor limits. That year also saw the abolition of the Regulations for Interest Rate Management, which stipulated that the minimum loan rate should not be higher than the maximum deposit rate. Banks have since been encouraged to set their own prime rates and, in addition, there has been a reduction of the types of deposit accounts from thirteen to four.

Since the promulgation of the new Banking Law on 19 July 1989, both the ceiling and floor limits for interest rates on all deposits and loans have been abolished, and interest rate liberalisation completed. The interest rate recommendation committee has been dissolved. After interest rate liberalisation, the three major commercial banks acted as price leaders for a while, with their prime rates differing from one another as well as from the new private banks, which began to appear in late 1991.

Legislation requiring the central bank to lift controls on trade-related transactions on current account was enacted on 15 July 1987, freeing to a large extent the foreign exchange market. Under that law, people in Taiwan can hold and use foreign currencies freely, and investors can purchase foreign currencies up to US$1 million per transaction, with an annual limit of US$5 million, for placing in foreign currency deposit accounts or for remittance abroad. This legislation can be said to be revolutionary in comparison to the earlier limit of only NT$5,000 per year which could be remitted overseas. Apart from this relaxation, people in Taiwan are allowed to hold foreign currency deposits for their own purposes.

On capital inflows, an amount of US$50,000 per year per person was set as the maximum limit. The initial ceiling of US$50,000 on inward remittances was said to be temporary, and the reason for this was to fend off hot money flowing into Taiwan's overheated stock market. By 1992, the limit had been resettled at US$3 million per year for both inward and outward remittances.

Since late 1983 foreigners have been able to invest indirectly in Taiwan's stock market by purchasing shares in four Taiwan Funds issued abroad. This indirect investment constituted the first phase of a three-phase plan to permit the entry of foreign capital into Taiwan's securities market. Phase two of the plan would allow foreign institutional investors to invest directly in the local market, and the final phase would be the total liberalisation of direct investment by all foreign investors.

The Taipei foreign currency call-loan market began operation in August 1989. The objective of setting up this market was, in the short run, to provide an efficient mechanism for banks and for non-financial institutions to make transactions in foreign currencies. For this purpose, the central bank provided foreign exchange to facilitate the short-term lending and borrowing of foreign currency funds by banks. Taken together, a total of fourteen currencies in the forex market are traded in the call-loan market. A long-term goal is for the Taipei foreign currency call-loan market to work as a mechanism to internationalise Taiwan's financial system, thus contributing to the development of Taipei into a regional financial centre.

In order to see this goal realised earlier, the Taipei Foreign Exchange Market Development Foundation signed linkage agreements first with a Singapore money brokerage house in February 1990, and then with two money brokerage houses based in Hong Kong in August 1991. In March 1992, it took a further action to start an on-line link-up with a Japanese international money brokerage house, Yagi Euro. All these moves to expand the scope of the Taipei foreign currency call-loan market to Singapore, Hong Kong and Tokyo have undoubtedly been geared to furnish Taipei with a network that will help it function as a financial centre in the Asia–Pacific rim.

THE POLITICAL SIGNIFICANCE OF THE 1980s FINANCIAL DEREGULATION

The previously mentioned serious labour shortages in manufacturing, together with a liberalised political setting which encourages union activism, might well in themselves have explained the lack of enthusiasm of the business sector for domestic investments. However, without the assistance of the 1980s financial liberalisation, the relocation of Taiwanese labour-intensive industry to Southeast Asia and the Chinese mainland would not have developed at such an astonishing speed. And without that massive outflow of investment, Taiwan's economic and financial strength in the international (or at least regional) community would not have become so conspicuous.

The acceleration of capital outflow to Southeast Asia and mainland China

The outflow of Taiwanese capital that started in 1984 became inter-nationally visible by 1987. In the latter year alone, off-shore investments approved by the government increased by 80 per cent and reached US$102 million. Ever since, the pace of capital outflow has accelerated. Within a six-year period from 1986 to 1991, all Taiwan's outward investments, registered and non-registered included, amounted to US$19 billion (Liu, 1993). The figures for government approved projects were US$218.7 million in 1988, US$931 million in 1989, US$1.55 billion in 1990, US$1.66 billion in 1991, and US$887.3 million in 1992. Of the total approved off-shore investments between 1987 and 1992, 43 per cent went to Asian countries, 33 per cent to the United States and 16 per cent to Europe. These remarkable figures (which, of course, do not include unapproved invest-ments) make Taiwan the ninth largest supplier of foreign investment capital in the world.

These figures do not include a majority of small and medium enterprises which invested in Southeast Asia either. With reference to the statistics provided by the governments in Southeast Asia, the total amount of Taiwanese investments in this region exceeded US$12 billion, with 41 per cent placed in Malaysia, 28 per cent in Thailand and 23 per cent in Indonesia.

Between 1986 and 1992, US$13 billion of Taiwanese capital moved to Thailand, Malaysia, Indonesia and the Philippines, with thousands of Taiwanese firms establishing operations in these countries. By country, Taiwanese investments in Malaysia amounted to US$5.5 billion, in 800 manufacturing projects. Among foreign investors in Malaysia, Taiwan ranked third in 1987, behind Japan and Singapore. By 1992, Taiwan was ahead of Singapore and second only to Japan in supplying foreign capital to Malaysia. Thai government statistics indicate that Taiwanese capital invested in Thailand reached US$3.7 billion in 1992, in approximately 2,000 operations. A further US$2.8 billion worth of investment applications was lodged in 1993. Again, Taiwan was second only to Japan in current investments in Thailand.

Table 6.10 Outflow of government-approved Taiwanese capital by region: 1987–93

	Southeast Asia*	Europe	United States
1987	14,787	214,322	70,058
1988	52,729	96,574	123,335
1989	276,873	314,438	508,732
1990	529,768	282,681	428,690
1991	690,097	161,421	297,795
1992	280,269	164,963	193,026
1993	205,774	209,974	529,063
Total	2,050,297	1,444,373	2,150,699

Source: Monthly Statistics on Overseas Chinese and Foreign Investment, Technical Cooperation, Outward Investment, Outward Technical Cooperation and Indirect Mainland Investment, Republic of China, Investment Commission, Ministry of Economic Affairs, December 1993

Note: Southeast Asia includes Indonesia, Malaysia, Thailand and the Philippines

Table 6.11 Government-approved Taiwanese investments in Southeast Asia: 1987–93 (in US$ 000)

	Malaysia	Thailand	Indonesia	Philippines
1987	5,831	5,366	950	2,640
1988	2,708	11,886	1,923	36,212
1989	158,646	51,604	311	66,312
1990	184,885	149,397	61,871	123,607
1991	442,011	86,430	160,341	1,315
1992	155,727	83,293	39,930	1,219
1993	64,542	109,165	25,531	6,536
Total	1,014,350	497,141	290,857	237,841

Source: Monthly Statistics on Overseas Chinese and Foreign Investment, Technical Cooperation, Outward Investment, Outward Technical Cooperation for the Republic of China, Investment Commission, Ministry of Economic Affairs, December 1993

In 1988, Taiwan became the biggest foreign investor in the Philippines. Total investments exceeded US$100 million, constituting 23 per cent of all foreign capital. From 1986 to 1992, total Taiwanese investments in the Philippines reached US$430 million. During the same period, Taiwan placed US$3.3 billion in Indonesia, covering 800 projects.

The implications of these huge capital outflows to Taiwan's own financial markets development are multifaceted. As Taiwanese investors

Table 6.12 Taiwanese investment approved by host country in Southeast Asia (in US$ million)

	Malaysia	Thailand	Indonesia	Philippines
1987	91.00	307.58	8.40	9.04
1988	313.00	859.94	914.00	109.87
1989	815.00	892.20	157.00	148.69
1990	2,383.00	782.69	618.30	140.65
1991	1,314.21	583.46	1,056.50	11.61
1992	602.00	289.92	563.30	9.27
Total	5,518.21	3,715.79	3,317.50	429.13

Source: Outward Investment from Taiwan, ROC, Investment Commission, Ministry of Economic Affairs, 1993

Table 6.13 Taiwanese investments in Southeast Asia

	Malaysia	Thailand	Indonesia	Philippines
Direct investment: 1987–92	US$5 billion	US$3.4 billion	US$2.8 billion	US$0.4 billion
Industry	garments, electronics	handbags, footwear, ornaments, toys, chemicals	garments, shoemaking, woodworking, engineering, electronics and construction	garments, fishery, footwear, pulp and paper
Number of firms	800	2,000	800	–

Source: ibid.

place funds overseas, the need for more flexible financial markets and products will be ever increasing. Not wanting to be caught by a rising NT$ as experienced in the second half of the 1980s, Taiwanese firms would want to hedge as much of their overseas investments as practicable. If such hedging facilities were not to be available at home, they would be looked for somewhere else, such as Hong Kong. This demand pressure will continue to be exerted on Taipei to more rapidly open up its financial economy and provide the regulatory environment conducive to financial activities.

The large capital flows between Taiwan and the outside world also present similar pressure. Containing capital flows has been seen to be neither desirable nor feasible. To pre-empt unwanted side-effects of this surging capital traffic on the internal economy, the government must formalise the financial system as quickly and broadly as possible in order to bring the capital flows to the surface and apply macroeconomic policy appropriately. Information has become paramount, and a less than fully formalised market will not provide information to the extent desired.

Relations with the mainland

As Southeast Asian economies prosper, wage rates continue to rise rapidly. China and Vietnam, with their low-wage environment, seem to stand out against ASEAN economies as potentially better destinations for foreign investment. From 1988 to 1991, Taiwanese investment in Vietnam amounted to US$784 million (in sixty-two projects), or about 20 per cent of total foreign capital (US$3.9 billion) placed in that country. This share made Taiwan the largest foreign investor there.[5]

Similarly, the PRC has attracted a substantial (though mostly invisible) part of Taiwan's capital outflow. In its race to lay the international capital network, Taiwan gained an opportunity to assess the investment environment in mainland China in 1987, when the Taipei government lifted the ban on family visits to relations in the PRC. By the end of 1991, Taiwanese investments in the mainland had topped US$3 billion. A Japanese source estimated that the true figure was probably five times that amount, most having made its way into the PRC through Hong Kong or another third country. According to the PRC's official statistics, from 1979 to 1991, the largest amount of foreign investments flowing into China had been from Hong Kong and Macau, at US$27.8 billion, followed by the US (US$4.6 billion) and Japan (US$3.5 billion). Taiwan was ranked fourth, claiming just US$2.4 billion worth (Gao, 1993). In 1992, however, Taiwan's rank was up to second.

Nevertheless, regardless of what figures are used, it is clear that the intensified economic relations between Taiwan and the PRC (Table 6.14) have grown to the extent that some provincial governments in the southeastern part of China have declared the NT$ an acceptable medium of exchange. Before 1992, Taiwanese companies transferring funds to the mainland had first to convert NT dollars into US$ and then convert them again into renminbi (RMB). This was changed in June 1992, when the authorities in Fujian decided to accept the NT$ as a payment instrument for trade with Taiwan.[6] In September 1992, the People's Bank of China, the PRC's central bank, recommended the acceptance of the NT$ as a currency for payment to the state-operated Friendship Stores. Many banks in the mainland have since been granted the authority to provide NT$ deposits to facilitate Taiwanese investment in the mainland. This development has reduced extra expenses on currency conversions, thus encouraging Taiwanese capital to be drawn into the PRC.

Table 6.14 Taiwanese indirect investments in mainland China by region: 1991–92 (in US$ 000)

	1991	*1992*	*Total*
Shenzhen	43,386 (24.9%)	40,947 (16.6%)	84,333 (20.0%)
Guangdong	19,564 (11.2%)	24,748 (10.0%)	44,312 (10.5%)
Xiamen	17,657 (10.1%)	20,339 (8.2%)	37,996 (9.0%)
Guangzhou	7,141 (4.1%)	18,130 (7.3%)	25,271 (6.0%)
Shanghai	21,393 (12.4%)	17,373 (7.0%)	38,766 (9.4%)
Beijing	5,975 (3.4%)	5,612 (2.3%)	11,587 (9.3%)
Fuzhou	10,496 (6.0%)	5,428 (2.2%)	15,924 (3.8%)
Others	48,364 (27.8%)	114,415 (46.3%)	162,779 (38.7%)
Total	173,976	246,992	420,968

Source: Cross Straits Monthly Economic Statistics, Mainland Affairs Council, Taipei, ROC, March 1993

Table 6.15 Taiwanese investment in mainland China by industry: 1991–92 (in US$ 000)

	1991	*1992*	*Total*
Rubber and Plastics	54,428 (31.3%)	56,364 (22.8%)	110,792 (26.3%)
Food and Beverage	19,308 (11.1%)	46,415 (18.8%)	65,723 (15.6%)
Electronics	31,568 (18.1%)	37,837 (15.3%)	69,405 (16.5%)
Textile	13,631 (7.8%)	18,776 (7.6%)	32,407 (7.7%)
Metal	9,704 (5.6%)	17,147 (6.9%)	26,851 (6.4%)
Chemicals	2,977 (1.7%)	14,586 (5.9%)	17,563 (4.2%)
Others	42,542 (24.4%)	55,867 (22.6%)	98,409 (23.4%)
Total	174,158	246,992	421,150

Source: Cross Straits Monthly Economic Statistics, Mainland Affairs Council, Taipei, ROC, March 1993

Direct investment by Taiwan in the mainland is still banned and all investments must be undertaken indirectly through a third country (usually Hong Kong). By 1992, mainland China had become Taiwan's fifth largest export market and Taiwan the mainland's official second largest investor. In the first four months of that year alone, Taiwan's Ministry of Economic Affairs received a registration of 2,582 cases for mainland investments worth US$837 million. Most of the investments have been concentrated in manufactures such as bicycles, footwear, plastic products, metal products and electrical appliances (Table 6.15). At the same time, the tremendous increase in trade between mainland China and Taiwan through Hong Kong also made Hong Kong Taiwan's third largest export market. As interdependency between the three Chinese communities grew, the formation and then consolidation of a greater Chinese common market appeared to some as inevitable.[7]

In January 1992, about a hundred government officials and academics gathered in Hong Kong to discuss the prospect of creating a Chinese economic zone that would encompass the ethnic Chinese territories of Hong Kong, Macau, Taiwan and Southeastern coastal China, particularly Guangdong and Fujian provinces. However, despite cultural, familial and linguistic proximities which may enhance intraregional economic links, two major obstructive elements working against the formation of the greater Chinese zone stood out: the first was the difference in provincial origins among the Chinese groups (for example, Guangdong for Hong Kong Chinese, and Fujian for Taiwanese); and the second was the historical, geographical and political gulf between them (a fact that has tended to escape those who see the China Basin in simple ethnic terms).

Most diverged among the various Chinese states have been the PRC and Taiwan. The testy political relations between these two have not changed fundamentally with the advent of capital market development. If anything, Taiwan's competitive spirit will now be called into force even more fiercely than before as the PRC has been stirred from a forty-year slumber. With the prospect of mainland China as a potential economic superpower, Taiwan's modernisation of its own economy has taken on more urgency. Which means that the internationalisation of Taiwan's capital market engenders two national security objectives. One is to outperform the PRC in financial management, thus shifting the race from real economy performance to the more sophisticated sphere of financial economic activity; and the other is to create a regional and international capital network so that any attempt by the PRC to take over Taiwan by force would entail significant repercussions to regions far beyond the China Basin.

The dilemma faced by Taiwan's officials is not simple. As trade relations between the mainland and Taiwan intensify, there looms large a tendency of reliance by Taiwan's gradually diminishing labour-intensive economy on mainland China as a market for its exports as well as a manufacturing base for its products. This has increased fears that Taiwan would become more vulnerable to political pressures from Beijing. In an attempt to steer Taiwanese investments away from excessive concentration in China, Taipei has adopted several measures including investment seminars on and business tours to Southeast Asia. Taiwan has also offered loans to Southeast Asian nations to improve their infrastructure and to establish industrial zones for Taiwanese capital to be used. In 1990, Taiwan's Retired Servicemen

Engineering Agency (RSEA) spent US$100 million in Malaysia to develop a 82-hectare Sungai Petani Industrial Park in Kedah State into an electronics manufacturing zone which attracted thirty Taiwanese companies. In 1991, the RSEA built another Free Trade Zone in Malaysia's Ipoh City to house light industries. For the same reason, Taiwan has agreed to provide up to US$20 million to develop an industrial site at the former US naval base at Subic Bay in the Philippines.

Taiwan's aspiration for a sovereignty free of mainland intervention has manifested itself in more ways than economic ones. International relations moves taken by Taipei have included the establishment of the International Economic Co-operation and Development Fund in 1988, the provision of funding commitments to multilateral development organisations such as the Asian Development Bank, the Inter-American Development Bank and the European Bank for Reconstruction and Development, and recent campaigns for membership of the General Agreement on Tariffs and Trade (GATT) and for rejoining the United Nations.

TAIWAN: A REGIONAL CENTRE IN THE MAKING

The strong outflows of Taiwanese capital have greatly changed Taiwan's economic profile and role in the regional, if not international, community. The implications of this capital export to Taiwan's own financial markets development has been multifaceted. Mention has been given to the need for more flexible financial markets and products in order to pre-empt further financial activity drain offshore. Continued strong export performance has underpinned Taiwan's stock of international reserves, which is approaching US$100 billion, making Taiwan the largest reserve-holder in the world, a position that undoubtedly will help the country raise its profile in the international capital market.

But possessing the capital is not sufficient to catapult a country to financial centre status. The experience of Japan in the last ten years shows amply that it takes more than just bulk capital to make a country central in the operational market of that capital. Australia carries net foreign debt worth 40 per cent of its GDP and yet Sydney can be classified as a regional financial centre. Taiwan, for its aspiration as a regional centre to be achieved, will require a thorough transformation of its financial system and regulatory framework. Reforms in the financial sector since the last decade have been in the right direction, although no more rapid or comprehensive than other places such as Indonesia, Malaysia or Singapore. Taipei lags Singapore in building up a critical mass of major international or regional financial institutions operating from its own territory. In this regard, Hong Kong remains the centre to beat, where 140 of the world's most influential financial institutions chose to place their regional headquarters despite outrageous site costs.

Nevertheless, there are several factors in favour of Taipei. First, the residual uncertainty surrounding post-1997 Hong Kong. While this uncertainty has been diminished to a large extent over the last few years by the successful transformation of the PRC into a market economy – with its fair share of rising pockets of wealth and income inequalities – flares of PRC's dismissive attitude towards human rights as the West understands them have frequently re-ignited concerns. Taiwan would obviously gain from every bit of instability emanating from the PRC's handling of Hong Kong. The strategic capital linkages that Taiwan provides to the Southeast Chinese coast and Southeast Asian region could also serve a purpose in expanding the client base for a Taipei centre. Successful industrialisation has given Taiwan a broad manufacturing base, which is at a stage conducive to financial deepening. Perhaps more than the trade and investment links with mainland China's Southeast coast, where a large chunk of Hong Kong's manufacturing base also resides, Taiwan could carve out for itself a niche market in the PRC by concentrating in the Northeast as well as the hinterland. Taipei could become the springboard into those regions of the PRC, and a go-between for China Basin–Southeast Asian activities. Financial services could then be built around these specialities. This strategy implies that a complementary relationship between Hong Kong and Taipei as dual regional centres may turn out to be more mutually beneficial than a competitive one.

Which leads to the adoption of measures that would make Taipei at least as attractive as Hong Kong to foreign participation in the domestic financial markets. There is no shortage of East Asian countries yearning to be financial centres on the one hand, and politically autarkic on the other. Such dichotomy has never worked. So far, the Central Bank of China has seemed to learn from others' experiences. It has announced a number of broad based initiatives to upgrade Taiwan's financial system. They are:

1 constructing an office building to accommodate international monetary institutions;
2 improving the telecommunication system in Taiwan;
3 attracting international financial money dealers and other financial institutions to deepen participation in Taiwan's financial markets subsequent to enlarging the foreign exchange call-loan market with foreign currencies other than the US dollar, Deutschmark, and yen;
4 expanding the role of the Monetary Personnel Training Centre to train more banking and non-banking personnel;
5 establishing an international currencies exchange in Taipei for a number of monetary products including foreign currency futures and options;
6 reopening the forward foreign exchange market, which had closed only a few days after its inception and opening;
7 creating a gold market and permitting the export of gold.

Liberalising the formal financial markets will eventually draw Taiwan's own informal market to a close. The speed and extent of this closure depends on those in the deregulation of the financial system. It will also depend on comprehensive non-financial initiatives, such as those surrounding the regulatory framework in Taiwan. Laws and regulations governing trading and settlement, company disclosure and intellectual property rights, profit repatriation and transfer pricing, investor protection as well as derivative products, would need to be clear, objective and enforceable.

Even more central is the issue of Taiwan's long-term relationship with the PRC itself. It is doubtful that multinationals would flock to Taiwan to establish trading and investment houses while the two Chinas continued to refuse to sanction official partnership. Taiwan's biggest drawcard, like Hong Kong's, is mainland China. If Taipei could corner the north while leaving southern China to Hong Kong, it might be half-way to achieving its goal.

In summary, will Taiwan's 1980s financial reforms be seen as setting a landmark to turn Taipei into an international financial centre in the Asia–Pacific by the end of this decade? The answer lies in the authorities' forceful implementation of a well formulated scheme for the sophistication of Taiwan's technical financial markets and regulatory system, and a constructive relationship with Beijing. Without any of these, Taiwan's plan to become a regional centre would be just another NIC's wish.

NOTES

1 By the end of 1993 the Postal Savings system had 1,585 branches all over Taiwan and it started in 1982 to redeposit its deposits into the Central Bank and other banks such as the Chiao Tung Bank, the Farmers' Bank of China, the Cooperative Bank of Taiwan, and the Medium and Small Business Bank of Taiwan to extend credit to rural customers and small businesses (Lee, 1990, p. 177; Liang, 1991; Semkow, 1992).

2 By the end of 1993, there were seven investment and trust companies with a total of 60 branches: Cathay Investment and Trust Company (12), Taiwan First Investment and Trust Company (13), the Overseas Investment and Trust Corporation (7), China United Trust and Investment Company (13), Taiwan Development and Trust Corporation (9), Asia Trust and Investment Corporation (5), and China Development Corporation.

3 At the end of 1993, there were 27 life insurance companies and 23 property and casualty insurance companies.

4 The LSL was passed in 1984 in the legislature without serious resistance from the legislators who sided with the interests of capital. The greatest contribution of the LSL resides in the fact that it specifies the rules regarding payments for bonuses, overtime, retirement and severance.

5 Chiu, 1992, p. 8.

6 Tseng, 1993, p. 37.

7 Lim, 1992 and Wei, 1992.

REFERENCES

Baum, J. 1993, 'Successful Bonding', *Far Eastern Economic Review*, 22 July, p. 60.
Chang, Chi-cheng. 1990, 'Financial Liberalisation in the Republic of China', in *Pacific-Basin Capital Markets Research*, S.G. Rhee and R.P. Chang (eds), North-Holland: Elsevier Science Publishers BV.
Chen, Elaine. 1992, 'Easy Come, Easy Go: Money Across the Strait', Sinorama 17(9), pp. 18–23.
——. 1993, 'The Chinese Road to Riches – Rotating Credit Associations', *Sinorama* 18(9), pp. 36–43.
Chiu, Paul C.H., 1992, 'Money and Financial Markets: The Domestic Perspective', in *Taiwan: From Developing to Mature Economy*, Gustav Rains (ed.), Boulder: Westview.
Chu, J.J., 1993a, 'Political Liberalisation and the Rise of Taiwanese Labour Radicalism', *Journal of Contemporary Asia* 23(2), pp. 173–188.
——. 1993b, *The Political Economy of Post-1980s Taiwanese Foreign Investment*, ARC Working Paper 21, Asia Research Centre, Murdoch University.
——. 1993c, *A Sociological Analysis of the 1990s New Rich in Taiwan*, ARC Working Paper 29, Murdoch University.
Gao, Kung-lian. 1993, *The Relations between Taiwan and Mainland China: Present and Future* (in Chinese), Council of Mainland Affairs, Taipei.
Hsieh, Tsong-lin. 1993, 'Taiwan's Foreign Exchange Policy', paper presented at the conference on *Taiwan's Economic Success: Trade, Finance and Foreign Exchange*, Monash University, Australia.
Kuo, Cheng-tian. 1992, 'The PRC and Taiwan: Fujian's Faltering United Front', *Asian Survey*, pp. 683–695.
Kuo, Shirley W.Y., 1990, 'Liberalisation of The Financial Market in Taiwan in the 1980s', in S.G. Rhee and R.P. Chang (eds), op. cit.
Lee, Sheng-yi. 1990, *Money and Finance in the Economic Development of Taiwan*. London: Macmillan.
——. 1993, 'Taipei as a Financial Centre', paper presented at the conference on *Taiwan in the Asia–Pacific in the 1990s*, the Australian National University, Australia.
Liang, Kuo-shu. 1991, 'Background and Lessons of Financial Reform in the Republic of China', *Industry of Free China* LVXXI (10), pp. 37–41.
Li, Luara. 1992, 'A Niche in Time – A New ROC for the Future', *Sinorama* 17(8), pp. 27–34.
Lim, Linda. 1992, 'The Emergence of a Chinese Economic Zone in Asia?' *Journal of Southeast Asian Business* 8(1), pp. 41–46.
Liu, Christina Y. 1992, 'Money and Financial Markets: The International Perspective', in Gustav Rains (ed.), op. cit.
——. 1992, 'Liberalisation and Globalisation of the Financial Market', in *Taiwan's Enterprises in Global Perspective*. New York: M.E. Sharpe.
McKinnon, Ronald I. 1973, *Money and Capital in Economic Development*, Washington DC: Brookings Institution.
San, Gee. 1993, 'Taiwan's Economy and Trade', paper presented at the conference on *Taiwan's Economic Success: Trade, Finance and Foreign Exchange*, Monash University, Australia.
San, Gee and Hui-mei Tsai. 1993, 'New Taiwan Dollar Fluctuations and Taiwan Trade', paper presented at the conference on *Taiwan's Economic Success: Trade, Finance and Foreign Exchange*, Monash University, Australia.
Semkow, B. Wallace. 1992, *Taiwan's Financial Markets and Institutions: The Legal*

and Financial Issues of Deregulation and Internationalisation, London: Quorum Books.

Shaw, Edward S. 1973, *Financial Deepening in Economic Development*, New York: Oxford University Press.

Shieh, Samuel C. 1992a, 'Financial Liberalisation and Internationalisation: The Development of Taipei as a Regional Financial Centre in Asia', *Industry of Free China* LXXVII(6), pp. 27–38.

——, 1992b, 'The Outlook for Taipei as a Regional Financial Centre in Asia', *ICBC Economic Review* 266, pp. 1–20.

Skully, Michael. 1993, 'Finance and Foreign Trade: An Asian Comparison', paper presented at the conference on *Taiwan's Economic Success: Trade, Finance and Foreign Exchange*, Monash University, Australia.

Tseng, Osman. 1993, 'The NT Dollar Moves Across the Straits', *Free China Review* 43(1), pp. 36–39.

Wang, Jiann-chyuan. 1991, 'The Informal Sector and Policy in Taiwan', *Industry of Free China* LXXVI (11), pp. 69–78.

Wei, Ting. 1992, 'The Regional and Internal Implications of South China Economic Zone', *Journal of Chinese Studies and International Affairs* 28(12), pp. 46–72.

Yang, Ya-hwei. 1993, 'Taiwan's Trade and the Financial System', paper presented at the conference on *Taiwan's Economic Success: Trade, Finance and Foreign Exchange*, Monash University, Australia.

Yun, Eugenia, 1993, 'Do-It-Yourself Banking', *Free China Review* 43(8), p. 26.

Chapter 7

The political economy of Korean foreign direct investment in Southeast Asia

You-Il Lee and Moon-Joong Tcha[1]

INTRODUCTION

Over the last three decades, Korea has experienced the most successful economic growth in the developing world. The average real annual growth during the period between 1962 and 1991 exceeded 9 per cent, and radical changes in the economic structure saw a move away from previous import substitution policies. The state implemented major economic reforms – such as the adoption of more realistic exchange rates, centralisation of import controls, and the introduction of export incentives – that encouraged industries to look to global markets and to develop the country's comparative advantage such as low production costs and, until the early 1980s, a relatively compliant workforce. Consequently, agriculture's contribution to the gross domestic product (GDP) dropped from 36 per cent to 13.8 per cent and the share of manufacturing increased from 25 per cent to 50 per cent between 1962 and 1985.[2] These elements have converted the image of Korea from that of an underdeveloped country in the 1960s to that of a newly industrialising country (NIC) by the late 1970s.

A significant consequence of Korea's economic development has been an increase of investment in Southeast Asia where, since the late 1980s, it has emerged as one of the largest investors. In 1992, Korean foreign direct investment (FDI)[3] in the region stood at over US$1.2 billion: more than twice the sum total of FDI in the period between 1968 and 1985 (US$570 million). In the period between 1986 to 1988, 96.2 per cent of Korean FDI went to Indonesia. Despite this dramatic increase, however, internationalisation of Korean capital is still at an early stage; the 1990 figure (US$820 million) represented no more than 0.4 per cent of Korea's gross national product (GNP) – US$238 billion.

A large number of Korean investments realised in Southeast Asia are small- and medium-sized and engaged in labour-intensive manufacturing industries like textiles, footwear, garments and toys. Korean FDI by manufacturing firms in the region has shown remarkable growth since 1988, especially in Indonesia. The total amount of Korean FDI (US$48.17 million) in 1988 alone was 91.7 per cent of the cumulative total of Korean FDI in the region prior to that year. Almost half of that amount (US$23.74 million) went to Indonesia. A clear difference from the past pattern (the 1970s and early 1980s) of Korean FDI has been a shift from previously concentrated resource areas such as mining, forestry and fisheries.

Several studies have attempted to explain this relatively recent phenomenon, ranging from micro-level to macro-level variables. These include factors like rapid wage increases, revaluation of exchange rates and the government's loosening up of the foreign exchange control law in response to expanding current account surpluses since 1986. These analyses correspond to the theoretical explanations of Japanese FDI, which place FDI behaviour in the changing patterns of a nation's comparative advantages. But this provides only a partial picture. Most approaches based on the trends in Korea's economic growth concentrate on economic factors as probable determinants of FDI behaviour. Those studies tend to ignore or downplay the nature of industrialisation and the socio–political factors *driving* FDI. In other words, in examining the recent surge of Korean FDI, a critical analysis of various socio–economic and political difficulties faced by Korea in the 1980s should be taken into account.

This chapter discusses the political economic dynamics of development in Korea and the origins of Korean investment in the region, first in Southeast Asia and very recently moving to Northeast Asia. We begin with the historical background of Korean industrialisation, then analyse various aspects of the dramatic change (including traditional economic causes) and the nature of Korean FDI in recent years. We then follow this with a critical look at how Korea's industrialisation strategy since the 1960s has changed, with particular emphasis on the domestic political economy of the 1980s, not only economic but also social and political, not only domestic but also international. This section also discusses how and why the various environments of the 1980s relate to Korea's aggressive move to Southeast Asia, particularly to Indonesia. The chapter concludes with a comparative discussion of Korean FDI *vis-à-vis* the Japanese experience of the 1960s and 1970s and what the future direction of Korean FDI could be.

THE NATURE OF KOREAN INDUSTRIALISATION WITH PARTICULAR REFERENCE TO RAPID ECONOMIC GROWTH PERIOD OF THE 1960s AND 1970s

The withdrawal of Japan from Korea in 1945 following the defeat in World War II as much as the Korean War (1950–1953) destroyed almost all of the country's existing industrial facilities as well as physical infrastructure. The Korean economy in the 1950s was largely dependent on the United States (US) aid – reaching nearly 70 per cent of Korea's total imports and 75 per cent of total fixed capital formation. Between 1946 and 1976, US aid topped US$5.74

billion, in addition to the US$6.86 billion in military aid. Forty-five per cent of the non-military aid was given during the import-substitution industrialisation (ISI) period of 1953–62.[4] As a traditional agricultural economy, more than 60 per cent of the labour force was employed in the primary sector, and the government pursued an import substitution policy combined with high tariffs and quota restrictions. This period was characterised as an endless vicious circle of low income, low saving, low investment, and low production. The annual average growth rate of GNP during the ISI phase was 3.7 per cent and that of GNP per capita was only 0.7 per cent.

Consequently, when Major-General Park Chung-Hee came to power through the military coup of 16 May 1961, the Korean economy was in dire straits. Per capita GNP in 1961 was a mere US$82, and Korea suffered from chronic balance of payments difficulties, saturation of the domestic market, inflation, and no significant export industries. Perhaps the most powerful attraction of the newly established military regime to the Korean people was the promise of rapid economic growth. However, the emergence of the Park regime resulted in important and fundamental structural changes in the postwar Korean political economy. This can be termed export-oriented industrialisation (EOI), a phase realised through an active introduction of foreign capital, an alliance between the government and business groups, and the political and economic alienation of the lower class.

First, Park reoriented economic reform away from ISI towards EOI and capital accumulation. As Cumings and Haggard argue, this transition can in part be explained by America's new economic policy in the early 1960s towards Korea, reducing economic aid and emphasising 'self-sufficiency'.[5] But the rapprochement with Japan in the early 1960s also shaped Korean economic policy. The normalisation of Korea–Japan relations driven by the Park regime in an effort to solve external balance difficulties, brought about the massive inflow of Japanese capital – US$40 million in short-term credit to Korea in 1962, followed by US$37 million long-term credit in 1963.[6] More important than the amount, however, is the subsequent Japanese capital integration with Korea's markets, providing the latter with a vital source of capital for its EOI programme. This swap in capital sources, from foreign aid to foreign investment, proved to be the catalyst for Korea's economic emergence.

In order to achieve fast EOI, Park introduced various economic reforms. These involved a revaluation of the currency (about 12 per cent) and the establishment of a Free Export Zone for industries such as electronics and motor vehicles. Furthermore, the government provided exporters (industry or firms) ample autonomy for their export activities such as tariff-free access to the imported intermediate inputs and automatic access to bank loans.[7]

The implementation of these reforms resulted in the emergence of, in Cumings' term, BAIR or Bureaucratic Authoritarian Industrialising Regime. By this, he means a regime that is 'ubiquitous in economy and society:

penetrating, comprehensive, highly articulated, and relatively autonomous of particular groups and classes'.[8] We would also add that it is an ideal structure for governments that lack legitimacy to achieve social control with coercive force.

This is particularly true in the government's complete control over financial institutions. During the period between 1961 and 1980, the government owned most of the important banks, including the Bank of Korea, five nation-wide commercial banks, six special banks, and the two development banks (the Korea Development Bank and the Export–Import Bank).[9] government involvement in the financial sector in this period was remarkable, ranging from low-level personnel policy, salary reviews and budgets, to setting ceilings for individual banks, controlling their operating funds and interest rates.

In addition, Park's creation of the Economic Planning Board (EPB) in June 1961 strengthened the government's autonomy over the whole process of EOI programmes. The EPB controlled the entire budget and dictated the levels of foreign borrowing and direct investment. It also held the power to screen and monitor the various activities of foreign investors. Furthermore, the establishment of the Korean Central Intelligence Agency (KCIA) added to the regime's power by the Agency engaging directly in various societal sectors, through its extensive roles ranging from traditional intelligence gathering and secret police functions to implementation of economic policy.

Other than its control of the economy, the government maintained a tight grip on the business sector. Using the corporate sector as the engine of rapid economic growth, the regime provided a variety of incentives and encouragement to assist the rapid expansion of business conglomerates or *jaebeol*[10] (e.g., cheap credit and the suppression of labour unions and organisations). Business sector refusal to follow government-initiated strategies was dealt with in a number of ways including threatened tax audits and cancellation of import and export allowances.[11]

The relationship between labour and the government is another example of the interventionist regime. The Park regime's policy towards labour was repressive. Shortly after taking power, Park froze wages, prohibited strikes and dismantled labour unions.[12] As Amsden quoted, 'labour issues [were] handled by the Administration of Labour Affairs, which reports directly to KCIA'.[13]

Emphasis on labour repression was the central pillar of the Park regime's strategy of rapid industrialisation. Since the adoption of EOI required a large infusion of foreign capital, it was crucial for the government to demonstrate a secure labour environment. And as Korea's comparative advantage lay in low-labour costs, the maintenance of low wages and labour discipline was essential for the success of EOI based on labour-intensive manufactured products.

In short, the government's strong hold on hard-working, low-cost and disciplined labour, the reliance on foreign capital and the creation of bureaucracies and the *jaebeol*, have all contributed to Korea's remarkable export performance and government-led capital accumulation. We would venture to say that Korea's competitiveness would have been diminished had any one of these factors been absent. However, the past decade has witnessed a substantial change in the nature of the Korean political economy as major components driving the country's rapid economic growth in the 1960s and 1970s have become retrogressive factors in the mainstream, new orthodoxy of the 'late-industrialisation model'.[14] These factors include

1 the high vulnerability to protectionist measures;
2 high dependence on technology from advanced nations like Japan and the US;
3 deterioration in the domestic situation (frequent labour unrest causing sharp increases in wages and workday losses).

These have become the major threat to Korea's export competitiveness in low-wage, labour-intensive industries. As such, the rate of export growth fell from 24.8 per cent in 1988 to 2.8 per cent in 1989, 4.2 per cent in 1990, 10.5 per cent in 1991, and 6.8 per cent in 1992 respectively.[15] While Korea's long-standing comparative advantages of earlier times have proven to be no longer viable by the late 1980s, the successful operation of offshore holdings emerged as one of the critical determinants of Korea's sustained economic growth.

Korean FDI both in value and number of projects for the most recent five or six years has exceeded that recorded for the previous four decades. Particularly, as was in the case of Japanese FDI of the 1970s (a point that will be discussed in detail later), the last decade has seen an enormous expansion of Korean FDI by firms in labour-intensive light and small scale industries. And most of this investment has concentrated in less-developed countries like Southeast Asia. As mentioned earlier, various studies have seemingly traced the factors behind this relatively recent phenomenon. These include rapid wage increases, exchange rate realignments, current account surpluses and marketing strategies, as well as indicators of economic growth (GNP per capita and GNP growth rates) that have directed Korean firms to foreign markets. However, these factors represent more or less economic syndromes and do not say much about the underlying developments that had caused those economic variables to change. The mutation in the Korean political economy in recent years proved that Korean FDI may have had much to do with internal social change – such as state–society and state–labour relations in the late 1980s – and external factors as well as some economic variables. But before demonstrating this link, it would be useful to look at the changing general patterns and characteristics of Korean FDI.

KOREAN FDI: PAST AND PRESENT PATTERNS AND CHARACTERISTICS

Korean FDI by year and industry

The history of the Korean FDI is relatively recent. Its first move was made in 1968 with resource investment in Indonesia. It was during the EOI (the 1960s and 1970s) phase of growth that some of the externally oriented Korean firms began to make outbound direct investment to ensure continued expansion of their industrial exports. Particularly, Korea's need for natural resources (e.g., crude oil, coal) underlay the strong motivation for Korean firms' early resource investments such as in mining, forestry and fishing.[16] The highest rate of Korean FDI in Southeast Asia occurred in these industries in this period, largely due to the region's abundance of natural resources, low-wage labour and geographical proximity. In other words, since Korean exports depended heavily on labour-intensive goods, the early period of Korean FDI was aimed at expanding, not replacing, home-based industrial production and exports by securing raw material overseas.

The defensive mode of Korean FDI during this period can be traced to other elements. First, capital accumulation within Korea was at such a low level, partly due to the balance-of-payments problem, that the government had sought to restrain the outflow of capital, except in the cases where the outflow was seen to contribute to the expansion of export markets or the acquisition of natural resources in the long term. Second, Korean firms were technologically inferior to developed economies' counterparts, suffering from a chronic shortage of capital and lacking the managerial experience necessary to operate manufacturing projects outside Korea. Third, the Park regime's 'export-first at any cost', or *suchul gangkuk*[17] (strong nation through export) policy in the 1960s and 1970s, drove firms to concentrate on pursuing exports rather than seeking to produce overseas. Table 7.1 shows the evolution of Korean FDI and its significant increase since 1985.

From 1988, Korean FDI in resource extracting industries, particularly the mining sector, started to lose its dominance as the total amount of FDI in manufacturing sectors surpassed it as is shown in Table 7.2. In 1990, FDI in manufacturing industries accounted for about 50 per cent of total investment while the mining sector accounted for 15 per cent. The resources portion did not exceed 19 per cent even with the inclusion of forestry and fisheries. Of course, this does not necessarily mean that investments in resource extracting sectors, in dollar terms, are shrinking, only that rapid

Table 7.1 Korean FDI by number of projects and value

Year	No. of projects	US$ million
1968–75	70	49
1976–78	220	107
1979–81	321	173
1982	352	289
1983	401	386
1984	432	444
1985	443	476
1986	475	633
1987	534	966
1988	668	1,119
1989	899	1,444
1990	1,243	2,335
1991	1,673	3,372
1992	2,090	4,389

Source: Bank of Korea, *Jugan Haeoetuja Jeongbo* (Weekly Report on FDI), Bank of Korea, Seoul, 27 February 1993, p. 31

Note: Amounts and the number of projects are the cumulative total

expansion of FDI in manufacturing sectors has made the relative portion of resource investments decline.

Investment in the trade sector has to be noted here. Since 1980, except for 1984, this sector has never experienced any reduction in investment. In 1990, investment in the sector increased by 250 per cent compared to 1989 and accounted for 21 per cent of total FDI, which was even greater than the total of the resources sector. The relative change in FDI in these three major areas of manufacturing, mining, and trading, over this period is illustrated in Figure 7.1 and Table 7.2.

An important characteristic of Korean FDI is the size of the investment per case, which in 1990 was less than $3 million overall. Throughout the listed period, resource extracting sectors showed relatively high per project investment (US$8 million average) while that in the manufacturing sector averaged less than US$2 million. These data throw doubt, at least in the Korean case, on the argument that the size of an imperfectly competitive firm (such as in a monopoly or oligopoly case) is motivating FDI through the firm's ability to realise economic (i.e. abnormal) profits. Except for a couple of manufacturing FDI directed to North America, the size of these investments per project is too small to realise the 'advantage from imperfect competition' (or economies of scale) view. This phenomenon is most prominent in Korean FDI in Southeast Asia.

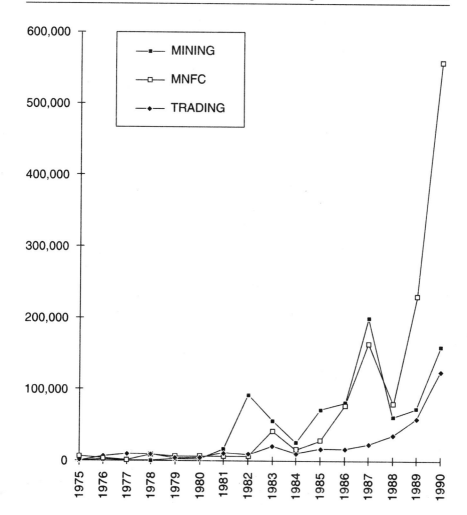

Figure 7.1 Korean FDI by major recipient sector

Notes: Figures refer to US$
MNFC = Manufacturing

Distribution of Korean FDI by region

For Korea, two major destinations of FDI are North America and Southeast Asia. Table 7.3 indicates the direction of Korean FDI from 1980 to 1990. In 1990, almost 80 per cent of Korean FDI was directed to those two regions while accumulated FDI to these two regions by the same year accounted for almost 70 per cent of total accumulated foreign direct investment. From 1982 to 1991, North America has consistently been the destination of the

Table 7.2 Korean FDI by industry, in US$ million

Year	Primary industry		Manufacturing industry		Trade		Others[a]		Subtotal	
1968–87	593	(80)	332	(132)	114	(357)	126	(178)	1,165	(747)
1988	79	(7)	82	(68)	43	(69)	20	(32)	224	(176)
1989	149	(11)	280	(147)	61	(79)	80	(32)	570	(269)
1990	185	(24)	489	(192)	220	(78)	65	(45)	959	(339)
1991	137	(27)	599	(277)	233	(94)	155	(56)	1,125	(453)
1992[b]	137	(27)	412	(221)	275	(65)	89	(26)	913	(339)
Sub total	1,280	(176)	2,194	(1,037)	946	(742)	535	(369)	4,956	(2,323)

Source: Korean Trade Promotion Corporation (KOTRA), *Giyeopeui Jeonryaksarye* (Case Study: A Firm's FDI Strategy), Seoul, KOTRA, 1993, p. 448

Notes: ( ) refers to the number of cases
     [a] Construction, transportation, real estate, and service sectors
     [b] January to August

largest part of Korean FDI. Southeast Asia, which has been the next largest destination since 1981 except for 1986, eventually caught up with North America in 1992 by absorbing US$556M compared to North America's share of US$392M. Since 1988, FDI from Korea directed to Southeast Asia has consistently increased. By contrast, FDI to North America started to show a slightly declining trend after peaking at an annual US$482M in 1990. Figure 2 illustrates the changes in Korean FDI to these top two destinations between 1975 and 1992. Except for these two regions, Korean FDI to the rest of the world has shown insignificant growth throughout this period.

Major Korean investments in Southeast Asia have been carried out in the clothing, garments and electronics sectors, and the size of the average investment is relatively small, a strong contrast to North America. Throughout the whole period, per project investment value in Southeast Asia was less than 30 per cent of that in North America. In accumulated dollar terms, North America attracted 50 per cent of total Korean FDI value (or US$528M) by the end of 1990, although collecting only 16.4 per cent (82 projects) of the total number of projects. Electronic and electricity (US$40M with 15 projects), steel (US$240M with 4) and transport (US$139M with 3) are three major industries which Korean FDI has concentrated in North America.

One distinctive characteristic of Korean FDI in Southeast Asia is that Indonesia has been the most favoured destination in this region by Korean firms, absorbing a considerable part of the total. The following section turns to this phenomenon by looking more closely at aspects of Korean FDI in Indonesia.

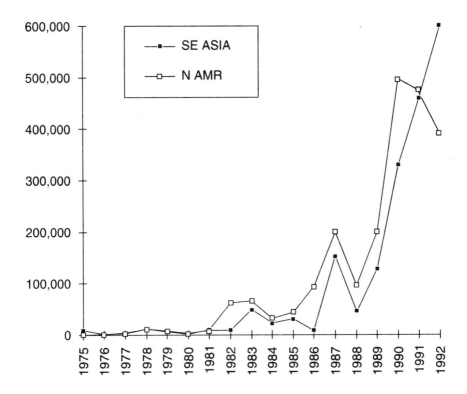

Figure 7.2 Korean FDI to Southeast Asia and North America

Notes: Figures refer to US$
        SE Asia = Southeast Asia
        NAMR = North America

Korean FDI in Indonesia

From 1982 to 1990, Korean FDI directed to North America was always significantly more than that to Asia. In 1991, the gap began to disappear and in 1992, Korean FDI to Asia, which rose by 30 per cent year on year, was greater than that to North America, which declined by 15 per cent. The manufacturing sector has been the major target for Korean FDI to Asia, including Indonesia. In accumulated terms, at the end of 1990, FDI to Asia's manufacturing sector accounted for 61 per cent (US$801M) of total FDI ($1279M) to this region. The mining sector was the second largest receiver, accounting for 19 per cent (US$ 248M).

As can be observed from Table 7.4, Indonesia is the most important destination for Korean FDI. This applies especially to the manufacturing sector. In accumulated terms, at the end of 1990, Indonesia took US$179M

Table 7.3 Korean FDI by region, in US$ million

	SEA		MSA		NA		Europe		Others		Total	
1968–87	278	(211)	18	(57)	449	(280)	75	(78)	345	(121)	1,165	(747)
1988	42	(70)	14	(15)	99	(58)	19	(17)	50	(16)	224	(176)
1989	130	(129)	55	(28)	283	(72)	20	(17)	82	(23)	570	(269)
1990	300	(189)	36	(25)	435	(86)	95	(22)	93	(17)	959	(339)
1991	431	(272)	42	(36)	463	(88)	92	(39)	97	(18)	1,125	(453)
1992*	400	(236)	27	(20)	320	(47)	75	(26)	91	(10)	913	(339)
Total**	1,581	(1,107)	192	(181)	2,049	(631)	376	(199)	758	(206)	4,956	(2,323)

Source: Korean Trade Promotion Corporation (KOTRA), *Giyeopeui Jeonryaksarye* (Case Study: A Firm's FDI Strategy), Seoul, KOTRA, 1993, p. 449

Notes: SEA = Southeast Asia
NA = North America
MSA = Middle and South America
( ) = Number of projects
* = January to August 1992
** = the cumulative total

Table 7.4 Korean FDI to Southeast Asia and Indonesia, US$ 000

Year	Southeast Asia[1]	Indonesia[2]	World total
1980	1,588	1,471	21,095
1981	9,897	1,800	40,077
1982	8,674	5,122	129,375
1983	28,912	11,963	113,163
1984	10,821	5,686	56,975
1985	16,861	6,307	117,822
1986	1,680	1,319	171,999
1987	129,463	126,131	397,235
1988	37,349	20,472	212,919
1989	121,512	75,390	492,496
1990	306,264	163,979	1,019,744
1991	431,300	170,005	1,125,364
1992	555,700	164,408	1,218,395

Source: Bank of Korea, *Overseas Investment Statistical Yearbook*, Seoul, Bank of Korea, 1993, p. 12

Notes: [1] = All Southeast Asian countries including Indonesia
[2] = The portion of Korean FDI to Southeast Asia invested in Indonesia

of Korean FDI, with 117 projects, which was larger than the total of all other countries in Asia including Thailand, the Philippines, Malaysia, China and Sri Lanka. By number of projects, investment to Indonesia exceeded that to the US (71 for the latter destination in 1990) but lost out in accumulated value terms, reaching only 51 per cent of FDI to the USA ($349M in 1990). These figures confirm that the per project size of Korean FDI to Indonesia is relatively small compared to North America. From Indonesia's viewpoint, by the end of 1993, Korea was the fourth largest investor in terms of total investments and next only to Japan in terms of total number of projects.

A noted characteristic of Korean FDI to Asia is found in the structure of the investment. Korean firms investing in Indonesia concentrate on labour-intensive, light industries such as fabrics, clothes, shoes and stuffed toys. Recently, it was reported that the investment has been diversified and expanded to sectors such as chemicals, processing woods and some electronic goods (KTPC: 1991). It is also notable that FDI to Indonesia since 1990 has been relatively stable while that to Asia has risen. Accordingly, Indonesia's weight in Asia declined to 30 per cent in 1992 from 96 per cent in 1987. Economic and political economic explanations for Indonesia's role as a major destination for Korean FDI are looked at in the following sections. Figure 7.3 depicts the size of Korean FDI to Southeast Asia and Indonesia.

THE POLITICAL ECONOMY OF KOREAN FDI: FACTORS AND DETERMINANTS

Prevailing theories of FDI have concentrated on the behaviour of multinational firms. These include Hymer's and Kindleberger's industrial organisation theory, Buckley's and Casson's internalisation theory, and Vernon's and Well's product life cycle theory, among others.[18] The essential and common characteristic of each of the approaches is that FDI is carried out by a firm with a profit maximisation incentive. Investing firms are presumed to make their decisions by considering all available information and situations. Because the firms investing abroad will meet indigenous firms that possess various kinds of advantages (cultural, legal, economic, institutional), the entering firms must have critical incentives or specific advantages (marketing, technology, skilled personnel) to dominate the local firms and extract maximum profits.[19]

Traditional FDI analyses suggest several incentives for FDI: vertical integration, horizontal integration and marketing strategies (tariff evasion and establishment of export bases), etc. They illustrate some economic variables which are considered to affect firm's FDI decisions, ranging from micro-level variables (e.g. R&D expenditure) to macro-level variables (e.g. GNP of investing firm's country). In explaining the significant increase in Korean FDI in recent years, Korean economists have tended to see the

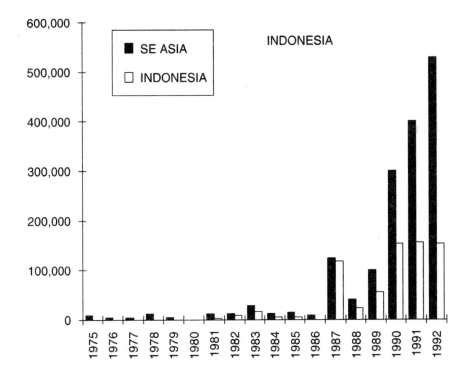

Figure 7.3 Korean FDI to Southeast Asia and Indonesia

Notes: Figures refer to US$
SE Asia = Southeast Asia

changes in economic variables such as wage rates, exchange rates, current account balances and marketing strategies, as main factors. This section thus begins with a brief overview of the 'economic variable effect' school of thought.

Approaches to economic incentives of FDI

Since World War II, theories of FDI have been developed to replace the neoclassical capital arbitrage theory of portfolio investment based on interest rate differentials that maintains that international capital flows are driven by these rate margins. In general, explanations of FDI by Western economists in the 1960s and 1970s understood FDI as a strategy undertaken by multinational corporations (MNCs).[20]

For example, in his industrial organisation (IO) theory, Hymer argued that FDI is a profit-seeking strategy of oligopolistic MNCs with firm-specific intangible advantages such as access to marketing, technology, skilled personnel and credit. The central thesis of this approach is that the 'imperfection in the capital market' is the major incentive for a firm to make an overseas direct investment.[21] This argument has been elaborated further by other economists such as Caves and Vernon who have been interested in the internalisation process of the transaction costs by which MNCs can minimise market transaction costs and evade taxation through FDI. This approach posits that the firm-specific advantage over local firms is the most critical determinant in the relocation process of production.

Apart from Western theories of FDI, a group identified as the Japanese school, such as Kojima and Ozawa, contended that the market itself is incapable of dealing with global adjustment and recommended government intervention to boost adaptive efficiency.[22] Central to this theory is the notion that government-led structural adjustment provides assistance to FDI.

In empirical studies examining how the economic factors affect FDI behaviour in the real world, economists have considered the above economic variables as valid explanatory variables, and have adopted some of them. In the section below, utilising available recent economic data on Korea and some selected countries, we examine the effects of economic variables on the progress of Korean FDI.

Data and variables

The Korean FDI data are obtained from various sources: the annual FDI amount for the overall period comes from *Korea Economic Indicators*. More specific FDI data (e.g., by region or by industry) are collected from *Research Material Series* (particularly No. 92–2 and No. 92–9) by the Korea Export–Import Bank and *Economic Statistics Yearbook* by the Bank of Korea. The prospective explanatory variables used in this study are the exchange rate, the volatility of exchange rate, current account balance, Korean stock market index, per capita GNP, wage index and exports from Korea to Indonesia. Exchange rates are from *International Financial Statistics* by IMF, volatilities are obtained from those exchange rates, and trade related variables are from *Direction of Trade Statistics* by IMF, and all other variables are from *Economic Statistics Yearbook* and *Korean Economic Indicators*.

Other things being equal, it is expected that Korean FDI will increase as Korean currency becomes stronger relative to the destination country's currency. Devaluation of the Korean currency against the destination country's currency will increase the cost of production, thereby the FDI incentive will shrink. Froot and Stein, in their study of foreign investment in the US, showed that FDI is the only type of capital inflow that is statistically negatively correlated with the value of the US dollar. As the value of the dollar increases, foreign countries invest less in the US.[23] They also found that the manufacturing industries, particularly chemicals, receive the strongest effects from the change of exchange rates. After utilising more disaggregated data to the level of individual industries, they concluded that exchange rate effects appear to be pervasive. Therefore, the exchange rate between the US dollar and Korean won will be used in the empirical equation for Korean FDI to North America and to the world, and the exchange rate between the won and Indonesian rupiah for Korean FDI to Indonesia.

Harvey explained that the exchange variance adds uncertainty to international trade, and one way to avoid that uncertainty is to 'skip' the exchange market and engage in FDI.[24] Therefore, the effect of the exchange variance is assumed to be positive. Studying US FDI throughout the world, he adopted more independent variables such as the sales amount, the exchange rate variance, the ratio of expenditure for research and development and advertising, plus retained earnings over total sales and the top tax bracket for corporations in the host country. His empirical results showed that expected exchange rate variation is significant for machinery except electrical when Canada is included and for machinery, chemicals, and transportation when Canada is excluded. In the case of overall FDI, the exchange rate variance is significant with the expected sign for FDI to the world but Canada is used as a dependent variable. Therefore, the volatilities of the exchange rate (Korean won/US dollar and Korean won/Indonesian rupiah) are adopted as explanatory variables in this study.

The importance of per capita GNP and GNP growth rates has been well surveyed by Root and Ahmed:

> The importance of per capita GDP corresponds with similar finding by Reuber. The selection of the GDP growth rate is somewhat surprising. In both the Scaperlanda/Mauerand Bandera/White studies the GDP or GNP growth rate was found to have little significance). Reuber detected only a weak, inconclusive relationship between changes in GDP and direct-investment inflows. . . . The absolute size of GDP is a poor indicator in many developing countries. . . . The absolute size of GDP is more likely to reflect population size than per capita income.[25]
>
> (Root and Ahmed 1979: 757–8)

In our study, per capita GNP is adopted as an independent variable. If we consider that most Korean FDI is concentrated on the resource extracting or labour-intensive sectors, particularly in the case of Southeast Asia, the lower wage level in those countries will be attractive. The wage rate is thus tested in our empirical study, and in the later section, it will be reconsidered in detail when political economic reasons are analysed.

Wealth effect can be a factor in FDI behaviour. Stock market index and current account balance in the investing firm's country are considered as factors giving wealth effects to decision makers. Therefore, those variables are utilised here.

At the more disaggregated level, i.e. at the firm's level, variables such as assets, advertising intensity, labour intensity, R&D expenditure and product diversity are used as independent variables. Grubaugh showed that the functional form chosen to estimate a probability function can make a significant difference in the inferences and that intangible asset, size and product diversity are positively correlated with the probability of becoming a multinational.[26] Unfortunately, the significance of those variables for each firm's choice is not tested in our study because those data in the dis-aggregated level are not available and our main concerns are on the effects of the economy-wide and political economic variables.

Empirical results

Korean FDI to the world

Six prospective independent variables are collected and the correlations are examined as shown in Appendix, Table (7)A1. Assuming that the US dollar has been the major currency in the world trade and financial system, the US dollar to Korean won is used as an exchange rate (this assumption stands in this study also because Korean FDI, other than to Asia, has been mainly to North America). The volatility of the exchange rate for every year is derived from the exchange rate in every month and the mean exchange rate for the year.

Appendix Table (7)A1 reveals strong correlation among some variables, especially, KSTCIND (stocks), KPCGNP (GNP) and KWAGEIND (wages). It is not surprising that KPCGNP and KWAGEIND have a very high level of correlation because they are considered to be related to each other and represent the overall economic situation of the country. As the Korean economy has achieved consistent economic growth, KPCGNP and KWAGEIND showed very high correlation with a time trend.

Account must be taken of KSTCIND which experienced very similar movement to the other two variables until 1990. However, it has started to move downward since then, which was different from the changes in KPCGNP and KWAGEIND. As accurate data for the recent movement of KSTCIND since 1990 are not available at this stage, only the data before 1991 were used in the above table. In this case, it brings out a serious multicollinearity problem among independent variables if we use KSTCIND for the same regression with KPCGNP or KWAGEIND (correlation between KSTCIND and KPCGNP is 0.962 and KSTCIND and KWAGEIND is 0.917). Therefore, even if there is no consensus on the theoretical relationship between KSTCIND and the other two variables, KSTCIND will not be used together with KPCGNP or KWAGEIND in this study.

Exchange rate, volatility and current account balance do not show strong correlations with any other variable. Therefore, the significance of these variables with one of 'wealth effect variables' (KSTCIND, KPCGNP and KWAGEIND) is examined from three regressional forms. The results of estimation by ordinary least squares are reported in Appendix Table (7)A2. For all regressions, the models fit very well. R^2 and Adjusted R^2 ranged from 0.74 to 0.92 and F-values for all regressions are significant in the 1 per cent level. Regression (3) containing KWAGEIND performs the best, resulting in the highest R^2, adjusted R^2 and F-value. Variables related to the economic situation of Korea (KSTCIND, KPCGNP and KWAGEIND) are all significant in the 1 per cent level. Significant level of b_4 (the coefficient of KPCGNP) is 0.08 per cent while c_4 (the coefficient of KWAGEIND) is 0.06 per cent. Two variables directly related to the economic situation of Korea appear to work very well. However, it is still controversial if the Korean stock market has its own effect on FDI because the significance of a3 (the coefficient of KSTCIND) might come from its high level of correlation with the other two variables throughout the sample period. It would be helpful to reconsider this problem when more data on KSTCIND are obtained.

Neither KEXR (exchange rate) nor VAKEXR (variance of exchange rate) is significant in the 10 per cent level in any regressional model. We cannot draw any evidence that the exchange rate or the variance of the exchange rate affects FDI from Korea to the world. Figures 7.4 and 7.5 respectively show the relation between FDI and the exchange rate and FDI and the exchange rate volatility from 1980 to 1992.

Korea's current account has a significance in regression 1 in the 10 per cent level, but the sign is unexpectedly negative. Variables adopted in regression 2 are available for the 1980–92 period and the regressional results are in Appendix Table (7)A3. With two more sample periods, KCABM and KPCGNP become significant in the 5 per cent level, a constant term is significant in the 10 per cent level, but KEXR and VAKEXR are still insignificant. The negative effect of the current account balance on FDI should be noted. The common belief among some economists in Korea that the increase of trade surplus leads FDI to the world is not supported by the empirical work. Figure 7.6 illustrates the changes in the current account of and FDI from Korea from 1980 to 1992.

From 1980, Korea's current account deficits gradually decreased and then the balance started to swing to surpluses from 1986, accelerating in 1987. As Korean FDI until 1987 in general followed the same trend as the current account, it might not be wrong to say that Korean FDI and the current account balance had high correlation until 1987. However, after 1987, the movements in the two variables are completely different from each other. The current account surplus hit a peak in 1988, and thereafter started to go the other way, recording the largest deficit (since 1980) in 1991, while FDI has been increasing consistently. Therefore, we do not have any strong evidence to argue that Korean FDI has been led by the current account.

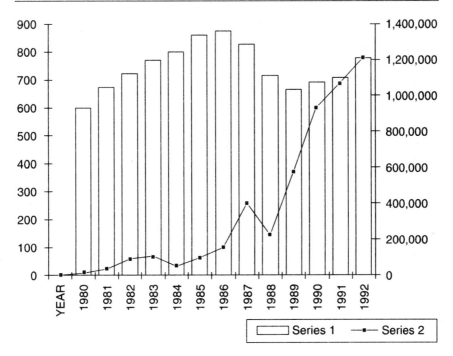

Figure 7.4 Korean FDI to the world and the exchange rate

Notes: Series 1 = Exchange rate (Korean won/US$)
Series 2 = Korean FDI to the world

Per capita GNP appears to be very important in explaining Korean FDI. Accurate data on KSTCIND are not available after 1991, even though it is widely accepted that KSTCIND already started to decrease after 1989. Since 1980, the Korean stock market has experienced a stable rise in the stock index, which soared up considerably from 1986 to 1989. This uptrend clearly has co-movement with that of per capita GNP (and that of FDI). However, since 1989, it (KSTCIND) has declined and kept the downtrend until 1993, a virtually opposite picture to the movement in FDI. Figure 7.7 presents Korean KSTCIND and FDI movements for the relevant period.

Korean FDI to North America

The same forms of regressions are performed for Korean FDI to North America. As that area can be categorised as the US dollar block, all independent variables utilised for the regression for the world are used again. R²s and adjusted R²s are very high for three regressions. The exchange rate and the volatility of the exchange rate, which are expected to be more significant than the regression with FDI to the world, do not

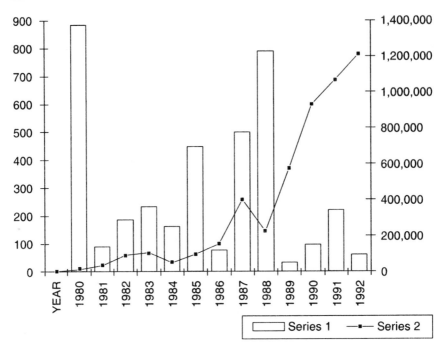

Figure 7.5 Korean FDI to the world and the exchange rate volatility

Notes: Series 1 = Exchange rate variance
Series 2 = Korean FDI to the world

show any significance. Neither of them significantly explained Korean FDI directed to North America for the sample period. KSTCIND, KPCGNP and KWAGEIND are significant in the 1 per cent level in all regressional equations. KCABM is significant in equations (1) and (2) but not in (3). The sign of KCABM is again negative which means that the Korean current account historically has given negative effect on FDI. These results are summarised in Appendix Table (7)A4.

Korean FDI to Indonesia

Indonesia has been the main destination of Korean FDI in Asia. This sub-section examines if some macroeconomic variables could explain this phenomenon. First, the correlations among prospective variables are obtained in Appendix Table (7)A5. It is the same as the cases for the world and North America that three independent variables, KSTCIND, KWAGEIND and KIPCGNP display close correlation with each other. It would be useful if we could use the wage (or wage index) ratio between the two countries. However, the wage data in Indonesia is not available.

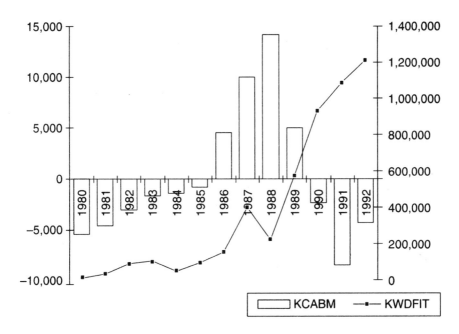

Figure 7.6 Korean FDI and the current account

Notes: KCABM = Korea's current acount in $M (left vertical axis)
          KWDFIT = Korean FDI to the world in $000 (right vertical axis)

Per capita GNP (KIPCGNP: in this case, the ratio of Korean per capita GNP to Indonesian per capita GNP in US dollar terms) data for the two countries still have a very high level of correlation with KSTCIND and KWAGEIND. The exchange rate used here (IKEXR) is the Indonesian currency (Rp). to the Korean won, and the variance of the exchange rate is derived based on the exchange rate as before. The exchange rate for the two countries indicates high correlation with those three variables which are considered to have a high correlation with time. Figure 7.8 depicts the change of the exchange rate of the won and Rp. to the US dollar since 1980. While the won has been relatively stable *vis-à-vis* the US dollar, the Rp. has experienced two large-scale devaluations in 1983 and 1986. As a result, the Rp. has consistently lost its priority to the Korean won which it had held before 1983. Therefore, the Rp./won exchange rate has increased (the Korean won has become stronger against the Indonesian currency) over time and has high correlation with a time trend.

Excluding variables which are considered to be highly correlated with one another to escape the multicollinearity problem, we can have four regressional formulae of which results are summarised in Appendix Table (7)A6.

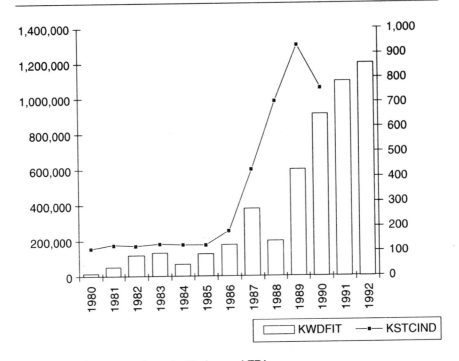

Figure 7.7 Korean stock market index and FDI

Notes: KWDFIT = Korean FDI to the world in $000
KSTCIND = Korean stock market indicator

The first regression shows the highest fitness of the model in both R^2 and adjusted R^2 terms. It also has the highest F-value of which the significant level is 5 per cent. F-value of (4) is also significant in the 5 per cent level while that of (3) is significant in the 10 per cent level. F-value of (2) is not significant in the 10 per cent level. VAKIEXR and KCABM have not been significant in any regression. The exchange rate is used in (1) where the coefficient has an expected positive sign and significant in the 1 per cent level. It confirms that Korean FDI to Indonesia has been impacted strongly by exchange rate changes between the two countries. This result indicates that with other things being equal, each unit depreciation of the Indonesian currency against the Korean won induces US$85.07M of additional Korean FDI to Indonesia.

In regression (2), the stock market index replaced the exchange rate. The variable has a coefficient with an expected sign and is significant in the 5 per cent level. Korea–Indonesia per capita GNP is used in (3) and the coefficient of the variable has an expected sign with the 5 per cent significance level. In the last regression, because the wage index of Indonesia is not available, the wage index of Korea is used and the

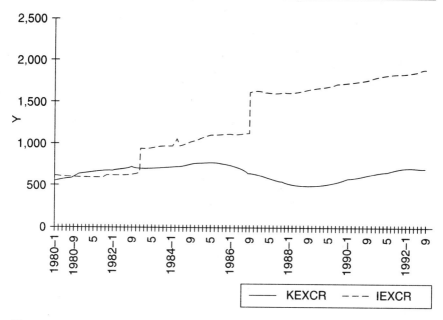

Figure 7.8 Exchange rate of Korean won and Indonesian Rp. to the US$

Notes: KEXCR = Korean exchange rate to US$
IEXCR = Indonesian exchange rate to US$

coefficient is significant in the 5 per cent level. As most Korean firms investing in Indonesia have concentrated on labour-intensive sectors, the effect of the relative wage levels between two countries on FDI flow must be examined. With recent wage data for the selected period, this topic will be revisited in the later section.

The results of regressions for 1980–90 indicate that only the variables correlated with a time trend are shown to be significant. As the exchange rate of the two countries and the Korean current account data are available up to 1992, the same regression as (1) is carried out for the longer period. Appendix Table (7)A7 is the result of that regression.

Adding two more sample periods (1991 and 1992), the fitness of the model increases notably. The constant term and coefficients of the exchange rate and Korean current account balance show slight changes and significance increases considerably. However the coefficient of VAKIEXR still remains insignificant. The exchange rate is significant in the 1 per cent level. The fluctuations of the exchange rate and Korean FDI to Indonesia over time are depicted in Figure 7.9.

The Korean current account turns out to be significant in the 5 per cent level. It was not significant even in the 10 per cent level in the former regression for 1980–90. This variable appears to have a very strong negative

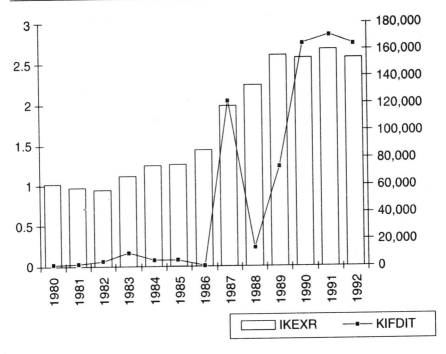

Figure 7.9 Exchange rate and FDI to Indonesia

Notes: IKEXR = Exchange rate Indonesian Rp./Korean won (left vertical axis)
KIFDIT = Korean FDI in Indonesia in $000 (right vertical axis)

effect on FDI, similar to the case for Korean FDI to the world, and it is reconfirmed by the high significance of the exchange rate that variables related to overall growth in the Korean economy have a positive effect on FDI.

As we can see from Figure 7.3, Korean FDI to Indonesia, after a dramatic increase in the 1980s, has been rather stable since 1990, but the overall FDI flowing to Asia has continued to rise. It might imply that Indonesia has lost its relative attractiveness as a destination for Korean FDI. We can raise two questions. How did Indonesia begin to lose its comparative advantages, and which country has gained from Indonesia's loss?

Before proceeding on this path, however, we recall that the start of our chapter mentioned the possible importance of non-market factors, which may in part explain the recent shift of Korean capital from Indonesia to other countries such as China and Vietnam. In the next section, therefore, we go back to the 1980s and look at these non-market factors, and ask how Southeast Asia, especially Indonesia, had come to emerge as the most favourable destinations for Korean firms in the late 1980s.

INTERNATIONAL ENVIRONMENT AND POLITICAL ECONOMIC CHARACTERISTICS OF KOREAN FDI IN THE 1980s

There are qualitative factors which we consider to be important in understanding the behaviour of Korean FDI, by industry or by region, even though by their nature we have not been able to adopt them in the regression analyses. This section scrutinises how those factors have affected FDI by looking at certain time series and cross-sectional data.

International environment for Korean FDI

One of the major contributing factors to Korea's rapid economic growth is exports. It is also true that Korea's outward-looking development policies made it heavily dependent on trade. With more than 40 per cent of GNP accounted for by exports, Korea has been highly vulnerable to shifts in the global economy. In particular, its heavy dependence on the markets of the United States has made it more sensitive to US protectionism. In 1988, the US alone accounted for more than 35 per cent of Korea's total exports.[27] As the saying goes, if Washington sneezes, Seoul catches a cold.

However, in the last decade, the long-standing intimate relationship between the US and Korea entered a patently different phase from that of the 1960s and 1970s, as the US entered an era of economic difficulty. The sudden rise in the exchange rate of the US dollar in the early 1980s weakened its international export competitiveness. This resulted in its international accounts reverting to deficit from 1982. The annual deficit reached US$10 billion in late 1984, accompanying a rapid decrease in net US holdings of foreign assets.[28]

Unlike the US economy in the 1980s, which was suffering from balance-of-payments problems, Japan emerged as the most influential creditor in the world due to a decrease in international oil prices and the low exchange rate of the yen. Japan's current account surpluses in 1984 reached US$35 billion. Importantly, in this context, 80 per cent of Japan's trade surplus was with the US.[29] This created severe trade friction between the two countries, which eventually led to the Plaza Accord of 1985, and triggered a steep revaluation of the yen.

In reaction to the burgeoning US trade deficit, the late 1980s saw the beginning of US criticism of the NICs, including Korea. As of January 1989, Washington excluded these nations from the General System of Preferences (GSP) and imposed Voluntary Export Restraints against such industries as textiles, apparel, shoes, television sets and steel in an effort to reduce chronic US trade deficits.[30] This was further reinforced by the steep appreciation of NIC currencies.

In addition to the Plaza Accord, which brought a 40 per cent appreciation of the yen against the US dollar, the Louvre Accord of 1987 resulted in a swift up-valuation of the Korean currency by more than 8 per cent in 1987 and 15 per cent in 1988.[31] These exchange rate realignments played a critical role in not only reducing Korea's penetration of the US market but also in reducing Korea's competitive advantages. However, as noted earlier, the direct relationship between the exchange rate and Korean FDI is found only in the case of investment to Indonesia. The appreciation of Korean currency appeared to have insignificant effect on its FDI to the US.

Wages, labour disputes and Korean FDI

At the same time, the newly emerging economies (NEEs) such as Indonesia, Malaysia and Thailand experienced economic growth similar to what the Asian NICs achieved in the 1960s and 1970s. Taking advantage of their cheap and abundant supply of labour (less than US$1 per hour as late as 1990, see Table 7.5) and their increasingly positive foreign investment policies (that sometimes courted foreign investors to a fault),[32] the NEEs superseded Korea's main export industries like textiles, shoes, clothing, and toys. For example, in terms of export markets in the footwear industry, Korea had to relinquish its comparative advantage (low price) to other developing countries (e.g., Indonesia and China). In 1992 the export price per unit of Korean footwear sold to the US market was US$13.46, whereas China's per unit cost for the same product was US$4.35, Indonesia's US$7.47, and Taiwan's US$8.42.[33]

This rapid increase in wages in Korea compared to other Asian developing countries was partly due to the rise in labour disputes in Korea. The effect of labour disputes on FDI may be manifested in various ways. It increases political and economic instability and deters domestic investors from investing in domestic industry or markets. Another consequence may be pressure on wage rates. Labour struggles usually aim at improving working conditions for those in jobs, including higher wages, and it is clear that was the case in 1980s Korea. Competitiveness in many of Korea's

Table 7.5 Wages per hour in textile industry by country, unit: US$

Country/Year	1980	1989	1990
Korea	0.78	2.87	3.22
Thailand	0.33	0.68	0.92
Indonesia	–	0.23	0.25
Malaysia	0.43	0.82	0.86
Philippines	–	0.64	0.67

Source: C.Y. Ahn, 'Dongnama Gyeongjega Ddeooreugo Itdda' ('The Emerging Power of Southeast Asian Economies'), *Sin Dong A*, June 1992, p. 395

export industries, particularly in the labour-intensive, simple manufactured product categories, was eroded. In addition, we have to consider another important but not easily observable effect of labour dispute on the cost, such as the increase of the fringe benefits. All of them make domestic investment less attractive and lead to higher FDI.

Consequences of Korea's economic development with special reference to domestic politics of the late 1980s

One of the most distinctive features of Korea's exceptional economic growth since the early 1960s can be seen in the authoritarian state's conscious exclusion of popular sectors (i.e. the middle stratum of professionals, skilled workers, business people and farmers). This was particularly evident in semi-skilled and unskilled manufacturing labour sectors and stemmed from the political and economic decision-making process in the name of *godo seongjang* (high-speed growth). This process has seen two major developments in Korea's political economy:

1 the main element of Korea's successful and effective export-oriented and labour-intensive industrialisation has been the maintenance of a low-cost and disciplined labour;
2 the social and political repression and hostility towards labour, especially organised labour, formed the key not only to the decline in its bargaining power, but to a rise in the government's power over the economy and society.

Equally important is the failure by both the Park Chung-Hee (1961–79, Third and Fourth Republic) and the Chun Doo-Hwan (1980–88, Fifth Republic) regimes to pay adequate attention to qualitative changes in the social environment, thereby creating considerable inconsistency between economic and social progress. During the Chun era, various measures aimed at restricting labour's political power were much harsher than those during the Park period. For example, the new Trade Union Law of 1980 decentralised the union movement to the company level and gave the government rights to change the existing union structure at any time. The new Labour Disputes Adjustments Law renovated the state's power in labour disputes, and banned all types of involvement by external organisations (e.g. church groups and students) in labour actions.[34] The failure of the government in recognising the emerging importance of popular sectors during the rapid industrialisation stage played a leading role in the build-up of enormous popular discontent, which became a major social crisis, critically affecting the structure of Korean industry and trade in the late 1980s. This was highlighted by the nation-wide pro-democracy movement in June 1987, the '87 *Yuweol Minjuhwa Hangjaeng* ('87 June Struggle for Democratisation), which led to such events as Chun's decision to name his close military and personal friend Roh Tae-Woo – then the Chairman of the Democratic Justice Party (DJP) – as his successor. In fact, mounting popular protests played a crucial role in drawing President Roh's (1988–92, Sixth Republic) abrupt announcement (so-called *Palchil Yukigu Seonyeon* – 29 June Declaration of '87) of the government's intention to repeal its restrictive labour regulations, and to allow for media freedom and direct presidential election.

In particular, the Roh package included freedom of labour union formation and activism. This opened a new chapter in the entire history of government–labour relations in Korea. As such, for the first time, the minimum daily wage was finally legislated, and the new labour law guaranteed the three rights of labour (union organisation, collective bargaining, and collective acting). In addition, the new legislation called for non-interference by the state in industrial actions by the workers.[35] As an alternative to the state's puppet organisation (Federation of Korean Trade Unions), the Federation of Democratic Labour Unions was established. Moreover, the number of unions increased at a remarkable rate – 1,400 new unions in 1987 alone, and the total number reached approximately 8,000 in 1990.[36]

These new developments led to an unprecedented wave of labour activism. The consequence of alienation created by decades of labour repression and exploitation was manifested in an explosion of protests and strikes, demanding 'better pay, more time off, safety equipment, the abolition of sexual and occupational discrimination, the abolition of morning physical exercise, better food at lunch, and more freedom in choosing their clothes and hairstyles'.[37]

Shortly after the Roh announcement, more than 3,700 labour disturbances took place, with 2,552 strikes in August alone.[38] As shown in Table 7.6, these numbers exceeded the total number of labour disputes in the entire period between 1960 and 1986. The following description characterises the costs of labour disputes:

> The 1987 strikes caused a loss of 8.2 million working days, with an additional 3.4 million in the first ten months of 1988. In 1988, the loss of production was calculated to be US$3 billion; lost exports were US$7 billion. In the first ten months of 1989, lost production was estimated to be US$5.5 billion; lost exports were US$1.15 billion. Both the Daewoo and Hyundai (Korea's leading business groups) motor companies fell far short of their production targets during periods of labour unrest. Hyundai Heavy Industries claimed that it lost US$6 million in sales daily during its extended strike in 1989.[39]
>
> (Kearney 1991: 123–4)

The biggest blow to the low-wage and export-oriented Korean economy came in the form of the massive wage rises after June 1987. Between 1986

Table 7.6 Number of labour strikes in Korea: 1971–89

Year	No. of strikes
1971–79	3,359
1987	3,749
1988	1,873
1989	1,616

Sources: Jung-En Woo, *Race to the Swift*, 1991, p. 112; and *Asian Finance*, July 15 1991, p. 39

and 1989, wages increased by 60 per cent in Korean currency terms, and 90 per cent in US dollar terms.[40] In particular, wages in the manufacturing sector soared faster than average income movements; for the first seven months of 1988 average income increased by 16.5 per cent while manufacturing wages rose 21.2 per cent. This was despite the government's mandatory guideline for wage increases that stipulated such changes should not exceed single digits, a guideline which had been kept for twenty years.[41] The dramatic surge in labour costs resulted in the sharp fall in Korean export competitiveness. The rate of Korean export growth, for example, fell from 24.8 per cent in 1988 to 2.8 per cent in 1989, 4.2 per cent in 1990, 10.5 per cent in 1991, and 6.8 per cent in 1992.[42]

The rapid wage increases, which failed to allow for productivity and prices growth, resulted in the regression of light industries. The percentage of light industries in pure manufacture between 1988 and 1991 showed a 5 per cent drop (to 38 per cent) from the period of 1985–87. This provided a decisive incentive for wage-conscious Korean (manufacturing) firms to seek alternative low-wage labour, with low associated costs of employment (welfare health benefit, workers' compensation for injury and infrastructural development of occupational requirements), overseas.

STRUCTURE OF FDI

It has been argued that Korean FDI has been relatively small-scale, particularly FDI to Southeast Asia. In order to confirm the hypothesis that the labour-intensive sector has been more vulnerable to labour disputes, the number of labour strikes and the figures on FDI are compared. The relation between the two sets of figures is reflected in the sudden increase in small-scale, and labour-intensive investments in the low-labour-cost Southeast Asian countries, which also enjoyed low levels of labour unrest. While 132 projects (17.6 per cent of total FDI) or some US$332 million (28.5 per cent) were realised in the manufacturing sector between 1968 and 1987, 905 projects (57.4 per cent) or US$1,861 million (49 per cent) were invested in that sector over the next five years.[43] This new phase of Korean FDI had been carried out by small-scale investors; 35.2 per cent of the total number of projects, or a mere 4.9 per cent of total investment value, was made by small and medium-sized companies before 1985. These figures soared to 58.7 per cent and 26.8 per cent respectively between 1986 and 1990. In 1991, 66.8 per cent of all foreign investment projects were undertaken by small to medium-size investors.[44]

The following commentary by the director of the Hyosung Group provides an insight into this development:

> The labour unions seem to dislike it but the fact is that because of the growing strength of South Korean unions there will be more factories built out of South Korea. That is their fault. They can ask for 20 per cent or 30 per cent wage rises, but they will be killing themselves. More jobs will be leaving South Korea.[45]

(Clifford and Moore 1988: 89)

Another statement made by an executive of a (Korean) footwear company further consolidates the sentiment:

> Our company had to leave for Indonesia after our factory in Pusan (the second largest city after Seoul in Korea) suffered heavy losses last year (1988) following a prolonged workers' strike. . . . Indonesia is a heaven because workers are paid US$50–60 a month, compared with the US$350 a month we used to pay Korean workers.[46]

(Guat 1989: 46)

Therefore, we may conclude that the countries with a negligible labour union power, as well as a low labour cost, become very attractive destination of Korean FDI after it experienced frequent labour disputes. As shown in Table 7.7, Korean FDI by manufacturing firms in Southeast Asia showed remarkable growth since 1988. Most have concentrated in Indonesia, the country that provided the lowest rate of labour cost among ASEAN nations. As such, the total amount of Korean FDI (US$48.17 million) in 1988 alone equalled to 91.7 per cent of total cumulative Korean FDI in the region prior to 1987. Almost half of that amount (US$23.74 million) shifted to Indonesia, whereas Malaysia, where labour cost was relatively higher than in the others (Indonesia, Thailand and the Philippines), appeared unattractive to Korean firms.[47]

Moreover, Korean investors who were 'small-scale, wage-conscious and labour-intensive', would prefer countries that provided the comparative advantages of low wages and more effective labour control.[48] Indonesia had been the best 'fit', because it had the lowest wage rate and the most politically disciplined labour force – that is, until in very recent years when Vietnam and China loomed as even cheaper-labour destinations. In 1990, the minimum wage rate per day in Jakarta (Rp. 2100, which was equivalent

Table 7.7 Korean FDI in ASEAN by manufacturing industry, US$ 000

	1973–85		1986		1987	
	No. of projects	Value	No. of projects	Value	No. of projects	Value
Thailand	3	1,871	1	45	2	997
Indonesia	5	11,993	–	–	3	2,349
Malaysia	4	26,488	1	588	1	240
Philippines	2	2,009	–	–	1	2,062
Singapore	2	3,908	–	–	–	–
Total	16	46,269	2	633	7	5,648

	1988		1989		Total	
	No. of cases	Amount	No. of cases	Amount	No. of cases	Amount
Thailand	14	16,098	14	13,363	34	32,374
Indonesia	22	23,744	53	76,383	83	114,469
Malaysia	4	3,301	15	33,858	25	64,475
Philippines	4	4,529	14	8,758	21	17,358
Singapore	1	500	–	–	3	4,408
Total	45	48,172	96	132,362	166	233,084

Source: K.S. Bae and S.I. Hong, *ASEAN Jegukeui Tujahwangyeonggwa Urieui Jinchuljeonryak* (Investment Environment of ASEAN Countries and Korea's Strategy), Seoul, Korean Institute for Economics and Technology (KIET), 1990, p. 75

to US$1) was less than half that of Thailand (90 baht, or US$ 3.50), less than a sixth of the wage rate in Malaysia (about US$6–7), and also significantly lower than the rate in the Philippines (89 pesos per day, or US$3–4).[49]

Yoon-Hwan Shin provides another valuable insight into why Korean firms had preferred Indonesia to any other Southeast Asian countries despite Indonesia's poor infrastructure, such as a relatively unskilled labour force, ineffective procedures and prevalent corruption in the bureaucracy.[50] He argues that the political structure of Suharto's Indonesia in which entrepreneurs or businessmen were highly dependent on government power, provided a more comfortable atmosphere than any other country to the Korean businessmen who had long been accustomed to the strong government and bureaucracy and pervasive red tape.[51] As he correctly puts it,

To be sure, Korean businesses have also been influenced in their decision to invest in North America, the most favoured region for Korean FDI, by Korea's strengthening organised labour and the appreciating won. But the prime motivation has been more or less defensive and aimed at circumventing the protectionist measures and pressures threatened by the American government'.[52]

(Yoon-Hwan Shin 1992: 4–5)

By contrast, those who moved to Southeast Asia, particularly to Indonesia, were motivated by factors like cheaper labour and the desire to avoid the increasingly militant labour movement at home, and to overcome the increasing labour shortage in Korea deriving from reduced incentives for the so-called three D works (dirty, difficult, and dangerous) undertaken by semi-skilled or unskilled workers.[53] The latter investments were made predominantly in such highly labour-intensive, light manufacturing industries as textiles, particularly garments and weaving, leather goods, and footwear.

However, Korean FDI behaviour in Southeast Asia has already created various problems, least of all labour strikes. According to the Indonesian Ministry of Manpower, the industrial actions by Indonesian workers against their foreign bosses including Korean bosses have been rising in recent years. In 1991 ninety instances of labour unrest were reported, compared to sixty in 1990, in Indonesia; most of which were in manufacturing.[54] A crucial point is that most cases of labour unrest in Indonesia are attributed to such industrial issues as maltreatment of local workers, low pay and compulsory overtime. According to recent research (January 1993) conducted by Korean Trade Promotion Corporations (KOTRA), in examining thirty-three Korean firms which had successfully invested in Southeast Asia, preliminary investigation of the feasibility and future prospects of the investments and the smooth relationship between labour and management were claimed to be the most powerful factors behind the firms' success.[55] Nevertheless, the numbers of labour strikes in Korean–Asian joint ventures, particularly in manufacturing industries (textile, shoes and garments), continued to increase. For example, in February 1993, the largest labour strike (600 workers) in a Korean–Vietnamese joint venture since the emergence of socialism in Vietnam was reported to have been caused by 'long-working hours, poor pay and mistreatment by their foreign bosses'.[56]

It would be dangerous to view these developments as a result of Korean firms' often ad hoc, improvisatory and unsystematic posture. But the Korean FDI behaviour so far, particularly in Southeast Asia, shows what a Korean journalist refers to as a 'gipsy pattern'[57], seeking short-term profits, low wages and a compliant workforce. This impression is further reinforced when one takes a close look at the recent shift (1992 onwards) of Korean capital from Southeast Asia, particularly from Indonesia, to socialist countries like China that provide still cheaper labour costs (incomes, raw materials and industrial site costs) than Southeast Asian countries, and with fewer labour union conflicts. As of November 1992, Korean FDI worldwide by small-and medium-sized firms amounted to around US$1.1 billion, in 1,979 projects. Of these, 60 per cent (US$677 million and 979 projects) were located in Asia. Among Asian countries China ranked top in terms of number of projects (92 per cent of which were in manufacturing industries); of other Asian countries, Indonesia with 163 projects, the Philippines with 103 projects and Thailand with 58 projects.[58]

Within this context, the success story of Japanese FDI in the 1960s and 1970s provides numerous implications for the present picture of Korean FDI. The section below will focus on major characteristics of Japanese FDI in the period, particularly on the way in which the Japanese government and other institutions led successful operation of FDI. A thorough analysis of the post-war Japanese capitalism, such as the role of the government in economy through industrial policy, the banking system and the government's relations with business, finance and labour, provides a good insight into the way in which FDI has been a crucial determinant behind the pre-eminence of Japanese economy.

JAPANESE FDI OF THE 1960s AND 1970s: LESSONS AND IMPLICATIONS

The experience of Japanese FDI in the 1960s and 1970s suggests various implications for the future direction of Korean FDI. During this period various structural changes occurred in Japan. It was crucial that Japan began to promote industrial change, rather than simply protecting struggling industries. Steps were taken to conserve energy and promote an orderly reduction in production capacity in certain traditional and energy intensive industries like steel and petrochemicals. Incentives were devised to encourage the growth and development of new areas like electronics, assembling and processing industries. But how do we explain this quick, quiet and successful transformation? A careful examination of the mechanisms such as the *sogo shosha* (trading companies) and the role of the state, underlying the success of Japanese FDI will provide the reason why. In other words, the lesson from the Japanese FDI experience is how the Japanese state and enterprises utilised the FDI strategy from a national economy standpoint and how they achieved the level of sophistication in industries that were losing comparative advantages. The following section will examine how relative the Japanese model is to Korean FDI of the late 1980s.

Japanese FDI, starting from 1951, was relatively small and limited (under US$100 million average) until the early 1960s. In this period, due to the nation's lack of natural resources, the acquisition of raw materials played a major motivation in the process of FDI. However, with the advent of rapid economic growth (the 1960s and 1970s), Japanese FDI entered a new phase. Between 1962 and 1967, it recorded a three-fold increase in the

Table 7.8 Japanese FDI by year

Year	No of Projects	Amount (US$ M)
1951–70	3,733	3,576
1971	904	858
1972	1,774	2,338
1973	3,093	3,494
1974	1,912	2,395
1975	1,591	3,280
1976	1,652	3,462
1977	1,761	2,806
1978	2,393	4,598
1979	2,694	4,995

Source: S.L. Shon, *Ilbongiyeopeui Haeoejikjeoptujawa Gukjejeonryak* (Foreign Direct Investment of Japanese Firms and Their Strategies of Globalisation), Seoul, KIEP, 1990, p. 75

annual average figures over the earlier two decades. Particularly during 1972–73, Japanese FDI in both project number and value exceeded the cumulative total of the twenty-one-year period to 1971.

As was the case of Korean FDI in the late 1980s, a distinctive feature of Japanese FDI in the period of rapid economic growth was the rapid increase in FDI in manufacturing sectors such as textiles, chemicals and electrical machinery. In particular, most of them went to Southeast Asia, including Korea and Taiwan. The intensive processes of relocation of production to foreign countries were manifold. Japan's chronic difficulties with its balance of payments had been overcome. It was also facilitated by substantial liberalisation of outward foreign direct investment from 1967, and considerable assistance from statutory bodies, including the Overseas Economic Co-operation Fund and the Export–Import Bank of Japan.

The rise in Japanese FDI can also be traced to factors like the threat to Japanese exports from industrialised countries, erosion of Japanese comparative advantage *vis-à-vis* other developing countries like Korea and Taiwan, and anxiety about raw materials. Although there was a curb on Japanese FDI in the mid-1970s (1974–77) due to the oil shock of 1973–74, FDI continued to play a critical role in Japan's capacity to maintain its economic momentum in the 1980s. Indeed, after 1984, with large increases in trade surpluses since 1981, Japan emerged as the world's largest capital exporter.

It was Kojima who first attempted to theorise about Japanese FDI based on changes in the Japanese economy and its relation to the national welfare

Table 7.9 Japanese FDI by sectors, in per cent

Sector	Year	1951–61	1962–67	1968–71	1972–73	1974–77	1978–81
MFT	Amount	36.3	34.8	24.7	38.1	33.7	34.3
	NP	25.2	42.6	40.0	39.1	31.2	34.0
NRD	Amount	44.6	28.1	33.1	29.1	27.9	21.1
	NP	14.2	9.6	9.7	7.2	9.9	7.3
T&O	Amount	19.1	37.1	42.2	32.8	38.4	44.6
	NP	60.6	47.8	50.3	53.8	59.0	58.7

Source: Eui-Jung Kang, *Ilbonhaeoetujaeui Seonggyeok Bunseok: Muyeokgwa Haeoetuja* (The Analysis of the Characteristics of the Japanese FDI: Trade and FDI), unpublished Masters Dissertation, Seoul National University, Korea, p. 17

Notes: MFT = Manufacturing
NRD = Natural Resource Development
T&O = Trade and Others
NP = Number of Projects

of the investing and home countries. He argued that Japanese FDI in low-labour cost and resource-rich developing countries has been directed, to a large degree, to industries which were in decline in Japan and in which the recipient countries were acquiring a comparative advantage. This kind of investment usually leads to the increase of exports to Japan from the developing host countries and to an upgrading of industrial structure on both sides (complementary relationship). Thus, the Japanese FDI is trade oriented and 'development oriented', and is different from American type investment which is, in Kojima's term, 'anti-trade oriented investment'.[59] In other words, Kojima seemingly argued that whereas Japanese FDI started from the concept of altruism for the welfare of the global economy, America's (namely the US's) was simply individualistic and 'totally oblivious of social costs and benefits'.[60]

Although Kojima's argument is useful in understanding the FDI behaviour of the transfer of industries requiring labour-intensive and standardised technology from the developed to the developing world, it may have nothing to do with the complementarity of industrial development that he refers to, or with the neoclassical thesis that free trade automatically generates development between poor and rich economies (the 'international division of labour' school). As Roemer points out, Japanese FDI of the 1960s and 1970s came about through fortuitous circumstances in which there was no alternative but to relocate labour-intensive industries offshore and develop brain- and capital-intensive industries at home, or go bankrupt. According to Roemer, 'Southeast Asia has been Japan's main sphere of influence, and labour-intensive investment is the natural type of investment to make in that area, and a large, unsaturated domestic market made foreign expansion in the advanced sectors less critical during the 1960s'.[61]

An extended theoretical development of Kojima's hypothesis can be located in Ozawa (1979).[62] Like Kojima, Ozawa examines Japanese FDI within the macroeconomic framework, arguing that the mainspring of Japanese FDI lay in the changing structure of domestic industries caused by internal and external economic factors as a result of rapid industrialisation. These factors include 'uncertain supplies of overseas resources, scarcity of labour and industrial sites at home, and the ever-deteriorating environmental conditions'. These, in fact, forced the government to adopt certain policies to encourage the growth of high-tech industries at home and encourage the relocation of labour-intensive and pollution-prone industries offshore.[63]

In short, to Ozawa, the main driving forces behind Japanese FDI were the inevitable consequences of macroeconomic change, both internal and external. Japan's poor natural resources and heavy reliance on the export of labour-intensive manufactured goods in the 1960s and 1970s determined that success in export-led industrialisation in the next stage required extensive Japanese FDI.

Both Kojima and Ozawa's insight into the relationship between a nation's comparative advantage and its FDI within the relative factor endowments is useful in understanding how the changes of domestic industrial structures affect FDI behaviour. Interestingly, motives and determinants of Japanese FDI in accordance with its rapid economic development in the 1960s and 1970s are very much similar to those of Korean FDI of the late 1980s. However, it seems that where the Japanese model differs from the Korean model is in the particular features of the Japanese industrial network, such as the role played by trading companies and the government in the operation of FDI. These features warrant a little further discussion.

Sogo shosha and jonghap sangsa

The Japanese *sogo shosha* has often been translated into English as 'general trading company'. But a close examination of their role in overseas investment reveals this translation to be inappropriate. A particular feature of the *sogo shosha* is their organising ability, based on skilled personnel in both top and middle management, that is usually associated with a high level of diversification. In the 1970s the big nine *sogo shosha* among more than 8,000 trading companies in Japan[64] dominated the country's overseas transactions (47 per cent of Japan's exports and 55 per cent of its imports in 1977).[65]

The *sogo shosha*'s leading role is largely facilitated by the existence of the gigantic corporate conglomerates, popularly known as *zaibatsu* or *Keiretsu*, such as Mitsui, Mitsubishi and Sumitomo. The big *sogo shosha* in the 1970s and the 1980s invested not only in raw materials development but also in commerce, finance, insurance, services and all sectors of manufacturing. An important point to be made here is that those firms moved into export markets from domestically well-established industries. Any Japanese firm that could succeed in cut-throat competition among various economic sectors at home – such as banking, the *sogo shosha* and numerous subcontract and affiliate firms – was well positioned to compete successfully with foreign firms in overseas markets. This was facilitated by various official measures such as QC (quality control), TQM (total quality management) and ZD (zero-defect) amongst others.

In the case of Korea, however, the situation was somewhat different. Various problems rooted in the rapid expansion of exports in the mid-1970s provided a strong incentive for the government to establish trading companies. These problems included excessive competition within domestic firms, over-dependence on government subsidies and expansion of in-experienced and under-capitalised, small-scale manufacturing exporters.

With these problems in mind, the Korean government established thirteen trading companies, known as *jonghap sangsa* (a direct translation of *sogo shosha*) in the mid-1970s. In theory the main objectives of these were to expand exports, seek new markets and provide a proper export channel for small- and medium-sized manufacturers. However, the Park regime's strong drive for exports eventually made the *jonghap sangsa* focus almost exclusively on their export function.

Although the *jonghap sangsa* contributed substantially to Korean exports (handling more than 40 per cent of all exports in the 1970s), excessive emphasis on the export function retarded functional diversification of trading companies such as that of products and regions. In fact, the government's strong export policy, particularly of heavy industrial products, bred a favoured group of big firms, thereby widening the discrepancy between the big and small-to-medium firms. These large conglomerates were influential also because they were capable of meeting the government's requirements for membership of the *jaebeol*, such as paid-in-capital of US$2.5 million, US$50 million exports per annum and the establishment of ten overseas branches.[66] Furthermore, unlike the case of *sogo shosha*, the ability of Korean trading companies to finance trade transactions or invest in long-term projects were severely limited. This is simply because the government controlled virtually all public and private banks and banned the *jonghap sangsa* from setting up or taking over any banks.[67]

The government

The role of Japanese government is one of the more fundamental factors in the smooth operation of Japanese FDI. Reference to the government in this context should focus on the highly effective bureaucracies such as the Ministry of International Trade and Industry (MITI), the Ministry of Finance and the Economic Planning Agency. MITI has to an overwhelming degree externalised the risk for business ventures in that it makes available information regarding Japan's economic position in relation to the world economy. For instance, information is freely supplied to Japanese firms irrespective of the latter's size (and to some extent, to foreign firms). This information base (involving indicators such as market share, demand growth and import competition) is constantly updated. This information dissemination role, in fact, falls squarely within the sphere of operations of the Japan External Trade Organisation (JETRO), an agency under the MITI umbrella.

To further facilitate this objective, the bureaucratic organs have used administrative guidance,[68] protective legislation, financial incentives and disincentives, and threats and directives to channel the Japanese private sector towards a direction that is in line with broad strategic goals. This economic management aspect has incorporated a consultative mechanism between bureaucrats, big business and industrial bodies to generate a broad consensus towards the economic objective.

In this context, the government performs the key role of signaller, which has credibility in facilitating businesses' planning, with the latter understanding that their decisions will be integrated into the national strategy. This has the effect of minimising the possibility of bottlenecks and amounts to a coordinated and integrated system of economic management, focused upon international competitiveness as well as serving the Japanese nation.

The government's role in promoting new technology and dealing with the declining industries at home is also relevant. Dore describes the Japanese government's three major roles in the development of high-tech industries:

1 to finance research, but also to direct and co-ordinate the research effort of private industry under the administrative guidance of the MITI;
2 to accelerate the fiscal and monetary incentives to private enterprise provided by tax measures and the lending policies of the major state banks (Japan Development Bank, the Export–Import Bank of Japan, Small Business Finance Corporation);
3 through direct intervention, to reduce internal competition and coordinate rationalising measures to enhance the international competitiveness of a Japanese infant industry.[69]

Equally important, these measures were aimed at promoting commercialisation of the fruits of R&D rather than the R&D activity itself. The government provided various kinds of grants and funds to promote new frontier industries, with major organisations such as the Agency for Industrial Science and Technology (AIST) undertaking the research mission as communicated through the MITI, although the latter did not have official control of research bodies' activity. These research organisations carried out basic research in areas closely related to industrial technology where higher education institutions were unable to provide, helping in the transfer of technology to small- and medium-sized firms and in the development of applied technology for public goods. Anti-pollution technology, for instance, is a necessity but one for which the private sector could not be relied on to conduct sufficient R&D.

In short, the success of Japanese capital exports and of building a strong basis for a great leap towards high technology in the 1970s was a result of close cooperation among 'private banks, government financial agencies as well as the *sogo shosha* and the manufacturers themselves'.[70] In other words, although the rapid industrialisation based on exports resulted in rapid domestic industrial restructuring, the active involvement of the government and close linkage among industrial networks such as the big enterprises and their affiliates made the operation of FDI and the development of high-tech industries a success. Compared with their Japanese counterparts, the role of the Korean government in FDI has also been quite different. That is, there has existed an intentional negligence by both the Korean government and the *jaebeol* in fostering the development of high-tech industries at home.

The Korean government and the jaebeol

Though the EOI strategy brought about rapid economic growth, it also produced a strong tendency for excessive dependence by Korean firms on Japan and the US for critical components in manufacturing export products such as technology and machinery. This was an unsurprising phenomenon given the developing status of the Korean economy and its focus on exports. Nevertheless, this excessive reliance on overseas physical and intellectual capital could induce domestic businesses to overlook their own R&D obligations. In addition to Korea's three leading motor companies' high dependence on foreign companies – 15 per cent Mitsubishi ownership of Hyundai, 50 per cent of Daewoo Motors by General Motors, and Mazda's 8 per cent and Ford's 10 per cent equity in Kia motors – 90 per cent of new technologies that Korean firms adopted in 1991 came from foreign countries, mostly Japan and the US.[71] Another example is that, in 1988, against the government's strong wish to have 1.86 per cent of GNP spent on research and development, the ratio came to only 0.4 per cent.

Because of the lack of local investment in R&D, resulting over time in Korea's decline in competitiveness in the global market, FDI in low-labour cost regions became the most attractive option for Korean firms to maintain export market shares. Instead, in close collaboration with the government, the *jaebeol*, which should have been able to bring about further advance in the industrial structure, continued to put great effort into pursuing short-term profits through investing in speculative assets such as real estate and golf properties.[72] It seems that to Korean business people, 'R&D means pouring money into ventures where the returns are long-term and the outcomes uncertain'.[73] Furthermore, the consistent monopolistic and oligopolistic dominance of the *jaebeol* in the domestic market is still prevalent. As of 1 April 1992, there were altogether seventy-eight *jaebeol* which consisted of a total of 1,056 affiliated industrial firms. Whereas during the period between January and October 1992, the number of company shutdowns or cessations reached 598, 90 per cent of which came from small-to medium-sized manufacturing firms, largely due to their weak financial and technological capabilities which have meant that small- and medium-sized manufacturing firms have had to look offshore for their businesses' viability.[74]

CONCLUSION

This chapter's study of the economic reasons for Korean FDI shows that some variables, such as wage rate and per capita GNP, could explain the whole Korean FDI experience well, while others are only partially significant. For instance, FDI to Indonesia was influenced by exchange rates but that to the world was not. There was no evidence that Korea's current account surpluses played a major role in accelerating FDI, in contrast to the widespread belief in the literature on Japan that such a link exists.

The chapter argues that the sudden, large increase in Korean FDI in the late 1980s was fundamentally rooted in the changing structure of the domestic political economy (state–labour relations, for example) rather than in some economic factors (e.g. external balance surplus) that underlay the Japanese FDI experience of the 1960s and 1970s. The beginning of severe labour unrest and phenomenal increases in wage rates became the major factor behind Korea losing its comparative advantage in labour-intensive industries. This, in turn, became the major push factor in the surge in Korean FDI. Furthermore, the *jaebeol* and their affiliated firms that have been expanding under the patronage of the government could not find a proper way of dealing with their labour problem. In fact, without substantial negotiation with workers these sectors began pursuing a relocation of production offshore. The region that best fitted Korean requirements was, of course, low-wage Southeast Asia, where labour problems had also been negligible.

It would be true that Korean FDI, especially to Southeast Asia, has accompanied the structural adjustment of Korean economy, which has experienced a period of transformation from a labour-intensive, light-industry oriented economy to a capital- or technology-intensive, heavy-industry oriented economy. However, the dramatic increase in Korean FDI to Southeast Asia cannot be described as a systematic process in terms of structural economic adjustment. Instead, it has been a haphazard reaction to political economic developments at home during the 1980s. The government's changed policy agenda was more related to the government's previous mismanagement of the emerging metamorphosis of government–society relations, a condition stemming from the government's past economic policy that emphasised rapid industrialisation through exports. The radical eruption of the civil society in the period of political thawing played a leading role in persuading Korean firms, especially small- and medium-sized firms – whose business is heavily dependent on cheap labour and exports, and are thus susceptible to frequent labour disputes – to seek countries like Indonesia for the provision of cheaper productive inputs. The move to such FDI recipient countries was reinforced by the availability of existing labour-exploitative structures in those countries, such as authoritarian labour control and the tradition of clientelism between government and business.[75]

Appendix

Table (7)A1.1 Correlation among independent variables: 1980–90

	KEXR	VAKEXR	KCABM	KSTCIND	KPCGNP	KWAGEIND
KEXR	1.000	−0.209	0.299	−0.259	−0.167	−0.038
VAKEXR	−0.209	1.000	0.290	−0.080	−0.175	−0.255
KCABM	0.299	0.290	1.000	0.573	0.461	0.429
KSTCIND	−0.259	−0.080	0.573	1.000	0.962	0.917
KPCGNP	−0.167	−0.175	0.461	0.962	1.000	0.987
KWAGEIND	−0.038	−0.255	0.429	0.917	0.987	1.000

Notes:
KEXR   Exchange rate (=US dollar/Korean won)
VAKEXR   Variance of exchange rate
KCABM   Korea's current account balance
KSTCIND   Korean stock market indicator
KPCGNP   Korean per capita GNP
KWAGEIND   Korean wage index (1985=100)

Table (7)A1.2 Korean FDI to the world: 1980–90

Regressors	Regressions		
	1	2	3
CONSTANT	−1377 (−1.82)	−820 (−1.65)	−381 (−0.89)
KEXR	1.58 (−1.83)	5.58 (1.03)	−0.05 (−0.10)
VAKEXR	0.13 (0.57)	0.04 (0.23)	0.04 (0.24)
KCABM	−0.03 (−2.26)	0.02 (−1.77)	−0.01 (−1.30)
KSTCIND	1.30 (4.57)	– (–)	– (–)
KPCGNP	– (–)	0.23 (6.28)	– (–)
KWAGEIND	– (–)	– (–)	5.92 (6.62)
R^2	0.85	0.91	0.92
Adj.R^2	0.74	0.85	0.86
Regression F-value	8.30 (0.01)	15.03 (0.00)	16.66 (0.00)
Durbin-Watson	2.04	2.23	2.24

Notes: Numbers in the parentheses are t- or f-statistics
Units in US$ million for FDI, KPCGNP and KCABM
Regression 1: $KFDI_t = a_0 + a_1 IKEXR_t + a_2 VAKIEXR_t + a_3 KCABM_t + a_4 KSTCIND_t + u_t$
Regression 2: $KFDI_t = b_0 + b_1 IKEXR_t + b_2 VAKIEXR_t + b_3 KCABM_t + b_4 KPCGNP_t + v_t$
Regression 3: $KFDI_t = c_0 + c_1 IKEXR_t + c_2 VAKIEXR_t + c_3 KCABM_t + c_4 KWAGEIND_t + w_t$
where $KFDI_t$ is Korean FDI at year t, a_0, b_0 and c_0 are constants and u_t, v_t and w_t are error terms

Table (7)A1.3 Korean FDI to the world: 1980–92

Regressors	Coefficient	T-statistics	Significant level
CONSTANT	−738.59	−2.16	0.06
KEXR	0.49	1.20	0.27
VAKEXR	0.01	0.06	0.95
KCABM	−0.01	−2.63	0.03
KPCGNP	0.22	13.54	0.00

Note: $R^2 = 0.96$, Adj.$R^2 = 0.95$, F-value = 54.93 (Sig.level = 0.0), D-W = 2.45

Table (7)A1.4 Korean FDI to North America: 1980–90

| Regressors | Regressions | | |
	1	2	3
CONSTANT	−709.37 (−1.65)	−466.44 (−1.73)	−245.33 (−1.04)
KEXR	0.80 (1.63)	0.32 (1.11)	0.02 (0.08)
VAKEXR	0.07 (0.60)	0.04 (0.45)	0.04 (0.47)
KCABM	−0.02 (−2.11)	−0.01 (−2.01)	−0.01 (−1.61)
KSTCIND	0.64 (3.93)	–	–
KPCGNP	–	0.12 (5.86)	–
KWAGEIND	–	–	2.98 (6.15)
R^2	0.79	0.89	0.90
Adj.R^2	0.66	0.82	0.83
F-value	5.81	12.23	13.40
Durbin-Watson	2.07	2.00	2.00

Notes: Numbers in the parentheses are t- or f-statistics
Units in US$ million for FDI, KPCGNP and KCABM
Regression 1: $KNAFDI_t = a_0 + a_1 KEXR_t + a_2 VAKEXR_t + a_3 KCABM_t + a_4 KSTCIND_t + u_t$
Regression 2: $KNAFDI_t = b_0 + b_1 KEXR_t + b_2 VAKEXR_t + b_3 KCABM_t + b_4 KPCGNP_t + v_t$
Regression 3: $KNAFDI_t = c_0 + c_1 KEXR_t + c_2 VAKEXR_t + c_3 KCABM_t + c_4 KWAGEIND_t + w_t$
where $KNAFDI_t$ is Korean FDI to North America at year t, a_0, b_0 and c_0 are constants and u_t, v_t and w_t are error terms

Table (7)A1.5 Correlation among independent variables: 1980–90

	IKEXR	VAKIEXR	KCABM	KSTCIND	KIPCGNP	KWAGEIND
IKEXR	1.00	−0.27	0.62	0.97	0.99	0.95
VAKIEXR	−0.27	1.00	−0.33	−0.25	−0.24	−0.38
KCABM	0.62	−0.33	1.00	0.57	0.55	0.43
KSTCIND	0.97	−0.25	0.57	1.00	0.99	0.92
KIPCGNP	0.99	−0.24	0.55	0.99	1.00	0.92
KWAGEIND	0.95	−0.38	0.43	0.92	0.96	1.00

Table (7)A1.6 Korean FDI to Indonesia: 1980–90

Regressors	Regressions			
	1	2	3	4
CONSTANT	−92.61 (−2.35)	−9.69 (−0.38)	−56.33 (−1.61)	−75.71 (−2.11)
IKEXR	85.07 (3.51)	–	–	–
VAKIEXR	−0.01 (−0.15)	−0.02 (−0.20)	−0.02 (−0.21)	0.04 (0.51)
KCABM	−0.003 (−1.27)	−0.002 (−0.65)	−0.002 (−0.80)	−0.001 (−0.31)
KSTCIND	–	0.15 (2.43)	–	–
KIPCGNP	–	–	18.20 (2.96)	–
KWAGEIND	–	–	–	1.00 (3.42)
R^2	0.67	0.50	0.63	0.65
Adj.R^2	0.52	0.29	0.42	0.51
F-value	4.65	2.33	3.36	4.41
Durbin-Watson	2.54	2.50	2.67	2.77

Notes: Units in US$ million for KIFDI, KPCGNP, IPCGNP and KCABM
Regression 1: $KIFDI_t = a_0 + a_1 IKEXR_t + a_2 VAKIEXR_t + a_3 KCABM_t + a_4 KSTCIND_t + u_t$
Regression 2: $KIFDI_t = b_0 + b_1 IKEXR_t + b_2 VAKIEXR_t + b_3 KCABM_t + b_4 KWAGEIND_t + v_t$
Regression 3: $KIFDI_t = c_0 + c_1 IKEXR_t + c_2 VAKIEXR_t + c_3 KCABM_t + c_4 KPCGNP_t + w_t$
Regression 4: $KIFDI_t = d_0 + d_1 IKEXR_t + d_2 VAKIEXR_t + d_3 KCABM_t + d_4 KWAGEIND_t + e_t$
where $KIFDI_t$ is Korean FDI to Indonesia at year t, a_0, b_0, c_0 and d_0 are constants and u_t, v_t, w_t and e_t are error terms

Table (7)A1.7 Korean FDI to Indonesia, 1980–92

Variable	Coefficient	T-statistics	Significant level
CONSTANT	−98.20	−3.36	0.01
IKEXR	89.56	5.94	0.00
VAKIEXR	−0.01	−0.21	0.84
KCABM	−0.004	−2.31	0.05

$R^2 = 0.82$, Adj.$R^2 = 0.75$, F-value = 13.28, Durbin-Watson = 2.53

NOTES

1 The authors wish to acknowledge the critical comments on the earlier drafts of this chapter by Ky Cao, Ken Clements, Stephen Frost, Richard Robison, and Larry Sjaastad.

2 Yang-Sae Lee, 'The Role of Government in Trade and Industrialisation', *Korea Institute for Economics and Technology (KIET) Occasional Paper*, 88–05, March, 1988, p. 4.

3 The term FDI is problematic: there are two main definitions. The most widely adopted is the World Bank's. According to the Bank, FDI is understood as an investment made to acquire 'a lasting interest in an enterprise operating in an economy other than that of the investors' or 10 per cent or more possession of stocks of enterprises operating outside the investor's country (S. Thomsen and P. Nicolaides, *The Evolution of Japanese Direct Investment in Europe*, New York, Harvester Wheatsheaf, 1991, pp. 37–38). However, in this study the term 'Korean FDI' is defined according to the Korean Foreign Exchange Control Law. Accordingly, Korean FDI includes the establishment of local incorporation through 20 per cent or more possession of stocks of enterprises operating outside the investor's country, real estate investment for the purpose of foreign business, and joint venture investment for the purpose of development of natural resources. The ultimate purpose of these kinds of investments is to participate in the business management and to acquire a lasting interest in local firms. This definition distinguishes FDI from other forms of capital movement like loans and credit investment (foreign portfolio investment) made for the purposes of acquiring dividends or interest which do not result in Korean control of foreign firms. Therefore, whereas portfolio investment is simply an international capital movement, FDI, although a capital movement, involves transfers of marketing expertise, technology etc.

4 Stephan Haggard, *Pathways from the Periphery: The Politics of Growth in the Newly Industrialising Countries*, Ithaca and London, Cornell University Press, 1990, p. 55, and S. Haggard and Tun-Jen Cheng, 'State and Foreign Capital in the East Asian NICs', in Frederic C. Deyo, ed., *The Political Economy of the New Asian Industrialism*, Ithaca and London, Cornell University Press, 1987, p. 87. See also Jung-En Woo, *Race to the Swift: State and Finance in Korean Industrialism*, New York, Columbia University Press, 1991, pp. 45–46.

5 Haggard, *Pathways from the Periphery*, pp. 61–62.

6 Woo, *Race to the Swift*, pp. 85–86.

7 Alice Amsden, *Republic of Korea – Country Study*, World Institute for Development Economics Research of the United Nations University, Helsinki, Finland, 1987, p. 111.

8 B. Cumings, 'The Origins and Development of the Northeast Asian Political Economy: Industrial Sectors, Product Cycles, and Political Consequences', in F. Deyo, ed., *The Political Economy of the New Asian Industrialism*, p. 71.

9 R. Luedde-Neurath, 'State Intervention and Export-oriented Development in South Korea', in G. White, ed., *Developmental States in East Asia*, London, Macmillan, 1988, p. 76.

10 Woo provides a clear and precise definition of the *jaebeol* as 'a family-owned and managed group of companies that exercises monopolistic or oligopolistic control in product lines and industries', Woo, *Race to the Swift*, p. 149.

11 R.P. Kearney, *The Warrior Worker: The Challenge of the Korean Way of Working*, New York, Henry Holt & Company, 1991, p. 40.

12 F. Deyo, 'State and Labor: Modes of Political Exclusion in East Asian Development', in F. Deyo, ed., *The Political Economy of the New Asian Industrialism*, pp. 188–189.

13 Amsden, *Republic of Korea*, pp. 107–108.

14 See C. Johnson, 'Political Institutions and Economic Performance: The Government Business Relationship in Japan, South Korea and Taiwan', in F. Deyo, ed., *The Political Economy of the New Asian Industrialism*, pp. 136–164.

15 *Dong A Ilbo*, 5 January 1993.

16 Sung-Hwan Jo, 'Overseas Direct Investment By South Korean Firms: Direction and Pattern', in K. Kumar and M.G. McLeod, eds, *Multinationals From Developing Countries*, Lexington, Mass., D.C. Heath, 1981, pp. 59–62, see also Yoon-Dae Euh and Sang H. Min, 'Foreign Direct Investment From Developing Countries: The Case of Korean Firms', *The Developing Economies*, 26(2), June 1986, pp. 154–155.

17 All translations from Korean are by the authors, and follow guidelines stipulated by the Korean Ministry of Education.

18 For a summary of these theories, see K. Kumar and M.G. McLeod, eds, *Multinationals From Developing Countries*, Lexington, Mass., D.C. Heath, 1981, chapters 1 and 2; see also S. Lall, *The New Multinationals: The Spread of Third World Enterprises*, Chichester, John Wiley & Sons, 1983, pp. 1–18.

19 S. Hymer, *The International Operations of National Firms: A Study of Direct Foreign Investment*, Cambridge, Mass., MIT Press, 1976, pp. 24–27, and Pasuk Phongpaichit, *The New Wave of Japanese Investment in ASEAN*, Singapore, Institute of Southeast Asian Studies, 1990, pp. 6–7.

20 P. J. Buckley and M. Casson, *The Future of the Multinational Enterprise*, New York, Holms and Meier Publishers Inc., 1976 and C.P. Kindleberger, *American Business Abroad: Six Lectures of Direct Investment*, New Haven, Conn., Yale University Press, 1969. See also, S. Lall, *The New Multinationals*.

21 Hymer, *The International Operations of National Firms*, pp. 26–27.

22 K. Kojima, *Direct Foreign Investment: A Japanese Model of Multinational Business Operations*, London, Croom Helm, 1978 and T. Ozawa, 'International Investment and Industrial Structure: New Theoretical Implications from the Japanese Experience', *Oxford Economic Papers*, No. 31, 1979, pp. 72–92.

23 K. Froot and J. Stein, 'Exchange Rates and Foreign Direct Investment: An Imperfect Capital Markets Approach', *Quarterly Journal of Economics*, 106(4), November 1991, pp. 1191–1217.

24 J. Harvey, 'The Determinants of Direct Foreign Investment', *Journal of Post Keynesian Economics*, 12(2), Winter 1989–1990, pp. 260–272.

25 F. Root, and A. Ahmed, 'Empirical Determinants of Manufacturing Direct Foreign Investment in Developing Countries', *Economic Development and Cultural Change*, 27(4), July 1979, pp. 757–758.

26 S. Grubaugh, 'Determinants of Direct Foreign Investment', *Review of Economics and Statistics*, 69(1), February 1987, pp. 149-168.

27 L. Tai and D. Lee, 'The Composition and Direction of Korea's Foreign Trade', *Asian Profile*, 19(1) 1991, p. 17.

28 Bank of Korea, *Josa Tonggye Weolbo*, Seoul, Bank of Korea, 1991, p. 29.

29 Ibid.

30 W. Bello and S. Rosenfeld, *Dragons in Distress*, San Francisco, A Food First Book, 1990, p. 9; and Tun-jen Cheng and Stephan Haggard, *Newly Industrialising Asia in Transition*, Berkeley, Institute of International Studies, 1987, p. 4.

31 *Asian Finance*, 15 July 1991, p. 44.

32 For example, in the period between 1988 and 1991 since adoption of new policy reforms in terms of foreign direct investment in Indonesia the total amount of approved FDI in Indonesia reached US$26.7 billion exceeding those for the previous twenty years between 1967 and 1987. Hadi Soesastro, 'Foreign Direct Investment in Indonesia', paper presented at the Third Joint Research Conference on Asia Pacific Relations, Kuala Lumpur, Malaysia, 5–7 July 1992, p. 11.

33 *Dong A Ilbo*, 31 December 1992.

34 For more detail, see F. Deyo, 'State and Labor', pp. 188–189, and Kearney, *The Warrior Worker*, pp. 112–118.

35 Although the three rights of workers were elucidated in the labour law of 1980, they were only 'within the scope defined by law'. In fact, under both the Park and Chun regimes Korean unions did not have monopoly powers, and the capacity of workers to resist measures concerning pace of work was extremely weak; the state prohibited third parties (e.g., university students, dissident activists) from helping and meddling in labour disputes. Jae-Youl Kim, 'Democratisation in South Korea', in James Cotton, ed., *Korea Under Roh Tae-Woo*, St Leonards, N.S.W, Allen and Unwin, in association with the Department of International Relations, RSPacs, Australian National University, 1993, p. 50.

36 Kearney, *The Warrior Worker*, p. 123 and Kim, 'Democratisation in South Korea', p. 51.

37 Kearney, *The Warrior Worker*, pp. 123–124.

37 Ibid., p. 123.

39 Ibid., p. 131.

40 Ibid.

41 Jonathan Moore, 'Squeezed by Success', *Far Eastern Economic Review*, 16 March 1989, p. 8, and Yong Sook Lee, 'Industrial Subcontracting and Labour Movement', *Journal of Contemporary Asia*, 23(1) 1993, p. 39.

42 *Dong A Ilbo*, 5 January 1993.

43 Computed from the Ministry of Finance, data quoted in Korean Trade Promotion Corporation (KOTRA), *Giyeopeui Haeoetuja Jeonryaksarye* (The FDI Strategy of An Enterprise: a Korean Case), Seoul, KOTRA, 1993, p. 448.

44 Ibid., p. 68. For a comprehensive analysis of the recent trend of Korean FDI, see Export–Import Bank of Korea, *Jugan Haeoetuja Jeongbo*, No. 759, 19 September 1992, pp. 1–23.

45 Quoted in Mark Clifford and Johnathan Moore, 'Overseas Attractions', *Far Eastern Economic Review*, 16 March 1988, p. 89.

46 Quoted in Ooi Guat, 'Economic Rocket Goes Off Course', *Asian Business*, June 1989, p. 46.

47 Kwang Seon Bae and Seok Il Hong, *ASEAN Jegukeui Tujahwangyeonggwa Wurieui Jinchuljeonryak* (Investment Environment of ASEAN Countries and Korea's Strategy), Seoul, KIET, 1990, p. 76.

48 Ibid., p. 5.

49 Chris Manning, 'Approaching the Turning Point? Labour Market Structure and Change Under Indonesia's New Order', paper presented at the Conference on

Indonesia Paradigms for the Future, Asia Research Centre, Murdoch University, Australia, 22–23 July, 1993, p. 8.

50 Yoon-Hwan Shin, 'Korean Direct Investment in Indonesia and Its Political Implications: A Critical View', paper presented at the Centre for Strategic and International Studies, Jakarta, Indonesia, 23 July 1992, p. 7.

51 Ibid., p. 9.

52 Ibid., pp. 4–5.

53 According to the Korean Ministry of Labour, the labour shortage tends to increase at a rapid speed; 1.8 per cent in 1985, 3.5 per cent in 1988, and in 1991 it marked 5.5 per cent. Particularly, the rate for semi-skilled workers was much more serious, at 20.1 per cent. In terms of industries, harsh working condition sectors like textile and leather sectors suffer the severe labour shortage. World Bank, *Korea: Country Economic Memorandum*, World Bank, 1992, pp. 59–60.

54 *Asian Intelligence*, No. 371, 1992, p. 6.

55 *Dong A Ilbo*, 20 January 1993.

56 Murray Hiebert, 'Industrial Disease', *Far Eastern Economic Review*, 2 September 1993, p. 16.

57 Interview with a Korean journalist, 7 May 1993.

58 *Hanguk Gyeongje Sinmun*, 27 November 1992.

59 See Kojima, 'Direct Foreign Investment', chapters 4, 5 and 6.

60 K. Kojima and T. Ozawa, 'Micro-and Macro-Economic Models of Direct Foreign Investment: Toward A Synthesis', *Hitotsubashi Journal of Economics*, 25, 1984, p. 1.

61 Quoted in Young-Kwan Yoon, 'The Political Economy of Transition: Japanese Foreign Direct Investments in the 1980s', *World Politics*, 43(1) 1990, p. 9.

62 Tsutomo Ozawa, *Multinationalism, Japanese Style*, Princeton, Princeton University Press, 1979, and T. Ozawa, 'International Investment and Industrial Structure'.

63 Ozawa, 'International Investment and Industrial Structure', p. 88.

64 Jon Woronoff, 'Japan's Ubiquitous Traders Have a Finger in Every Pie', in *Asian Business*, July 1982, p. 19.

65 Toshikazu Nakase, 'Sogo Shosha, The Japanese Conglomerate', in Jomo ed., *The Sun Also Sets*, Malaysia, Institute for Social Analysis (INSAN), 1983, p. 85.

66 Karl J. Fields, 'Trading Companies in South Korea and Taiwan', *Asian Survey*, 29(11),1989, p. 1076.

67 Ibid., p. 1081.

68 Administrative guidance refers to the authority of the state, that is implicit in the laws that established the various ministries, which is used to issue directives, requests, warnings, suggestions and encouragement to particular firms or industry under its jurisdiction. C. Johnson, *MITI and the Japanese Miracle*, California, Stanford University Press, 1982, pp. 242–274.

69 Ronald Dore, *Flexible Ridigities*, London, The Athlone Press, pp. 135–138.

70 G.C. Allen, *The Japanese Economy*, London, Weidenfeld and Nicolson, 1981, p. 175.

71 *Asian Finance*, April 1991, p. 17, and *Choong Ang Ilbo*, 11 November 1991. See also Rob Steven, *Japan's New Imperialism*, London, Macmillan, 1990, pp. 159–161.

72 Bello and Rosenfeld, *Dragons in Distress*, p. 115.

73 Michael Selwyn, 'R&D: A Matter of Survival', *Asian Business*, January 1992, p. 25.

74 *Dong A Ilbo*, 6 January 1993.

75 Shin, 'Korean Direct Investment in Indonesia', pp. 8–13.

REFERENCES

Ahn, C.Y. 'Dongnama Gyeongjega Ddeooreugo Itdda (The Emerging Power of Southeast Asian Economies), *Shin Dong A*, June 1992.

Allen, G.C. *The Japanese Economy*, London, Weidenfeld and Nicolson, 1981.

Amsden, Alice *Republic of Korea – Country Study*, World Institute for Development Economics Research of the United Nations University, Helsinki, Finland, 1987.

Amsden, Alice *Asia's Next Giant: South Korea and Late Industrialisation*, New York, Oxford University Press, 1989.

Asia Watch, 5(2) 1993.

Asian Finance, April 1991.

Asian Finance, 15 July 1991.

Asian Intelligence, No. 371, 1992.

Bae, Kwang Seon and Seok Il Hong *ASEAN Jegukeui Tujahwangyeonggwa Wurieui Jinchuljeonryak* (Investment Environment of ASEAN Countries and Korea's Strategy), Seoul, Korea Institute For Economics and Technology, 1990.

Balassa, B. *The Newly Industrialising Countries in the World Economy*, New York, Pergamon Press, 1981.

Bank of Korea *Josa Tonggye Weolbo* (Monthly Report on Statistics), Seoul, Bank of Korea, 1991.

Bank of Korea *Jugan Haeoetuja Jeongbo* (Weekly Report on FDI), Bank of Korea, Seoul, 27 February 1993

Bello, W. and S. Rosenfeld *Dragons in Distress*, San Francisco, A Food First Book, 1990.

Blomstrom, M. *Foreign Investment and Spillovers*, London and New York, Routledge, 1989.

Calderón-Rossell, J. 'Towards the Theory of Foreign Direct Investment', *Oxford Economic Papers*, 37(2) June 1985, pp. 282–291.

Cheng, Tun-jen and Stephan Haggard *Newly Industrialising Asia in Transition*, Berkeley, Institute of International Studies, 1987.

Cheng, Tun-jeon and Lawrence B. Krause 'Democracy and Development: With Special Attention to Korea', *Journal of Northeast Asian Studies*, 10(2) 1991, pp. 3–25.

Choong Ang Ilbo, 11 November 1991.

Chu, J.J. 'The political economy of post-1980s Taiwanese foreign investment,' *Asia Research Centre Working Paper*, No. 21, 1993, Asia Research Centre, Murdoch University, Australia.

Clifford, Mark and Johnathan Moore 'Overseas Attractions', *Far Eastern Economic Review*, 16 March 1988.

Cumings, B. 'The Origins and Development of the Northeast Asian Political Economy: Industrial Sectors, Product Cycles, and Political Consequences', in F. Deyo, ed., *The Political Economy of the New Asian Industrialism*, Ithaca and London, Cornell University Press, 1987, 44–83.

Deyo, Frederic C. 'State and Labor: Modes of Political Exclusion in East Asian Development', Frederic C. Deyo, ed., *The Political Economy of the New Asian Industrialism*, Ithaca and London, Cornell University Press, 1987, pp. 182–202.

Dong A Ilbo, 1 April 1992.

Dong A Ilbo, 31 December 1992.

Dong A Ilbo, 5 January 1993.

Dong A Ilbo, 6 January 1993.

Dong A Ilbo, 20 January 1993.

Dore, Ronald *Flexible Ridigities*, London, The Athlone Press, 1987.

Euh, Yoon-Dae and Sang H. Min 'Foreign Direct Investment From Developing

Countries: The Case of Korean Firms', *The Developing Economies*, 26–2 June 1986, pp. 149–168.

Export–Import Bank of Korea *Jugan Haeoetuja Jeongbo* (Weekly Report on FDI), No. 759, 19 September 1992.

Far Eastern Economic Review, 10 October 1991.

Fields, Karl J. 'Trading Companies in South Korea and Taiwan', *Asian Survey*, 29(11), 1989, pp. 1073–1089.

Froot, K. and J. Stein 'Exchange Rates and Foreign Direct Investment: An Imperfect Capital Markets Approach', *Quarterly Journal of Economics*, 106(4), November 1991, pp. 1191–1217.

Goto, A. and R. Wakasugi 'Technology Policy', in R. Komiya, M. Okuno and K. Suzumura eds, *Industrial Policy of Japan*, Tokyo, Academic Press Inc., 1988.

Grubaugh, S. 'Determinants of Direct Foreign Investment', *Review of Economics and Statistics*, 69(1), February 1987, pp. 149–168.

Haggard, Stephan *Pathways from the Periphery: The Politics of Growth in the Newly Industrialising Countries*, Ithaca and London, Cornell University Press, 1990.

Hankuk Gyeongje Sinmun, 27 November 1992.

Harvey, J. 'The Determinants of Direct Foreign Investment', *Journal of Post Keynesian Economics*, 12(2), Winter 1989–1990, pp. 260–272.

Hasan, P. *Korea: Problems and Issues in a Rapidly Growing Economy*, Baltimore, The Johns Hopkins University Press, 1976.

Hiebert, Murray 'Industrial Disease', *Far Eastern Economic Review*, 2 September 1993.

Hymer, S. *The International Operations of National Firms: A Study of Direct Foreign Investment*, Cambridge, Mass., MIT Press, 1976.

Ichiyo, Muto 'Japan INC. At A Crossroads: US–Japan Relation, Politics and Labour', in Jomo, ed., *The Sun Also Sets*, Malaysia, Institute For Social Analysis (INSAN), 1983, pp. 47–65.

Insker, Ian 'Structural Change, the Multifunctional Polis and Japanese R&D for Australia', *Journal of Contemporary Asia*, 20(3), 1990, pp. 312–329.

Jo, Sung-Hwan 'Overseas Direct Investment By South Korean Firms: Direction and Pattern', in K. Kumar and M.G. McLeod, eds, *Multinationals From Developing Countries*, Lexington, Mass., D.C. Heath, 1981, pp. 53–77.

Johnson, C. *MITI and the Japanese Miracle*, California, Stanford University Press, 1982.

Johnson, C. 'Political Institutions and Economic Performance: The Government Business Relationship in Japan, South Korea and Taiwan', and F. Deyo, 'Introduction', both in F. Deyo, ed., *The Political Economy of the New Asian Industrialism*, Ithaca and London, Cornell University Press, 1987, pp. 136–164.

Kang, Eui-Jung *Ilbonhaeoetujaeui Seongkeok Bunseok: Muyeokgwa Haeoetuja* (The Analysis of the Characteristics of the Japanese FDI: Trade and FDI), Unpublished Master's Dissertation, Seoul National University, Korea, 1987.

Kearney, Robert P. *The Warrior Worker: The Challenge of the Korean Way of Working*, New York, Henry Holt and Company, 1991.

Kim, Jae-Youl 'Democratisation in South Korea', in James Cotton, ed., *Korea Under Roh Tae-Woo*, St Leonards, N.S.W, Allen and Unwin in association with Department of International Relations, RSPacs, ANU, 1993, pp. 42–52.

Kim, S.J., Y.K. Min and J.W. Yoo *Haewaetoojayei Hyunhwanggua Jeongchaekkuaje* (Foreign Direct Investment and Its Policy Questions), Seoul, KIEP, 1992.

Kim, Y.M. *Hankuk Hyeondae Jeongchisa* (A History of Contemporary Korean Politics), Seoul, Eulyu Munhwasa, 1992.

Kohlhagen, S. 'Exchange Rates Changes, Profitability, and Direct Foreign Investment', *Southern Economic Journal*, 44(1), July 1977, pp. 43–52.

Kojima, K. 'A Macroeconomic Approach to Foreign Direct Investment', *Hitotsubashi Journal of Economics*, June 1973, pp. 1–23.

Kojima, K. *Direct Foreign Investment: A Japanese Model of Multinational Business Operations*, London, Croom Helm, 1978.

Kojima, K. and T. Ozawa, 'Micro- and Macro-Economic Models of Direct Foreign Investment: Toward A Synthesis', *Hitotsubashi Journal of Economics*, 25, 1984, pp. 1–20.

Koo, Hagen 'Middle Class and Political Struggle in the East Asian Industrialisation', paper presented at the annual meeting of the American Sociological Association in San Francisco, 1989.

Korean Trade Promotion Corporation (KOTRA), *Giyeopeui Jeonryksarye* (Case Study: A Firm's FDI Strategy), Seoul, KOTRA, 1993.

KOTRA, *Giyeopeui Haeoetuja Jeonryaksarye* (The FDI Strategy of An Enterprise: a Korean Case), Seoul, KOTRA, 1993.

Kumar, K. and M.G. McLeod eds, *Multinationals from Developing Countries*, Lexington, Mass., D.C. Heath, 1981.

Lall, S. *The New Multinationals: The Spread of Third World Enterprises*, Chichester: John Wiley and Sons, 1983.

Lee, C.H. 'On Japanese Macroeconomic Theories of Direct Foreign Investment', *Economic Development and Cultural Change*, 32(4) 1984, pp. 713–723.

Lee, Yong Sook 'Industrial Subcontracting and Labour Movement', *Journal of Contemporary Asia*, 23(1) 1993, pp. 24–40.

Lim, D. 'Fiscal Incentives and Direct Foreign Investment in Less Developed Countries', *The Journal of Development Studies*, 19(2), January 1983, pp. 207–212.

Luedde-Neurath, R. 'State Intervention and Export–oriented Development in South Korea', in G. White, ed., *Developmental States in East Asia*, London, Macmillan, 1988.

MacMillan, C.J. *The Japanese Industrial System*, New York, Walter de Gruyter, 1985.

Magaziner, I.C. and T.A. Hout *Japanese Industrial Policy*, Berkeley, Institute of International Studies, University of California, Berkeley, 1980.

Manning, Chris 'Approaching the Turning Point? Labour Market Structure and Change Under Indonesia's New Order', paper presented at the Conference on Indonesia: Paradigms for the Future, Asia Research Centre, Murdoch University, Australia, 22–23, July 1993.

McClintock, B. 'Recent Theories of Direct Foreign Investment', *Journal of Economic Issues*, 22(2), June 1988, pp. 477–484.

Moore, Jonathan 'Squeezed by Success', *Far Eastern Economic Review*, 16 March 1989.

Nakagawa, Yatsuhiro and Nobumasa Ota *The Japanese-Style Economic System*, Tokyo, Foreign Press Centre, 1981.

Nakase, Toshikazu 'Sogo Shosha, The Japanese Conglomerate', in Jomo, ed., *The Sun Also Sets*, Malaysia, Institute For Social Analysis (INSAN), 1983, pp. 83–86.

Nester, W. *The Foundation of Japanese Power*, London, Macmillan, 1990.

Ozawa, Tsutomo. *Multinationalism, Japanese Style*, Princeton, Princeton University Press, 1979.

Ozawa, T. 'International Investment and Industrial Structure: New Theoretical Implications from the Japanese Experience', *Oxford Economic Papers*, 31(1), 1979, pp. 72–92.

Park, Chong-Min 'Authoritarian Rule in South Korea: Political Support and governmental Performance', *Asian Survey*, 31(8) 1991, pp. 743–761.

Phongpaichit, Pasuk *The New Wave of Japanese Investment in ASEAN*, Singapore, Institute of Southeast Asian Studies, 1990.

Ragazzi, G. 'Theories of the Determinants of Direct Foreign Investment', *International Monetary Fund Staff Papers*, 20(2), July 1973, pp. 471–498.

Ramstetter, E. *Direct Foreign Investment in Asia's Developing Economies and Change in the Asia-Pacific Region*, Boulder and Oxford, Westview Press, 1991.

Root, F. and Ahmed, A. 'Empirical Determinants of Manufacturing Direct Foreign Investment in Developing Countries', *Economic Development and Cultural Change*, 27(4), July 1979, pp. 751–767.

Selwyn, Michael 'R&D: A Matter of Survival', *Asian Business*, January 1992.

Shah, A. and J. Slemrod 'Do Taxes Matter for Foreign Direct Investment?', *World Bank Economic Review*, 5(3), September 1991, pp. 473–491.

Shin, Yoon-Hwan 'Korean Direct Investment in Indonesia and Its Political Implications: A Critical View', paper presented at the Centre for Strategic and International Studies, Jakarta, Indonesia, 23 July 1992.

Shon, S.L. *Ilbongiyeopeui Haeoejikjeoptujawa Gukjejeonryak* (Foreign Direct Investment of Japanese Firms and Their Strategies of Globalisation), Seoul, KIEP, 1990.

Smith, Michael, J. McLoughlin, P. Large and R. Chapman *Asia's New Industrial World*, London, Methuen, 1985.

Soesastro, Hadi 'Foreign Direct Investment in Indonesia', paper presented at the Third Joint Research Conference on Asia Pacific Relations, Kuala Lumpur, Malaysia, 5–7 July 1992.

Steven, Rob *Japan's New Imperialism*, London, Macmillan, 1990.

Tai, L. and D. Lee 'The Composition and Direction of Korea's Foreign Trade', *Asian Profile*, 19(1) 1991.

Takeo, Tsuchiya 'The Japanese Sphere of Influence: Multifunctional Investment in Asia', *AMPO*, 16(1 and 2), 1984, pp. 28–59.

Tanaka, K. 'On the Effects of Direct Foreign Investment', *Kobe University Economic Review*, No. 37, 1991, pp. 61–84.

Thomsen, S. and P. Nicolaides *The Evolution of Japanese Direct Investment in Europe*, New York, Harvester Wheatsheaf, 1991.

Tin, Ooi Guat 'Economic Rocket Goes Off Course', *Asian Business*, June 1989, p. 46.

Torrisi, C. 'The Determinants of Direct Foreign Investment', *Journal of Economic Development*, 10(1), July 1985, pp. 29–45.

Woo, Jung-En *Race to the Swift: State and Finance in Korean Industrialism*, New York, Columbia University Press, 1991.

World Bank *Korea: Country Economic Memorandum*, World Bank, 1992.

Woronoff, Jon 'Japan's Ubiquitous Traders Have a Finger in Every Pie', in *Asian Business*, July 1982.

Yoon, Young-Kwan 'The Political Economy of Transition: Japanese Foreign Direct Investments in the 1980s', *World Politics*, 43(1) 1990.

Chapter 8

Tax regimes in East Asia
A comparative review

Gitte Heij

INTRODUCTION

Tax systems in the Asian region can be approached from different angles, including overall tax rates, tax exemptions and incentives, tax treaties[1] and specific incentives for foreign investors. These issues must all be analysed to accurately evaluate whether a country is attractive as an investment destination relative to another.

The taxes themselves are, of course, the main cost but they are not the only costs in any given tax system. To obtain a more complete picture, one has to look at other aspects such as clarity of the tax rules (for example, the transparency of taxation of financial instruments), access to information and procedures for objection and appeal. These can be described as the costs of compliance, briefly discussed below.

Given the medium- to long-term nature of investment returns, another important aspect is possible tax policy changes during the term of the investment. Is it likely that certain tax incentives will be introduced to encourage certain sectors? Are new types of taxes likely to be introduced or are rates of existing taxes likely to be changed?

In this chapter these three aspects – tax policy, the general taxation system and costs of compliance – are discussed for six countries. Some conclusions are drawn for each country in relation to its capital market.

It should be noted that much of the information given in this chapter is of a 'principle' character. The specific tax consequences of the more sophisticated financial instruments would have to be judged on a case by case basis, and would sometimes involve individual tax rulings by the tax authorities concerned. But even so, given the poor legal framework in certain countries, ruling results in past cases cannot always be interpreted as probably binding for present or future cases of a similar nature. The rapid evolution and change in the financial sector of East Asia, in terms of institutional and market structure and prudential framework, can make specific analysis of tax issues at times counter-productive.

Having said that, besides looking at the current general structures of taxation in various countries and the principles behind these structures, attention is paid to the factors and environment that are compelling governments to reform their tax systems. We will try to provide the reader with several case studies so that a practical insight can be gained.

Given the inconsistent availability of data, the chapter will deal with countries in a disproportional manner. Some will be discussed at greater length than others.

General trends

The competition between the different Asian countries in order to attract foreign capital and technology has always been intense – indeed more so in recent years as financial markets were deregulated – and taxation plays a vital role in maintaining competitiveness. There are many ways to attract foreign investment. Some countries believe that a transparent and simplified tax system with low tax rates is sufficient to attract foreign investment, while others give special incentives for certain investment sectors. Both trends will likely continue in the future. Overall, it may be stated that the development towards a more simplified tax system with lower corporate tax rates seems to be applicable for all countries.

As some governments face a continuing increase in their deficits, while corporate tax rates are lowered, other taxes will be introduced in order to meet revenue needs. A general sales tax (GST) or value added tax (VAT) has recently been introduced in China and Singapore, while Indonesia and Taiwan already had a VAT, and Malaysia and Hong Kong are considering its introduction. Increasingly, other taxes will also be introduced or extended to fund government budgets. Due to increasing public sector funding needs, there will be a trend towards stricter measures to curb more control on tax evasion and fraud.

How successful governments will be in raising tax compliance depends on several factors directly related to the society as a whole. The effectiveness and motivation of government administrations, the political will of the government to simplify the tax system and increase compliance, and the tools needed to check tax assessments and relevant information, detect tax evaders and properly punish those who do not comply with the laws will all play a part.

Costs of tax compliance

To comply with a law the taxpayer has to fulfil certain conditions. For example, the bookkeeping of a taxpayer has to be in accord with the requirements of the tax law. Assessment forms need to be filled in, often with the assistance of an expert, and tax planning needs to be done, again probably with the assistance of experts. These tax compliance costs can be defined as: 'those costs incurred by taxpayers or third parties, notably businesses, in meeting the requirements imposed upon them by a given tax structure (excluding payment of the tax itself and any distortion costs arising from it)'[2]

Although such costs are difficult to measure and have not been the subject of much research in the past (Pope 1991: 251), they are important elements that need to be taken into account by any significant investor.

These include the costs of change, i.e. costs caused by the introduction of a new tax or major changes in a given tax system. For example, a company may need a new computer system, or staff may need training to deal with a new tax or information system.

Regular costs include:[3]

- costs of tax planning;[4]
- fees for tax consultants[5] and time spent on administration to conform with the requirements of the taxation department;
- uncertainty about tax liabilities and the costs associated with this;
- costs involved in the appeal mechanisms;
- associated overhead costs including the costs of maintaining and storing records as required by the tax authorities;
- costs of collecting, remitting and accounting for tax on the products or profits of the business and on the wages and salaries of its employees;
- costs of acquiring the knowledge to enable this work to be done including knowledge of legal obligations and penalties.

These costs can be minimised if information about taxation is free, readily available and easy to understand. Information can be improved if tax officials' advice to taxpayers is clear and consistent. The methods and timing of tax returns and tax payments should be convenient to the taxpayer, preferably in accord with the period of business accounts. (When business years are from July–June, the tax department should designate the same period rather than, say, the calendar year, as the tax year). Clarity of legislation could be enhanced by tax officials giving advance rulings. This need for clarity and effective implementation is seen as a very important factor by many leading capital market players in the Asia–Pacific Region.[6] Where consistency in legislation and interpretation is lacking, appeal mechanisms need to be simple and relatively inexpensive. All these measures do significantly reduce the costs of compliance, and their absence will obviously cause either of two things to happen: business reluctance in making investments outside the narrowly defined safe market segments; or raising the 'hurdle rates' for such investments to prohibitive levels, leading to a high degree of distortion in resource allocation.

COUNTRY ANALYSIS

People's Republic of China

Policy

The Chinese Ministry of Foreign Economic Relations and Trade (MOFERT) has the following specific goals for foreign investment:[7]

- encouraging agriculture, infrastructure and service sector investments over the next ten years;
- attracting more investment in the inland areas;
- increasing project size;
- granting large land development projects to foreigners.

Tax incentives in order to attract foreign investment play a role in achieving these goals. The introduction of the special economic zones (SEZs) is one of the significant tax (and other) benefits to foreign investors. The special treatment of foreign investment in these special economic zones results in a tax system that is much more favourable for foreign investors than domestic investors.[8]

Since the start of January 1994, a unified tax system has been introduced in China, unifying the different types of taxes for foreign and domestic investors. The new tax system has as major goals an increase in the revenue of the central government and the unification of the tax regimes for local state enterprises and foreign companies. Many aspects of the new 1994 tax laws remain unclear, and further clarifications may not be available until the system is applicable for a period of time.

The reorganisation of the Chinese tax system by the State Tax Bureau in China has replaced the domestic income tax system. Before 1994, three income tax laws were applicable to Chinese domestic enterprises. The first applied to state-owned enterprises, the second to collective enterprises, and the third to private enterprises.[9] The Bureau replaced these three income taxes with a single one applicable to all three types of enterprise (with a maximum rate of 33 per cent). However, lower and preferential tax rates in the SEZs have remained intact. The general impression of the new tax system is that foreign companies will pay higher taxes than under the former tax laws and Chinese companies will see their tax burden reduced.[10] The various indirect taxes under the old system have merged into one unified turnover tax applicable to all enterprises, domestic and foreign. Before 1994 a value added tax (VAT)[11] was only imposed on domestic industry.

Tax revenue forms a major source of funds in the Chinese central government budget. In 1990, around 73 per cent of the total revenue had its source in taxes.[12] Tax revenue has not been increasing at the same level as economic growth, leading to rising central government budget shortfalls. It is estimated that in recent times the Chinese tax administration uncovers tax evasion worth about US$1.4 billion each year, while at least US$17.54 billion remains evasive.[13] The rapid economic reforms have demanded drastic changes in the taxation system, including homogenisation of the more than fifty types of different taxes previously in place as well as the removal of some taxes. This is not an easy task since not only would legislation need to be reformed, but the whole supporting administrative structure – of institutions and officials, at central, provincial and even local levels, all of which are critical to the successful implementation of tax reform – would need to be overhauled. The autonomy of the provinces has become a major problem: the World Bank estimates that the national government in Bejing is collecting a decreasing amount of tax revenue because the prosperous provinces keep a large part of the tax revenue for themselves.[14] Various data confirm this estimation for the period 1981–93.[15] In 1981 57 per cent of the total tax revenue went to the central government; in 1992, it was only 38.6 per cent.[16] This decrease in central government revenue means less capacity to redistribute financial resources to the poorer provinces and less power over the relatively wealthy coastal provinces.

The major problems with the taxation system include tax evasion, non-uniform profit tax rates, violence against official tax collectors, and the levy of additional, often illegal, taxes in the form of various surcharges by local authorities.[17] Other shortcomings include different tax penalties under different tax laws and regulations, and the weak apparatus that handles the tax collection. The lack of authority of the tax administration contributes to its low enforcement capacity. Corruption is a protracted problem in itself, as some local governments or tax officials do use tax revenue to line their own pockets.[18]

In addressing the problem of low tax compliance and a weak tax administration, the government introduced the Tax Collection and Administration Law (TCAL), which came into force in January 1993. However, laws do not suddenly change deeply ingrained habits. It is difficult to reform any tax administration system because 'the tax administration reflects social and economic conditions such as literacy, income distribution and attitudes toward government authority'.[19] Any tax administration will reflect the strengths and weaknesses of that society as a whole and, therefore, expectations of the impact of the new TCAL should not be too high. Work ethics as dictated by the TCAL law call for tax officials not to seek or accept bribes or engage in malpractices for selfish ends. Instead, tax officials must be devoted to their duties.[20] But these new rules clearly do not necessarily create an environment conducive to fair and effective administration within a short to medium time frame.

Although the new TCAL is a step in the right direction towards a more effective tax system, it is no more than one step on a long road. Therefore,

Li's prediction that the TCAL will effectively safeguard tax enforcement and legitimise the rights and interests of taxpayers, seems premature. The problem of local authorities giving unauthorised tax exemptions and reductions to foreign enterprises has prompted the central government to announce, in August 1993, that all foreign enterprises be re-registered. The government is also intent on sending inspection teams all over the country to check out illegal practices.[21]

The rapidly expanding number of SEZs is another problem the government is attempting to solve. At the time of writing the government plans to close down 1,000 of these out of a total of more than 1,200. Unauthorised zones have been established by local governments in a bid to attract foreign investment. Some have been criticised for lack of genuine development prospects and for wasting valuable fertile land. The 200 remaining SEZs will be reviewed and there is the possibility that more zones will be closed down.[22] It is planned that taxation rules that apply in the SEZs for foreign companies will be unified. This is aimed at standardising tax rates and other tax incentives between the different SEZs, which have been competing among themselves for foreign capital.

It is not clear if the facilities of SEZs will continue in the medium-term future under the new tax laws. The government has given the guarantee that the facilities of the SEZs will remain intact but it is not clear for how long. Some expect that the government will choose to head in the direction of a tax system that supports certain types of industry instead of a system that favours geographical areas such as the SEZs.[23]

General income tax structure before 1994

Domestic and foreign companies

Domestic companies were liable for income tax under differing rules depending on whether they are collective enterprises or private enterprises. State-owned enterprises are subject to a range of taxes besides income tax.

Under the Foreign Investment Law of April 1991 all foreign investments are taxable under the same regime. Joint ventures and wholly owned foreign companies both fall under the Enterprise Income Tax (EIT). EIT is also levied on foreign enterprises with establishments in China.

Resident and non-resident taxpayers   Individuals residing in China for more than five years are seen as resident taxpayers and are subject to Chinese income tax on their worldwide income. Non-resident taxpayers are only taxable on their China sourced income.

The Foreign Investment Law distinguishes two types of taxpayers, foreign investment enterprises (including equity joint-ventures and co-operative joint ventures), and wholly foreign-owned enterprises established in China.

Foreign companies with their head office in China will be seen as resident taxpayers. This means that they would be taxable in China on worldwide income, although taxes paid abroad are creditable. Joint ventures with a head office in China are taxed on their worldwide income.

Wholly foreign-owned companies with establishments or sites in China are only taxable on their Chinese sourced income. Representative offices and business agents are included in the term establishments.

Taxable income under corporate income tax Taxable income includes profits, interest, dividends, rentals, royalties and other income, calculated according to the accrual method. This means that taxable income is calculated from the time when income is earned, and liabilities accrue on the date on which they become due and payable, even when the actual payment takes place in the following tax year.

Capital gains tax There is no specific capital gains tax. However, in calculating their taxable income, enterprises have to include their capital gains in the income of the enterprise. This happens automatically, as the accrual method has to be used by companies to compute their taxable income.

Withholding tax Foreign companies without an establishment in China are, in theory, taxed on income sourced in China, such as dividend, interest and royalties. This is generally paid via a final withholding tax,[24] with the possibility of a reduced final withholding tax rate for royalties. Withholding tax is levied at a rate of 20 per cent, (when a tax treaty applies rates are reduced or exemption may be given) unless the income is derived from the Open Cities (OC), in which case the withholding tax rate is reduced to 10 per cent. An exemption may be given to withholding tax on dividends paid out by export 'enterprises' or 'technologically advanced enterprises' under regulations of the Ministry of Finance.

However the rule that dividend remitted abroad is subject to withholding tax, is not implemented. It remains unclear if implementation will be realised in the short or medium term future.

Transfer pricing Transactions between related parties including wholly foreign-owned enterprises or foreign joint-ventures have to be at arm's length, as if the parties are independent of one another.

Tax incentives

A tax incentive is given to production-oriented investment enterprises with terms of operation of ten years or more. These enterprises enjoy a two-year exemption from income tax in the first and second profit making year. Lower tax rates may be applicable for subsequent years (see also Tax rates).

Incentives are also given to foreign companies in the SEZs, OCS and other designated investment areas (see 'Tax rates' below).

Special tax arrangements are available for branches of foreign banks, but approval has to be given by the tax authorities. Chinese/foreign joint-venture banks and finance companies with paid-up capital or working funds of more than US$10 million, remaining in operation for more than ten years, are exempt from enterprise income tax in the first profit making year and will be given 50 per cent reduction of tax in the following two years. The incentive is only available when the capital or funds are not reduced for ten years.[25]

Tax rates

Domestic enterprises   State-owned enterprises are subject to income tax at a uniform rate of 55 per cent for large and medium-size enterprises whereas small enterprises are taxed at a rate between 10 and 55 per cent. The conditions for being classified as a small enterprise differ between regions and economic sectors. Collective enterprises are subject to an income tax rate varying between 10 per cent and 55 per cent. Private enterprises are subject to income tax rates of 7–60 per cent.

Resident individuals   Individual resident taxpayers are subject to income tax rates between 5 per cent and 45 per cent.

Foreign enterprises   Under the Enterprise Income Tax the tax rate is 30 per cent on taxable income. An additional 3 per cent local tax rate on taxable income is imposed.

Special Economic Zones   Rates are different for companies in the SEZs, Open Cities and other designated investment areas. The rates on taxable income are 15 per cent for companies in a SEZ, and 24 per cent in an OC. However, the latter rate can be reduced to 15 per cent if the enterprise is engaged in projects involving high technology, energy, transportation, or port construction, or if the investment made by the foreign investors exceeds US$30 million with a scheduled long-term investment plan. With-holding tax will be reduced in these Open Cities to 10 per cent and local taxes may in some cases not be imposed by local governments.

Others   In all other cases, income derived from sources in China is subject to a final withholding tax of 20 per cent. This rate applies to any passive income from inside China.

Other taxes Other taxes include Urban Real Estate Tax, Customs Duty and the Turnover Tax, the latter including a Consolidated Industrial and Commercial Tax. In total, China has more than fifty types of federal and local taxes.

Capital markets For the Shanghai capital market and the Shenzhen capital market, a stamp duty of 0.3 per cent is levied.[26]

The government is considering introducing an additional 0.3 per cent transaction tax for transaction in the securities markets.

General income tax structure since January 1994

Domestic and foreign companies

Foreign and domestic companies are, since the first of January 1994, taxable under the same regime of income tax. However, lower preferential rates remain for the SEZs. A special category under the new system is the service businesses, including finance, construction, communication and transportation firms. Also included in this category are entertainment centres such as bars, dance halls, teahouses, golf courses. This category will be subject to reduced rates. This incentive for financial service businesses can be seen as an attractive element of the new Chinese income tax system.

The Chinese government assured foreign funded companies that in case there is an increase in their tax liabilities under the new laws, the government will give refunds for the excessive amount paid. Preferential business-income taxes, if applicable, for these companies will remain, according to Jin Xin, Director-General of the State Administration of Taxation.[27]

Individuals, Chinese and foreign, are taxable under an individual income tax levied on wages, salaries, revenues from individual businesses, contracts, rentals, royalties, interest, dividends and property transfers.

Dividends Dividends received by foreign investors from foreign investment enterprises are exempt from tax.[28] The same rule is applicable for dividends or bonuses received by foreign nationals from Chinese–foreign equity joint ventures. This incentive is significant, particularly for Hong Kong investors who invest in foreign joint venture companies, as there is an exemption from tax on dividends in China and no tax liability on dividends in HK as the dividends do not have their source in HK.

Foreign enterprises and foreign nationals receiving dividends or bonuses from B shares or shares in Chinese enterprises listed overseas are provisionally exempt from tax.

Capital gains tax The new income tax includes taxation of capital gains, deductions being allowed for acquisition costs. The capital gains realised with stock transactions or the sale and development of real estate will be taxable. In July 1993, the tax authorities issued a notice concerning the taxation of capital gains from share transfers or equity interests by foreign enterprises.[29] Net gains obtained by foreign investment enterprises with the selling of shares and/or equity interest in Chinese enterprises is taxable in China. The same rule applies if the foreign company has set up establishments or sites in China which conclude transfers with shares and/or equity interest. Net losses are deductible. Gains are defined as that portion of income in excess of the paid-in capital.

The situation is different for gains received by foreign enterprises from the transfer of so-called B shares or shares in a Chinese company that is listed overseas. These gains are provisionally exempt from income tax.

However, it remains unclear if the Chinese tax authorities will be able to implement these tax rules. The rules require a highly effective administrative system to trace and calculate these capital gains, especially in the field of stock transactions.

Exempted from capital gains tax are those residential property developers who earn less than 20 per cent profit.

Tax incentives   The government has given the promise that it will give some exemptions to ease the conversion to the new tax system for foreign investors. However, no details have been given yet as to what these exemptions contain and how they will apply.

Tax rates

All enterprises, state-owned and private-owned as well as foreign, are subject to income tax at a uniform rate of 33 per cent. Service businesses are taxable at a rate of 3–20 per cent. The rate is 3 per cent for transport, construction and communication. Entertainment businesses are taxable at the maximum rate of 20 per cent. Individuals, foreign and Chinese are subject to income tax at progressive rates up to 45 per cent.

Special Economic Zones   The advantaged tax rates as existing under the pre-1994 system remain intact under the new tax system. However, the policy of closing down a large number of economic zones still continues under the new taxation laws.

Repatriation of profits

There is no tax levied on repatriation of after-tax profits transferred out of China (this is in contrast to, for example, Indonesia).

Other taxes

Value added tax The former Consolidated Industrial and Commercial taxes are replaced by a value added tax. The VAT is heavily influenced by the European type of VAT and is levied on production at each stage of manufacturing. The rate for the VAT is 6 per cent for small scale businesses, 13 per cent for food, newspapers, books, gas, coal and agricultural products and 17 per cent for other products.

Exempted from VAT are those products that will be exported. Included are capital inputs for agricultural production, birth-control products, imports for scientific research, special imports for the handicapped and for diplomats.

Consumption tax A consumption tax is levied on luxury items such as alcohol, tobacco, petrol, cosmetics and cars. The rates vary and can go up to 45 per cent.

Tax treaties

China has tax treaties with more than thirty countries including Australia. The tax treaty between China and Australia reduces the withholding tax rates for dividends to 15 per cent and for interest to 10 per cent.

Costs of tax compliance

Costs include the lack of clarity and uncertainty of tax treatment (which makes tax planning difficult). The introduction of a range of new tax laws is another cost, as the introduction of new laws, even when they are cost-reducing in the long term, carry extra immediate costs (see costs of compliance, general heading). The 1994 tax laws contain many uncertainties such as the applications of the new VAT and the problems involved with the recent devaluation of the Chinese currency, the renminbi. The VAT will cause major administrative burdens on foreign companies, as it is a tax that requires intensive administration and skills. Other uncertainties include the duration of the tax benefits of the SEZ, as it is not clear how long these tax incentives will last. The government has assured foreign investors refund of any increases in their tax payments from 1994. In May 1994, the State Tax Bureau of China issued a notice outlining details concerning a tax concession for foreign companies burdened with excess VAT and Consumption tax. The concession is applicable until 1999.[30]

Although the new TCAL is a step in the right direction towards a more effective tax system, it will in the short to medium term not change tax compliance costs significantly.

Conclusion

Changing the tax system was necessary in order to fund a larger proportion of the Chinese budget and to make the tax system more transparent, efficient and suitable for the changing economy. Although the government sees foreign investment as an important factor in the country's economic development, the number of SEZs will be diminished and controls are to be stricter. It is also doubtful how long these SEZs will last. The policy thrust is to improve central government monitoring of the regulatory regime, in itself a positive feature for continued foreign investment in the long run. Unification of the different tax systems is just implemented, but this will have a high chance of succeeding only if the national government is able to induce the provincial governments to follow the same direction.

The problems the tax administration is facing are severe. The laws are not uniformly applied, bribery is common and local governments play a major role in the unequal and sometimes unpredictable application of the tax laws. This insecurity and lack of clarity, and the introduction of new tax laws, given the state of flux in the taxation regime, make the costs of tax compliance significant for those who do comply with the laws. Needless to say, these perceived and real costs have created a significant group of tax evaders, who, by sometimes acquiescing to the unofficial desires of officials at the local and provincial levels, in turn magnify the difficulties faced by the central government in attempting to reform the system.

The general compliance problems highlight a dual issue in China. Due to the imposition of greater transparency on them, public companies are generally paying higher taxes (as well as incurring tax compliance costs) than unlisted firms. This acts as a deterrent to domestic companies wanting to list in China, deferring the 'officialisation' of the domestic capital market. Thus, not only is taxation reform a much needed task for government finance purposes – in broadening the tax base, catching a higher percentage of potential revenue, etc. – it is also a prerequisite for the continued development of China's capital market.

As long as transparency and consistency remain lacking in the tax system, and future developments in tax laws remain highly uncertain, investing in China and operating in its capital market will be relatively high-risk ventures. Although more clarity on tax issues can be expected when China's derivatives markets are further developed, the tax administration will then be confronted with the taxation problems of more sophisticated instruments. At the present time, the lack of transparency and consistency explains much of the global portfolio investment activity in recent years, in hiking on China's growth prospects but using the Hong Kong share market, rather than China's own, as a vehicle.

Hong Kong

Policy

In contrast to China, Hong Kong has the reputation of being a very attractive place for investment from a taxation viewpoint. Indeed, taxes are so low as to be of little concern for investors, whether individuals or companies. Furthermore, the tax system is well administered.

In 1984, the United Kingdom and the People's Republic of China (PRC) signed a Joint Declaration stating that the PRC will take over the sovereignty of Hong Kong (HK) in 1997. In that year Hong Kong will become a Special Administrative Region of China. The Joint Declaration states that the present social and economic policies will stay unchanged until 2047. The so-called Basic Law sets out the constitution of HK after 1997 and in this law it is specifically stated that HK will have the same low rates of taxation.

What are the options for the pre-1997 future? The prediction is that it will be very unlikely that a capital gains tax on securities, or any extra tax incentives, will be introduced. Some analysts expect the introduction of some form of general sales tax or value added tax (VAT) in HK.[31] The first reason for this expectation is that the existing Profits and Salary Tax is narrowly based, but constitutes the major source of tax revenue. Economic fluctuations will tend to have a direct impact on this revenue source, making it vulnerable. The second reason is possible developments in the field of a Value Added Tax in the PRC. The PRC is considering the option of an EC-style VAT, which will replace the present indirect taxes. The extensive trade between China and Hong Kong means that it would be difficult not to introduce a VAT also in HK once this tax was introduced in the mainland – quite apart from the political question of whether China would be willing to exempt Hong Kong, the richest enclave in China, from such a VAT.

Another development that may influence the pre-1997 future is the current official tendency to leave a large percentage of people out of the tax net in HK. At present, less than half of the labour force of 2.5 million are actually paying any form of Salary Tax (income tax for employees). With increasing budget expenditures on education, health and social security, infrastructure and environment, revenues will have to be raised from some source. Although there has been firm opposition to any increase in rates, the increase in revenues might have to come from such an increase in tax rates, unless a broader tax base could be realised.[32]

While Hong Kong may have an image of a low tax paradise, the tax system is well enforced. Tax audits are part of Hong Kong's tax system.[33] The system of 'Field Audits'[34] has been in place in HK since June 1991. The field audits look at small to medium-size taxpayers which have suspicious accounts, heavily qualified auditor's reports or an unrealistically low turnover in comparison to other businesses in similar sectors and circumstances. The team of auditors is small (thirty-six in October 1992) but the first results, up to March 1992, were encouraging. As the government is looking to increased tax revenues, the field audits are a welcome measure to ensure maximum tax compliance.

General income tax structure

The general rule is that Hong Kong only taxes income that is earned in or derived from Hong Kong (the so-called territorial concept). The law regulating income tax is the Inland Revenue Ordinance (IRO) and includes all the provisions regarding profits tax, salaries tax and property tax.

The IRO imposes three separate taxes:

1 profits tax
2 salary tax
3 property tax.

Each of these taxes has their own assessment and administrative obligations. There are no other taxes on income.

Profits tax

Residents and non-residents are taxed on profits under the following three conditions:[35]

- when they carry on or are deemed to be carrying on a trade, business or profession in HK;
- the profits to be charged must be from that trade, business or profession;
- profits must be profits arising in or derived from HK.

Foreign income, income with no source in Hong Kong, is generally not taxable in Hong Kong. The accrual system of calculating income is followed.

The above mentioned conditions provide opportunities for significant tax savings by organising transactions in such a way that they are considered to be offshore. The crucial question is whether income has its source in Hong Kong or not. This is especially the case with increasing investments in China by HK firms, whereby around 80 per cent of the HK industrial base has been moved to Southern China. The point of dispute is whether profits made from the sale of goods produced in China, but sold via HK, derive from a source outside HK. The Commissioner of Inland Revenue has issued a Practice Note in order to clarify this issue.[36] The Note states that it is necessary to determine where the taxpayer effected the relevant purchase and sales contracts. The term 'effected' is described as the place where the actual steps took place which led to the existence of the contract. However, problems remain as some of the rules are open to question.

An important court case in regard to this issue is the Privy Council decision in the case of *Commissioner of Inland Revenue v. Hang Seng Bank Limited*, 1990, in which was stated:[37]

> The guiding principle, attested by many authorities, is that one looks to see what the taxpayer has done to earn the profit in question. If he has rendered a service or engaged in an activity such as the manufacture of goods, the profit will have arisen or derived from the place where the service was rendered or the profit making activity carried on. but if the profit was earned by the exploitation of property assets as by letting property, lending money or dealing in commodities or securities by buying and reselling at a profit, the profit will have arisen in or derived from the place where the property was let, the money was lent or the contracts of purchase and sale were effected.
>
> (Bramhall 1992: 189)

Thus profits from the purchase and sale of listed shares are seen as having their source at the location of the stock exchange where the shares concerned were traded. This conclusion is based on the rationale that sales and purchases on an exchange can only be performed by those agents who physically trade on the exchange, negotiate and conclude the contracts concerned.[38] It seems fair that this rule applies equally to all listed securities, including debt instruments. This appears to be in contrast to transactions that are concluded off-exchange, for example private transactions not effected through foreign brokers. However, the Inland Revenue Department does not make a distinction between on-exchange and off-exchange transactions.

The rules for listed shares do not apply for unlisted shares. In the case of non-listed shares the normal rules relating to trading profits are applicable. This means that the decisive factor here is where the taxpayer effected the relevant purchase and sales contracts.

Cases in which it may be clear if income is onshore or offshore include: an overseas company that carries a business in HK via an agent will be taxable on the HK source of income; persons or companies that instruct an agent in HK to buy and sell shares as part of a business of dealing in securities, will be subject to tax on any profits; if a person or company in Hong Kong instructs agents overseas to buy and sell securities and commodities in overseas markets, the profits arising in respect of that overseas activity will not be subject to Hong Kong profits tax.

Dividends See 'exemptions'.

Interest Interest is taxable in HK if it falls within the scope of one of the HK taxes. For instance, a profits tax is levied on interest derived from HK by a company carrying out trade or other business in HK (Section 15 IRO).

Interest is not defined in the law, but the general interpretation is that when the source of interest originates in HK, the interest may be taxable. Interest received from outside HK is taxable when received by or accrued to a financial institution as a result of carrying on a business in HK.[39] This is an exception to the general rule that income is only taxable if derived from HK.

The taxation of some sources of interest may change in the near future if the government is serious about attracting investment in the private debt securities market. There is speculation that the government may remove the stamp duty and tax on investments in the corporate debt securities denominated in HK dollars. This removal would bring this market in line with the government securities market.[40]

Capital gains Capital gains are generally not taxable in Hong Kong. However, a profits tax may be levied in case of profits deriving from speculative transactions if they can be shown to be an 'adventure' in the nature of the trade. An important court case in this regard is the 13 November 1990 Privy Council decision in *'Waylee' v. Commissioner of Inland Revenue*. The issue was whether a sale of shares by a banking group was a sale of capital assets or an adventure in the nature of trade. The case was as follows:[41] Waylee was a subsidiary of Hong Kong and Shanghai Banking Corporation Limited (the Bank). In 1975, Hutchison International Limited (HIL) was in financial difficulty and heavily indebted to the Bank. To rescue HIL, the Bank agreed to purchase new shares in HIL through Waylee. The shares purchased by Waylee represented 30 per cent of HIL's issued share capital. HIL then gave the Bank effective control as long as the Bank held no less than 20 per cent of HIL's issued shares. In 1979, Waylee disposed of its shares in HIL following an unsolicited offer from a third party.

In reaching its decision in favour of Waylee, the Privy Council relied on the fact that the Commissioner of Inland Revenue had not challenged the Bank's policy of holding long-term investments through subsidiary companies. The Privy Council was satisfied that the shares in HIL were a long-term investment made in line with that policy. Moreover, the shares' long-term nature was supported by the fact that they were not used or expected to be used as part of the Bank's circulating capital held to meet depositors' demands.

Derivatives[42] For the tax application of all derivatives, the following condition applies in Hong Kong; it has to be a Hong Kong source revenue transaction. This condition applies for the taxability, deductibility of payments and the possibility of tax relief for certain payments.

Commodity swaps[43] Relief is available for payments made under the swap. Receipts under the swaps are taxable and the fees paid in consideration for arranging a commodity swap are deductible.

Currency options[44]   In Hong Kong currency options are for tax purposes treated as separate contracts from the underlying currency. Premiums paid to obtain an option are subject to relief. A relief is given when the premium becomes payable.

Currency swaps[45]   Payments made under this type of swap are subject to relief on an accrual basis. Receipts are taxable and fees made to arrange the swap are deductible. A currency swap which is matched economically with an underlying asset or liability will realise a matched position for tax purposes.

Financial futures[46]   Gains realised on this type of futures are taxable and losses are relievable. The system of the accrual basis is applicable.

Forward rate agreements[47]   Payments made in connection with this type of agreements are generally deductible and receipts are taxable. However they are not deductible or taxable when the transaction is offshore in nature or is a hedge against non-deductible interest expenses.

Interest rate caps[48]   Deductions are available for the premium paid by the buyer of the agreement. The payments made by the writer of an interest rate cap agreement are not regarded as interest and are deductible for the writer.

Interest rate options[49]   Premiums paid to acquire such options are relievable. This relief is not dependent upon the option being exercised or not.

Interest rate swaps[50]   Payments made under interest rate swaps are subject to relief, which is available on an accrual basis. Receipts under this type of swap are taxable but fees paid for arranging the swap are deductible. Also deductible are payments made to terminate the swap. Hong Kong generally determines the source of the payments by the location at which the recipient carries on business.

Zero coupon bonds[51]   Relief is available to the issuer of zero coupon bonds on an accrual basis. In Hong Kong the investor is not taxed on the discount as it accrues. The tax treatment of gains or losses arising on disposal or maturity is dependent on the tax status of both the issuer and the investor.

Head office expenses   Head office expenses are accepted as deductible by the tax authorities as long as the amount is reasonable. However, there has to be a relationship between the amount deducted as expenses and the profits earned in Hong Kong. Thus, deducting 90 per cent of the Hong Kong profit as head office expenses would not be acceptable.

Withholding tax   There is no withholding tax on interest and dividends. Nevertheless, profits tax is sometimes levied on non-residents via their resident agent. The tax generally applies where the non-resident uses a resident agent to sell goods in HK. The agent is ordered to withhold and pay up to 1 per cent of gross sales revenue to the tax authorities. The non-resident is entitled to submit a tax return at the end of the taxable year to calculate a final tax liability.

Tax incentives   There are no specific tax incentives for foreign or local enterprises or certain types of investment, since the tax system itself is seen as an incentive for enterprise and investment.

Tax exemptions   Dividends paid from profits subject to profit tax are not taxable in the hands of shareholders. Dividends from overseas companies are not subject to tax either, because they do not have a HK source. Interest derived from funds deposited abroad are also tax-exempt. This exemption is only given to companies that are not financial institutions.

Royalty payments are exempt when they have no sources in Hong Kong. Otherwise, they are subject to profit tax.

Tax rates for profit tax   A profit tax is levied at a flat rate of 15 per cent on all businesses run by individuals whereas companies have been taxed at 17.5 per cent since 1 April 1992. From 1994–1995 the rates are reduced from 17.5 per cent to 16.5 per cent. This reverses the 1 per cent increase in the profits tax rates for companies which took place in 1992.

Repatriation of profits

There is no restriction on the repatriation of profit of a Hong Kong company and no taxes are levied unless the profits can be classified as royalties with their source in Hong Kong.

Salary tax: employees

Visitors who stay less than sixty days in HK are not subject to salary tax. The tax treatment of employees is rather favourable as fringe benefits are lightly taxed. The general rule is that fringe benefits are not taxable unless they can be converted into cash or represent an employee's personal liability assumed by the employer. The tax paid is the lesser of:

- a tax rate of 2 per cent to 25 per cent (from 1994–95 the top rate is 20 per cent) on net chargeable income* derived from employment
- a flat rate of 15 per cent on net assessable income*

*net assessable income is cash remuneration plus all taxable benefits less charitable donations. Net chargeable is net assessable income less personal allowances and charitable donations.

Property tax

Persons owning buildings or land in HK have to pay a property tax, levied according to the value of their property.

Other taxes

Besides the above mentioned taxes a number of other taxes and duties are imposed under various Hong Kong ordinances. Stamp duty is levied at a rate of 0.3 per cent on share transfer. This used to be 0.4 per cent but was reduced in the budget for 1993–1994. However no stamp duty is payable if the transfer is not required to be registered in Hong Kong or if it concerns a foreign exchange transaction. Stamp duty is also levied on the transfer of property.

Tax treaties

Hong Kong does not have any tax treaty,[52] and although the territory is not a sovereign state, the tax treaties between the United Kingdom and other countries are not applicable to HK. It has been reported that HK will ask the approval of China to enter into tax treaties with other countries.[53] The PRC has concluded more than thirty tax treaties but it seems unlikely that these agreements will be equally applicable for HK after 1997. It seems likely that HK itself will be allowed to enter into tax treaties with major trade partners.

Costs of tax compliance

The Commissioner of Inland Revenue issues Departmental Interpretation and Practice Notes, and Information Pamphlets, in order to assist with the practical application and administration of the tax laws. However, this information can be used as guidelines only and does not form part of the law. Upon request, the Inland Revenue Department will provide advance ruling which may come within the scope of the anti-avoidance provisions of the IRO.[54] These services do minimise the costs of tax compliance, but there remain cases where the tax treatment is unclear. The issue of whether income is onshore or offshore is one such case, especially with the increasing trade and investment between China and Hong Kong. Compliance costs will increase further if a VAT is introduced, since a VAT involves not only starting costs, as is usual with the introduction of a new tax law, but also requires intensive administration afterwards.

Conclusion

Hong Kong's tax system can be described as one of the most favourable in the world. There is the possible introduction of a VAT, which may cause short-term uncertainties and temporary and permanent costs, but the general clarity of the tax system and the quality of information disseminated by the tax department is likely to minimise these extra costs of tax compliance.

The lack of restrictions on the entry and repatriation of capital and profits and dividends, combined with low corporate income tax rates, makes investing in Hong Kong's capital market (especially in its equity market) highly attractive. This tax-attractiveness is further enhanced by the general (with some exceptions) tax exemption on dividends, royalties or capital gains.

Unfortunately, it remains unclear what the post-1997 tax regime will be like, even though some promises are given that the tax rates will remain low. This contentious state means HK's investment fortune risks being increasingly tied to those of the PRC, whereby instability in the mainland for whatever reason might cause some degree of capital flight out of HK (to a third destination) as a result. Conversely, as long as China is perceived by the international market as remaining committed to market reform, mainland economic growth will be reflected in that of HK's equity and debt markets turnover.

Malaysia

Policy

Since the late 1980s, the Malaysian government has faced a decline in tax revenues. The government sees this decline as a result of an excessively narrow tax base and the large number of exemptions and reliefs given to promote investment.[55] It felt that drastic measures had to be taken in order to stop this declining tax revenue trend.

In his budget for 1992, the Minister of Finance proposed a new investment promotion policy. This focuses on high technology activities and capital intensive industries combined with the reduction or removal of many tax incentives and exemptions previously provided to promote investment.[56] However, the Minister of Finance recognised that there might be cases where a 100 per cent tax exemption would be given to projects which were deemed vital to the national interest or involving heavy capital investment and high technology. The Malaysian government's recent policy change reflected its view that tax incentives are only one factor attracting foreign investors and that other factors such as political stability, good infrastructure and a trained labour force are equally important. Although tax incentives still play some role in the promotion of investment, more value has been given to the reduction, with effect from 1993, in corporate tax rates to 34 per cent and the abolition of the 2 per cent development tax.[57] The Minister of Finance indicated that there might be further reductions in corporate tax rates to 25–28 per cent, possibly in connection with further reductions in tax incentives and a move towards indirect taxes.[58]

In the 1989 budget, the government expressed its intention to introduce a value added tax (VAT) to overcome the weaknesses of the current sales tax system and to expand the revenue base.[59] Since then, the services tax has been extended, in preparation for the ultimate introduction of a VAT. A VAT is believed to increase net tax revenue in the long term, despite the already reduced income tax rates. The introduction of a VAT can be seen as a positive development for investors, since it will be accompanied by a further reduction in the rates of direct taxes.[60]

There are tax incentives in the area of capital market, including the tax exemption for interest paid to non-residents and to individuals from government securities or bonds, and corporate bonds (not being convertible loan stocks) issued by companies listed on the Kuala Lumpur Stock Exchange. This indicates the government's policy of promoting domestic savings and stimulating the domestic bond market. The exemption for non-residents attempts to attract capital (as well as foreign know-how) into the domestic bond market and further develop its scope and scale in an effort to integrate the local market with the world structure.

General income tax structure

Resident and non-resident taxpayers A company is classified as a resident taxpayer if the control and management of its business or one of its businesses is exercised in Malaysia.

Corporate income A resident company is not only taxed on Malaysian-sourced income but also on its foreign earned income when repatriated to Malaysia.

Dividends For resident taxpayers dividends are taxable as income in the hands of the shareholders. Dividends are subject to a withholding tax of 34 per cent. This tax may be creditable against their final tax liabilities payable at the end of the tax year.

There is no withholding tax on dividends paid to either residents or non-residents. This is because of the imputation system Malaysia applies, whereby the dividend is grossed up by the 34 per cent income tax rate that is levied on the underlying profits of the resident company paying the dividend. The 34 per cent tax can be claimed as credit against final tax liabilities of the taxpayer who received the dividends. This rule is not applicable for dividends paid out of profits, which are not subject to Malaysian tax laws. Such dividends are subject to an extra income tax of 34 per cent which is not creditable.

Non-residents receiving dividends from a Malaysian company out of its tax exempt funds, i.e. pioneer company dividends, are not subject to Malaysian tax on those dividends.

Interest   There is a withholding tax of 20 per cent on payments of interest to non-residents. However, payments of interest to non-residents by banks and financial institutions are exempt from withholding tax. Interest is taxable at a flat rate of 20 per cent in the form of a final withholding tax on interest paid to non-residents.

Interest paid to individuals from government securities or bonds, corporate bonds (not being convertible loan stocks) issued by companies listed on the Kuala Lumpur Stock Exchange or rated by Rating Agency Malaysia Bhd, is exempt from income tax. Interest on savings bonds issued by the Central Bank with a guaranteed return of 48 per cent on maturity is also exempt from tax, regardless of the term of the bond.

Taxation problems have arisen with the introduction of commercial papers and zero coupon swaps. The tax authorities seem to treat a discount and an interest payment as the same. However, from a tax point of view a distinction has to be made between interest payments and a discount.[61] With the issue of a discounted bond, the sum of money involved is advanced at a discounted face value of the bond (or other security). The issue or subscription price will be different from the redemption price on maturity, the difference being the discount and not the interest, although to calculate the discount a formula involving interest is used. The distinction can be clarified when using the example of the payment made to a non-resident, in which case the interest is subject to a withholding tax while the discount is not. The distinction is explained in the court case *Willingale v. International Commercial Bank Ltd* [1978] STC 75:[62]

> The difference between the price at which the bank buys the bill and the bill's face is something referred to as a 'discount'. A discount however, is different from interest; it is not earned nor does it accrue from day to day.

> (Wong 1993: 5)

But that is not the only problem in relation to discounted securities. Another issue occurs when the question regards at what time the borrower can claim the discount.[63] At the time of issue, or at the maturity date, or over the period of the security? This should be determined according to the general tax provision: when was the discount incurred in producing the income? According to Malaysian law deductions are permitted if classified as 'all outgoings and expenses wholly and exclusively incurred during that period in the production of income'. It seems that the discount is 100 per cent deductible at the time of issue.

Capital gains No capital gains tax is levied in Malaysia except when capital gains are obtained from the transfer of land, buildings and rights/ interest attached to them, which are subject to Real Property Gains Tax. Therefore, capital gains from the transfer of shares in a so-called 'real property company' will also be subject to the Real Property Gains Tax.

From the perspective of investors, therefore, gains or profits are taxed according to the source from which such gains or profits are derived. The pertinent sources of taxable income specified by the Income Tax Act fall into six broad categories: business income, dividends, interest, discounts, royalties and premiums.

Thus, gains or profits from transactions in money-market or capital market instruments are taxed according to the source from which the gains or profits are derived. It follows for example, that the profits or gains of a passive investor in the stock market are not ordinarily subject to income tax because they are considered as a capital transaction. However, a share trader who carries on the business of selling shares is liable for income tax on profits and gains originating from the trade.[64]

Withholding tax A withholding tax is levied from non-resident taxpayers on interest and royalties at a rate of 20 per cent.

Tax incentives

Pioneer status One of the many tax incentives is the so-called 'pioneer status', which can be granted for an initial five years to companies establishing or participating in a promoted activity such as agriculture, hotel and tourism business and gazetted manufacturing. The status entitles the company to tax exemption of 70 per cent of its income for five years from the production date. A five-year tax holiday is also granted to companies engaged in research and development or in areas of new and emerging technology. For those pioneer status companies, 85 per cent of their statutory income is exempt from tax for a five-year period.

The government introduced in 1994 new tax incentives to support industrial expansion into the Eastern Corridor, Sabah and Sarawak.[65]

Investment tax allowance An investment tax allowance up to 60 per cent may be given in respect of qualifying capital expenditure incurred within five years from the date of approval of the project. The allowance can be seen as an alternative to the pioneer status and focuses on capital intensive industries with a long starting period.[66]

The decision to grant the above mentioned tax incentives will be made according to priorities termed as promoted activities or promoted products as determined by the Minister of Trade and Industry.

In the 1991 budget the government announced incentives in the field of outgoing investments, to encourage Malaysian investors to look overseas, particularly in sectors where Malaysia has expertise.[67] Several incentives for export were already available prior to 1991 and are still applicable. In summary, the following export incentives apply:

1 export credit refinancing scheme, giving credit at lower interest rates;
2 abatement of adjusted income of 50 per cent of export sales, granted to resident manufacturing companies exporting Malaysian manufactured products;
3 export allowance of 5 per cent of the value of exported sales to trading companies which export products manufactured in Malaysia;
4 double deduction of export credit insurance premiums;
5 double deduction for promotion of exports, with certain expenses able to be deducted twice by the resident company, including costs of overseas advertising, other PR activities overseas, export research and the maintenance of an overseas sales office for the promotion of exports.

The Minister of Finance announced in 1993 that some incentives need to be revised, and he proposed the abolishment of export abatement and export allowance from the year 1994.[68]

Besides the above mentioned incentives two other important measures available under the Income Tax Act of 1967 apply.

• Reinvestment allowance, applicable until the end of 1995, for those companies which are not eligible for pioneer status; the allowance given is 40 per cent of the expenditure on plant, machinery and industrial building;
• incentives for research and development in industry, allowing double deduction for certain expenditures related to research.

Tax rates

Corporate tax is levied at a rate of 34 per cent on income derived or accrued from Malaysia (except petroleum companies). For petroleum companies a special tax is levied at 45 per cent on profits derived from petroleum operations under the Petroleum (Income Tax) Act of 1967.

Personal income tax rates vary between 2 per cent and 34 per cent. This is a reduction from previous rates of 4 per cent to 35 per cent. By setting the maximum rate for corporate and personal income tax at the same level, the government aims to prevent tax evasion by individuals structuring their personal income in a fashion allowing them to describe it as corporate income. The reduction, introduced in 1993, followed the lowering of corporate tax rates.

Repatriation of profits

There is generally no limitation on repatriating profits and capital out of Malaysia.

Other taxes

Stamp duty Stamp duty is levied on the sale of any stocks, shares or marketable securities. This is computed on the price or value on the date of transfer on every M$100 or fractional part of M$100. The stamp duty is 30 cents, or 0.3 per cent.

Sales tax Currently a sales tax is levied at 5–15 per cent on goods sold or imported into Malaysia.

Other taxes generally applicable in Malaysia include customs duty, excise duty, service tax, sales tax and entertainment tax.

Tax treaties

Malaysia has concluded tax treaties with over thirty countries. The tax treaty with Australia reduces the withholding tax rate on interest to 15 per cent.

Costs of tax compliance

The taxation of a large number of financial instruments is not always clear in Malaysia. In case of cross-border financial instruments, the problems are even greater due to a lack of sophistication in the tax treatment of these instruments, for example, with the introduction of commercial papers and zero-coupon swaps. The possible introduction of a VAT will increase costs of tax compliance in the same way outlined in previous sections, both temporarily, due to the introduction of a new tax, and permanently as the system of VAT requires significant administration.

Conclusion

Malaysia's corporate tax rate of 34 per cent cannot be classified as very attractive compared to neighbouring countries. It is probable that these rates will be reduced in future. However, Malaysia will have some way to catch up since a reduction might not be sufficiently competitive, as other countries with already lower tax rates are considering further cuts themselves.

Incentives are given, for example, in the field of domestic bond markets. Although it is arguable whether Malaysia's tax policy will hinder the development of new instruments in the market, problems have to be faced in regard to the unclear taxation rules for financial instruments.

The introduction of a VAT could be a positive development for investors as the rates of direct taxation might be further reduced. However, as noted, the introduction of a VAT, in order for it to be gainful, will require efficiency in implementation on the part of the authorities. The direction for the government to take, as in other emerging markets, should be to streamline the tax system and make it more effective, like Hong Kong's. Tax rate reductions are attractive preliminary moves to encourage foreign capital and technology inflow. Of longer term consequence are the consistency and transparency of the tax regime, how speedily the system expedites appeals and disseminates information and replies to enquires. In this regard, a higher level of training for tax officials and a better organisational structure for tax administration are prerequisites.

Indonesia

The Indonesian government provides few income tax incentives for approved foreign investments. However, there are some reliefs, including the exemption or reduction of import duties on capital goods. The government promotes certain investments in remote areas, including most parts of Kalimantan, Sulawesi, East and West Nusa Tenggara, East Timor, Maluka and Irian Jaya. Industrial endeavours promoted by the government are oil and gas exploration, and mining. Primary production also promoted by the government in this way includes the establishment and management of plantations growing hardy plants (crops with a growth period of more than one year). Special tax advantages may be applicable for these government-promoted sectors. There are also some specific tax breaks for geothermal resources industries as well as for the shipping, fishing, banking, leasing and insurance sectors. In October 1994, the Indonesian House of Representatives approved an income-tax bill containing a clause giving the government power to grant tax 'facilities' to investors in 'certain' industries or locations. It remains unclear what type of incentives will be granted. The new tax bills are applicable from 1995.

A recent move by the government is the increase in tax rates on time deposits from 15 per cent to 35 per cent (from 1995 30 per cent), resulting in an equal tax treatment of interest and dividends. This is aimed at stimulating a dormant stock market, by transferring savings from deposit accounts to the equity market. A more competitive move might have been to cut corporate and dividend taxes to 15 per cent rather than raise deposit taxes.

To compete with neighbouring countries, Indonesia has lowered its top corporate and individual tax rates from 35 per cent to 30 per cent, applicable from 1995 with the potential for a further reduction to 25 per cent by Ministerial Decree.

Given the inefficiencies embedded in Indonesia's tax collection system, the World Bank reported that the country's actual tax revenue remains low in comparison with its neighbours' and in proportion to Indonesia's own potential revenue. The bank estimates that the actual potential tax revenue ratio is:

- 50 per cent for income tax (personal and corporate)
- 55 per cent for value added tax (VAT)
- 60 per cent for property tax

In countries with more developed tax systems, these ratios average 80–85 per cent.[69]

The source of government revenue has changed since tax reforms were implemented in 1984. In that year, only 24.7 per cent of government expenditure was funded by non-oil tax revenue (NOTR). By 1990, 39.9 per cent of the government's expenditure had its source in NOTR. This trend in increasing government reliance on NOTR to fund its budget can be projected to continue in the foreseeable future, given the on-going trend decline in world oil prices (especially in real terms) since the 1970s.

The state budget for 1992–93 and the draft budget for 1993–94 depend heavily on a large increase in tax revenue. President Suharto said at the beginning of 1993 that the country's development should be financed by the most reliable and least risky development funds, namely funds from domestic sources.[70]

The largest revenue increase in 1993–94 is projected to come from income tax sources, by a large 35.9 per cent. The second largest rise in non-oil revenue will be from the VAT, due to an increase by 5.9 per cent for 1993–94.[71] Tax revenue is scheduled to rise further over 1993–94 due to legal changes such as the broadening base of the VAT, the increase in sales tax on selected luxury goods, and adjustments to taxes on interest earned by corporations from money held in term deposits.[72]

It seems that the potential for extending the tax base is nearly exhausted. The high rate of non-compliance and the low ratio of filing make it unlikely that attempts at further broadening the tax base will be fruitful. A country only has so much room to manoeuvre autonomously, especially when it comes to structural changes that may affect directly or indirectly its capacity to access global capital.

Further increases in (income) tax revenue, therefore, would have to come from better enforcement and compliance.[73] Mar'ie Muhammad, former Director General of Taxation, claimed that there was great scope for improvement in Indonesia's tax system in terms of compliance. This includes overcoming such major shortcomings such as inadequate legislation, poor organisational structure, inefficient manpower and the incidence of corruption.[74]

It is apparent that drastic change in the tax administration is required. The administration is no more than a reflection of the society at large. Salaries and general levels of education – factors impacting on the issue of bribery – within the administration may not change as long as those changes are not realised more generally in the society. The problems that the Indonesian tax administration is facing are protracted, however, given their diverse and complex nature. Yet the administration's very important role in the nation's fiscal health calls for particular attention to be paid to the monitoring of those protracted problems. For instance, weak supervision at most bureaucratic levels and officials' limited knowledge of fiscal and legal matters present hurdles to any attempt to improve tax policy implementation or rule application.

An important factor in the collection of tax revenue is tax compliance, which involves the willingness of taxpayers/potential taxpayers to pay taxes. Citizens' perception of their government contributes partly to this willingness. The protection accorded by the government to some taxpayers or taxpayer groups does discourage compliance at large. There needs to be a serious overhaul of the relationships between the government and these groups in order to establish a degree of level playing field in the tax system, where all taxpayers should be (and are seen to be) treated fairly.

Tax evasion and fraud cannot be separated from the above mentioned issues. Efficient detection is an important aspect of tax collection, but this aspect encounters two problems: first, the use of penalties as a tool will only be effective if the chance of getting caught is reasonable and the size of the penalty substantial. A weak tax administration, and poor auditing and information systems, mean that the instruments to enforce the law are rarely there; and second, detection only deals with the methods or approaches of tax enforcement, not the fundamental reasons behind non-compliance. Unless, as has been said, a more equitable and perhaps less invasive (in terms of size of the tax take) system becomes apparent to the large majority of the populace, non-compliance (resulting at times in punishing tax liabilities for certain taxpayer categories) will remain an intractable problem.

General income tax structure

Resident and non-resident taxpayers Indonesian limited liability companies, including the foreign joint-venture (the so-called PMA company), are considered to be resident tax subjects. A permanent establishment is considered a resident taxpayer. An individual is considered to be resident in Indonesia if he or she is present in Indonesia for more than 183 days, whether or not in succession, in any 12-month period, or if he or she resides in Indonesia with the intention of staying there.

Taxable income   The ITL of 1984[75] covers all forms of income for resident and non-resident taxpayers. As a general rule, there is no distinction between organisations and individuals. Both corporate and individual income tax are covered uniformly by the ITL.

Taxable income is generally determined on the accrual basis. The cash basis may be used by small individual entrepreneurs.

Income is defined (Article 4 ITL) as: any increase in economic prosperity received or accrued by a taxpayer, whether originating from within or outside Indonesia, that is used for consumption or that increases the wealth of such taxpayer, in whatever name and form, including:

- wages, salaries, commissions, bonuses, pensions or other compensation for work performed;
- honorariums, lottery prizes and awards;
- gross profit from business;
- gains from the sale or transfer of property;
- interest;
- dividends, in whatever name and form;[76]
- royalties;
- rents from property.

The list is not exhaustive as any increase in economic prosperity for a taxpayer may be seen as income.

Although business income as such is not specified in the ITL, it is considered as income from business activities, whether performed by an entity or a private entrepreneur or by an independent profession.

Resident taxpayers are taxable on their worldwide income, within or outside Indonesia. Non-resident taxpayers are taxed only on their Indonesian sourced gross income.

Interest and dividends   Dividends and interest are part of the taxable income for resident taxpayers. A pretax is paid via a withholding tax of 15 per cent on dividends and interest received by resident individual taxpayers. The withholding tax is creditable at the year end against other tax liabilities.

A final withholding tax of 20 per cent is levied on dividends received by foreign recipients. Interest payments are treated in the same manner. If a tax treaty applies the rates may be reduced to 10 per cent or 15 per cent.

Convertible bonds   The gains received by switching convertible bonds from bond into shares is seen as taxable income in Indonesia and subject to withholding tax of 20 per cent if the holder or bearer is a non-resident. The gains from the transaction are taxable in the year of conversion. However, when a tax treaty applies, generally the gain will not be subject to tax in Indonesia but only in the country of residence of the holder or bearer.

Floating rate notes Income from floating rate notes are treated as interest and the normal tax rules for interest apply, even if the interest rates vary.

Warrants The gain from the sale of warrants is taxable for resident taxpayers as it is considered the realisation of a capital gain. It seems that non-residents are not taxable for these gains, especially when a tax treaty is applicable. Gains from the sale of the original bond which once carried the warrant are also taxable to the holder of that bond who becomes the beneficiary of the gains. Again, it seems logical that only resident taxpayers are taxable for this gain. The interest on the original bond is taxable and so is any dividend declared. Both are taxable according to the general rules.[77]

Capital gains All capital gains accrued or realised by resident taxpayers are in principle taxable. However, due to limited administrative capacity, the application of the law is not always feasible. In 1994, non-resident taxpayers were not taxed on capital gains.[78] However, in October 1994 the government issued a new tax bill that is applicable from January 1995. Under the new legislation sales of capital assets by foreign owners will be subject to a 'transaction tax'. This is proposed to be a final transaction tax of 20 per cent. It remains unclear how this new legislation will affect foreign shareholders in Indonesia.

A Permanent Establishment (PE), thus a resident taxpayer, may be created when foreign investors use Indonesian brokers (or other agents) to perform on their behalf, unless the agent is carrying on its own business acting independently. An important aspect is if the agent is acting partly or wholly in the name of the foreign investor, then the agent does not qualify as being an independent agent, but is considered as a PE of that foreign investor. Offshore funds using an agent, broker or underwriter have to be aware of this and should use an independent agent where possible. However, no guarantee can be given as to whether or not activities are classified as activities creating a PE, so this remains a grey area.

Withholding tax The system of withholding tax plays a very important role in the Indonesian tax system. For resident taxpayers, withholding tax is a prepayment of the tax due at the end of the taxable year. The tax paid during the year via the withholding tax will be credited against the tax due at the end of the taxable year. For non-resident taxpayers, withholding tax is the final tax and not creditable against other tax liabilities in Indonesia. The withholding tax is imposed at source and is collected via a third person.

Take, for example, a withholding tax on wages. In this case, the employer is obliged to withhold the tax before the wage is paid to the employee. The employer transfers the withholding tax to the taxation department and at the end of the taxable year the withholding tax paid is creditable against the tax due by the taxpayer.[79]

Employees earning more than the minimum tax-free income have to pay income tax. This income tax is paid during the year via withholding tax rates of 15 per cent, 25 per cent or 35 per cent (from 1995 30 per cent) on monthly employment income (Article 21 ITL).

If a resident taxpayer pays out to another resident taxpayer dividends, interest, rent, and royalties, the former has the duty to collect an advance payment withholding tax of 15 per cent of the gross amount. Technical and management fees, and other income connected with the use of assets, are subject to 9 per cent withholding tax on the gross amount of payments. This tax is creditable against year-end tax liability in Indonesia.

If a resident taxpayer pays out to a non-resident taxpayer dividends, interest, rent, royalties, technical and management fees, that resident taxpayer has the duty to collect a final withholding tax of 20 per cent of the gross amount (this rate is different under the tax treaties). 'Final' means it cannot be credited against other tax liabilities in Indonesia.

Tax rates

For resident corporate taxpayers, including permanent establishments, which are classified as resident taxpayers, tax rates vary between 15 per cent and 35 per cent. The corporate tax rates also apply to resident individual taxpayers but there is a deduction permitted for exempt income. From 1995, the top corporate and individual tax rates will be reduced to 30 per cent.

Repatriation of profits

Repatriation of after-tax profits of a PE (branch) to the head office abroad is subject to a final withholding tax of 20 per cent unless a tax treaty is applicable, in which case the rate is reduced to 15 per cent. Repatriation of dividend is also subject to the above mentioned rules on taxation of dividend (subject to 20 per cent final withholding tax unless a tax treaty is applicable, when the rate drops to 15 per cent).

Other taxes

Import tax Import tax[80] is levied at rates varying from nil for essential goods to 100 per cent and more for some consumer goods and also goods which are produced locally.[81] The latter includes ready-made clothes, shoes, some foodstuffs, dinner ware, video cassette recorders and tapes. Services are not subject to import and/or export tax.

Export tax An export tax is levied at rates up to 30 per cent or a specified amount denominated in US dollars. An export tax surcharge on specified commodities is levied at the rate of 20 per cent.

Value added tax   The Value Added Tax Law covers: the transfer of taxable goods and the rendering of taxable services, the importation of most taxable goods,[82] and the export of specified services.[83] Retailers are not required to charge VAT unless they are large-scale retailers. There are special VAT rules for foreign aid projects.[84] The VAT rate is 10 per cent on the sales price of the goods transferred or taxable service rendered, or 10 per cent of the import value of taxable goods/services imported.

Sales tax on luxury goods   A number of goods are subject to the Luxury Goods Sales Tax. This tax is only imposed once upon import or at the manufacturing stage. The rates are 10 per cent, 20 per cent or 35 per cent.[85]

Stamp duty   Share transactions in Indonesia are subject to stamp duty payable at the rate of Rp 1,000 on transactions having a value of more than Rp 1,000,000, and Rp 500 on transactions having a value of Rp 100,000 to Rp 1,000,000. Transactions having a value of less than Rp 100,000 are not subject to stamp duty.

Minor taxes   Minor taxes include:

- tax on land and buildings
- motor vehicle tax
- transfer duty on motor vehicles
- tax on the transfer of ships.

Tax treaties

Indonesia has more than twenty tax treaties. This includes a tax treaty with Australia reducing the withholding tax rates for dividends to 15 per cent and for interest to 10 per cent. (See also under the following section on costs of tax compliance).

Costs of tax compliance

The new legislation of 1984 involved a number of changes. The income tax base, including individual and corporate tax, was broadened, and tax rates significantly reduced. The exemptions for mainly high income earners were abolished. The next step, a luxury sales tax and a Value Added Tax (VAT), were gradually introduced from 1985. The Land and Building Tax and the new stamp duty law were implemented in 1986. A lot of attention was paid to ensuring simplicity of the 1984 tax laws, and to making them easily applicable in practice. The major law in respect of foreign investors is the income tax law. The income tax law was designed to avoid any complicated juridical tax bases. The design of the law has to a certain degree succeeded in avoiding a difficult juridical base with the introduction of a withholding tax system and the system of self assessment. Nominally, simplicity in the Income Tax Law can be seen as achieved, although there are some unclear points.[86] Unfortunately, there are areas that still cause problems, most of them directly linked to the problems within Indonesia's tax administration system.

The Director General (DG) of Taxation in Indonesia has the task of formulating tax policy, but the DG is not always a tax law specialist. Thus, where there are problems of interpretation and application of tax law, the DG is not always able to issue clear and constructive guidelines. Confusion about legal interpretation can continue for years because of non-intervention on the part of the Director General.

This confusion is widespread in the field of capital market instruments, for instance, the tax treatment of premium paid by the shareholders. A change in its form as an element of capital cannot change its character as income. However, Mansury (Indonesia's Assistant Minister of Finance for Revenue Affairs, when this chapter was written) argues that where shares are issued at premium, the premium is not taxable; however, if the premium is converted into equity capital and therefore bonus shares are issued, the distribution of the bonus shares will be subject to income tax, as it is considered as dividends.[87]

With the development of the capital market in Indonesia still in its early stage, not many decrees or circulars of the tax administration have been issued to clarify the tax treatment of more sophisticated financial instruments, most of which do not exist anyway. The lack of clarity in taxation may play a constraining role in the potential development of the derivatives markets.

Tax audits

The main criterion for auditing a company is if the company claims to have paid excessive tax (Government Regulation 31/1986), i.e., audits mainly take place when a company asks for a tax refund. Tax audits have the reputation of being very inconvenient and time-consuming for the taxpayer, which is a further disincentive for taxpayers contemplating seeking a refund.

Objections and appeal process   In case the taxpayer disagrees with the assessment, an objection can be made at the district tax office where the taxpayer is registered. The objection may be reviewed by the regional or head office, which can be very time-consuming, due to bureaucratic practices, staff shortages and lack of specialist knowledge on the part of officials.[88] In objection cases, the decisions of the former Director General, Mar'ie Muhammad, who was under pressure to meet the revenue targets set out by the government, were in most cases in favour of the tax administration.[89]

If the decision goes against the taxpayer, the dispute can be taken to the Supreme Court for tax matters in Jakarta, the MPP. This option involves lengthy court procedures, with, for the litigant, the added disincentive that the money equivalent to the disputed tax must be deposited for up to several years in non-interest bearing accounts (this is in contrast to Hong Kong, where interest is paid on the disputed sum). The MPP is external to the Directorate-General of Taxation. Court members are appointed by the President on the recommendation of the Supreme Court and the Chamber of Commerce. When an appeal procedure starts, a response is requested from the DG, which can take months or even years.[90] After receiving the response, the MPP can take further time before making a decision. The tax court cases, although not published, are often in favour of the taxpayer and the independent Supreme Court has been accused, from the government side, of bias.[91] The fact that the court cases are not published means that they cannot be used as guidelines for the tax administration and taxpayers.

Tax treaties

Indonesia has concluded more than twenty tax treaties with other countries. Although not explicitly stated in Indonesian law, it was generally accepted that tax treaties take precedence over national law. Notwithstanding this silent convention, the Indonesian Taxation Department issued in March 1993 a circular stating that prior approval would be required from the Indonesian taxation department for the application of the tax treaty. The approval is given in the form of a 'Certificate of Rate Reduction' or 'Certificate of Exemption'. The approval is only given if certain documents are provided by the taxation departments of the foreign countries. If there is no prior approval the tax treaty is not applicable. This Indonesian Taxation Department rule has received much criticism from inside the country as well as from abroad, including foreign governments. The non-automatic application of the tax treaties is against the commonly accepted conventions of international tax law. It creates much practical and administrative frustration and a lot of uncertainty.

Conclusion

The Indonesian tax policy does not have an extensive system of tax incentives such as those that exist in some East Asian countries, however, this may change under the new 1995 legislation. Corporate tax rates in Indonesia will be reduced in 1995 to maintain international competitiveness. This lowering in tax rates will coincide with a widening of the withholding tax system and further limitation of deductions, while the base for indirect taxes will be broadened. This seems a necessity as the government sees non-oil related tax revenue as the most important source of budget funding. However, it remains unclear how the government is planning to achieve its very high revenue targets without paying more attention to the low levels of tax compliance and the structural problems within the tax administration.

The costs of tax compliance can be significant as the tax administration is not always able to interpret tax laws, the application of the tax treaties is restricted and the procedures for objection and appeal are expensive and time-consuming. The lack of clarity in tax rules, especially those concerning the capital market, and the risks that offshore funds face in being treated for tax purposes as a PE in Indonesia, further contribute to these costs. The latest tax changes will further contribute to this lack of clarity.

The final withholding tax of 20 per cent (unless a tax treaty applies, in which case the rate is 15 per cent or 10 per cent) on dividends and interest paid out to non-residents and the relatively high corporate tax rates, combined with the above mentioned costs of tax compliance, makes Indonesia's capital market not as attractive as, say, Hong Kong or Singapore.

Singapore

Policy

The Singapore government makes very active use of tax incentives to attract foreign capital and direct these capital flows to sectors determined by itself. The government issues a new range of incentives with almost every new annual budget. The tax incentives aimed at attracting financial institutions and international banks to Singapore, as well as promoting shipping business and trading activities and simplifying the repatriation of income earned abroad, are the result of government policy which promotes investment abroad by Singaporean companies. This promotion is seen as a necessary step to create a stronger external dimension to the Singaporean economy.

Over the past decade there have been numerous tax incentives or concessions granted to the finance sector. This trend is expected to continue. It has become increasingly evident that the taxation of financial instruments will converge with international practice. Tax incentives are used to encourage international companies to use Singapore as a base and thereby take advantage of Singapore's financial institutions and services.

The Singapore government has made serious attempts to expand its catchment of tax revenue, to include as large a proportion of the labour force as possible in its income tax system. In 1988, more than 70 per cent of employees paid income tax.[92] This is the opposite of the situation in Hong Kong, where there is a tendency to leave a large percentage out of the tax net.[93] Singapore uses a system of one-off rebates on the total income tax liability. This indicates that the system of rebates is seen as more flexible and a better instrument than lower tax rates in motivating the work force. The system of rebates also gives the government more control over the tax policy,[94] as it is flexible and easily changed.

One of the latest major developments in the Singapore tax system is the introduction from 1 April 1994 of a General Sales Tax (GST). The government sees the introduction of a GST as a necessary source of government revenues,[95] given its policy decision to keep the corporate income tax rates low (see Tax rates, p. 292), in view of international competition. As part of the policy to keep professionals in Singapore and to attract skilled labour from abroad or persuade those who studied abroad to return to Singapore, individual income taxes are also kept low.

The GST is largely based on the system applicable in New Zealand and the principle is rather similar to that of the system of Value Added Tax in the United Kingdom and other OECD nations.

A positive point of the introduction of a GST is that the government will have a much broader tax base. This broader base increases the flexibility with which the government can respond to economic and social developments.[96] It also diminishes the vulnerability of the revenue levels from economic fluctuations.

The vast number of tax incentives are implemented by an even larger number of agencies, which enjoy considerable discretion in implementing the incentives. Unfortunately, not much is known about public finance matters, as the government sees information regarding taxation as a strategic policy tool and not suitable for public exposure. Therefore, it is not known if the tax incentives have been successful in achieving their purposes of promoting certain investments, how frequently the incentives are used and what type of activities are eligible for tax incentives. It could be argued that there is a need for greater transparency in the application of the Singapore tax system[97] in order to better evaluate the net benefit of current practices economy-wide. The lack of such transparency represents an obstacle to corporate tax planning, a necessary activity for companies to keep themselves commercially competitive. With the growing internationalisation of business, this secrecy characteristic in parts of Singapore's tax administration has become more conspicuous. Improvement in this area of Singapore's tax system is, therefore, being called for.

General income tax structure

Resident and non-resident Resident companies are considered to be resident if the control and management of the business is exercised in Singapore. Individuals are classified as resident taxpayers when they reside in Singapore for 183 days or more during the tax year.

Taxable income   Income is only taxable according to the Income Tax Act if it is accrued in, derived from or received in Singapore. Like Hong Kong, Singapore adopted the territorial concept. Included in income are gains or profits from a trade or business, dividends, interest, rents, royalties, commission fees, premiums and any other profits of an income nature. The accrual basis of accounting is used.

Problems have occurred involving unit trusts,[98] as to whether gains or profits derived from the disposal of securities are taxable as income or are seen as capital gains, in which case the profits are not taxable. The Singaporean Income Tax Act[99] defines that the profits of disposal of securities held for a certain period would be seen as capital in nature and thus not taxable.[100] This rule only applies to an investment company approved by the Ministry of Finance. The problems arise for unit trusts around the holding period. Those who invest in unit trusts have the right to reclaim their units at any time. There is no fixed holding period, as managers of those funds are obliged to redeem the units if asked by their investors. In order to solve this problem, a new scheme was introduced in 1989, which only applies to approved unit trusts (which have to be Singapore residents) and deals with the gains and profits arising from the disposal of securities. According to the scheme, 10 per cent of the profits from the disposal of securities is taxable. The other 90 per cent of the profits is not taxable as long as it is distributed to individuals and foreign investors who may be individuals as well as corporate entities.

Resident individual taxpayers are not only taxed on their income derived from Singapore but also on their income earned overseas but received in Singapore. A Singaporean working abroad may be treated as resident of Singapore if he intends to return to Singapore. Thus any overseas income received in Singapore is liable to tax. This tax barrier to working overseas has been recognised and the IRAS, since 1993, has allowed Singaporeans the choice of being treated as non-resident for any year of assessment, on condition that the individual has worked abroad for at least six months in any calendar year.[101] If this option is not chosen, the taxpayer will be treated as resident.

Dividends   Dividends are taxable for resident taxpayers as income. There is a tax at source that is levied on paid-out dividends. Dividends declared by a company from a fund of exempt profits are also exempt in the hands of the recipient.

Singapore does not have a dividend tax for non-residents, and dividends carry no further tax liabilities when received by non-residents.

Interest   Interest is taxable at a rate of 27 per cent, levied via a final withholding tax for non-residents.

Capital gains tax There is no capital gains tax (although recurring receipts from a business will almost always be subject to tax as income). Unfortunately, it is neither clear nor consistent as to whether certain transactions are regarded as income received from capital gains or as normal income.[102] Frequent buying and selling of property, including bonds and stocks, may result in the taxpayer being treated as a dealer in property, in which case gains from dealing are taxed as income.

Non-residents may be protected (against taxation of capital gains as part of income) under a tax treaty when they are not carrying on a business through a permanent establishment.

Exchange gains or losses are taxable upon realisation. Generally unrealised capital gains or losses are not taxable or deductible.[103]

Derivatives[104] For the deductibility of payments involving all derivatives the following condition applies: the payments have to be classified as revenue expenses. But then the payments may be subject to relief or may be deductible in Singapore. Generally the payments are not subject to value added tax, unless specifically mentioned under the separate headings.

Commodity swaps[105] Relief may be available for payments made under commodity swaps. The receipts under the swaps are taxable in Singapore. Fees paid in consideration for arranging a swap are not deductible, unless they are connected with a trade. Payments under commodity swaps may be subject to VAT.

Currency options[106] This type of option is treated as a contract separately from the underlying currency. Relief may be available for the premiums paid to acquire an option, and when the premium becomes payable.

Currency swaps[107] Relief can be given for payments made under a currency swap. This relief is generally available on a paid basis but the tax authorities may allow the accrual basis for banks and/or financial traders. Fees paid to arrange the swap are deductible. The payments under these swaps may be subject to withholding tax, unless the swap is between Asian Currency Units and a non-resident, and no Singapore dollars are involved in the swap.

Financial futures[108] Gains and losses realised on these futures are taxable and relievable in Singapore. The paid basis applies, but exceptions can be made as described under currency swaps.

Forward rate agreements[109] Deductions are available for payments made with this type of agreement, and receipts are fully taxable. The payments may be subject to withholding tax unless the condition as described under currency swaps applies.

Interest rate caps[110] Deductions are available for the premium paid by the buyer of an interest rate cap agreement. The payments made by the writer of an interest rate cap agreement are regarded as interest payments and a withholding tax will be applicable unless the condition as described under currency swaps applies. The payments made by the writer are deductible.

Interest rate options[111] Relief is available for premiums paid to acquire the options. This relief is not dependent upon the option being exercised.

Interest rate swaps[112] Provided that the payments are for the purpose of acquiring income, relief is available for payments made under interest rate swaps. This relief is obtainable on an accrual basis. Fees paid to arrange the swaps and to terminate the swaps are only deductible if the agreement is entered into in the course of a trade. Otherwise it is uncertain whether relief is available for those payments to arrange the swaps, while payments to terminate the swaps are not deductible. The payments are generally regarded as having their source where the payer is resident or trades. The payments are subject to withholding tax unless the condition as described under currency swaps applies.

Zero coupon bonds[113] Relief is available to the issuer of the bonds on maturity or payment. Generally the discount will only be taxed when realised on the earlier of disposal or maturity. Banks may be taxed on an accrual basis. The balance of gains or losses arising on disposal or maturity may be regarded as interest in nature and thus taxable or deductible, particularly in the case of banks. The discount payable is subject to withholding tax.

Withholding tax Resident companies receiving income from other resident companies are not subject to any withholding tax requirements. Interest, royalties, rentals from movable properties, management and technical fees paid to non-residents are subject to withholding tax in Singapore. The rate of withholding tax may be reduced when a tax treaty is applicable. There is no dividend withholding tax in Singapore.

The issue of withholding tax can be relevant in the securities business, when a domestic issuer is required to withhold tax on interest on certificates, deposits, notes or bonds payable to a non-resident. Non-residents include subsidiaries of foreign companies as the branches are controlled by the foreign companies. The Inland Revenue Authority of Singapore (IRAS) has given an administrative concession in certain cases,[114] for example, in the case of interbank Asian Currency Unit transactions and of branches of foreign banks and merchant banks which obtained withholding tax waivers although they are classified as non-resident taxpayers.

Tax incentives

Other incentives to attract foreign investment are given to approved Finance and Treasury Centres. Included in these tax incentives are:[115]

- the exemption of withholding tax on interest and similar payments between banks;
- the facility of the Asian Dollar Market to exempt from withholding tax any interest earned by non-residents on foreign currency deposits and approved Asian dollar bonds;
- the exemption of withholding tax, since 1987, on interest paid by Singapore International Monetary Exchange (SIMEX) members to non-residents on margin deposits for transactions in gold, financial futures and gold futures;
- the exemption from withholding tax, since 1989, on qualifying swap payments;
- the tax incentive given to banks, in 1991, to maintain general provisions;
- the 10 per cent concessional tax rate for offshore futures and options income was extended to include income from spot transactions which hedge futures positions.

Tax exemptions

There is a tax exemption for intermediaries on income from offshore loans syndicated in Singapore, and a 10 per cent concessional tax rate for offshore banking, fund management, managing and underwriting international securities, foreign securities trading, trading in futures and options, offshore insurance and offshore leasing income.

In 1992 the RAS Commodity Exchange (RASCE) started, as a centralised and regulated exchange for trading in commodity futures. In the same year the Singaporean Budget Statement issued a set of tax incentives for the RASCE and its members.[116] The general rule is that interest paid out by members of RASCE to non-resident members of RASCE or non-resident clients of members of the RASCE is subject to withholding tax. However, to increase the attraction of RASCE, the following tax exemptions are granted:

- RASCE members paying out interest to non-resident clients on margin deposits for all futures transactions on the RASCE;
- RASCE interest payments to non-resident members on their margin deposits, security deposits and adjusted net capital.

Corporate tax rates

From the year of assessment 1994 the top rate is 27 per cent. The government has further given a commitment to reduce the rate to 25 per cent in the long term.[117]

For resident individuals, the top rate for personal income tax is 33 per cent, with varying degrees of reduction in other brackets. This will result in individual income tax rates varying from 3.5 per cent to 33 per cent, with a total of fourteen tax brackets. Non-resident individuals are taxed at a flat rate of 27 per cent.

Repatriation of profits

In contrast to Indonesia, for example, there is no restriction on the repatriation of profits of local branch or subsidiary.

Other taxes

Goods and Services Tax A Goods and Services Tax was introduced from 1 April 1994. The rate is 3 per cent and is not expected to change for the first five years.[118] In terms of goods and services coverage, the base for the GST is very broad, with exemptions only for certain financial services and the sale and lease of residential land and buildings. To simplify the system, and pre-empt complaint of administrative burden on small businesses, the GST only demands registration of business entities with a turnover of more than S$1,000,000. This threshold is much higher than in, say, Japan, Indonesia or the United Kingdom,[119] and means that around 80 per cent of business entities will escape the GST net. The negative offset for these exempt businesses is that their GST-added inputs will thus not be claimable as credit for GST. Only export businesses are accorded the so-called zero rating, allowing them to claim GST refunds for exported goods. It is expected that the GST will not be extended to interest, dividends or commissions.

Stamp duty Stamp duty is levied on the transfer of shares, at a rate of 0.2 per cent. It is levied regardless of whether residents or non-residents are involved in the taxable transfer. But the transfer has to be executed or received in Singapore. The transfer of shares is taxable for stamp duty but not the changes in ownership or legal title for other securities as these securities change via delivery. It is believed that with the trend towards scripless trading, stamp duty will in the long term disappear.[120]

Other taxes are customs duty, taxes on motor vehicles, property taxes, skills development fund levy, entertainment duties, and foreign workers levy.

Tax treaties

Singapore has tax treaties with twenty-nine countries, including Australia. Under the treaty, withholding tax on interest is reduced to 10 per cent.

Costs of tax compliance

The Inland Revenue Authority of Singapore has taken over the functions of the Inland Revenue Department since September 1992. This takeover was, according to the government, necessary to generate more autonomous personnel and financial management. The IRAS works as an agent for the government and is responsible for the assessment, collection and enforcement of the major taxes in Singapore. The IRAS is focusing on improving the level of services to taxpayers. It set up a Taxpayer Services Branch to provide one-stop services. The IRAS publishes administrative statements and interpretation and practice notes, in order to improve the clarity and quality of information for taxpayers. In 1992, the IRAS introduced a field audit programme (similar to the HK field audits system).

The costs of compliance involved in the introduction and existence of a GST are potentially significant. The administrative apparatus which businesses with a turnover of more than S$1 million will need to maintain in order to comply with the GST must be borne in mind. The introduction of a GST system will likely make the Singaporean tax system more complicated and increase the costs of compliance.[121] The aforementioned lack of clarity on whether certain transactions are to be regarded as income received from capital gains or as normal income, will contribute to these costs.

Conclusion

The overall Singaporean tax burden can be described as light and the system rather transparent compared to some of its neighbouring countries. However, there is confusion regarding the types of activity that are eligible for tax incentives.

As the IRAS is trying to offer better service to taxpayers, there are some areas that are in need of improvement such as the issue of capital gains. The costs of compliance will increase with the introduction of a GST.

The tax policy vis-à-vis Singapore's capital market does provide strong incentives for this market to develop, and contribute to Singapore's continuing improvement in establishing itself as a regional financial centre. Tax breaks given to the Asian Dollar Market, the Singapore International Monetary Exchange, swap payments and offshore futures and options are among the clearest examples.

Singapore's relatively stable political system, plus explicit assurances that tax policy will remain unchanged in the medium term, further consolidate the state's status as a competitive financial centre servicing the international capital market. This is an advantage that Hong Kong may to some extent cede as 1997 approaches, an uncertainty that Hong Kong's currently very favourable tax system may find at times difficult to compensate for without dual effort expended by other domestic sectors (and by Beijing) in trying to retain the Territory's competitive edge.

Taiwan

Policy

The Taiwanese government sees a need to encourage domestic private investment, especially for the purpose of industrial upgrading, and is planning to introduce more tax incentives for the high technology sector. A five-year exemption from corporate income tax may be available for large companies in this sector.[122] In March 1993, the introduction of tax credits was announced to encourage the transportation and communication sectors to invest in production automation machinery, new pollution control equipment and related technology.[123]

From 1 January 1990 income tax on capital gains from transactions in shares and bonds, whether listed or unlisted, was abolished (the introduction of this capital gains tax in 1988 was an attempt by the Taiwanese authorities to slow down an overheated domestic market). A proposal to reintroduce tax on capital gains derived from the sale of non-listed shares was removed from the bill in 1992.[124] However, in October 1993, the ruling KMT announced that a capital gains tax would be introduced in 1994. The announcement came as a reaction to a proposition by Taiwan's Financial Committee to cut the transaction tax on share sales by half to 0.3 per cent.[125]

The Central Bank would like to stimulate investment in treasury bonds and asked the Ministry of Finance (MOF) to provide certain tax incentives, for example, a lower flat tax rate of 20 per cent on interest income from these bonds. No specific tax provisions have yet been formulated for other capital market instruments such as futures and options given the newness of these derivatives markets, but the MOF has indicated willingness for the tax structure of Taiwan to follow international trends.[126]

General income tax structure

There are two taxes on income, the profit-seeking enterprise income tax and the consolidated income tax, both of which are part of the Income Tax Law 1943 as amended. The first is applicable for any profit-seeking enterprise on its taxable income while the second type of tax applies to individuals.

Resident and non-resident taxpayers An enterprise whose head office is registered in Taiwan is subject to income tax as a resident taxpayer on all of its income, irrespective of source. Non-resident taxpayers are only subject to tax on income derived in Taiwan.

Taxable income: enterprises Included in taxable income are profits from the carrying on of an enterprise in Taiwan, dividends, interest and royalties. Companies are required to account for income and expenditure on the accrual basis.

Financial institutions are taxable on their profits and are also subject to the business turnover tax. The institutions are allowed to create a reserve for bad debts, as long as the reserve does not exceed 1 per cent of the outstanding loans

Individuals Individuals are only taxable on their Taiwanese sourced income, whether resident or non-resident. For non-residents the tax is levied via a withholding tax.

Dividends Dividends are deemed to have their source in Taiwan when distributed by companies which are registered and incorporated according to the Taiwan company law, or government authorised foreign companies operating in Taiwan.

Dividends are taxed at 35 per cent unless they are from a foreign investment approved by the government, in which case a rate of 20 per cent is applicable. The dividend derived from such investments may be remitted without restrictions. The remittance must be made at the exchange rate established on the foreign exchange market.

Interest Included in the definition of interest is interest from: government debts, various kinds of short-term commercial papers (e.g. treasury bonds with a maturity period of less than one year), bills of exchange accepted by banks, commercial promissory notes, other short-term certificates of indebtness approved by the Ministry of Finance, transferable time deposit certificates issued by banks, and corporate bonds.[127]

Capital gains Generally gains derived from transactions in property and property rights are taxable as normal income. The government has introduced a capital gains tax, starting in 1995, as it sees a need to raise revenue as well as to come down on excessive stock speculation and widespread tax evasion by stock investors. The scope of the new capital gains is not clear as yet.[128]

Withholding tax Generally income paid to a foreign profit-seeking enterprise which has neither a fixed place of business nor a business agent within Taiwan is subject to final withholding tax between 15 per cent and 35 per cent. Included in the definition of income are dividend and interest.

The withholding tax on profits realised on short-term commercial paper at its maturity date, in excess of the selling price at the issuing date, is a final tax. This means the withholding tax on short-term papers is not creditable against the company's final tax liabilities at the end of the taxable year.

Tax exemptions

Financial institutions dealing in commercial paper which deposit funds in banks, trusts investment companies or other financial institutions for fund management purposes are not taxable on the interest earned on these deposits, unless the interest derives from short-term commercial papers as discussed above under 'withholding tax'.

Certain types of interest are exempt from tax:[129]

- interest derived from loans offered to the government or legal entities within Taiwan by foreign governments or international financial institutions for economic development;
- interest derived from financing offered by foreign financial institutions to their branch offices and other financial institutions within Taiwan;
- interest derived from loans extended by foreign financial institutions to legal entities within Taiwan for financing important economic construction projects under the approval of the Ministry of Finance;
- interest derived from low-interest export loans offered to or guaranteed for legal entities within Taiwan by foreign governmental institutions and foreign financial institutions specialised in offering export loans or guarantees;
- interest received by individuals on savings of a compulsory nature made in accordance with a law or ordinance.

Tax rates

Corporate income tax for domestic enterprises is levied at a rate from 15 per cent to 25 per cent. Foreign enterprises are taxed at the same rate as domestic enterprises if they have a business in Taiwan or if they maintain a business agent in Taiwan. Resident individual taxpayers are taxable at a rate between 6 per cent and 40 per cent.

The withholding tax rates vary according to the different sources of income and domestic and foreign enterprises. In summary the following rates apply for domestic companies on Taiwan-sourced income:

- Company dividends and other forms of profit distribution   15 per cent
- Commission   10 per cent
- Interest   10 per cent
- Short-term papers   20 per cent
- Rental income   15 per cent
- Royalties and technical service fees   15 per cent

Rates applicable for foreign companies on Taiwan-sourced income:

- Company dividends and other forms of profit distribution (20 per cent if the investment is approved by the government)   35 per cent
- Commission   20 per cent
- Interest paid on loans made by an international banking institution to an individual or entity within Taiwan   15 per cent
- Other interest   20 per cent
- Rental income   15 per cent
- Technical service fees subject to the deemed income rule   20 per cent
- Royalties and other technical service fees   20 per cent
- Capital gains from the disposal of property   25 per cent
- All other income   20 per cent

The withholding tax paid by non-resident taxpayers is creditable against other tax liabilities in Taiwan. The only exception is the rule for short-term commercial papers, as discussed under 'withholding tax'.

Repatriation of profits

A branch whose foreign head-office is recognised by the Ministry of Economic Affairs, is allowed to repatriate after-tax profits to the foreign head-office free of tax.

Other taxes

Business turnover tax The tax is levied on the taxpayer's gross business income from the sale of goods or the rendering of services within Taiwan. Subject to the tax are financial institutions such as banks, insurance companies, trust and investment companies, securities houses and bro-kerage firms. The rate varies for these types of business between 1 and 5 per cent.

Securities transaction tax A securities transaction tax is levied on securities trading. Taxable transactions include the buying and selling of bonds (unless they are government bonds), shares, debentures and other securities. The rates are:

- 0.15 per cent (previously 0.3 per cent) of the transaction price for a transaction in shares issued by a company
- 0.1 per cent of the transaction price for a transaction in corporate bonds and other government approved securities (e.g. certificates issued by the securities investment trusts).

Tax treaties

Taiwan is not recognised as a country de jure by the United Nations and has only one income tax treaty (with Singapore). There are other more limited agreements mainly regarding shipping income with nine other countries, and one agreement regarding shipping and air transport income with the USA.

Conclusion

Although the corporate tax rate of 25 per cent can be classified as attractive, the taxation of dividend income by non-residents is at a rather high rate of 35 per cent (or 20 per cent as mentioned earlier, see p. 298) and is in contrast with, for example, Hong Kong or Singapore. This feature distinguishes Taiwan's equity market as a less attractive one than the other two.

Currently there is no capital gains tax, but such a tax will more than likely be introduced in the near future. There seems to be a trend towards more tax incentives to develop the domestic bond market and future legislation is likely to stimulate the derivatives market. In order to remain competitive, the Ministry of Finance may reduce or even abolish taxation of dividends.

GENERAL CONCLUSION

Corporate tax rates differ significantly among the six countries (see Table 8.1). Hong Kong has the lowest rates, with Taiwan and Singapore following closely behind, while higher rates are levied in Indonesia, Malaysia and China.

Differences are also noticeable in tax incentives policy. Singapore, for example, gives specific incentives for its capital market, in contrast to, say,

Table 8.1 General corporate tax rates for resident taxpayers: 1994

Country	Tax rate %
China	33 (reduction available in Special Economic Zones and Open Cities)
Hong Kong	16.5
Malaysia	34
Indonesia	35 (30 from 1995)
Singapore	27
Taiwan	25

Note: Indonesia and Taiwan have progressive rates of tax, only the top rate is mentioned. Tax incentives may be available, see the separate country headings.

Hong Kong, whose government upholds an impartial view of the tax system and sees it as favourable enough.

Both approaches carry advantages: Hong Kong's simplicity, clarity and neutrality in taxation make the system (from the perspective of costs of tax compliance) highly efficient. On the other hand, Singapore's system relies on breaks and encouragement and could at times prove costly to businesses in terms of seeking consultancy advice. Nevertheless, once they have operated within the system for a lengthy period of time, businesses do come to learn where to obtain better value for their investments. Foreign companies and investors would find it easier to transplant their operations or transfer their capital to Hong Kong than to Singapore, where substantial reading of local government policy and tunes is required.

For all the countries discussed, it can be said that governments have invested a great deal of effort in ironing out many inconsistencies in their tax regimes; clarifying terms of reference and definitions, and simplifying clauses; improving their systems' equity aspect, by trimming traditional approaches so as not to discriminate against particular market segments. A good example is Indonesia, where the abolition of favourable tax treatment of term deposits has resulted in a less unequal treatment of interest income and dividend income.

More specifically, the region's debt securities market is still to be developed. Taxation of interest and often involvement in withholding tax have constrained this market at a more primitive stage than seen in the equity markets (see Table 8.2 below). There is a strong need for a reduction in tax rates on interest as individual countries are seeking actively to promote both government and private sector debt issuance and trading.

The more developed economies unambiguously have more developed taxation systems, with Hong Kong, Singapore and to some extent Taiwan as examples. On the other hand, less developed countries, such as Malaysia and Indonesia, have less sophisticated means of dealing with new developments in the capital market. This can be seen in the latter countries' lack of clarity in tax rules and the difficulties they encounter in tax collection. However, some developed systems can be classified as more complicated: simplicity and clarity do not always coincide with increasing development in the economy, as is shown in the Singaporean tax system. Therefore the statement that costs of compliance are lower in more developed tax systems where clarity in rules is backed by reliable information that is freely available, such as in Hong Kong, may be applicable in many cases but should be applied with care.

Indonesia faces severe problems in its tax administration and tax compliance. Steps in the right direction have been made in the reform drives of the early 1980s, although much more effort needs to be exerted to catch up with the NICs. China is just beginning to develop its market based taxation system, and it will be a long time before the system could work according

Table 8.2 Withholding tax rates for foreign investors, without application of tax treaties: 1994

Country	Dividend	Interest	Capital gains	Comments
China	Unknown before 1994: 20% (10% in special cases)	Unknown before 1994: 20% (10% in special cases)	Does exist: rate 20% Before 1994: 0%	Total lack of clarity of tax rules
Hong Kong	0%	0%	0%	Tax rules clear in general
Malaysia	0% (imputation system)	20%, or 0% when payment by banks or financial institutions	0%	Tax rules in regard to financial instruments not clear
Indonesia	20%	20%	0%	Some lack of clarity about tax rules
Singapore	0% (imputation system)	27% (unless exempt)	0%	Tax rules fairly clear, however uncertainties remain
Taiwan	35% or 20% when foreign investment approved by the government	20% or 0% when interest paid by banks	0%. May be introduced in the near future: tax on listed shares of 0.6% for individuals above certain limiit; 6–40% for unlisted shares for individuals and institutional investors	Tax rules clear in general

to international standards. A complete intellectual framework and administrative infrastructure is required, and it is of little surprise to witness the nation at present struggling with a just introduced new tax regime full of ambiguities and uncertainties.

Besides Hong Kong, inconsistent tax rule application and interpretation is evident, at various levels, in all other countries. This handicap is hindering the development and trading of more sophisticated financial instruments such as futures, options and swaps. Taiwan and Singapore are striving to develop their capital markets from an operational viewpoint by introducing significant stabilising and internationalising factors (e.g. Singapore's promise of no sudden change).

There is a general trend towards indirect taxes (see Table 8.3). Indonesia

Table 8.3 Application of VAT or GST

Country	Application
China	VAT on the production and the sale of products at each stage of manufacture
Hong Kong	Considering following Chinese system
Malaysia	Considering a VAT
Indonesia	VAT applicable at a rate of 10%
Singapore	Goods and Services Tax with a broad scope, applicable at a rate of 3%
Taiwan	Gross business receipts taxt 0.1–25%* VAT applicable at a rate of 5%

Note: *Applicable for financial institutions and small-scale enterprises

introduced a VAT in the 1980s and is trying to further broaden this tax base over the next few years. Singapore introduced a GST system in 1994, helping to alleviate the corporate tax burden. Awareness of international competition seems to play an important role in keeping corporate tax rates down (Hong Kong and Singapore), or reducing them (Indonesia and Malaysia). This shift to indirect taxes may increase overall costs of tax compliance, as the introduction of a VAT requires intensive lead-in effort and on-going administration. However, the lowering of corporate tax rates is a significant positive offset, especially for large entities such as public companies.

In conclusion, it seems clear that, in the medium term, the six countries described will continue to pursue tax policies aimed primarily at integrating their domestic markets with the global one and attracting an increasing share of foreign capital, with the secondary objective of possibly using tax instruments to direct these capital flows towards certain desired sectors or market segments.

NOTES

1 The term tax treaty is used in this chapter, and has the same meaning as the term double taxation agreement. Both terms are commonly used. The main goal of a tax treaty is to allocate the taxing rights on income occurring from international transactions between two countries (IBFD 1992: 249).
2 Sandford 1989: 10.
3 Sandford 1989: 13.
4 One could argue that those costs are incurred in order to avoid taxes and therefore should not be included in the costs of compliance. However from a commercial point of view, these costs are inevitable in order to be competitive.
5 Research done in the United Kingdom showed that around half of the total costs of tax compliance for corporate tax were spent on external advisers (Sandford 1989:140).

6 Arthur Andersen 1993: 70.
7 IBFD 1993: 34.
8 Li 1993: 269.
9 In practice it can be hard to distinguish between collective and private enterprises.
10 Tabakoff 1994: 4.
11 According to the IBFD tax glossary a value added tax is:

> A specific type of turnover taxation. In its purest form VAT is a tax on all final consumption expenditures for the supply of goods and services. Although VAT ultimately bears on individual consumption of goods and services, it is collected by sellers in each stage of the production and distribution process. VAT is a percentage tax levied on the price each firm charges for the goods or services it supplies.
>
> (IBFD 1992: 270)

This type of tax is different from a sales tax (general sales tax=GST) which can be described as:

> A tax imposed as a percentage of the price of goods (and sometimes services). The tax is generally paid by the buyer but the seller is responsible for collecting and remitting the tax to the appropriate authorities.
>
> (IBFD 1992: 218)

VAT and sales tax appears in many different forms. Sometimes it is hard to make a distinction between the two, for example, when a VAT is only levied in the last stage of the production and distribution process; another example is the GST system in Singapore that is partly based on the VAT system in the United Kingdom. The six countries discussed in this chapter have already or are intending to introduce some form of VAT or General Sales Tax. Both types of taxes are classified as indirect taxes.

12 IBFD 1993: 28.
13 Li 1993: 312.
14 Lague 1993: 11.
15 In 1979 the national government collected tax worth 34 per cent of GDP, in 1993 only 19 per cent of GDP was collected by the government in Bejing. There seems to be the risk that Bejing could become irrelevant as regional governments gain so much in wealth and power.
16 Zuckerman 1994: 1.
17 IBFD 1993: 28.
18 Li 1993: 311.
19 Mansfield 1990: 139.
20 Li 1993: 314.
21 APTIRC 1993: 55.
22 APTIRC 1993: 55.
23 Zuckerman 1994: 4.
24 According to the IBFD Tax Glossary:

> Withholding tax is a tax on income imposed at source, i.e. a third party is charged with the task of deducting the tax from certain kinds of payments and remitting that amount to the government. . . . Withholding tax may be provisional or final. If provisional, the amount withheld will be credited against the taxpayer's final tax liability and adjusted accordingly. If final, no subsequent adjustments will be made.
>
> (IBFD 1992: 274)

Withholding tax is often preferable because it is a third person who collects the money before it comes into the hands of the taxpayer. For example, a withholding tax on wages: in that case the employer is obliged to withhold the tax before the wage is paid to the employee. The employer transfers the money to the tax department. This mechanism makes it easier to control the tax money and to collect it. The number of taxpayers and information points would be smaller and the earnings potential for each investigation far greater than it would be for audits of individuals who do not pay their taxes via a withholding system. Taxpayers (or potential taxpayers) who do not follow the withholding system include some types of businesses (not including the service professions), people not employed by anybody and independent bodies. For example in the United States, over 90 per cent of all personal income tax liabilities is collected through withholding via a third party (Gordon 1990: 465).

The term 'final withholding' tax means that the taxes withheld are not creditable against other tax liabilities at the end of the fiscal year

25 IBFD 1993: 164.

26 Other fees levied are:

> Shanghai market: commission: 1 per cent; transaction fee: par value × quantity × 0.1 per cent; clearing fee: USD 4.00 or multiple. Shenzhen market: commission: 0.7 per cent; SSE levy: 0.05 per cent; registration fee: 0.3 per cent of shares face value (for purchase only); settlement fee: 0.1 per cent between 185.00 and 625.00; bank charges: 0.15 per cent.

27 *Asian Wall Street Journal* 13 January 1994: 3.

28 APTIRC 1994: 13.

29 See the 21 July 1993 Notice, 'Concerning the Levy of Income Tax on Gains From Share (Equity Interest) Transfers and on Share Dividends Derived by Foreign Investment Enterprises, Foreign Enterprises and Foreign Nationals', by the State General Administration of Taxation (APTIRC 1994: 12).

30 Aptirc News Service, October 1994: 71.

31 APTIRC 1993: 222.

32 APTIRC 1993:223.

33 Harris 1992: 313.

34 Audits can be distinguished between 'desk or office audits' carried out in the tax office or 'field audits' carried out on the taxpayers' premises or elsewhere outside the tax office (IBFD Tax Glossary 1992: 18).

35 These three conditions are defined in the court case *Commissioner of Inland Revenue v Hang Seng Bank Ltd.* [1991] IAC 306. The court case is controversial and has been criticised in other court cases, including the Hong Kong Court of Appeal case *Wardley Investment Services Ltd v Commissioner of Inland Revenue* of December 1992, which partly deviates from the case of the Hang Seng Bank as it sees the third condition as formulated in the Hang Seng Bank case as unnecessary. Another important case related to this issue is the *Commissioner of Inland Revenue v HK TVB International Ltd*, [1992] 3 WLR 439.

36 The Hong Kong Inland Revenue Department issued, in November 1992, a Departmental Interpretation and Practice Note No. 21, which discusses the problematic issue of source of profits.

37 Bramhall 1992: 189.

38 Olesnicky 1993: 230.

39 The following rules for the taxation of interest can be distinguished (Departmental Interpretation and Practice Note No. 21, November 1992, Commissioner of Inland Revenue HK):

Interest received on offshore loans initiated, negotiated, approved and documented by an associated party outside HK and funded outside HK is not taxable in HK.

Interest received from offshore loans initiated, negotiated, approved and documented by the HK institution and funded by it in/from Hong Kong are taxable for their total amount, 100 per cent.

Interest received from offshore loans initiated, negotiated, approved and documented by an associated party outside HK but funded by the HK institution are taxable for half of their amount, 50 per cent.

Interest received from offshore initiated, negotiated, approved and documented by a HK institution but funded by offshore associates, under certain conditions, are taxable for half of their amount, 50 per cent.

Interest on certificates of deposit are taxable for the full amount.

40 Arthur Andersen 1993: 138.
41 IBFD 1991: 36.
42 Part of the information under this heading is based on the publication *Derivatives, An International Tax Survey*, 1994, KPMG.
43 A commodity swap can be defined as an arrangement under which two parties agree to exchange a contractual principal amount of a given commodity, for a defined period, at an agreed upon price, but without taking physical delivery of the underlying commodity. Generally, during the time of the swap, regular payments are made based on the principal amounts exchanged (KPMG 1994: 51).
44 A currency option can be defined as a contract between a buyer and a seller, in which the buyer is given the option to exercise its right to buy or sell a specific amount of one currency at a predetermined price on or until a certain future date (KPMG 1994: 51).
45 Currency swaps can be defined as arrangements under which two parties agree to exchange specified amounts of two different currencies for a defined period (often between 5 to 10 years). During this period a series of interest payments will be made based on the amounts exchanged (KPMG 1994: 51).
46 Financial futures can be described as futures contracts when the underlying commodities are specific derivatives whose prices depend either on an interest rate, exchange rate or an index. Futures contracts are transferable contracts to buy or sell a set amount of a commodity on a specific future date at a price agreed upon under the terms and conditions of recognised exchange (KPMG 1994: 51).
47 Forward rate agreements can be defined as an agreement in which two parties agree on the interest rate to be paid on a notional deposit of a specified maturity at a specific future date, the seller agreeing to compensate the purchaser who in turn agrees to pay over the difference between the agreed and prevailing rate if the rate falls (KPMG 1994: 52).
48 Interest rate caps can be defined as agreements placing an upper limit on the rate of interest payable on a variable rate borrowing. Interest rate caps can be traded quite separately from the borrowing to which they relate (KPMG 1994: 52).
49 An interest rate option can be defined as an agreement between a buyer and a seller, which gives the buyer the option to buy or sell a specified derivative at a predetermined price on or until a certain future date (KPMG 1994: 52).
50 Interest rate swaps can be defined as agreements between two parties to exchange streams of payments over a period of time. An interest rate swap involves the exchange of interest payment streams of differing character in accordance with predetermined rules and based on a notional principal amount (KPMG 1994: 52).

51 Zero coupon bonds can be defined as discount securities which pay no interest during their life. The return to the investor is the amount by which the redemption value at maturity exceeds the original discounted purchase price (KPMG 1994: 52).
52 The only exception is a limited Double Tax Agreement between HK and the United States concerning the taxation of shipping profits.
53 APTIRC 1993: 30.
54 IBFD 1992: 17.
55 Sivalingam 1993: 5.
56 Included were the reductions of tax advantages of the Pioneer Status, Investment Tax Allowance, Abatement of Income for Export and Export Allowance. Some tax incentives were entirely abolished (Sivalingam 1993: 7) such as those for location, small scale, compliance with policy on capital participation or employment and the use of indigenous materials.
57 Sivalingam 1993: 8.
58 Singh 1993: 29.
59 Singh 1993: 30.
60 Wong 1993: 2.
61 Wong 1993: 4.
62 Wong 1993: 4.
63 Wong 1993: 5.
64 Arthur Andersen 1993: 201.
65 Wong 1994: 322
66 Sivalingam 1993: 2.
67 APTIRC September 1993: 62.
68 Sivalingam 1993: 7.
69 World Bank 1992: 46.
70 *The Australian*, 19 March 1993.
71 Heij 1993: 6.
72 World Bank 1992: 46.
73 Asher 1990: 51.
74 *Business Times*, 6 December 1989.
75 The ITL was promulgated in December 1983 and has been applied since 1984.
76 An exception is made for payments to banks and non-bank financial institutions.
77 Mansury 1993: 210.
78 In October 1989, a circular was issued by the taxation department, confirming that Indonesian tax in respect of capital gains on publicly listed shares will not be imposed on foreign individuals and foreign entities if they are non-residents and the capital gains are not effectively connected with a Permanent Establishment (PE) of such individuals or entities in Indonesia.
79 In Australia, and also in the United Kingdom, there is a similar system whereby every employer is generally required to make tax instalment deductions from all payments of salary and wages to individual employees; these deductions are credited against the employee's tax liabilities at the end of the taxable year. This system is known as the PAYE (pay-as-you-earn) system.
    Apart from the PAYE system, the other tax system available to Australians is the system of provisional tax payable on non-salary and wages income of the current year. Provisional tax is used not only in Australia but also in Indonesia.
    In Indonesia a withholding system exists for resident and non-resident taxpayers. For non-resident taxpayers this is a final withholding tax, and no credit will be given in Indonesia. In Australia the withholding tax is imposed on certain interest, dividends and royalties paid to non-residents.

80 Import and export tax is generally levied on goods, not on services so financial services are not subject to these taxes.

81 Imported goods can be exempted from import duty under Customs Law. Examples of such goods include those for the oil/gas sector and foreign aid projects.

82 There are exceptions under the VAT. Foreign investment companies may seek deferment of VAT on capital goods under the so called Masterlist facilities granted by the Capital Investment Coordinating Board (BKPM). If imported goods are exempt from import duty such goods are also exempt from VAT.

83 Batam Island is a specially designated bonded zone for foreign investment companies, and is situated outside the Indonesian customs area.

84 For several aid projects conducted with government customers various sections of VAT are borne by the government.

85 Imported goods which are exempt from VAT or eligible for VAT deferment are also exempt or subject to deferment in the case of the luxury goods sales tax.

86 Gunadi 1992: 210.

87 Mansury 1993: 207.

88 Gunadi 1992: 213.

89 Unfortunately, there are no figures given by the Ministry of Finance regarding decisions. The information is obtained from tax firms, consultants and research centres who all agree that the Director General very rarely decided in favour of the taxpayer.

90 Gunadi 1992: 214.

91 This view is confirmed by different sources such as legal and accountancy firms and the research institute Institute Bisnis Indonesia.

92 Asher ed. 1992: 113.

93 Harris 1993:223.

94 Asher 1992: 113.

95 Although the budget shows a significant surplus, the government wants to maintain this surplus as a necessary tool for its growth strategy.

96 Asher 1993: 219.

97 Lim 1988: 257.

98 Thio Su Mien 1992: 412.

99 See Section 10A of the ITA.

100 The holding period is defined in the Income Tax (Approved Investment Companies) Regulations 1990.

101 APTIRC 1993: 25.

102 Asher ed. 1992: 124.

103 Except in the case that the exchange is of a capital nature realised with the settlement of account with the supplier of a fixed asset (Chia 1994: 348).

104 Part of the information under this heading is obtained from the publication *Derivatives, An International Tax Survey*, 1994, KPMG.

105 See note 43.

106 See note 44.

107 See note 45.

108 See note 46.

109 See note 47.

110 See note 48.

111 See note 49.

112 See note 50.

113 See note 51.

114 Thio Su Mien 1992: 411.

115 Arthur Andersen 1993: 254.
116 Ang 1993: 15.
117 Aptirc 1993: 91.
118 Asher 1993: 212.
119 Asher 1993: 212.
120 Thio Su Mien 1993: 413.
121 Asher 1993: 218.
122 APTIRC March 1993: 18.
123 Aptirc May 1993: 34.
124 IBFD 1992: 1.
125 Mark 1993: 13.
126 Arthur Andersen 1993: 291.
127 IBFD 1992: 28.
128 The rate expected is to be 0.6 per cent.
129 See Article 4 of the Income Tax Law of Taiwan. The rules set out in this Article overlap to a great extent the exemptions mentioned under the 'Statute for Borrowing and Guarantees by government for External Debts to Achieve Social and Economic Development', which exempts interest on several types of offshore loans from income withholding tax when paid to non-residents.

REFERENCES

General: Costs of tax compliance

Pope, J., 1991, Book review of 'Administrative and Compliance Costs of Taxation' by Sandford C, Godwin M, Hardwick P, *Australian Tax Forum*, 8, pp. 251–57.
Sandford, C., Godwin, M., and Hardwick, P., 1989, *Administrative and Compliance Costs of Taxation*, Fiscal Publications, Bath, UK.

China

APTIRC, 1993 and 1994, *APTIRC Bulletin News Services*, several issues, Asian–Pacific Tax and Investment Research Centre (APTIRC), Singapore.
Andersen, Arthur, 1993, *Asia and the Pacific . . . A Tax Tour*, Arthur Andersen.
Andersen, Arthur, 1993, *Asia/Pacific Capital Markets; A Vision of Change*, The Economist Intelligence Unit, London.
Gordon, R.K., 1990, 'Income tax compliance and sanctions in developing countries', in *Readings on Taxation in Developing Countries*, ed. R. M. Bird and O. Oldman, Duke University Press, Durham.
Gordon R.K., 1992, 'Tax administration concerns in the reform of substantive personal income tax law in emerging economies', *Bulletin of The International Bureau for Fiscal Documentation*, April.
International Bureau for Fiscal Documentation (IBFD), 1992, *International Tax Glossary*, IBFD, Amsterdam, The Netherlands.
IBFD, 1993, *Taxation and Investment in the People's Republic of China*, IBFD Amsterdam, The Netherlands.
Lague, David, 1993, 'Bejing struggles to whip boom provinces into line', *The Weekend Australian*, 13–14 November.
Li, Jinyan, 1993, 'The New Law on Tax Administration', *Bulletin of the International Bureau of Fiscal Documentation* (IBFD), May, pp. 263–277, IBFD Amsterdam.
Li, Zhi Hui, 1993, 'An Analysis of China's Tax Policies and System for Enterprises

with Foreign Investment and Foreign Enterprises', in *APTIRC Bulletin*, July, Asian–Pacific Tax and Investment Research Centre (APTIRC), Singapore.

Li, Zhi Hui, 1993, 'China: A New Legislation for Tax Collection and Administration', in *APTIRC Bulletin*, August, Asian–Pacific Tax and Investment Research Centre (APTIRC), Singapore.

Mansfield, C.Y., 1990, 'Tax Reform in Developing Countries, the Administrative Dimension', *Bulletin of The International Bureau for Fiscal Documentation*, March, pp. 137–43.

Minter, Ellison, Morris, Fletcher, *Doing Business with China, a Legal Guide*, Australia.

Ramaer, Joost, 1993, 'Corrupt China onder curatele van Spartaanse koppensneller', *de Volkskrant*, 28 August, The Netherlands.

Tabakoff, Nick, 1994, 'Beijing's tax our burden', *The Australian Financial Review*, 11 January, Australia, p. 4.

World Bank, 1990, *China Revenue Mobilization and Tax Policy*, A World Bank Country Study, World Bank, Washington, DC.

Zuckerman, Laurence, 1994, 'China's New Taxes Puzzle Foreigners', *Asian Wall Street Journal*, 3 January 1994, pp. 1 and 4.

Hong Kong

APTIRC, 1993, *APTIRC Bulletin News Services*, several issues, Asian–Pacific Tax and Investment Research Centre (APTIRC), Singapore.

Andersen, Arthur, 1993, *Asia and the Pacific . . . A Tax Tour*, Arthur Andersen.

Bramhall, Vincent, Murdie, Bill, Nesbitt, Gavin, Rae, Simon, 1992, 'Hong Kong', in *International Securities Law*, Euromoney Publications, London.

Harris, Ian, 1992, *Tax Audits in Hong Kong*, paper presented at the 9th Asian–Pacific Tax Conference, November 1992, Asian–Pacific Tax and Investment Research Centre (APTIRC), Singapore.

Harris, Ian, 1993, 'An evening talk to APTIRC members', *Aptirc Bulletin*, June 1993, Asian–Pacific Tax and Investment Research Centre (APTIRC), Singapore.

IBFD, 1992, *Taxation in the Asian Pacific Region, Chapter Hong Kong*, IBFD Amsterdam, The Netherlands.

Inland Revenue Department, 1992, *Departmental Interpretation and Practice Note No. 21, November 1992*, Commissioner of Inland Revenue HK

Olesnicky, Michael, 1993, 'Hong Kong: Source of Profits – The New Practice Note', in *Aptirc Bulletin*, June, Asian–Pacific Tax And Investment Research Centre (APTIRC), Singapore.

Malaysia

Andersen, Arthur, 1993, *Asia/Pacific Capital Markets; A Vision of Change*, The Economist Intelligence Unit, London.

International Bureau for Fiscal Documentation (IBFD), 1993, *Taxation in the Asian–Pacific Region, Chapter Malaysia*, IBFD, Amsterdam, The Netherlands.

Sivalingam S., 1993, *Malaysia: Tax Incentives for Inbound Investments: Towards Greater Selectivity?*, 8th Asian–Pacific Tax Programme July 1993, Asian–Pacific Tax and Investment Research Centre, Singapore.

Sing Veerinderjeet, 1993, 'The 1993 Budget and Recent Developments', in *Bulletin*, January, International Bureau of Fiscal Documentation, Amsterdam.

Wong, Barry, 1994, 'Investing in Malaysia: New rules and new incentives', *Aptirc*

Bulletin, September, Asian–Pacific Tax and Investment Research Centre (APTIRC), Singapore.

Wong, Barry, 1993, *Malaysian Tax and Investment Update: Recent Development*, 8th Asian–Pacific Annual Tax Programme July 1993, Asian–Pacific Tax and Investment Research Centre, Singapore.

Indonesia

Asian–Pacific Tax and Investment Research Centre (APTIRC), 1984, *Indonesian Laws and Supplements*, APTIRC, Singapore.

Asian–Pacific Tax and Investment Research Centre (APTIRC), 1993, *Taxation in the Asian–Pacific Region*, APTIRC, Singapore.

Asher, M. G., 1990, *Reforming the tax system: A case study of Indonesia*, processed by the Department of Economics and Statistics, National University of Singapore, Singapore.

Asher, M.G. (ed.), Rolt, S.C., Ariff, M., Khan, M.H., 1992, *Fiscal Incentives and Economic Management in Indonesia, Malaysia and Singapore*, Asian–Pacific Tax and Investment Research Centre, Singapore.

Heij, Gitte, 1993, *Tax administration and compliance in Indonesia*, Asia Research Centre, Murdoch University, Western Australia.

Heij, Gitte, 1993, *Doing business in Indonesia: a tax guide for the Australian investor*, Asia Research Centre, Murdoch University, Western Australia.

International Bureau for Fiscal Documentation (IBFD), 1993, *Taxation in the Asian–Pacific Region*, IBFD, Amsterdam, The Netherlands.

International Bureau for Fiscal Documentation (IBFD), 1992, *International Tax Glossary*, IBFD, Amsterdam, The Netherlands.

Mansury, D.R., 1993, 'Tax Treatment of Financial Instruments (Hybrid Instruments) in Indonesia', in *Aptirc Bulletin*, June, Vol. 11, No. 6, Asian–Pacific Tax and Investment Research Centre, Singapore.

World Bank, 1991, *Indonesia developing private enterprise*, Country Department V, Asia Regional Office, Report No. 9498-IND, 9 May.

World Bank, 1992, *Indonesia: Growth, Infrastructure and Human Resources*, Country Department III, East Asia & Pacific Regional Office, Report No. 10470-IND, 26 May.

Singapore

Ang Chiew Leng, 1993, *Administration of the Income Tax Act and the Economic Expansion Incentives (Relief from Income Tax) Act: Recent Developments*, 8th Asian–Pacific Tax Programme, July 1993, Asian–Pacific Tax and Investment Research Centre, Singapore.

APTIRC, 1993, *APTIRC Bulletin*, several issues, Asian–Pacific Tax and Investment Research Centre, Singapore.

Andersen, Arthur, 1993, *Asia/Pacific Capital Markets; A Vision of Change*, The Economist Intelligence Unit, London.

Asher, M.G., 1993, 'The Proposed Goods and Services Tax (GST): Implications for Singapore's Fiscal System', in *Aptirc Bulletin*, June, Vol. 11 No.6, Asian–Pacific Tax and Investment Research Centre, Singapore.

Asher, M. G. (ed.), Rolt S. C., Ariff M., Khan M. H., 1992, *Fiscal incentives and economic management in Indonesia, Malaysia and Singapore*, Asian–Pacific Tax and Investment Research Centre, Singapore.

CCH, 1991, *Singapore Master Tax Guide*, CCH Asia Limited, Singapore.

Chia, William, 1994, 'Singapore: Tax treatment of exchange gains and losses', *APTIRC Bulletin*, Asian–Pacific Tax and Investment Research Centre, October, Singapore

Lim, C.Y. and Associates, 1988, *Policy Options for the Singapore Economy*, Singapore, McGraw–Hill Book Co.

Minter, Ellison, Morris, Fletcher, 1992, *Doing Business with South-East Asia, A Guide for Australian Business*, Australia.

Ow, A.S.S, 1992, *Developments in Tax Administration in Singapore*, paper presented at the 9th Asian–Pacific Tax Conference, November 1992, Asian–Pacific Tax and Investment Research Centre, Singapore.

Thio, Su Mien, 1992, 'Singapore', in *International Securities Law*, Euromoney Publications PLC, London.

VanderWolk, Jefferson P., 1993, 'The Privy Council Wanders in the Wilderness', *Bulletin*, International Bureau of Fiscal Documentation, January, pp. 33–36.

Taiwan

Andersen, Arthur, 1993, *Asia and the Pacific . . . A Tax Tour*, Arthur Andersen.

Andersen, Arthur, 1993, *Asia/Pacific Capital Markets; A Vision of Change*, The Economist Intelligence Unit, London.

APTIRC 1993, *APTIRC Bulletin*, several issues, Asian–Pacific Tax and Investment Research Centre, Singapore.

Gordon, Richard and Summers, Victoria, 1992, *Taxation of investment funds in emerging capital markets: Theory, problems and solutions in the case of Taiwan*, Development Discussion Paper No. 436, Taxation Research Series No.2, International Tax Program, Harvard Law School, Cambridge, Massachusetts.

IBFD, 1992, *Taxation in the Asian Pacific Region, Chapter Taiwan*, IBFD Amsterdam, The Netherlands.

Mark, Jeremy, 1993, 'Taipei Plans to Tax Share Profits Again', *Asian Wall Street Journal*, 19 October, p. 13.

Chapter 9

Accounting regulation in East Asia

Phil Hancock and Greg Tower

INTRODUCTION

This chapter deals with accounting as an aspect of capital market's activities in Asian countries. It outlines the financial reporting rules which apply in some major Asian countries and financial centres. The People's Republic of China (PRC), Taiwan, Hong Kong and Singapore share a Chinese heritage, but the latter two, as well as Malaysia, are also strongly influenced by British rules, especially in regard to company law. Indonesia is uniquely influenced by Dutch legal traditions.

The objective of this chapter is to provide an overview of the financial reporting requirements that apply in Indonesia, Singapore, Hong Kong, Malaysia, the People's Republic of China and Taiwan. The implications of corporation law, stock exchange and the accounting profession's standards for financial reporting are discussed. While the chapter outlines the financial reporting requirements in each of these countries, it is not possible to provide more specific details on accounting regulation in each industry/sector in each country. The fast changing regulatory environment of East Asia has meant that accounting standards are being reviewed and redefined at a fast pace. As a result, practitioners will need to obtain up-to-date case-specific information from the host country in which they operate or intend to operate.

Multinational companies are caught between the host country's desire for more information and home government reporting requirements. Gray (1981) notes the perception of some users and multilateral organisations such as the United Nations, Organisation for Economic and Co-operative Development, the European Community, International Monetary Fund (and others) that market forces cannot be relied upon to ensure sufficient comparable information about multinationals. Accounting regulation is offered as a remedy (Cooper and Keim 1983).

INTERNATIONAL HARMONISATION

With the recent rapid globalisation of economic activities, differences in accounting practices between countries are regarded as an impediment to international trade and business expansion. Dissimilarities in national accounting standards have the potential to distort financial information and reduce the level of communication (Choi and Bavishi, 1982). As a result, increased attention is drawn to the need to eliminate or minimise such differences and it is argued that formal action has been taken to achieve harmonisation. Accordingly, accounting guidelines from several international bodies have been generated in the last two decades. For many countries, implementing the International Accounting Standards Committee's (IASC) rules is seen as politically more acceptable and practicable than adopting particular British or American standards (Baker, 1986). Furthermore, IASC standards have already been vetted by individual countries, a screening that would save Asian (and other regions' developing) countries from frequent future revisions.

Doost and Ligon (1986) state four significant obstacles to the trend towards international harmonisation: politics, nationalism, differing levels of sophistication, and the lack of a worldwide enforcement agency. Tower and Perera (1989) note that several authors have argued that the need for the IASC may decline in the future because of the efficiency of the international financial markets, which are spreading their full operations to East Asia and around the globe; asserting that the market place will demand and receive the amount of financial information it desires, thereby lessening the need for an international accounting entity. Perera (1985) also points out that the uniqueness of each country's business and social environment constitutes an obstacle to the unified imposition of an international body of standards.

It is thus unclear how successful or useful supranational accounting rules will become. The can enhance comparability and lower preparation and enforcement costs, but they may not always be appropriate for local usage. Be that as it may, the pressure for applying such rules in East Asia appears to be growing.

The trend in East Asia is towards the adoption of International Accounting Standards which are issued by the IASC. These standards are often a compromise between various countries' viewpoints and do allow for several different accounting methods. It can also be argued that the IASC standards have a distinct Anglo–American bias towards disclosure. The Anglo–American countries' large equity markets generate demands for a high level of disclosure. Other countries' positions (i.e., those with a greater emphasis towards debt financing) are not always heeded within the IASC, which generates concerns about the maintenance of a nation's sovereignty and protection of unique cultural attributes.

INDONESIA

Indonesian commercial law essentially comprises the Commercial Code of the Netherlands of 1847 as amended. Accounting requirements for listed versus unlisted public companies in Indonesia differ significantly. This Commercial Code and subsequent decrees do not provide for the submission of financial statements or accounting procedures, and do not require an audit for unlisted public companies. However, it is implicit in the Commercial Code that annual financial statements be prepared for presentation to the annual general meeting. Tax legislation in Indonesia relies very much on the Indonesian Accounting Principles (IAP) and thus companies are required to keep accounts and calculate income in accordance with IAP. In addition, matters such as accounting procedures and appointment of auditors are generally dealt with in the Articles of Association for most companies. Audits are mandatory for listed companies, banks, insurance companies, leasing companies, stockbrokers and underwriters.

The capital markets in Indonesia are regulated by the Capital Market Supervisory Board (BAPEPAM) which has wide ranging regulatory powers similar to the Securities and Exchange Commission (SEC) in the United States.

The Indonesian Association of Accountants issues Accounting Standards which are binding on all members of the Association.

Corporation law

Unlike in other countries, company law in Indonesia is much less detailed. In fact, there can be many aspects of company law and regulation with which a foreign investor would be familiar in other contexts, that simply have no counterparts in Indonesia.

The approach to law making in Indonesia is such that only the relevant elements required to be achieved by statute are written in the statute. Statutes are normally brief and general, leaving many aspects of what is meant by the statute to implementing regulations and to the relevant Minister. The relevant Minister for the capital markets is the Minister of Finance, who will often exercise his power by Ministerial Decree.

An important relevant decree for listed public companies was the Presidential Decree 53 and Ministerial Decrees 53 and 1548 issued in late 1990. These decrees contain three fundamental policy changes:

1 A Capital Market Supervisory Agency (BAPEPAM) was established so that the capital market in Indonesia could be guided and regulated in line with government policy.
2 Government regulatory and supervisory responsibility was consolidated in BAPEPAM as an agency working under and responsible to the Minister.

3 The private sector was considered to be capable of operating securities exchanges and be responsible for regulating their members under BAPEPAM guidance and supervision.

In relation to accounting and auditing standards, Section 2(n) of Decree 1548 gives BAPEPAM the authority to 'establish accounting rules which modify Indonesian Accounting Principles'. Section 2(o) allows BAPEPAM to give accountants orders in relation to their accounting and auditing activities in the capital market and to disqualify them or restrict their capital market activities.

Clearly, in relation to the regulatory requirements for financial reporting for listed public companies in Indonesia, the attitude and actions of BAPEPAM are significant.

Accounting profession

The accounting profession in Indonesia is represented by the Indonesian Association of Accountants (IAI). The IAI is a member of the International Federation of Accountants (IFAC) and reference is made to their pronouncements in any statement or principle issued by the IAI. Any statement or principle is binding on all members of the association. While BAPEPAM has the authority to establish accounting standards in the same way as the SEC in the United States, it is working with the IAI to develop accounting and auditing standards.

There is still a great deal of work to be done in the development of accounting standards in Indonesia. The country needs skilled personnel to develop such standards. The education of accountants in Indonesia is inadequate and many students travel overseas for their education. There is also an urgent need to improve the regulation of financial markets and financial reporting. The World Bank has allocated large sums of money in recent times to a project aimed at improving accountancy in Indonesia.

Accounting standards

General accounting principles are documented in the PAI (Prinsip Akutansic Indonesia) issued in 1984. This was based largely on Accounting Research Study No. 7 published in 1965 by the American Institute of Certified Public Accountants.

Since publishing the PAI, the IAI has issued several statements on specific matters and these are referred to as Statements on Accounting Standards (SAS). In addition to these standards, the IAI also issues statements of interpretation of Indonesian Accounting Principles.

Financial statements are prepared on the historic cost basis and the entity is assumed to be a going concern. The accrual method of accounting is used and transactions should be accounted for based on substance rather than form.

As previously mentioned, the IAI and BAPEPAM are endeavouring to move quickly to issue accounting standards on various issues not presently covered by an existing standard. This process will take considerable time as the gestation period for an accounting standard in countries like the USA and Australia can be from one to three years or even longer depending on the nature of the proposed standard. Furthermore, an apparent shortage of trained and skilled staff will mean that development will be slow.

The standards already issued by the IAI are, in general, similar to the accounting standards issued in Australia. Some of the major differences between accounting standards in Indonesia and Australia are summarised below:

- *Consolidation* In Australia control is defined as: 'the capacity of an entity to dominate decision-making, directly or indirectly, in relation to the financial and operating policies of another entity so as to enable that other entity to operate with it in pursuing the objectives of the controlling entity'. In Indonesia control is indicated by ownership of 50 per cent or more of the voting shares in an entity. It appears there is some doubt as to whether consolidation is mandatory in Indonesia and so many subsidiaries are still accounted for using the equity method.
- *Goodwill* There is no standard as yet in Indonesia. In Australia goodwill must be amortised over a period not exceeding twenty years.
- *Foreign currency translation* The standards are similar in both countries except that in Indonesia exchange gains or losses can be deferred when they result from a devaluation or revaluation of the Indonesian currency. The deferred gain or losses are then systematically amortised.
- *Revaluation of fixed assets* While this is permitted in Australia, it is only allowed by Indonesian Accounting Principles when the revaluation is approved by government regulation.
- *Inventories* Inventories are valued at the lower of cost or net realisable value in both countries. LIFO, FIFO or average cost can be used in Indonesia to determine cost. LIFO is not allowed in Australia. The method of determining cost should be used on a consistent basis.
- *Extraordinary items* The definitions are similar in Indonesia and Australia. In both countries the items are outside the ordinary operations of the entity. In Australia these items are also non-recurring while in Indonesia they are defined to occur rarely.
- *Income taxes* There is no requirement in Indonesia to provide for deferred taxation as required in Australia. Hence, only current taxes are normally recorded in the financial statements. Where deferred taxes are accounted for, the liability method is used. Tax losses can only be carried forward for five years.

BAPEPAM directives

There are two circulars which relate to the form and content of financial statements. These are:

- SE-24/PM/1987 issued 24 December 1987
- SE-05/PM/1992 issued 18 March 1992.

These directives require publicly listed companies to report to BAPEPAM and the public on an annual and semi-annual basis. The financial statements must include:

- a balance sheet
- a profit and loss statement
- a statement of retained earnings
- a statement of changes in financial position; and
- notes to the financial statements.

The statements must provide comparisons with the previous year and comply with Indonesian generally accepted accounting principles and directives issued by BAPEPAM.

Detailed formats of financial statements for public companies are provided in the BAPEPAM circulars. Generally, assets are classified according to their liquidity (current assets, investments, fixed assets, intangible assets and other assets). Liabilities are listed in order of the date they are due for settlement (current liabilities, long term liabilities and other liabilities). A summary of significant accounting policies must be disclosed, as in Australia.

All companies must provide six copies of audited financial statements in Bahasa Indonesia within 120 days of balance date to BAPEPAM. Proof of newspaper publication must also be given to BAPEPAM.

For shareholders, the companies must publish in the Indonesian newspapers both the profit and loss and balance sheet statements within 120 days of balance date. Companies are not required to send an annual report to all shareholders but are required to provide one at the annual general meeting and upon request.

BAPEPAM requires companies to provide short form unaudited financial statements with comparatives for the first six months of an accounting period. These profit and loss and balance sheet statements must also be published in at least one Bahasa Indonesian newspaper.

BAPEPAM also requires certain information which is thought to be relevant to the setting of share prices to be provided to shareholders and stock brokers in a timely manner. Some examples include mergers, acquisitions, acquisition or loss of important contracts and significant new products or inventions.

Materiality is defined in the BAPEPAM directives as:

- 5 per cent of total assets for assets

- 5 per cent of total liabilities for liabilities
- 5 per cent of total equity for equity items
- 10 per cent of revenue/sales for profit and loss items
- 10 per cent of profit before tax for the effect of transactions.

Prior period adjustments arising from the correction of calculation errors in a prior year, or errors in applying certain accounting principles, can be made direct to the opening balance of retained earnings. This is not permitted under Australian Accounting Standards.

The statement of changes in financial position can be based on the concept of funds as working capital or cash and cash equivalents. Hence, if cash and cash equivalents are used, the statement would resemble the cash flows statement required in Australia.

Stock exchanges

The Jakarta and the Surabaya Stock Exchanges are privately managed exchanges. On 22 May 1993, BAPEPAM issued regulation No. Kep-12/PM/ 1993 concerning procedures for Enacting Regulations by Stock Exchanges. This regulation gives BAPEPAM the authority to approve, amend or disallow proposed regulations from the stock exchanges, BAPEPAM is also drafting a Capital Market Act which many expect will give BAPEPAM the power to conduct capital market investigations in accordance with the Criminal Code. The listing requirements of the larger Jakarta Stock Exchange call for all companies to provide:

1 Annual reports audited by accountants registered with BAPEPAM which must be lodged within 120 days from the balance date.
2 Mid year reports which must be lodged within sixty days after the end of the company's first half year if reports from accountants are not included; or must be lodged within ninety days after the end of the company's first half year if reports from accountants are included.
3 Unaudited quarterly reports which must be lodged within sixty days of the company's first and third quarters of their financial year. The forms of these reports are not stipulated by the JSE. However, BAPEPAM does establish the form of the annual and half yearly reports. The form of the quarterly report is not stipulated by either body.
4 Continuous reporting requirements: the JSE also requires disclosure of any decision or the occurrence of any event or the receipt of any information which may influence the price of listed shares or an investor's decision about investing in the company's shares.

The JSE has provided the following non-exclusive examples of possible events which must be disclosed by the end of the second trading day after the event or decision:

(a) mergers, acquisitions, consolidations or the formation of joint ventures;
(b) share splits or the distribution of stock dividends';
(c) earnings and dividends announcements of an extraordinary nature;
(d) acquiring or losing important contracts;
(e) significant new products or inventions;
(f) changes in control or significant changes in the management of the company;
(g) announcement of redemption or repayment of debt instruments;
(h) significant sales of additional shares to the public or private placements;
(i) significant sales, purchases or changes in assets.

Stock exchanges in Australia also require immediate disclosure of important material events which are likely to be significant to investors.

Outlook

According to the results of a survey published by Arthur Andersen (1993), Indonesians believe 'that more capital market regulations will be introduced; these rules will be enforced more effectively; stricter accounting and disclosures will be required; and regulations will be made more transparent or more user friendly'.

As previously noted, the World Bank has committed resources to improve the development of the accounting profession in Indonesia. It is thus likely that more accounting standards will be issued, which should in the long term further improve the quality of financial reporting in Indonesia.

SINGAPORE

Singapore has a system of company law and an accounting profession similar to Australia's. The main regulating agency in Singapore is the Monetary Authority of Singapore (MAS), which is the central bank. There is also a Registrar of Companies, the Securities Industry Council and the Stock Exchange of Singapore which regulate the securities market.

Corporation law

The Singapore Companies Act provides for the establishment of public, private or exempt companies. Companies are required to file audited financial statements with the Registrar of Companies. An auditor must be a member of the Institute of Certified Public Accountants of Singapore. Exempt private companies are only required to submit a certificate signed by a director, the company secretary and the auditors indicating the company is solvent.

While no standard format is specified, the Ninth Schedule of the

Companies Act specifies certain information which must be disclosed. In addition the Act requires that the financial statement present a true and fair view of the company's results and its financial position.

The financial statements must include a balance sheet, profit and loss account, a statement of changes in financial position, a director's report and a director's statement. Consolidated financial statements are also required except in the case of wholly owned subsidiaries incorporated in Singapore.

Accounting profession

The professional accounting body in Singapore representing accountants is the Institute of Certified Public Accountants (ICAPS). The ICAPS issues Statements of Accounting Standards (SASs) which are generally identical to the International Accounting Standards.

The historical cost convention is followed in Singapore, although certain assets may be revalued. Therefore the financial reporting rules are similar to those in Australia.

- *Consolidation* similar approach to Australia except the definition of control in the Australian standard is broader, in that it includes the capacity to control.
- *Pooling of interests* this approach to accounting for business combinations is permitted in Singapore, but not in Australia.
- *Goodwill* no separate standard in Singapore, but the standard on consolidations requires any goodwill to be amortised over its useful life.
- *Foreign currency translation* very similar to the standard in Australia.
- *Prior period adjustments* these can be made against opening retained earnings in Singapore, where they must be included in operating profit/loss in Australia.
- *Revaluation* revaluation of assets is permitted in both Singapore and Australia. The two standards are very similar, except in the definition of recoverable amount.
- *Investments* while there is a standard in Singapore dealing with investments, there is no similar standard in Australia.
- *Extraordinary items* similar definition except that in Australia extraordinary items are non-recurring, whereas in Singapore they are not expected to recur frequently or regularly.

Members of the ICAPS are expected to comply with SASs issued in Singapore. However, they are not intended to be a comprehensive code of fixed rules and accountants are expected to use their professional judgement when applying the standards.

Stock exchange

Listed companies are required to file annual financial statements within one month of the annual general meeting and a half yearly report within three months of the end of the financial half year.

In addition to the above returns, there are some fairly onerous reporting requirements for listed public companies in Singapore.

A listed company must make an immediate public announcement of material information. Such information is likely to influence an investor's decision about whether to invest in the company's shares. The following list, which is not exhaustive, is an example of the type of events which could require an announcement.

- a joint venture, merger or acquisition;
- the declaration or omission of dividends or the determination of earnings;
- a stock split or stock dividend;
- the acquisition or loss of a significant contract;
- a significant new product or discovery;
- a change in control or a significant change in management;
- a call on securities for redemption;
- the borrowing of a significant amount of funds;
- the public or private sale of a significant amount of additional securities;
- significant litigation;
- the purchase or sale of a significant asset;
- a significant change in capital investment plans;
- a significant labour dispute or disputes with sub-contractors or suppliers;
- a tender offer for another company's securities.

There are other rules covering rumours, unusual market action and unwarranted promotional disclosure. The exchange has also set out guidelines for the content of media and other announcements.

HONG KONG

Accounting regulation in Hong Kong is influenced by two main sources. Core company law is based on the British model and accounting standards are closely modelled on the International Accounting Standards. The few differences in accounting rules between Australia and Hong Kong are mostly related to Australia's decision to not wholly adopt the IAS standards and Hong Kong's preference for less disclosure on certain issues.

Corporation law

The Companies Ordinance covers the operations of companies trading or incorporated in Hong Kong. It encompasses rules for the maintenance of books and the generation of financial statement disclosures. The 10th Schedule does not require a specific format but does detail the minimum disclosures required. Private (usually family run) companies have limited reporting obligations although a prospectus is required to be filed with the Registrar of Companies. Overseas companies must file their accounts with the Registrar of Companies on an annual basis (Stott, 1988).

Accounting profession

The Hong Kong Society of Accountants (HKSA) is the professional accountancy body in Hong Kong. It promulgates the accounting standards and guidelines for financial reporting.

Accounting standards

The going concern, accrual accounting and historical cost principles are followed in Hong Kong. Revaluations are allowed for certain non-current assets. Accounting methods inconsistent with the Statement of Standard Accounting Principles (SSAP) are to be disclosed in the notes along with a justification. Hong Kong has adopted most of the International Accounting Standards. The only real differences are the lack of a standard on related party disclosures and a limited segment reporting rule applicable only to listed companies. Other issues of note include:

- The control criteria is used for consolidation accounting but subsidiaries may be exempt where in vastly dissimilar lines of business. No official rule exists for joint ventures, but minority interest and detailed consolidation disclosures are required.
- Hong Kong companies can use equity investments for certain investee companies. This practice is effectively not allowed in Australia.
- Prior period adjustments are taken to the opening balance of retained profits whereas in Australia they are disclosed via the profit and loss account.
- Revaluations of non-current assets are allowed based on either a professional or director evaluation.
- The LIFO method of measuring inventory is not usually used.

Annual reporting

Companies incorporated in Hong Kong are required to appoint an auditor to report on the financial statements. The auditor must be independent and a member of the HKSA. The accounts are to provide a true and fair view of the state of affairs of the company as at the end of the financial year.

A balance sheet, profit and loss account and a cash flow statement[1] are all required on an annual basis for all companies incorporated in Hong Kong (even if listed elsewhere). However, Hong Kong companies that are wholly owned subsidiaries of overseas holding companies are not required to file annual reports unless they are listed on the Hong Kong stock exchange. Hong Kong companies are encouraged (in Australia they are required) to disclose their cash flow statement using the direct approach (reconciliation of beginning and ending balances), with the indirect method (reconciliation of cash flow to net profit given) to be disclosed via the notes.

International Accounting and Auditing Trends (1993) report a notable increase in financial accounting reporting and disclosures of Hong Kong industrial companies. They attribute this to a wider dispersion of ownership. Balance sheet information was generally rated quite highly whilst the shareholder data disclosure was less well regarded.

Stock exchange

The Stock Exchange of Hong Kong Limited (SEHK) provides the rules and regulations for financial reporting requirements for listed companies. The securities industry was troubled by the October 1987 crash. The Hong Kong exchange was the only major exchange that was forced to temporarily close. The Hay Davison Committee report resulted in a strengthened independent Securities and Futures Commission (Sihombing, Mahmood and Latimer, 1991). New stock exchange listing rules also came into effect in 1989 which established clearer lines of demarcation and removed some former anomalies. For instance, the pricing of new securities on a listing are now totally left to the issuer and financial adviser and the HKSE Listing Committee no longer has an input (Bramhall et al., 1992). Moreover, the normal administration of listing matters and reporting matters is left to the HKSE.

Bramhall et al. (1992) note that most of the listed companies are still family controlled, resulting in few hostile takeovers. The stock exchange listing requirements are similar to the London Stock Exchange 'Yellow Book'. Newly listed companies need to comply with both the HKSE requirements and the Companies registry regarding compliance with the Companies Ordinance.

1997

In 1997 the People's Republic of China will regain control over Hong Kong. It is unclear what effect that will have on the accounting system or financial markets in Hong Kong. In general, the Hong Kong accounting regulatory system is far more advanced than its PRC counterpart. However, the PRC's recent adoption of Enterprise Standards (see p. 327) is a movement towards the adoption of international accounting standards. The Hong Kong financial markets are likely to exert strong pressure on the PRC for the maintenance of an adequate flow of accounting information.

MALAYSIA

As a former member of the British Commonwealth, Malaysia has a system of company law and an accounting profession similar to Australia's.

Corporation law

The Malaysian Companies Act 1965 provides for the creation of both private and public companies. A private company has the words Sendirian Berhad or Sdn Bhd, meaning private, at the end of its name. A public limited liability company has the word Berhad or Bhd at the end of its name. The Act also provides for the creation of an exempt private company.

The Companies Act requires directors of public companies to present audited financial statements for approval by shareholders at the annual general meeting. The annual financial statements include a balance sheet, profit and loss statement, statement of changes in financial position and a directors' report. Where a company has subsidiaries, its annual financial statements in most cases will include consolidated financial statements.

The financial statements do not have to comply with any prescribed format. However, the statements must comply with the detailed disclosure requirements of the Companies Act (similar to the Schedule 5 requirements in Australia). The statements must also comply with the accounting standards approved by the Malaysian Institute of Accountants (MIA) and the Malaysian Association of Certified Public Accountants (MACPA). Finally, the financial statements under the Companies Act must give a 'true and fair view' of its financial position and results.

Some of the separate disclosures in the profit and loss statement include income from investments, interest payable on fixed loans, tax provisions, depreciation and movements in reserves. Balance sheet disclosures relate primarily to the classification of items into share capital reserves, assets and liabilities.

The financial statements of a public company must be audited and an auditor must be a member of the MIA and must be licensed by the government. The audited financial statements must be filed with the Registrar of Companies together with the directors' report and auditor's report.

Accounting profession

There are two bodies in Malaysia representing accountants. The Malaysian Institute of Accountants (MIA) represents similar constituents to the Institute of Chartered Accountants in Australia. The Malaysian Association of Certified Public Accountants (MACPA) has similar membership to the Australian Society of CPAs (ASCPA).

Approved accounting standards in Malaysia comprise the International Accounting Standards and Malaysian Accounting Standards issued by the MACPA and the MIA. These standards have to be adhered to by all public companies according to the Companies Act. There is also a professional obligation to comply with approved accounting standards. Technical bulletins similar to Accounting Guidance Releases are also issued by the accounting profession in Malaysia.

The adoption of most of the International Accounting Standards in Malaysia means that the financial reporting requirements in Australia and Malaysia are very similar:

- *Historical cost* assets are recorded at their historical cost.
- *Revaluations* are permitted but a public company must first obtain the approval of the Capital Issues Committee.
- *Consolidated statements* are required and the determination of a subsidiary uses a definition of control which is similar to the definition used in Australia.
- *Inventories* similar treatment to Australia, except that in Malaysia it is possible to use LIFO.
- *Prior period adjustments* can be adjusted against opening balance of retained earnings in Malaysia. All prior period adjustments are included in operating profit/loss in Australia.
- *Taxation* tax effect accounting is required in both Malaysia and Australia. The deferred tax benefit arising from tax losses can be carried forward in Malaysia when there is assurance beyond any reasonable doubt that future taxable income will be sufficient to allow the benefit of the loss to be realised. The criterion in Australia is one of virtual certainty in relation to future taxable income, i.e a company must be virtually certain that it will earn future taxable income sufficient to allow the benefit of a tax loss to be realised.
- *Superannuation plans and general insurers* there are some differences under the standards applicable to Australia and Malaysia for each of these two industries. In particular, the differences relate to the asset valuation methods and the determination of the liabilities in each industry.

Stock exchange

To obtain a listing on the Kuala Lumpur Stock Exchange, a company must obtain the approval of the Capital Issues Committee as well as the exchange itself. Companies are required to present half yearly and annual reports to the stock exchange. These accounts are to be on a consolidated basis and must comply with the accounting standards issued by the MIA and the MACPA.

Given the British background of Malaysia, the listing requirements are similar to those in Australia. There are certain restrictions on share ownership in Malaysia. For example, at the time of writing, native Malays must own at least 30 per cent of a corporation's equity and foreign ownership is restricted to 30 per cent.

PEOPLE'S REPUBLIC OF CHINA (PRC)

Accounting regulations are a relatively new phenomenon in China. They are being promulgated in an attempt to try and increase reporting uniformity amongst the maze of business ventures (especially in the southern provinces) currently conducted, both by domestic and foreign enterprises.

Corporation law

There are several legislated accounting requirements in China which apply depending on the particular business form chosen. The legal structure includes:

- Sino–Foreign Equity Joint Venture Law and regulations;
- Sino–Foreign Cooperative Joint Venture Law;
- Wholly Foreign-owned Enterprises Law and rules;
- Income Tax Law and regulations.

These laws have generated some confusion given that they were issued at different times and apply to different entities. The primary source of accounting rules stems from the Ministry of Finance. A series of Accounting Practices and Rules came into effect on 1 July 1992. These rules require that financial statements are prepared based on the historical cost principle. As with most other countries the principles of matching, going concern, consistency and accrual accounting are also followed. Reporting is to be in the Chinese language but a foreign language may be used concurrently (Touche Ross, 1988).

Lefebvre and Liang-qi (1990) note some problems with 'creative accounting' which are largely due to the tensions between a decentralised economy and a centralised but inefficient and inconsistent regulatory system. They note that the major difference between PRC financial reports and other countries rests with the difference in capital structure. Accounting anomalies were found in the determination of fund balances, expense adjustments and differing methods of book-keeping. Historically, enterprise funding in the PRC came from the state. As the enterprise funding source changes more emphasis is placed on internationally accepted accounting techniques.

Accounting standards

With an effective operating date of 1 July 1993, new Enterprise Accounting Standards were promulgated by the Ministry of Finance (Liu Zhongli, 1992). These new rules are part of the transformation from a socialist planned economy towards what is termed a socialist market economy (Liu Wei and Eddie, 1993). A key provision is the decison to turn state-owned enterprises into separate legal entities each responsible for profits and losses. The financial reporting emphasis is changed from disclosing fund balances to the reporting of assets, liabilities and net profit.

The Enterprise Accounting Standards cover all enterprises within the PRC. They encompass General Provisions, General Principles, Assets, Liabilities, Owners' Equity, Revenues, Expenses, Profit, Financial Statements, and Supplementary Provisions. The importance of historical cost accounting, accruals, comparability, timeliness and understandability are all emphasised.

There is less detail in the Chinese accounting rules in relation to their Australian counterparts. A comparison of the two systems leads to the following observations:

- Unlike the Australian concept of control, in China a company must consolidate an investee company if more than 50 per cent ownership is demonstrated. However, exceptions to mandatory consolidation accounting for all subsidaries are allowed for entities which have vastly different operations (similar to the USA rule), and where express exemption is given by the Ministry of Finance. Issues such as goodwill upon consolidation and minority interest are not covered (Coopers and Lybrand, 1993). Joint ventures and non-consolidated investee companies are typically accounted for at cost (although there are allowances for equity accounting where significant influence is demonstrated and where there is more than 25 per cent ownership by the investor company).
- Foreign currency transactions and translations are generally similar to Australian rules. Operating gains and losses are run through the profit and loss account. Reporting is based on the PRC currency (renminbi). However there are some differences in the accounting treatment for foreign currency transactions. Year end rates are to be used for the balance sheet, weighted average used for the Profit and Loss account and exchange differences are to be taken to a reserve. Disclosure of the foreign currency translation policies is not required.
- Unlike Australia, there is no requirement for disclosure of accounting policies, changing prices, subsequent events, related party disclosures, segment reporting, debt defeasance, contingencies, research and development costs, extraordinary items and tax-effect accounting.
- Non-current assets are shown at historical cost. Revaluations are not usually permitted. Intangibles are typically amortised on a straight line

basis whereas both straight line and accelerated methods are used for tangible non-current assets.
- Inventories are to be shown via the perpetual method.
- Prior period adjustments are taken to the profit and loss account in Australia whereas in China they are generally shown as an adjustment to undistributed profits.

Annual reporting

Foreign Investment Enterprises are required to file audited financial statements annually in accordance with the Ministry of Finance promulgations. The financial statements are typically based on a calendar year. The audit must be conducted by a registered Chinese Certified Public Accountant. Subsidiaries' accounts must be included.

The format of the annual reports is determined by the Ministry of Finance via a chart of accounts. Reporting exceptions must be given explicit approval from the authorities. A balance sheet and profit and loss account are required. Coopers and Lybrand (1993) note that these reports are required for three time periods: monthly, quarterly and annually. An international Statement of Changes in Financial Position (although this may change with the movement towards a cash flow statement) is required usually only on an annual basis.

TAIWAN

Taiwan is emerging as a major player in finance in Asia, with its US$80 billion foreign reserves and heavy investments in Continental Asia as shown in various chapters of this volume. In the 1980s rapid changes occurred in Taiwan's capital market and financial system. These changes have also had an effect on accounting rules and future direction of the country's accounting regulatory framework.

An important difference in Taiwan's approach to accounting regulation as compared to Hong Kong or the PRC is the American influence. This is especially notable in the structural arrangements of the accounting regulator and stock exchange enforcer.

Accounting profession

The accounting profession in Taiwan is represented by the National Federation of CPA Associations of China (NFCPAA). The role of the profession is established in the CPA Law. Originally, the NFCPAA was in charge of generating standards in Taiwan. In 1984 the Accounting Research and Development Foundation was established. The foundation was originally modelled on the USA experience with their Financial Accounting Foundation (the parent body to the Financial Accounting Standards Board).

Accounting standards

Accounting standards are generated by the Financial Accounting Standards Committee (FASC) of the NFCPAA. The accounting rules in Taiwan closely follow the International Accounting Standards. IASC rules are normally adopted soon after their release in Taiwan, especially those related to finance issues (such as interest capitalisation, foreign currency, debt restructuring etc). This is probably due to the large influence played locally by Taiwanese financiers.

Listed companies' annual reports are required to be audited on a semi-annual and annual basis. Financial statements are expressed in Chinese. Monthly sales figures are to be published and unaudited quarterly financial statements are also required.

Stock exchange

The Taiwan Stock Exchange (TSE) was originally created from the 1953 Land Reform as compensation for land redistribution (Park and van Agtmael, 1993). The TSE is owned by government controlled banks; it has a high trading value and approximately 200 listed entities. Their 1990 sharemarket crash was primarily related to the property investment sector (Chang, 1992). High volatility has been a trademark of the exchange, probably as a result of surplus funds and a limited number of shares. The vast informal banking sector creates problems of accountability and control. Pressures for greater disclosure and tighter regulation have been voiced.

The Securities and Exchange Commission (SEC) is an agency of the Ministry of Finance. All listed companies are required by the SEC to comply with the relevant accounting standards.

FUTURE DEVELOPMENTS IN EAST ASIA

One of the critical accounting issues confronting the accounting profession worldwide is the appropriate accounting treatment of financial instruments. The 1980s and 1990s have seen a rapid growth of derivative financial instruments such as swaps, futures and options in the more developed capital markets like Singapore and Hong Kong. Such growth has accentuated the need for the accounting profession and governments to issue authoritative pronouncements on the appropriate accounting treatment for financial instruments.

Due to the complex issues involved in accounting for financial instruments, the IASC has to date issued two exposure drafts in 1991 and 1994. It is likely that most countries in East Asia, and the rest of the world for that matter, will follow the accounting treatment proposed by the IASC. Some of the proposals in the IASC documents include:

- Recognition of a financial asset and financial liability arising from a financial instrument when substantially all of the risks and rewards associated with the asset or liability have been transferred to the enterprise and the asset or liability can be reliably measured.
- The financial asset and financial liability should only be offset for balance sheet presentation purposes when the enterprise has a legally enforceable right to set off the amounts involved and it intends to settle on a net basis or to realise the asset and settle the liability simultaneously.
- Compound financial instruments such as convertible debt should be initially recognised in its component parts of debt and equity.
- The financial assets and financial liabilities arising from financial instruments can be measured using either a benchmark approach or an alternative measurement model.
  The benchmark approach involves classifying financial instruments as:

  (a) investing and financing instruments which are measured at cost or amortised cost.
  (b) hedging instruments which are measured using the same method as applies to the item being hedged.
  (c) instruments which are not classified as one of the above are measured at fair (market) value.

  If enterprises choose the alternative measurement model then all financial asets and financial liabilities are measured at fair (market) values. Under this alternative model all gains and losses will normally be recorded in the profit and loss statement.

The IASC is expected to issue an accounting standard on financial instruments in 1995. Some critics have expressed concern that the IASC proposals may hinder the growth of the markets for some of the derivative instruments. For instance, if an enterprise is required to recognise a financial asset and a financial liability arising from a swap contract then it may choose not to enter the swap arrangement. Alternatively there is likely to be an increase in the use of netting arrangement in financial instrument contracts so that the resulting financial asset and financial liability qualify for set-off in the balance sheet.

Another important development in accounting which would have a significant impact on capital markets is the issue of measurement. While historical cost remains the primary measurement attribute in most countries, the possible move to fair or market values continues to be debated in the literature. There have already been moves towards fair values for disclosure purposes in the US (SFAS 107) and it is required for some industries in Australia (AAS 25 and AAS 26). The question of measurement is likely to appear on the agenda of the IASC as it continues to develop a conceptual framework of accounting. Ultimately this will impact on countries in East Asia.

Generally, in most of the countries in East Asia there will be a continuation of the development of more rigorous accounting standards in the future. This is particularly true of Indonesia, PRC, Taiwan and Malaysia. These same countries are also expected to continue to develop regulations covering all aspects of financial reporting for companies. An important issue in many of these countries is the need to increase the number of skilled people who are required to develop, monitor and enforce compliance with financial reporting regulations.

Various historical influences, notably the British, International Accounting Standards Committee, American, Chinese and Dutch were highlighted in this overview of accounting rules in certain Asian countries (PRC, Hong Kong, Taiwan, Indonesia, Malaysia and Singapore). Interested investors will find that many of the accounting rules are similar to those existing in Australia and other Anglo–American countries. At present a higher level of confidentiality of business arrangements can be maintained due to the reluctance of East Asian countries to reveal related party transactions. However, these rules are changing at a rapid rate and moving towards a greater adoption of international accounting standards. The dynamic nature of change is partially as a result of adoption of overseas pronouncements and partially related to domestic needs.

NOTES

1 Certain exemptions are allowed from the cash flow statement for small companies and certain industries such as shipping, banking and insurance (see Part III of the Tenth Schedule of the Companies Ordinance).

REFERENCES

Andersen, Arthur *Asia/Pacific Capital Markets: A vision of change*, The Economist Intelligence Unit, Jakarta, 1993.

Australian Accounting Standards Board and Public Sector Accounting Standards Board, Australian Accounting Standards 25, 'Financial Reporting by Superannuation Plans', August 1990.

Accounting Standards Review Board and Public Sector Accounting Standards Board, Accounting Standard 26, 'Financial Reporting of General Insurance Activities', December 1990.

Baker, S. 'Growing prestige of the IAS setters', *Certified Accountant*, 78(5), 10–11, May, 1986.

Bavish, V.B. (ed.) *International Accounting and Trends*, Third Edition, Center for International Financial Analysis and Research: Princeton, New Jersey, 1993.

Bramhall, V.E., Murdie, B., Nesbitt, G., Rae, S. and Johnson Stokes & Master. 'Hong Kong' in International Securities Law, Chapter 7, London: Euromoney Publications, 1992.

Chang, Y.H. 'Taiwan's accounting profession: A response to national economic growth', *The International Journal of Accounting*, 57–68, 1992.

Chia, R.M., Usman, M., Gondokusumo, S. and Wong, C.K. *Globalisation of the Jakarta Stock Exchange*, Prentice Hall, 1992.

Choi, F.D.S. and Bavishi, V.B. 'Diversity in multinational accounting', *Financial Executive*, pp. 45–49, August, 1982.

Cooper, K. and Keim, G.D. 'The economic rationale for the nature and extent of corporate financial disclosure regulation: A critical assessment', *Journal of Accounting and Public Policy*, 2(3), 189–205, Fall, 1983.

Coopers & Lybrand *International Accounting Summaries; 1992 Supplement*, John Wiley & Sons Inc., 1992.

Doost, R.K. and Ligon, K.M. 'How US and European accounting practices differ', *Management Accounting*, 67(4), 38–41, October, 1986.

Financial Accounting Standards Board, Statement of Financial Accounting Standards No. 107, *Disclosure About Fair Values of Financial Instruments*, December 1991.

Gray, S. J. 'Multinational enterprises and the development of international accounting standards', *Chartered Accountant*, 52(2), 24–26, August, 1981.

International Accounting Standards Committee, Exposure Draft E40, 'Financial Instruments', September, 1991.

International Accounting Standards Committee, Exposure Draft 48, 'Financial Instruments', January, 1994.

Lefebvre, C. and Liang-qi, L. 'Internationalization of financial accounting standards in the People's Republic of China', *The International Journal of Accounting*, 170–183, 1990.

Liu, Wei and Eddie, I.A. 'China's 1992 Enterprise Accounting Standards: Towards the Internationalisation of Accounting in China', International Accounting Group, Accounting Association of Australia and New Zealand annual seminar, Kakadu, 1993.

Liu, Zhongli. 'Enterprise Accounting Standards', Ministry of Finance of the People's Republic of China, Beijing, 1992.

Park, K.K.H. and van Agtmael A.W. *The world's emerging stock markets*, Salem, MA: Probus Publishing, 1993.

Perera, M.H.P. 'International accounting standards and the developing countries: A case study of Sri Lanka', (Research Report), University of Glasgow, Glasgow Business School, 1985.

Sihombing, J., Mahmood, N.R. and Latimer, P. *Business Law in Hong Kong, Malaysia and Singapore*, CCH Asia Limited, 1991.

Singapore Accountant, 'Hong Kong: Investment funds: New listing rules and quicker procedure', p. 36, February 1992.

Stott, V. *Hong Kong Company Law*, Pitman: London, 1988.

Touche Ross. *People's Republic of China: Tax and investment profile*, Touche Ross: New York, 1988.

Tower, G. D., and Perera, M. H. B. 'Closer Economic Relation Agreement (CER) between New Zealand and Australia: A catalyst for a new international accounting force', (Discussion Paper No. 96). Palmerston North, NZ: Massey University: Department of Accountancy, August, 1989.

Tritton, C. 'Accounting and Reporting Requirements in a Public Issue', paper presented to a conference on *Strategies for Successful Listing on the Indonesian Stock Exchange*, held in Jakarta, 15 July 1992.

Index